FAREWELL, TITANIC

FAREWELL, *TITANIC*

Her Final Legacy

CHARLES PELLEGRINO

John Wiley & Sons, Inc.

Design by Forty-five Degree Design LLC

Photo insert credits: pp. 1 (top left, top right), 2 (top left, top right), 13 (middle), Southampton City Council, courtesy of William MacQuitty; pp. 1 (bottom), 2 (bottom), 3, 5, 6, 8 (bottom), 9 (top), 14, Charles Pellegrino; p. 4 (top), James Cameron and Charles Pellegrino; pp. 4 (bottom), 10, 11, 16, Lori Johnston, NOAA; pp. 7, 8 (top), James Cameron; p. 9 (bottom), Leigh Bishop; p. 12, NOAA; p. 13 (top), courtesy of Walter Lord; p. 13 (bottom), Roy Cullimore and Charles Pellegrino; p. 15, Roy Cullimore

Published by John Wiley & Sons, Inc., Hoboken, New Jersey
Published simultaneously in Canada

For general information about our other products and services, please contact our Customer Care Department within the United States at (800) 762-2974, outside the United States at (317) 572-3993 or fax (317) 572-4002.

Wiley also publishes its books in a variety of electronic formats and by print-on-demand. Some content that appears in standard print versions of this book may not be available in other formats. For more information about Wiley products, visit us at www.wiley.com.

Library of Congress Cataloging-in-Publication Data
Pellegrino, Charles R.
    Farewell, Titanic : her final legacy / Charles Pellegrino.
        p. cm.
    Includes bibliographical references and index.
    ISBN 978-0-470-87387-8 (cloth); ISBN 978-1-118-19128-6 (ebk);
ISBN 978-1-118-19129-3 (ebk); ISBN 978-1-118-19130-9 (ebk)
    1. Titanic (Steamship)—History. 2. Shipwrecks—North Atlantic Ocean—History. I. Title.
    G530.T6P443 2012
    910.9163′4—dc23

                                                    2011049807

Printed in the United States of America

10 9 8 7 6 5 4 3 2 1

To the first responders and other rescuers—past, present, and future

Contents

Foreword

by Tom Dettweiler

When I first met Charlie Pellegrino, we of the Dr. Robert Ballard team were in hiding. We had just done the most incredible, wonderful thing: *we found the Titanic!* Our lives were suddenly turned upside down. Everybody wanted to know everything about it. We had, however, just experienced an event so exciting yet so disturbing that it was hard to relate to those who had not been there. The world's response was so overwhelming that we had to get away, return to our world of comfort, and return to sea, where life was on our terms and simpler. We had to escape, Bob and all of us, to give ourselves time to come back to reality, fathom what had been seen and accomplished, and put it into proper perspective, one we could deal with. So we set off on a research cruise designated as Argo-RISE, using our robotic sleds to explore the ridge systems in the mid-Pacific, where the planet is creating new volcanic material and new life, which then spreads toward the continents.

Upsetting this escape was the fact that Charlie was going with us with the goal of penetrating our team and finding out everything he could about how similar robots would someday travel into space and be used to explore the distant ice-covered oceans of Europa. As Charlie later told me, this cruise was a life-changing expedition for him. As we reviewed the *Titanic* pictures we had taken a few short weeks before and talked among ourselves about our find, Charlie was soon infected by the *Titanic* legend. His questions shifted from space to the *Titanic* and the voyage of discovery—the very thing we were hiding from.

What we soon realized was that Charlie's questions were coming from a place different from that of the questions we had been bombarded with at home. The question we had grown especially tired of was "Did you see any bodies?" Charlie was different. Instead of the morbid question about bodies, Charlie asked, "Did we see the *humans?*" In other words, did we see those little bits of evidence that told of their presence, the shreds that defined each individual's character and told his or her unique *Titanic* story—among them the story of the forward davit, still turned inboard, a testament to William Murdoch's futile attempt to launch the last lifeboat.

Charlie collected little bits of evidence from us and began piecing together the actual process the *Titanic* had gone through during the sinking, tracking the debris field backward in time to explain why the wreck appeared as it did on the bottom. Talking to Charlie was like a session on a psychiatrist's couch: he was able to draw out of us the precise things that had such an impact on us when we saw it live. The human drama we were seeing seventy-three years after the fact proved surprisingly disturbing, as our attention was drawn with increasing intensity to that cold Atlantic night in 1912. Finally Charlie was asking the questions that needed to be answered. This began a professional relationship between me and Charlie that has lasted more than twenty-five years, covering many discoveries and topics in ocean exploration, but always firmly tied together by a unique, direct perspective into the *Titanic* story.

When James Cameron was looking for someone to help develop the characters and add authenticity while making the movie *Titanic* I introduced him to Charlie. That led to another fruitful professional relationship, one that took Charlie down to the *Titanic* to experience firsthand the special hold that ship put on all of us, a mystery Charlie describes so well in this book. It's a unique club, and Charlie is one of the few individuals who is able to make his readers feel like a member.

The real treasure that Charlie shares with us in his three *Titanic* books—especially in *Farewell, Titanic*—is the intimate human details that resided in such places as the volumes of files accumulated by Walter Lord, the acknowledged dean of the *Titanic* story. For decades, *Titanic* survivors had shared their stories with Walter in personal correspondence, and Charlie's access to these files along with his forensic abilities to piece together events and evidence has woven an unprecedented, detailed account that takes you right to the decks of the *Titanic* on that horrible April night.

When my teenage son used to answer the phone and talk for half an hour or so before telling me the call was for me, I knew it was Charlie

calling. After I got off the phone, my son would spend hours enthusias-
tically telling me all the incredible things Charlie and he had discussed,
ranging from the bottom of the ocean to deepest outer space. It is
Charlie's ability to make science exciting and to put it into terms we can
all understand—and to bring out science's practical effects and often
long-ranging impacts—that will make *Farewell, Titanic* as much an
enjoyable, educational, and exciting read for you as it was for me.

I firmly believe that as the one-hundredth anniversary of the
Titanic's sinking approaches, her final chapters are now being written.
No one is better suited than Charlie to put the grand old lady to rest
with the impact and dignity that she deserves. Here is the real story of
the *Titanic*.

Tom Dettweiler is the scientist who, after building and operating a deep-ocean robot
that first mapped abyssal nodule fields, was brought to Woods Hole Oceanographic
Institute to work with Robert Ballard as co-designer of Argo, the robot that discovered
and filmed the *Titanic*. He also served as science officer aboard Jacques Cousteau's
research vessel, the *Calypso*. Dettweiler located the Japanese World War II submarine/
aircraft launcher I-52 and was awarded a medal for locating the Israeli submarine
Dakar. He is currently senior project manager for Odyssey Marine Exploration and has
turned much of his attention to research into explorations of the lost ships of the
Discovery Period, a venture analogous to our current voyages into space.

Preface

How strange to think that all of this began for me as just another interesting thing happening on the way to Jupiter.

In 1985, after the *Voyager* space probes started to support Jesse Stoff's and my models of new oceans under certain icy moons of the outer solar system, our designs for the Europa melt-through probe and the Titan probe (with Brookhaven physicist Jim Powell) made me aware of Tom Dettweiler's and Bob Ballard's still-evolving deep-ocean robot probe Argo. Argo was directly ancestral to the machines we intended to send as far afield as Titan. My baptism in the field of deep-ocean archaeology began with the expedition Argo-RISE, during a robotic reconnaissance of the same life-giving springs of the deep that Powell, Stoff, and I hoped one day to find under the icy surfaces of Europa, Ganymede, Enceladus, and Titan.

At the time, Ballard thought Stoff and me "a bit odd," we were later told. We contacted him in fall 1978, raving about his discovery of a deep-ocean food chain based on sulfides instead of sunlight. He had just opened up a window on the universe.

In the autumn of 1985, forensic archaeology was only an embryonic science developing in Pompeii's sister city, and the field of deep-ocean archaeology had not been invented yet. I joined the Argo-RISE expedition as someone whose focus was almost entirely on astrobiology. I boarded the Research Vessel *Melville* knowing so little about the *Titanic* that I had not even read Walter Lord's *A Night to Remember*. And yet I was surrounded by scientists and engineers who were shaken by what Argo had revealed to them only a few weeks before. Though the same robot had probed the graves of two nuclear submarines, there was something uniquely devastating about the *Titanic*'s empty lifeboat stations and the last davit head, pulled inboard in a desperate attempt to save the women and children in boat A. It's difficult now to convey the emotional impact I felt while studying those first fuzzy, robotic images aboard the *Melville* while surrounded by explorers who had just been through what Ballard described as "a minor nervous breakdown."

I wrote *Her Name, Titanic* in 1987 and resolved never to return to this subject again. At the end of the Ballard Era of *Titanic* exploration, in 1986, the ship had begun to emerge from the shadows of legend, gaining color and texture. The George Tulloch era of *Titanic* exploration began to resolve increasingly clearer images of what happened that night. The *Titanic* had become like a fractal equation: open the door to one question and your answers opened the doors to ten new questions. By the time Tulloch recovered the letters and diaries preserved in Howard Irwin's steamer trunk, revealing the story of a penniless world-wanderer who lived much like the Jack Dawson character in James Cameron's *Titanic*, I was hooked. No one who has seen the ship and said they were finished with it has ever been able to keep that vow; its mystique has a way of biting into a person and never letting go. Though I had said I was finished with the *Titanic*, I was already mainlining forensic archaeology.

Tulloch's French-American era of *Titanic* exploration became the subject of the second book in my trilogy, *Ghosts of the Titanic*. This artifact recovery period all but created the fields of forensic archaeology and bio-archaeology. The Russian-American-Canadian era (the Cameron era of *Titanic* exploration, and the subject of this book) began in 1995 with the deep-penetrating bot Snoop Dog, followed in subsequent years by a fleet of progressively smaller and more agile bots with names like Jake, Elwood, and Gilligan.

These bots have allowed us to penetrate deeper than ever before, into the rooms and the lives of *Titanic*'s people—from Edith Russell's stateroom through Maude Slocomb's Turkish baths, through the pantry areas, the firemen's quarters, and the previously ignored third class areas. Along the way, we have discovered postal workers' desks completely intact, in rooms inhabited by animals so strange that it sometimes took us years to fit them into phyla. We found great quantities of decorative wood in near perfect states of preservation and confirmed that what seventeen-year-old Jack Thayer saw rising near him as the bow submerged really was the multistory wooden structure of the Grand Stairway, floating up through the Crystal Dome.

We also discovered that due to the accelerating growth of the *Titanic*'s rusticle ("icicles" of rust) reef, the ship is becoming a house of cards avalanching section by section, year by year before our eyes. Though the *Titanic* is vanishing, I would never make a gross claim that forensic archaeology is finished on that deep-ocean prairie or that this is the last word on an unsinkable subject. This is merely the last book that could be written while survivors and at least some of their immediate family members were still alive and able to contribute details.

Among the people whose stories surface in this book—dovetailing with archaeology for the first time—are a Japanese efficiency expert falsely accused of getting past the women-and-children-first rule by entering a lifeboat dressed as a woman. You will meet a thirteen-year-old take-charge girl who saved her deaf mother and who spent seven of her last years as a sworn enemy of historian Walter Lord over an incident involving Charles Lightoller's whistle. Stewardess Maude Slocomb describes the terrible condition in which she found the Turkish baths, which were discovered in 2005 appearing almost as shiny and new as Maude had last seen them after she finished her repairs. A gateway to the lifeboats is still locked against third class. The story of a Chinese sailor found floating on a piece of wreckage might never have been told at all if a child and her mother had not cried out after Fifth Officer Harold G. Lowe, once he realized the survivor was a nonwhite, ordered his rowers to abandon him.

Most people know the stories of passengers in the luxurious first class regions of the ship. This is the first book that turns most of its focus away from the gilded regions of the *Titanic* toward the engineers, the Mediterranean passengers, and the successful nonwhites who were not permitted to purchase first-class tickets—including the largely unknown existence of an interracial couple aboard.

In addition to accounts from survivors and their families, forensic archaeological observations, including a census of open portholes, have been carefully cross-referenced with the American and British inquiries into the loss of the *Titanic* (which are generally referenced in this book under the heading "The Examination") to resolve such issues as the extent to which open portholes and Lightoller's open D-deck gangway door quickened the rate of the *Titanic*'s sinking.

Among the stories told for the first time in this book are the events that followed after we surfaced from the *Titanic* onto a Russian support ship, as the terrorist attacks of September 11, 2001, were about to commence. During the days that followed, while living through the inverse of what people in New York City experienced in 1912—awaiting word about missing family members, at the *Titanic*—I learned that not all of my family had survived in New York, while Russians and Americans helped me to prepare for my next job: applying the same physics I had been studying at the *Titanic* at ground zero.

This is also the first book to reveal something always discussed behind the scenes: how the explorers felt the presence of the people on the *Titanic* (often called "the quiet voices"), especially at the *Titanic*'s stern section. A widespread recurrence of this phenomenon has been experienced in the ruins of the World Trade Center.

One need not wonder about ghosts of the imagination to be drawn irresistibly into the mystique of the *Titanic*. The interconnected rusticle reef has turned the *Titanic*'s entire bow section into one of the largest and most intriguing organisms on Earth. The reef is also a timely warning: rusticle growth bands are a repository of year-by-year changes in the acidity and health of the oceans.

The changes being recorded from the Mediterranean to the deep Atlantic seem to be forcing us to recall survivor Eva Hart's last warning: that humans might be capable of repeating the futility of the *Titanic*'s final hours on a global scale. Hart knew how the statue builders of Easter Island had found a tropical paradise, yet by the year 1500 they made a desert of it. Surely, some doomed tribal elder must have warned against cutting down the last stand of healthy trees.

In the end, the story of the *Titanic* is as much about the future as about the past—warning us why there is no shortage of lost ships, lost cities, and lost civilizations for archaeologists to explore.

—Written at St. Paul's Chapel, New York City, August 8, 2011

Acknowledgments

First and foremost, as always, I thank John and Jane Pellegrino, Adelle Dobie, and Barbara and Dennis Harris. For conversations and information, lively debate, and even occasionally sharing adventures on the high seas (and deep under them), I thank Walter Lord, Bill MacQuitty, John Maxtone-Graham, and the *Titanic* families of Daisy Speddon, Frank Goldsmith, Helen Candee, Emily Badman, and Thomas Andrews. I thank survivors Frank Aks, Michel Navatril, Ellen-Betty "Marshall" Walker and her friend John Hodges, Eva Hart, Louise Pope, Marjorie Newell Robb, and Millvina Dean.

In the fields of primordial biology and astrobiology—which, by accident, led me to the *Titanic* and whose fields of study have resonated through the *Titanic* expeditions—I thank Harold C. Urey, Bartholomew Nagy, Claire Edwin Folsome, Francis Crick, Cyril Ponnamperuma, Sir Charles Fleming, James Powell, and Jesse A. Stoff. Astrobiology at the *Titanic* continued with Roy Cullimore and Lori Johnston, and later with Mark Newman. I am grateful to James Cameron, John-David Cameron, Rich Robles, Mike Cameron, Ken Marschall, Don Lynch, Ralph White, John Broadwater, Lewis Abernathy, Parks Stephenson, John Bruno, Ed Marsh, Bill Paxton, Charlie Arneson, Anthony El-Khouri, Takashi (Thomas) Tanemori, Sir Arthur C. Clarke, Father Mervyn Fernando, Holly McClure, George Zebrowski, and Pamela Sargent. I thank Georgyj M. Vinogradov, Lev, Lydia, Anatoly Sagalevitch, Victor Nescheta, Genya Cherniev, Barbara M. Medlin, Glen Singleman, and the entire crew of the good ship *Keldysh* (Ohana). I am also indebted to George Tulloch, Matt Tulloch, Paul Henry Nargeolet, William Garske, Paul J. Quinn, Barbara and Dave Shuttle (Dave is a descendant of Pearl Shuttle's family), Bill Schutt (and Janet and Billy), Steve Sittenreich, and Frances Kakugawa, Hideo Nakamura, Hidetaka Inazuka, and Kae Matsumoto (regarding Masabumi Hosono's family).

My thanks for the support of Don Peterson, Victor Chan, Ed Bishop, Dee Kenealy, Doug McClean, Steve Leeper, and the families of Tsutomu Yamaguchi and Masahiro Sasaki. Thanks also to Gioia Marconi Braga, Stephen Jay Gould, Rhonda Schearer, Jay Jonas, Richard Picciotto, Eugene Rice, Richard Meo, Sean O'Malley, Paul Mallery, John Morabito, the family and friends of Paddy Brown ("This is Ladder 3, and we are still going up"), Mary Perillo, Robert Vargas, Aaron Greenstein, Paul Hoffman, "Mary Leung and the Pellegrinoids," Robert Ballard, Tom Dettweiler, Haraldur Sigurddson, William N. Lange, Cindy van Dover, Ralph Hollis, David Sanders, John Salsig, Paul Tibbets of the WHOI *Alvin* crew, Stephane Pennec, Ken and Carl Olson, and Sharon Rutman. Thank you to Sharon, Tommy, Nancy, Patricia, Hannah, and the rest of the McAvinues. And, finally, my thanks and gratitude to Elaine Markson, Julia Kenny, Gary Johnson, Tom Miller, Kitt Allan, and Jorge Amaral.

1

⸏

Convergence

Long before the first handful of iron ore was drawn from the Earth, before the gods Zeus and Osiris were named and while mammoth hunters occasionally froze to death above deposits of pre-Jurassic coal, gentle snows around the rim of Baffin Bay, near Greenland, were being compressed and forged into something horrible. The Greenland ice sheets were already ancient when Spain's cave paintings were new. At the bases of glacial snouts, layers more than seventy thousand years old carried the scent of clay and gunflint chert, buttercups and grasses, and everything else the ice had managed to pry loose and drag away.

The end came swiftly. In no more than three months the ice shelf collapsed. Shaped by flaws and crevices that until now had lain mostly hidden, an ice block more than fifty stories deep was set free and began to move.

The iceberg did not begin its journey alone. From the maelstrom of disintegrating glaciers came an entire fleet of wandering islands, ranging from nuggets that could rest easily in the palm of a human hand to bluish-white monsters towering more than ten stories out of the water. Guided by neither compass nor rudder, they collided at random intervals, capsized, broke into pieces, and dissolved by inches as eddies brushed past their undersea ledges, tugging them into the current of the Labrador Sea, off the coast of Canada. The only escape from years of chaos was in a broad stretch of the North Atlantic that had become suddenly and incomparably quiet.

Fireman John William Thompson did not have time to think about what unseen giant had slapped the side of his bunk. At 11:40 p.m. Newfoundland Time on Sunday, April 14, 1912 (the fifth night of the *Titanic*'s maiden voyage), he was lying on his back and trying to pull himself fully awake for another midnight shift at the boilers when he "felt the crash with all its force up there in the eyes of the ship." Thompson and his friends were thrown sprawling from their double- and triple-tiered bunks. They were located on the starboard side of D deck, just ahead of the number 1 cargo hatch and the spiral stairs leading down to the boiler rooms.

On the opposite side of the bow's forward section, and three decks lower than Thompson, leading fireman Charles Hendrickson would have slept through the crash and its aftermath if he hadn't been jolted awake by his friend Ford. Simultaneously with the jolt to his shoulder, there came to him from the direction of the spiral stairs the bone-chilling sound of cascading water where a waterfall had no business being. Hendrickson would later describe for investigators how he rushed to the stairs just in time to see the lower deck being swallowed up by a green gush of foaming seawater; along with that deck, the passageway leading from the firemen's quarters into the front boiler rooms was also swallowed up. In theory, at least, if the impact did not kick the tracks of the watertight doors out of line, the rapid closing of the doors should have stopped the flood from reaching beyond the submerged passageway into the boiler rooms themselves. On this night, however, what should have been and what would be were often galaxies apart.

By the time Hendrickson reached the spiral stairs, the sea appeared to be erupting through a geyser somewhere on the starboard side. Overhead, Hendrickson saw the tarpaulin beneath the number 1 cargo hatch ballooning upward like a huge dome. The surge of air pressure—which measured the pulse of water rushing in from below—whistled through the firemen's quarters with ear-popping force.

Two levels above Hendrickson, in her bunk on E deck forward, stewardess Violet Jessop had just put aside her magazines and read a newly discovered prayer to her cabinmate, Annie Robinson. The prayer was reputed to be a safeguard translated from a scroll found in Jerusalem. Robinson commented that it was indeed a beautiful, albeit strangely worded, prayer. Just after she said this, a crash came from below, followed by a low rumble mingled with frightening undertones of ripping and crunching. The deck and the walls of the *Titanic*'s servants' quarters shivered, and the distant, normally steady vibration of the ship's engines changed in a manner that indicated the shafts were either locking up or trying to reverse or both.

"Sounds as if something has happened," Robinson said calmly. Jessop's initial response was to roar with laughter.

Between Hendrickson's and Jessop's decks, the shudder that awakened third-class passenger Albert Moss provoked confusion but no laughter. Moss likened it to a sudden hard docking, although he knew at once that it was nothing of the sort. Like Jessop, the thirty-year-old sailor could tell from an abrupt shift in the normally steady and comforting vibrations in the deck plates that the *Titanic*'s engines were operating neither steadily nor normally but were straining.

Moss supposed there was at least some small chance that he might be experiencing his second shipwreck in only four months. Last December 11, he had been second officer aboard the Harloff and Rodseth shipping line's *Hebe* when a hurricane formed out of place and out of season and the old freighter began to lose steam power and to founder. Moss managed to help everyone aboard to escape alive in broken and wave-swamped lifeboats.

Now, promoted to first officer, Moss was en route to join his next ship, the *Norheim*, when yet another steamer seemed to make a sudden swerve toward chaos, but he was not worried. Although the *Titanic* did not have the *Hebe*'s better ratio of seats in lifeboats to souls aboard, it was a far larger vessel, divided from stem to stern by damage-limiting watertight compartments. Whatever was happening to the *Titanic*, it could not possibly be as bad as the final voyage of the *Hebe*.

Down in the foremost boiler room (number 6), a system of watertight doors did indeed appear to have blocked the mini-tsunami that Hendrickson saw falling upon the firemen's tunnel. A hundred feet behind Hendrickson's position, boiler room number 6's front bulkhead stood against the flooded tunnel like an unbreakable dam.

During the seconds before Hendrickson was awakened, another leading fireman, Fred Barrett, was standing outside the foremost boiler room's number 10 stokehold, having already been present for the previous day's assessment of what should have forever remained a separate and forgotten crisis involving fire damage at the bottom of a steel bulkhead.

The starboard coal bunker near stokehold number 10 had raged with fire at the base of what was about to evolve from an ordinary, redundant bulkhead to a critical safeguard separating boiler room number 6 from boiler room number 5. Hendrickson would testify later that coal bunker fires were quite uncommon in ships at sea and that in fact, during his five years with the White Star Line, which owned the *Titanic*, he had never even seen a coal fire prior to the one that had burned during the *Titanic*'s maiden voyage. It had caused the steel to glow cherry red on the first day, April 10. The fire was not put out until the evening shift of Saturday, April 13. Hendrickson and at least three other men under Barrett's command had been working around the clock for more than seventy-two hours to put out the fire and shovel out every block of coal—whether inert or burning—and feed it into the furnaces.

Tonight, Sunday night, the places where the steel had glowed red were horribly apparent: in order for steel half an inch thick to emit a noticeably red glow, the bottom of the bulkhead must have reached a minimum temperature of 1,300 degrees Fahrenheit, shifting the iron crystals into a harder and less flexible alignment. The loss of flexibility should not have mattered very much as long as the bulkhead—its base dented and warped out of shape—was not called upon to do any great deal of extra work before it could be repaired in New York.

Barrett was located in a boiler room just forward of the fire damage when stoker George Beauchamp, standing nearby, saw the telegraph from the engineer's platform in the reciprocating engine room signaling with a red *stop* light. Very soon after the signal came a rumble from the starboard hull "like the roar of thunder," in Beauchamp's words.

"Shut the dampers!" Barrett hollered—an order that was shorthand for "cut off the air supply to the furnaces." The order had not yet been carried out, and other men were still relaying the message, when water began spraying into the compartment two feet above the floor plates. It seemed to Barrett that the lower margin of the ship's starboard side had suddenly developed a series of rents and at least one hole.

In the next compartment aft, boiler room number 5, John Shepherd, an engineer, watched a hole open up about two feet behind the fire-damaged bulkhead; this meant that the bulkhead itself (already rendered brittle at its base) had suffered a lateral, compressive kick from the iceberg. In spite of this, the men with Shepherd were not worried. The hole was small, no wider than the bottom of a beer bottle, and it appeared to be the damage farthest to the rear.

Boiler room number 5's pumps should surely have been able to handle it, from everything Shepherd, Barrett, and Beauchamp knew. The giant on the other side of the hull seemed to be losing strength as it pounded toward the rear along boiler room number 5. It had failed even to disturb the piles of coal in the boiler room's hind bunker. With the danger passing—and evidently weakening—the worst they expected was a detour to Belfast, Ireland, for repairs. The three of them knew that the ship would stand up well against any possible assault. The new science of compartmentalization was bound to keep them perfectly safe. In little more than an hour, only two of them would still be alive.

Directly above the ceilings of the foremost boiler rooms and the coal bunker fire, Norman and Bertha Chambers and their neighbors in first class noticed that their staterooms had remained unbearably hot throughout the voyage. Even after the bunker fire was extinguished, the heating problem persisted, so the Chamberses went to sleep that night with the porthole of their stateroom, E-7, wide open. At 11:40 they were awakened by ice rumbling through the opening and onto the bedroom floor. In E-25, a few staterooms back at the end of the hallway, James McGough was also awakened by chunks of ice falling through his open porthole.

About ninety feet away from E-7 and E-25, on the port side of the first smokestack, seventeen-year-old Jack Thayer had also tried to combat an inexplicable overheating of his room by leaving his porthole open. Because he was opposite the iceberg's impact along the starboard side, as well as two decks higher than the Chamberses, Thayer's perception of the collision was less dramatic. He merely felt the floor sway, as though the ship were being gently pushed from the starboard side in a new direction.

Some ninety feet behind Barrett and the dam at the front of boiler room number 5, the same shock of impact—which seemed to have been abating as it punched only one tiny hole in the boiler room and gently swayed the deck beneath Thayer's feet—came on again stronger when it roared through boiler room number 4. All of the lights in the compartment went out, and coal trimmer George Cavell thought that the impact would have knocked him completely off his feet had an avalanche of coal not buried him first. The earliest, ominous sounds of gurgling must also have started about the same moment, but Cavell was too busy rescuing himself from premature burial to take notice.

Minutes later, when boiler room number 4's electrician restored the lights, Cavell would begin to wonder if his escape from suffocation was only a brief respite. Water began rising steadily through spaces in the floor plates—rising definitely from somewhere below. Although boiler room number 4's bilge pumps would presumably be able to keep the sea from rising up to Cavell's waist, it was clear that the mischief being worked between the iron and the ice did not stop at the border between boiler rooms number 5 and 6.

Boulders of ice breaking away and bouncing along the ship's bottom had evidently begun inflicting damage along the *Titanic*'s double-hulled keel as well as along the ribbing and surface of the starboard side. The ice fall added up to a significant loss of weight along the iceberg's *Titanic*-facing side, and if at the moment of impact the ship was also riding over a submerged ledge of ice as well as abrading the berg's side, this same weight loss could have caused the ledge to rise slightly by the time it reached boiler room 4.

Under the ship's third smokestack, nearly 150 feet behind Cavell in boiler room number 4, fireman George Kemish had just checked the dials in boiler room number 2 when the crash came. The ship was running with a full head of steam—then accelerating gradually to twenty-three knots. Everything seemed to be working to perfection, until the telegraph signaled *stop*, and there followed "a heavy thud and grinding tearing sound," according to Kemish.

More than a hundred feet behind Kemish's compartment, among the steam engines between the third and fourth smokestacks, coal trimmer Thomas Patrick Dillon felt more than heard the impact. It came to him as "a slight shock," following the ringing of the alarm from the bridge by between two and "a few" full seconds. There was a lag time between the stop alarm from the bridge—the shouting out of the stop order to the men running the engines—and the relaying of a signal to stop feeding the boilers and to shut the dampers, which were 250 feet forward from Kemish's position, in Barrett's boiler room.

During this interval, the iceberg continued moving toward Dillon at approximately forty feet per second. The "slight shock" Dillon felt was merely the last note in a resounding chorus of ice chunks falling against the starboard hull. Near the ship's stern the impact felt so slight that virtually no one took it to mean anything serious.

For thirteen-year-old second-class passenger Madeline Mellinger, much in her life had already gone seriously wrong. She missed her father dearly, and her mother never spoke about the exact nature of the "mistake" he had made that ultimately drove him out of England. His last beautiful letter to Madeline had come from Christchurch, New Zealand, in 1909—and then there was only a desert of silence.

Madeline's father had been a journalist—"a genius whose extravagant high living brought the family to ruin," Madeline recalled. She remembered cheerless and cold-sounding words from early childhood, such as *divorce* and *auction sale*, followed by the loss of her family's home furnishings, all of the fine family heirlooms, and finally her home itself.

Madeline's mother, Elizabeth, had become a maid and traveling companion for wealthy families. She was eventually forced to send Madeline away to relatives and then to a girls' boarding school outside London. Now, at last, the sequence of disasters seemed to be abating. The year 1912 had become one of promise and adventure, once Elizabeth secured a permanent job with relatives of the Colgates, a family known, in those days, as "new money"—still in the process of making its fortune by turning powdery mixtures of chalk microfossils and peppermint oil into toothpaste.

Young Madeline was excited beyond imagining when her mother came up to London from Southampton to tell her that they would finally be reunited aboard the *Titanic* as traveling companions of a Colgate cousin on a trip to the United States. They would henceforth be living in Bennington, Vermont, and then in a new estate on Manhattan's West 57th Street.

The Mellingers' assignment to a second-class cabin proved no obstacle to dining invitations in first class, because their traveling companion, C. C. Jones, seemed to take a special liking to Madeline's educated and formerly wealthy mother. More than fifty years later, Madeline would tell historian Walter Lord that she suspected Jones wanted to become her stepfather.

Madeline was at first enchanted by the elegantly dressed people, intricate woodwork, and engraved glass of the dining areas, and then she became enchanted by Jones. "He came to our table—which was reserved," she would say later. "He had on a fur coat, full length, and I had never seen such a thing on a man. He gave me a golden sovereign (another first). Sunday, before lunch, he came over to our cabin in second class to bring pictures of lovely Bennington in spring, and to tell us what to do upon landing. We never saw him again alive."

The Mellingers' cabin was on the same deck as the open portholes of the Thayer and the Chambers staterooms, just behind the second-class dining saloon, on the starboard side. The iceberg passed directly outside the Mellingers' porthole. Elizabeth's hearing was very poor, but she felt the change in the engines below and possibly the straining of the propeller shafts, the last boulders of ice falling off the berg and bouncing against the starboard hull. Madeline was awakened by the sudden commotion of her mother springing from the lower bunk and climbing on top of a couch beneath the porthole. Elizabeth looked outside, saw nothing, and told Madeline she might as well go back to sleep.

In the same general region of second class, a multilingual Japanese man named Masabumi Hosono was dozing off at 11:40, having just completed a lucrative but long and distressing assignment helping Japan's allies in Russia to streamline the all but completely dysfunctional Siberian Railway. The *Titanic* was only the second leg of his long journey home, and even though Hosono could have afforded to seek greater comfort in one of the first-class cabins, nonwhites were unwelcome there, in accordance with the rules of the time. It did not seem to matter, for on the *Titanic*, second-class accommodations were the equivalent of first-class ones on many other liners.

Besides, Hosono had already seen enough inequities in Russia to consider himself exceedingly lucky. The rich lived in rooms decorated with gold, lapis, and the finest Baltic amber. There was no second class in Russia—and very little left over for the so-called underclass. Hosono had seen people walking barefoot during the incomparably cold Siberian winter. In boardinghouses, the occasional renting out of hallway spaces by the innkeepers meant the difference between freezing and survival.

Hosono had seen men trying to live a week on no more sustenance than lumps of sugar carried in their pockets. He did not need to know that in a corner of the *Titanic*'s third-class section, a steamer trunk bearing a carefully packed diary would preserve the record of a fellow world traveler named Howard Irwin, including his brief friendship with a Russian expatriate named Vladimir Lenin. As Hosono began drifting off to sleep, he already knew that a Leninesque revolution was in the air. He did not have to read Irwin's diary to confirm this.

Hosono did not understand the slight sensation of the floor rattling, as though the *Titanic* were a train riding over a series of split rail fasteners or some other defect in a long stretch of track. He guessed that it was nothing more than an engine cylinder encountering some difficulty wearing into its seatings. He did not hear a distinct crash, so he did not even consider the possibility of danger. He decided to ignore the rattling floor and let himself drift off more fully into sleep.

Quartered in the same cluster of suites, twenty-six-year-old architect and engineer Joseph Laroche was already in deep sleep. He was the cousin of soon-to-be Haitian president Tancrède Auguste and the son of the wealthy businessman Raoul Auguste. He was also one of the *Titanic*'s few passengers of African ancestry and the only such passenger married to a white woman, named Juliette. The engineer was traveling with his family to New York on the first leg of his return trip to Haiti. At 11:40, the Laroches' two little girls, Simonne and Louise, ages one and three, were asleep on the second-class cabin's couch, which had been designed for conversion into a bed.

Laroche had found the French relatively tolerant of interracial marriage, but in 1912 the friendliness and freethinking attitudes of the people seemed to end where competition in the job market began. Even when he could find work, Laroche too often received wages lower than the younger and less educated engineers, ostensibly because he was younger and less experienced. Juliette's father owned a wine business in France and had tried to assist the couple financially, but Joseph wanted to provide for his family on his own merits.

Laroche's initial plan, to be a successful engineer in France, was clearly not working. He was a believer in the old saying "If the first plan does not work, you've got to have another plan." Nature, of course, had a third plan he had never anticipated, although: he, Juliette, and little Simonne and Louise apparently slept through the iceberg's passing without noticing anything at all.

Above, in the first-class smoking room, passenger Spencer Silverthorne had settled into a large leather armchair and was browsing through a copy of the *Virginian* when he heard a series of loud thuds along the side of the ship. The loudest and nearest of the thuds came almost thirteen seconds after fireman Thompson was heaved out of his bunk, near the point of the bow. On the higher decks, and more than six hundred feet behind Thompson, the impact was not strong enough to splash a drink out of Silverthorne's glass or to upset a card game nearby, although it did shake his chair.

"We've hit something!" he cried, then he dashed outside just in time to see the iceberg gliding behind the ship, higher than the boat deck and still shedding "tons and tons of ice." There was now a widening margin of water between the cliff of ice and the wall of steel. Nonetheless, the avalanche continued. Silverthorne witnessed huge pieces of the cliff tumbling off and crashing into the sea as the berg appeared to be headed astern and away from the glare of the *Titanic's* lights.

Atop the after-bridge, near the very end of the *Titanic's* stern, quartermaster George Rowe had noticed the temperature dropping so quickly around 11 p.m. that whatever moisture was in the air through which he was steaming had begun crystallizing into what he called "whiskers round the light"—"that is," he would later write to Walter Lord, "[I saw] very minute splinters of ice like myriads of coloured lights" forming halos around deck lamps. Rowe could not wait for the man assigned to the middle watch to arrive at midnight so he could get out of the intense cold.

At 11:40, Rowe was struck by a curious motion of the deck, an interruption of the *Titanic's* otherwise steady glide through water that was dead calm and smooth enough to be full of reflected stars. It felt to him as though the ship were pulling alongside a dock wall—rather heavily, yet still with so slight a jar that he might not have noticed it at all had the North Atlantic been its usual turbulent self.

Rowe looked forward and saw what he at first mistook for a windjammer that had crossed the *Titanic's* path with all of its sails set, but as it came into the glare of the "whiskered" lights, he realized that it was an iceberg. Like Silverthorne, he saw a wall of ice that appeared to be rising along the ship's side now that great slivers of mass had fallen away. Far in front of Silverthorne and Rowe, and more than fifteen seconds earlier, witnesses near the bridge saw a berg that did not quite reach the boat deck. Rowe witnessed an iceberg that had already avalanched entire cliffs into the sea; it was rising about twenty feet *above* the boat deck, a hundred feet above the waterline.

The engines were trying to bring the propellers to a stop by then, but the effort seemed to make no difference, and the iceberg continued moving away from the back of the ship until at last it ceased to reflect anything from the *Titanic*'s lamps and became a receding silhouette, lost among the stars.

The immediate aftermath was deceptively peaceful, with neither the iceberg nor the ship appearing to have suffered greatly. Despite a combined release of energy that was capable of lifting the mass of fourteen Washington Monuments in a second, the rate at which the *Titanic*'s breached compartments began to flood would reveal to naval architect Edward Wilding that the total aggregate of punctures, rips, and parted seams added up to twelve square feet of openings to the sea—a surface area equal to approximately two sidewalk squares.

In many places (such as near the fire-damaged bulkhead, where Fred Barrett had been standing), the centers of the hull plates rattled and bent like parchment but did not break, except perhaps where blocks of ice had crumbled loose and gotten slammed between the iceberg and the hull, becoming focused impacts that sometimes allowed relatively soft ice to punch holes through steel plates already being deformed at points of severe ice ramming, in much the same manner that twenty-first-century antitank weapons would routinely pierce armor plate with relatively soft copper in focused bursts. The single hole in Barrett's empty coal bunker was consistent with this sort of damage.

The *Titanic* took the shock like a series of gunshots, stabs, and rivet-popping punches—with the impacted plates rippling somewhat like dolphin skin and occasionally becoming slightly concave, while the main body of the ship remained mostly on course. Outside the impact zones, the passengers and the crew had felt little apparent resisting shock, as though the *Titanic* were merely a human hand striking a glancing blow against a sharp instrument.

2

Far from Okay

Crushed and half sunk on the bed of the Atlantic, the *Titanic*'s entire stern section and most of its debris would eventually be found at latitude 41 degrees 43 minutes north and longitude 49 degrees 56 minutes west (just over 960 miles northeast of Manhattan). Only twelve hours before the convergence of the iceberg and the *Titanic*, a Marconi operator aboard SS *Mesaba* had radioed that ice was drifting southward into this same path:

> Latitude 41 deg. 50 min. north—Longitude 49 deg. 15 min. west, passed a quantity of bergs, some very large. Also, a field of pack ice about five miles long, with numerous bergs intermixed. . . . Had to steer about twenty miles south to clear it. The ice seemed to be one solid wall—[of bergs] at least sixteen feet high, as far as could be seen. In Latitude 41 deg. 35 min. north, Longitude 50 deg. 30 [min.] west, we came to the end [of the ice field], and we were again able to steer to the westward [toward the United States].

The airwaves were buzzing with such news. The steamer *La Bretange* reported, "Latitude 41 deg. 39 min. and Longitude 49 deg. 21 min. [through] 50 deg. 21 min., steamed through an ice field with numerous icebergs for four hours—7:30 to 11:38 a.m." At 11:52, another ship, the *Baltic*, reaffirmed what lay in the path of the *Titanic*'s final resting place, warning, "Icebergs and large quantity of Field Ice today at Lat. 41.51n Longitude 49.52w." The *Baltic*'s Marconi operator added that the German oil tank steamer *Deutschland*—also along the *Titanic*'s path at latitude 40 degrees 42 minutes north—was no longer under control, it was low on coal, and it was calling out to other steamers.

With the wisdom of perfect hindsight, no one later believed that these clear warnings of danger ahead could have been responded to with anything but increased vigilance.

Down in third class, close to the waterline and approximately forty minutes before impact, Neshan Krekorian became the first and only known survivor positioned low enough to witness the deadly fleet edge-on, along the horizon line. Located in quarters only two decks above the ship's waterline, he had gone to sleep in a room where heating problems were correctable only after his bunkmates opened both portholes. By 11 p.m., the temperature in the room had shifted from unbearably hot to unbearably cold.

When Krekorian arose from his bed to close the portholes (according to his report to the Hamilton, Ontario, *Spectator*, dated April 25, 1912), he saw distant dark shapes moving against the starry horizon. "I noticed many icebergs in the water of a comparatively large size," he said. "I thought little about them, however, despite the fact that they were the first I had ever seen, as they were hardly perceptible from the distance they were from the boat."

Several decks higher, the icebergs would not likely have been perceptible on the horizon at all. From where Krekorian stood, about twenty feet above the surface of the Atlantic, an iceberg standing seventy feet tall, half a mile away, would be barely discernible as a dark nub protruding above the horizon, moving against the backdrop of stars. Viewed from an angle almost sixty feet above Krekorian, on the *Titanic*'s bridge, an observer would be looking down upon that same iceberg—an invisible black shape lower than the horizon, silhouetted against black seas. Thirty feet above the bridge, in the crow's nest, where the *Titanic*'s two lookouts stood, a berg reaching even as tall as the bridge could remain undetectable until the ship was almost upon it.

How many icebergs the *Titanic* passed during the forty minutes between Krekorian's sighting and the moment of impact was a question answerable only with astonishment that the steamer had penetrated so deeply into the ice field without colliding with something much sooner.

Krekorian's mention of the two open portholes raised another question. A single F-deck porthole, if propped completely open until the sea reached it, would have increased the twelve square feet of initial iceberg damage by nearly 10 percent. Krekorian stated that he closed his two portholes, but how many other portholes of various widths on multiple decks were open because of excessive and otherwise uncontrollable heat from the boiler rooms, and how many of these remained open through the 11:40 p.m. crash and were then forgotten? The number could only be guessed at. One might just as well have asked how many angels could dance on the head of a pin.

At the critical moment, six decks above Krekorian's position, Fourth Officer Joseph Boxhall was walking toward the bridge, along the starboard side of the boat deck. He had just passed beneath the leading edge of the first smokestack and was abreast of Captain Edward J. Smith's quarters when he heard the three-bell warning from the crow's nest signaling that danger had been sighted directly ahead. At the same moment, he heard First Officer William Murdoch inside the bridge, shouting, "Hard astarboard!"

On the bridge, quartermaster Robert Hitchens received the order and began immediately to respond. Murdoch had come running indoors from the starboard wing bridge—apparently even before Boxhall heard the three bells from the crow's nest, for Boxhall did not see Murdoch outside, even though the open-air wing bridge on which Murdoch had been standing was directly in Boxhall's path, barely ten paces ahead.

Three stories lower than the crow's nest lookouts, Murdoch had been positioned nearer the sea's surface, and even though he was not at the optimum viewing point of Neshan Krekorian, he was at a lower, better angle than the lookouts for detecting the telltale shadow climbing above the horizon and eclipsing the stars.

From Boxhall's perspective, it was all over by the time he heard Murdoch's order to Hitchens. Simultaneously with that order, the engine telegraph was ringing an order for evasive action, from the bridge to the engineers' platform in the reciprocating engine room. Even as the impact occurred, Boxhall did not slow his stride toward the bridge. He felt the first jolts of the crash a startlingly short time after he heard the three bells from the crow's nest.

From the moment the three-bell alarm was sounded, Boxhall had scarcely more than twenty feet to walk before reaching the bridge—and yet, during that brief interval of ten steps, Murdoch's orders for turning the wheel could be heard, and the clash of ice and steel had already begun.

THE EXAMINATION

Boxhall would live to testify before the examiners (during the first of two official investigations into the loss of the *Titanic*, the American inquiry during the spring of 1912, followed quickly by the British inquiry). Boxhall stated that when he reached the bridge, he saw Murdoch still in the act of pulling the lever to close the watertight doors below. Fortunately—and contrary to self-perpetuating textbook dogma about the stop order disabling the rudder and all but guaranteeing that the *Titanic* could not be steered out of harm's way—the ship had enough forward momentum, even with all three propellers stopped, to carry it through Murdoch's avoidance maneuvers.

The point was moot; there was probably not enough time for the propeller blades to diminish the efficiency of the rudder by coming to a stop and switching a normally propulsive flow of water to chaotic turbulence and drag effects. According to Hitchens, Murdoch rushed in from the starboard wing bridge and gave the order, "Hard astarboard!" Sixth Officer James Moody repeated the order and Hitchens turned the wheel—"but during [this] time," Hitchens told an American examiner, "she [the ship] was crushing the ice—for we could hear the grinding noise along the ship's bottom."

Lookout Frederick Fleet told the same examiner that he rang the crow's nest bell and immediately called the bridge by telephone. The conversation was very brief.

"What did you see?" a voice on the other end asked.

"Iceberg right ahead!" said Fleet.

"Thank you," came the reply, and the officer hung up the receiver.

The interval between Fleet's ringing the bell and hanging up the phone could have occupied only five to eight seconds. Within this time frame—in which the countdown to impact probably began with Murdoch sighting the iceberg at least three seconds ahead of the crow's nest lookouts—Fleet thought the ship had started turning to port, and he watched the iceberg strike ahead of him, along the starboard bow. All of this occurred while he was still on the phone.

Fleet would later reiterate for Second Officer Charles Lightoller that "practically at the same time" he struck the bell, he noticed the ship's head moving under the helm. If Fleet's impression was correct, the *Titanic* began turning away from the danger even before Hitchens could turn the rudder, which suggests that the bow was striking the iceberg just as the crow's nest lookouts sighted it. Fleet believed that the first blow to the ship came from a submerged portion of the iceberg, because the *Titanic* not only *turned* toward the port side but also seemed to be *lifted* slightly in that direction by the ice.

At the moment Fleet rang the bell, quartermaster Alfred Olliver was standing between the second and third smokestacks, making adjustments to the compass tower's lights. Olliver immediately put down his tools and ran forward along the deck. He arrived on the bridge seconds after seeing the iceberg grinding along the starboard side, its pointed tip rising toward the boat deck. It seemed to him that the *Titanic* had begun to heave away from the ice while Murdoch shouted orders to the helm, but Olliver would testify later that he could not discern whether the engines and the rudder really changed the *Titanic*'s direction or whether "it was hitting the iceberg that stopped the way of the ship."

From the moment the iceberg was sighted, there was very little that could be done to save the ship. Conceivably, there was no time even to begin steering, and the *Titanic* struck at precisely the angle at which it was aimed when the countdown to zero began.

Quartermaster Olliver stood by in silent disbelief as First Officer Murdoch assured Captain Smith that all of the watertight doors were closed. Olliver also witnessed the skipper ordering the engines forward at half speed, for several minutes, during which the ship probably advanced about half a mile.

Able Seaman Joseph Scarrott had felt the entire forecastle shiver, almost simultaneously with the confusion of three bells warning of danger straight ahead, and amid enough vibration and pummeling of the hull to wake anyone in the berths below. Scarrott ran down several decks to tell a friend that something had just gone frighteningly amiss. A groggy voice told him to go away and not to come back unless it turned out to be something important.

By the time Scarrott climbed to the top of the forecastle, the *Titanic* was steaming smoothly forward again. There was freshly broken ice lying on the forecastle roof, and whole truckload amounts of ice were strewn along the starboard side of the well deck. When Scarrott looked over the rail, he saw an iceberg that he believed must have been the one the bow had just struck, passing not very far behind the bridge, but this could not possibly have been the case.

At a velocity of nearly forty feet per second, the iceberg that created the actual lesions and punctures in the hull had passed from the point of the bow, beyond the bridge and almost to the second smokestack, in all of ten seconds. Twelve seconds after that, it passed Quartermaster

Rowe on the after-bridge, then disappeared astern. The able seaman's trip two or three decks down to the crews' berths, his waking of a friend, the quick rebuke, and his return to the top deck took considerably longer than the ten-second interval in which the iceberg would have remained plainly visible from the forecastle.

Scarrott recalled for the examiners that several "minutes" might have been involved; and actual minutes must indeed have been involved in his mission of warning the sleeping crew on the lower decks. By the time he returned to the top, it seemed to him as though the ship was still trying to make an evasive, circling maneuver around the iceberg. Then the *Titanic* stopped, very near to its final resting place.

What Scarrott most likely saw was a second iceberg; because very soon after impact, the *Titanic* was steaming forward at half speed, through an ice field no less densely populated than the eastern fringe of bergs that Neshan Krekorian had observed nearly forty-five minutes earlier. The sighting of a second iceberg (if this was indeed what Scarrott saw) was certainly a powerful enough signal to the bridge that the *Titanic* must now be surrounded by hull-piercing bergs and that this would diminish even the hope of sighting another ship and steaming toward it, should the damage turn out to be life-threatening.

By this time, Swedish passenger August Wennerstrom and several of his traveling companions were finding the jolt that bounced them awake in the bow section more amusing than dangerous. They ran all the way back to the third-class smoking room, located just under the after-bridge, where Quartermaster Rowe remained at his post awaiting instructions from the bridge. Wennerstrom and his friends had hoped to find something to drink, to celebrate the exciting "talk of an iceberg," the stopping of the ship, and what was sure to be an extra day or two of better than average accommodations and all the free food one could eat.

Finding the smoking room's beer service closed down for the night, and with little else to do except wait and see if the *Titanic*'s engines were going to start up again, they lit cigarettes and played the piano. Even witnessing a group of Italian immigrants entering the room with life jackets and uttering prayers to Maria failed to darken their spirits. The Swedes sang louder and started dancing in a circle around the distressed Italians.

Far in front of the party in the smoking room, just a few steps to the rear of the spiral stairs on G deck, twenty-one-year-old Daniel Buckley had jumped out of his lower bunk the moment he felt the crash. Even as Quartermaster Olliver saw the helm reverse and the iceberg pass astern, water began running over Buckley's shoes. Colder than the steel deck plates, foot-cramping cold, the water was trying to rise against bed frames and cabin walls.

"You'd better get up," Buckley told his three cabinmates. "There's something wrong."

They had all been awakened by the collision, but they had all come aboard with total confidence in the world's largest new steamer, regarded by the press and by Edwardian culture to be the virtually unsinkable pinnacle of technology's achievements. Buckley's bunkmates merely laughed at him.

"Get back into bed," one of them taunted. "You are not in Ireland anymore."

Buckley put on some warm clothing and ran up, in his wet shoes, from G deck to the forwardmost of the ship's two well decks. He arrived not very far from the place where Joseph Scarrott had stood alone atop the forecastle, watching the *Titanic* come slowly to a stop after skirting what appeared to be a second iceberg. There were more people arriving on deck now, more and more of them. Few seemed to be taking the several tons of ice on the well deck very seriously. The icefall had occurred on what was normally an outdoor recreation area for the steerage passengers, and many of Buckley's fellow travelers were launching themselves into impromptu games of ice hockey and not-so-playful ice-ball fights.

Buckley's mind was working on an altogether different assessment of danger, and it occurred to him that life jackets might soon be needed on the playground, so he decided to head down again to G deck, where he knew he could count on coming back with at least four life jackets from his cabin. At the bottom of the stairs he encountered an unexpected barrier. The water had swallowed the stairs at least four steps deep and was lapping toward his feet as he watched. The four life jackets—along with everything Buckley owned that was not presently in his pockets—were already disappearing into the Atlantic.

In the next compartment forward, lamp trimmer Samuel Hemming discovered equally disturbing signatures of disaster. Although he was not quite ready to believe in signs that were plainly readable, he knew better than most people exactly what was occurring. More than four hours earlier, as he was leaving the bridge for some much-needed sleep, First Officer Murdoch had told him, "When you go forward, get the fore scuttle hatch closed." Hemming looked ahead, toward the hatch between the anchor chains. "There should be no glow coming from that," Murdoch explained, "as we are in the vicinity of ice, and I want everything dark before the bridge."

Hemming had closed the hatch himself before retiring to his bunk, but a burst of air pressure from below had blown it open again, at essentially the same moment the crash woke him. By the time he ran to an open porthole and looked outside, the iceberg had disappeared aft, leaving behind only the loud hissing of escaping air. Hemming traced the source of the hiss to the bottom of the forecastle head, in the store-room compartment nearest the point of the bow, immediately in front of the double-hulled sides of the locker where the anchor chains were stored. In this region of the ship, every hull section was doubly layered, from the very bottom all the way up the sides—yet underfoot, water was flooding into the tank space above the keel. Air was shooting out of the tank compartment as though through a high-pressure exhaust line. Lamp trimmer Hemming was now witness to the foremost damage caused by the collision.

By 11:50, ten minutes after impact, a carpenter came down to join Hemming. The lamp trimmer explained his findings: water seemed to be moving up from below, but he believed the ship to have survived in reasonably okay condition, because the anchor-chain locker and the front storage room appeared to be dry.

"No, it's far from okay," the carpenter replied. "She is taking water fast in cargo holds [number] 1 and 2 and all the way past the racquet court." He explained that the flooding was occurring as far back as boiler room number 6.

"What does this mean?" Hemming asked.

A boatswain climbed down behind the carpenter and explained exactly what it meant: "You'd better turn out [scramble out of here]. Anyone in this part of the ship has a half hour to live—the rest, not very much longer." The boatswain added that this assessment came from Thomas Andrews, the ship's designer. "But don't tell anyone," the boatswain commanded, adding that the designer and the skipper did not want panic to spread, creating the sort of rush on lifeboats that could easily kill everyone. "And so," the boatswain advised, "let's keep it to ourselves."

3

A Slight Trepidation

As the clock struck midnight, John Hardy and at least two other second-class stewards ran along a wood-paneled corridor, banging desperately on doors. Madeline Mellinger, the thirteen-year-old girl whose father had disappeared in New Zealand, was jolted awake a second time by an unexpected commotion—and by the deck steward's unusually high-pitched cry of "Get up! Put on warm clothes and hurry on deck with life jackets." Madeline jumped down from the top bunk and ran to the door, but by then the man had disappeared, and it was too late to ask what he was screaming about.

In later years, Madeline would realize that if she had failed to take the man's order seriously, or if the Colgates had left her behind in boarding school, she would have become motherless as well as fatherless, because her mother was all but completely deaf and did not hear the knock at the door. Obeying the order, Madeline took the life jackets down from the top of the wardrobe closet, shook her mother awake, and grabbed her hymnal (a going-away gift from her school) and a handful of precious letters. The doll she had hugged every night as she went to sleep was too large to carry with the rest of her load, so she tucked it gently into a storage hammock on the cabin wall.

As the Mellingers made their way toward the top deck and toward what was to become the remarkable journey of boat 14, Madeline did not yet believe that they were leaving their room for the last time, so she barely noticed that her mother was wearing only a nightgown and a heavy fur coat but no shoes. For years to come, she would often express feelings of guilt about her mother's frozen feet. She also began to feel bad about leaving the doll behind the moment she heard adults speculating that the water beneath the *Titanic* was more than two miles deep and that sunlight could never reach the bottom. Even when she was in her seventies, Madeline was haunted by thoughts of her childhood companion: images of her lovely doll sitting among silently deteriorating curtains and wall panels, all alone in the night—forever.

THE EXAMINATION

Among the moments Steward Hardy would keep coming back to, in his seventies, were the odd questions of his American examiners.

"When did you ship with the *Titanic*?" Senator Duncan Fletcher asked.

"I shipped with her on her last voyage," Hardy replied.

"In what capacity?"

"As second-class steward."

"Did anything unusual happen on that voyage?" the senator asked.

That probably depended, Hardy supposed, on whether being awakened by an iceberg and then being roused by Purser Reginald Barker from first class—who normally never came down to second class—counted as anything unusual. No, nothing out of the ordinary happened until about *that* time, Hardy told the senator.

The Antarctic explorer Sir Ernest Shackleton had no doubts about what happened to the *Titanic* and why. He knew that without moonlight over a dark sea on which no successions of waves were breaking at the feet of icebergs, there could be no starlight reflected from white foam and no disturbance of bioluminescent marine animals like comb jellies to reveal an iceberg a mile away. He knew from experience that on excessively calm nights sea ice became "black ice," and a skipper did not want the eyes of his ship looking down from an angle more then ninety feet high in the crow's nest, but rather from low in the bow of the ship, looking out from a point as near as possible to Krekorian's angle, across the surface of the sea toward the starlit horizon.

Shackleton also knew from experience that on a night with no wind, the sudden drop of air temperatures, which had sent the passengers indoors less than two hours before impact, was a clear indication that the *Titanic* was approaching an ice field, if the warnings from the *Baltic* and *La Bretange* were not already enough. Passenger Emily Ryerson had thought that Bruce Ismay, the *Titanic*'s owner, was rebuffing her after he showed her one of the ice warnings and after she responded with a suggestion that the *Titanic* should be slowed down, but Shackelton knew that had Ismay or anyone else in his industry listened to his passenger, he might never have been called to explain to Lord Mercey's committee how the *Titanic* came to be the subject of bio-archaeology for explorers of the future.

"And you think all these liners are wrong," the examiner asked the explorer, "in following the accepted standard of putting the danger quickly behind by going at top speed in regions where ice is reported?"

The examiner turned incredulous when Shackelton explained that in the vicinity of Antarctic ice he had slowed his research vessel—which had been built specifically to resist ice—to only four knots.

"Then where did *that* get you to?" the examiner asked.

"We got very near the South Pole, my lord." He did not have to emphasize that they got there and back alive.

The examiner pressed the question: Whether he was in an ice-breaker or in a ship whose floatability had been enhanced by dividing it into a series of watertight containers, would he slow down?

"I would slow down, yes," Shackelton replied.

"And supposing you were going twenty-one and three quarters to twenty-two knots?"

The explorer summed it up in thirteen words: "You have no right to go at that speed in an ice zone."

"I think the damage is serious," Barker said, and then he brought Hardy forward and showed him a flooded crew compartment stairwell in which the water was rising much faster than it would be in a small bath-tub with the faucets opened all the way. At the top of the stairs, a newly installed water fountain for the firemen and the coal trimmers was about to be overtaken by this unnatural indoor tide. Even after Hardy was asked to assist in closing additional watertight doors along F deck, he still had confidence that the *Titanic* would remain afloat.

Hardy had been advised by Barker to get the passengers on deck with their life jackets—"just as a precaution." As he ran along a second-class corridor, he personally woke passengers in at least twenty cabins by loudly banging on their doors while shouting, "Everybody on deck with life belts on, at once." He was most likely the mysterious savior who woke young Madeline Mellinger.

Unlike Madeline and her mother, the entire Laroche family had slept through the impact and were not awakened until a steward banged on the door and ordered them up to the top deck. To Juliette Laroche, the ship had seemed from the very first day to be "a monster," as she wrote in a letter to her father, posted from Queenstown, Ireland, on April 11, 1912. Although Juliette's nonwhite husband, Joseph, was not permitted to hold a first-class ticket, the prejudicial norms of the Gilded Age had played no role in the inception, from day one, of her belief that something wicked had come into her life, clothed in steel. Her concerns went deeper than the physical surroundings of second-class accommodations—which she found to be wonderful, externally. Indeed, Juliette echoed the consensus view that the arrangements in second class could not have been more comfortable were they traveling first-class on another ship.

"The boat set out [from France] while we were eating, and we could not believe we were moving," Juliette wrote to her father. She had thus far met only one other couple on the *Titanic* who could speak French, but this did not seem to matter to the children. Little Simonne had amused her mother by "playing with a young English girl who lent her [a] doll. My Simonne was having a great conversation with her, but the girl did not understand a single word."

Nevertheless, despite the comforts of the reading room from which Juliette posted her letter—"There is a concert here, near me: one violin, two cellos, one piano"— she wrote that there did indeed appear to be something monstrous about the ship, giving her and Joseph "a slight trepidation."

And now had come the loud bang at the door and a cry of warning. Joseph, who spoke English fluently, sought out a deck steward, an officer, or anyone else who might possess information. He came back with news that the *Titanic* had suffered an accident, and his instincts told him that the monster might sink. He bundled the children in warm clothing, gathered Juliette's money and jewels, and led the family toward whatever fate awaited them near boat 10, where Second Officer Charles Lightoller would soon be working under the twin assumptions that the new lifeboats were as frail and risky as older models and could be launched only half full. To him, this meant that what little space remained in the boats was not to be occupied by adult male passengers—and especially not by passengers of the second and third classes.

Another officer in command of the same string of portside lifeboats would soon be arriving on the boat deck to become a double barrier against Joseph Laroche's chances of survival. Fifth Officer Harold G. Lowe was a man very quick to draw his gun against nonwhites approaching the boats. He generally regarded them as dangerous and glaring, like animals.

Juliette had learned only recently, while planning for her family's new life in Haiti, that she was pregnant with their third child, who would now have the peculiar distinction of becoming a *Titanic* survivor who did not appear on any passenger lists.

Ellen Phillips, like the yet-to-be-named Joseph Laroche Jr., was absent on account of not having been born yet. Her father was Henry Marshall, but his real name was Henry Morley, and he was not married to his traveling companion, "Mrs. Marshall"—who was really his nineteen-year-old shop assistant, Kate Phillips—but to another woman. From the first seconds of impact, Ellen was embarking on one of the legal world's longest episodes of abandonment and delaying tactics. Her paternity and inheritance claims would remain unresolved from the beginning of one century into the beginning of the next. Though yet to be born, the daughter of Henry Morley was already heading into a maelstrom of broken promises, dying dreams, the emerging cruelty of a young mother on the path to insanity, the false hopes of a mad dash aboard the *Titanic* to a secret life in San Francisco, and a final parting gesture of devotion in the form of a blue sapphire necklace later to be called "Love of the Sea."

Behind them, in the countryside of Worcestershire, England, the Morley family's first confectionery and ice cream shop had been standing for more than three generations. At the time of his departure, Morley was leaving behind a business that had begun expanding into neighboring towns, and he was also leaving a twelve-year-old daughter—all for the sole purpose of spending the rest of his life with Mrs. Marshall.

Morley had sold his interest in two of the family's shops with the help of his brother. A portion of the proceeds was traveling with him aboard the *Titanic*, to be used as a down payment on a new life in the western United States. The rest of the money, as arranged with Morley's brother, would provide an income for the twelve-year-old girl he had resolved never to see again. Morley had also arranged, through his brother, for the rest of their family to believe that his trip to America—to the warmer, drier climate of California—was an attempt to find relief from what he had convincingly displayed as the potentially life-threatening health of his lungs.

Convincing people of such things was not difficult in those days. Common colds and even bruised thumbs often turned deadly, and the vow of "till death do us part" usually did not mean for very long. Stewardess Violet Jessop had lost two little brothers and her little sister to what by the last third of the twentieth century would be regarded as easily treatable infections. When Violet was a child, her parents had moved her to the mountains, based on the belief, similar to Morley's, that drier air and regular doses of creosote (a product of oil tar) and red wine would cure her nearly fatal lung infection. Jessop's lungs recovered, but her father died suddenly in 1903 from a simple infection, not quite having reached the age of forty.

According to plan, Morley was to board the *Titanic* as Henry Marshall and simply disappear.

By five past midnight, Morley and Phillips and the rest of the passengers who were awakened by Hardy and his junior stewards were filing past the second-class dining saloon and the library. Even below the decks, they could hear excess steam being vented from the pipes near the tops of the smokestacks, to prevent damage from the boilers that had been providing full-ahead power to engines that were suddenly standing idle.

Despite the alarming hiss from outside, the empty library was, in its own way, eerily silent. Fellow second-class traveler Lawrence Beesley—a schoolteacher who was headed now toward a destiny in the same lifeboat as Kate and her unborn daughter—would write later that he could look back across the years and recall every beautiful detail of the room, "with lounges, armchairs, and . . . writing bureaus round the walls of the room, and the [books] in glass-cased shelves flanking one side, the whole finished in mahogany relieved with white fluted wooden columns that supported the deck above." It seemed incomprehensible to Beesley that a mindless, rudderless mass of ice should be able "to threaten, even in the smallest degree, the lives of [so many] men and women who think and plan and hope and love."

Masabumi Hosono also passed the deserted library on his way to the boat deck. The Japanese efficiency expert who had streamlined the Manchuria Railway and the Trans-Siberian Express still had several pages of "On Board RMS *Titanic*" stationery folded into his coat pocket. Letters written earlier in the day and posted in a mailbox outside the library door were now bagged and already underwater in one of the bow section's sorting rooms. The stationery was durable rag-based paper, and the inks used in 1912 were indelible.

Given the right conditions, letters written by Hosono and other passengers during the first and last voyage—or stowed away by Howard Irwin's friend in what was to become an oxygen-starved environment— were about to enter the vault of the ages, allowing the *Titanic*'s people to speak clearly after a hundred years or more. In at least one case, the comparative resilience of the *Titanic*'s paper and ink (compared to the ship's bulkheads) would bring understanding to a family divided and even a measure of vindication mingled with joy and profound sadness.

For all of his efficiency, Hosono climbed toward the boat deck with at least a five-minute handicap behind Beesley, the Mellingers, the Marshalls, and the Laroches. Initially, he had not taken very seriously the sleep-disrupting sensation of the ship riding over a bad stretch of track or bumping up against a pier in the mid-Atlantic. For a while, he wondered why the engines slowed down to a stop, but he did not imagine that anything disastrous could be unfolding underfoot, so the man least likely to ignore the unexpected stowed away his own curiosity and drifted off peacefully to sleep. If Hardy knocked at his door, the efficiency expert only vaguely heard it. Not until a stranger pounded on the door did with near wood-cracking force did Hosono rise and ask impatiently, "What is it?"

He found a steward standing outside, holding a life jacket.

"What—?"

"You need to go up to the boat deck at once," the steward said, then thrust the life jacket at him and turned away.

"Wait!" Hosono called. "Tell me what has happened." But the steward did not answer and merely hurried away.

The complacency with which Hosono had greeted the first signals of disaster faded, and the efficiency expert dressed so hastily that he pulled on trousers, a coat, and a life jacket over the coat—but no shirt. When he arrived on the second-class promenade space, he was astonished to see the canvas covers being pulled off lifeboats and scores of passengers running agitatedly to and fro.

One of the boat-deck runners swore, "I'll fight death to the last if it comes." Another paused to joke that she had put on black stockings "to scare the sharks." On every one of them was tied a cork and canvas-wrapped life jacket—the white-painted "emblem of death at sea."

Hosono stopped several of the passengers, asking the same question: "What is the cause of this?" But no one seemed to know what had happened. He now understood that there was not a moment to lose, so when a sailor indicated that the lifeboats were to be cranked down to the lower decks and loaded from nearer the water's surface, he obeyed at once—even though the man's order seemed perplexing: "Listen carefully! Everyone race down to the third-class deck!" No one else seemed to be following Hosono down toward the rear well deck, and when the young railway manager looked up along the port side and saw that the keels of the lifeboats were still stationary above him, on the boat deck, he decided to turn back.

"No, you don't!" a crewman shouted, blocking his way. "The boat deck is for first- and second-class passengers only."

Suddenly, Hosono became acutely aware that he was shirtless and disheveled—and clearly a foreigner, probably even what the crewman considered to be a member of the "lower" races.

"But I hold a second-class ticket!" Hosono said sternly. He had put the ticket in his wallet, and he had left the wallet in his stateroom. At 12:15 a.m., Hosono realized that his troubles this night had only just begun.

Approximately three hundred paces forward, in the bow of the ship, Violet Jessop was no longer fighting a compulsion toward laughter. Here the manifestations of danger varied greatly, depending on which side of a watertight bulkhead one happened to be standing. At a quarter past midnight, the steam room and cooling rooms of F deck's Turkish baths were still quite dry; and just in front of the baths, although water in the swimming pool room was beginning to shift with the tilt of the deck, the exercise clock would continue keeping time for at least another half hour, along with the clock in the cooling room. Further forward, on the far side of the steel dam beneath the first smokestack, the lowermost portholes on F deck were already becoming submarine windows on whatever sea life was being attracted to the lights.

Jessop had firmly resolved not to express what had by now become an ever-present fear—a fear "wrapped" in her heart. The report from her roommate, Annie Robinson, was definitely not good. The water in the mail room was only six steps from overflowing onto the floors of E deck. Robinson had found the ship's carpenter looking down forlornly into the pond of floating mailbags. She asked him how serious the situation might be, but he seemed not to hear her at all.

The *Titanic*'s chief architect, Thomas Andrews, was more direct. "Tommy said we should put our life jackets on and let the passengers see us wearing them," Robinson explained. She added that she had told Andrews that such a display would appear rather mean—it would be excessively frightening to the passengers—and he had replied, "Well, if you value your life, put the jacket on."

Jessop had known Andrews aboard the *Titanic*'s older, almost identical twin sister ship, the *Olympic*. The news that the incident aboard the *Titanic* this night was developing into serious business—killing business—seemed every bit as unbelievable to Jessop as it was heartbreaking, "that this super-perfect creation was to do anything so futile as sink."

Her efforts to quash the fear in her heart and escape into disbelief were aided, at least to some degree, by a real foundation in history. Although she never mentioned it to her roommate and would never speak or write of it in future years, Jessop had been aboard the *Olympic* seven months earlier when it was rammed by HMS *Hawke*. The hole in the *Olympic*'s side was wider than a church door and more than two stories tall—a total surface area of damage far greater than the twelve square feet now pulling the *Titanic* down by the head—but the *Hawke* had pierced only two of the *Olympic*'s watertight compartments, and most of the damage was inflicted well above the water, at the level of the E- and F-deck portholes. A result of this accident was that the watertight bulkhead design seemed indeed to have rendered every *Olympic*-class vessel into a lifeboat in its own right. When Captain Smith transferred his command from the *Olympic* to the *Titanic*, a deadly complacency must already have slithered into him.

Despite her desire to disbelieve Robinson's report that their ship was indeed dying, Jessop's first concern was her duty to make sure that the passengers were comfortable and safe, no matter what chaos might (or might not) be coming their way. In a letter dated July 27, 1958, relating to a friend how her primary concern was always for the care of her passengers, she would write, "The unfortunate passengers of today get scant service in comparison." By the time she retired from the sea, the next generation of stewards and stewardesses had come to regard her as "quite out of date," Jessop explained, "because I regarded my passengers' comfort and well-being on board as greatly my responsibility."

Jessop and Robinson went from room to room along E deck and C deck, helping the passengers to select warm clothing to be worn beneath their life jackets, reiterating, in spite of Robinson's fear and in spite of the gradually increasing slant of the deck, that all of this late-night activity was merely a precautionary measure. Reassured, the passengers from first class began, only haltingly, their exodus up the grand stairway, quite unhurried and even joking about the great show of British adherence to unnecessary pomp and protocol.

Jessop noticed that several officers were peering down from the carved wooden railings near the crystal dome. Their faces looked exceedingly anxious about the lumbering parade, and it would occur to Jessop much later that they must have been loath to shout down to the people anything to indicate what they really knew was happening and perhaps to cause a stampede, but the officers undoubtedly wished that the parade would quicken its pace.

Passenger Helen Candee was among the few from first class who expressed a true foreboding about an approaching horror as she watched the parade ascending toward the crystal dome; she watched men and women dressed in fur coats and their finest hats, each clutching his or her life jacket of canvas and cork. It was, to Candee, the first trump—the very first dance in what was to become "a fancy-dress ball in Dante's Hell."

Candee's friend, Colonel Archibald Gracie, was a writer of history books who had not quite grasped the possibility that history was unfolding before his eyes and would soon envelop him.

As the nightly migration of krill, cephalopods, and strange fish that no one had yet named came up from seven-tenths of a mile and swarmed outside the still-shining bedroom lights of F deck's foremost portholes, Colonel Gracie found Frederick Wright at the top of the stairs and let out a laugh. Wright was the *Titanic*'s racquetball champion. Gracie had reserved the two-story ball court for a game at 7:30 a.m., and now he joked, "Hadn't we better cancel that appointment?"

Wright answered a very emotionally flat yes and hurried away toward the rear of the ship, as though he intended to get as far away as possible from the front deck spaces. The *Titanic*'s primary decks were lettered A through G, from the top deck down. The base of the racquetball chamber was located on G deck, five decks beneath the beds of the front cargo cranes. At 12:15, the water was already flowing across the ball court's floor, knee-deep on G deck. In another fifteen minutes, it would be up to the court's ceiling at the top of F deck.

Wright evidently knew what was happening to his ball court; Jessop did not. If she had known, she would certainly have ventured back at once, seeking out her friend Jim and his cat, Jenny. Jenny had lived through the *Hawke* incident, was another transfer from the *Olympic*, and had just presented the *Titanic* with her litter of kittens. Jenny and her kittens would ordinarily have become the official good-luck charms for the ship, in addition to serving as the galley's mousers.

"She laid her family near Jim, the scullion, whose approval she always sought and who always gave her warm devotion," Jessop later wrote. "This big, patient, overworked fellow, whose eyes did not match and whose good humor was contagious—often irritatingly so when you were not in the mood—seemed always to need something to be kind to.

"But Jim was quieter than usual and somewhat distracted [during] that trip. He had left behind a wife, generally as cheerful as himself but on this occasion annoyingly anxious that he should not join the new ship's crew. There was a reason, of course: The first and most important baby in the world was due to arrive soon. He did so much want to give in to her wish, for she demanded so little of him; but there was the one-room home to keep going, so Jim sailed on the *Titanic*, with a promise to bring a beautiful baby set from New York."

From everything Jessop knew of Jim, if he had been able to get near a lifeboat, his last act of kindness would have been to pass Jenny and her kittens along in a basket to a woman or a child, asking nothing for himself. The ship was officially in a state of being abandoned, and by now only chief baker Charles Joughin and a handful of others among Jim's bosses knew that twenty-two hundred human beings were about to be filtered through a peculiar Board of Trade mathematics that had allowed lifeboat space for only half of them.

Joughin set an example by refusing to take a seat in a lifeboat, even though as a man with sailing skills (and each of the lifeboats was equipped for conversion from a rowboat to a sailboat) he was assigned to take command of boat 10. Whatever warnings he had received about the ship's condition, and notwithstanding the grim arithmetic of the night, Joughin and his team refused to surrender. Instead, they made certain that there was food and water in the boats, and Joughin assembled a small crew of volunteers to follow him during repeated trips down to third class, seeking out women and children to fill the boats.

No one would know for certain whether Jim was among Joughin's crew of rescuers. If, after the work of warning and rescue was through, he eventually retired like Joughin to the pantry and galley area and prepared, as ship's surgeon Will O'Loughlin had suggested, to meet a quick death indoors when the liner finally plunged down, Jim would have been located between the third and fourth smokestacks. This was also the area where Jenny had presented Jim with her family; should he have been unable to give the mother and her kittens over to a lifeboat (an unusual and even heartwarming event that would surely have been recalled by survivors had it occurred), the safe and familiar kitchen area is the likeliest of places Jim would have retreated to, in the end, with the ship's cats.

Nearly a century later, maps of the *Titanic*'s debris would mark a quarter-mile-long swath strewn with cast-iron stoves, cooking utensils, and pantry goods. Deep-ocean archaeologists would name the region Hell's Kitchen. The galley and pantry debris could be traced backward to a point about two and a half miles away, where—in a moment that was nearly two hours away *after* Jessop had begun her journey toward the top deck and Hosono had found himself trapped on the well deck— the ship would split in two.

If Jim ultimately retreated to the pantry area, trying to give comfort to his helpless companions in the familiar surroundings of their home, then familiarity was only an illusion, doomed to evaporate during the very instant in which chasms yawned open in the floor and pulled apart the walls and drew Jim and his cats into the ocean with the tumult of dishes, wine crates, crockery, cheeses, ovens, knives, electric dishwashers, and all of the tools of an apprentice chef's trade billowing down with him in a remorseless gush.

4

∽

Night of the Lightning Dolphins

SEPTEMBER 2001
EXPEDITION *TITANIC XIII, MIR-2*, DIVE 10
DEPTH: 2.5 MILES

Lamp trimmer Samuel Hemming's hatch was still wide open, almost ninety years later and barely fifteen feet away from us. The anchor chains, although their features have been softened by a light dusting of deep ocean snow, seemed somehow brand-new. Beyond the range of our floodlights was the deck space where Dan Buckley watched people happily playing with pieces of the iceberg. All of the wood planking in that direction had since been reduced to a spongy pulp by bacteria and by scavenging invertebrates representing at least three different phyla.

No one really knows for sure how many species took part in the devouring of the deck. In its life after people and sunlight, command of the *Titanic*'s bow has been ceded to sea creatures like "gorgons" and eyeless crabs—along with the previously unknown "flashing Milk Duds," so named because of their size, shape, and color. The one that drifted past my viewport has defied classification. No sooner had it appeared than it flashed out in dazzling green light, and by the time my eyes recovered, it was drifting out of view.

Nice defensive mechanism, I guessed—but some of the large red shrimp and many of the prey-seeking fish we see down here lack eyes and are already blind. The flashing Milk Duds must be using blinding light against any number of large-eyed creatures, most of which we haven't seen yet, because they probably fled our own lights long before we crested the nearest hill.

No one would have believed, in April 1912, that so strange and wondrous a world existed in the "ever-black," or that the *Titanic* would come crashing down into it.

AUGUST 19, 2001
RUSSIAN RESEARCH VESSEL *KELDYSH*
EXPEDITION *TITANIC XIII*
APPROXIMATELY TEN MILES WEST OF THE *TITANIC*'S
LAST POSITION

We approached the site during the Chinese calendar's Week of the Dead. Half of my family is Chinese. Some are Buddhists, some are Christian—and one branch of our clan is Russian Jews. I myself am agnostic ("to lack knowledge"). Doubting Thomas—that's me. Still, in accordance with Buddhist philosophy, and with the instructions of Ma Leung, my mother-in-law, I agreed prior to this expedition to perform, on this date, a small ceremony in my stateroom in respectful acknowledgment of our approach to hallowed ground.

Only Big Lew Abernathy (who played a role essentially as himself—Big Lew—in the film *Titanic*) and microbiologist Lori Johnston knew about the ceremony. I had explained that according to Chinese tradition, ancestors' spirits were believed to walk among the living, sometimes inhabiting people's dreams or visiting places they would like to see.

Abernathy thought about this for a while: the thirteenth expedition to the *Titanic*, arriving during the Week of the Dead. "Oh, great," he said at last, laughing. "Now I know we're not getting back from this alive."

In accordance with Ma Leung's instructions, nothing of the ceremony was to be photographed. In accordance with the *Keldysh* fire regulations, I prepared the requisite ashes in advance in the chemistry lab. The "meal" for the offering included Skittles candy, grapes, and a Mars candy bar; the "libation" was coffee and Newfoundland Screech rum. The final offering included squares of brightly colored tissue provided by Ma Leung—sent out of my porthole and meant to land on the sea as the ship slowed to a stop.

The one-man ceremony turned out not to be quite so private as I had hoped. Shortly after we arrived on site, filmmaker James Cameron took one of the new 3-D cameras out aboard a Zodiac inflatable boat to film the *Keldysh*. In Newfoundland, he had paid to have the ship repainted for his documentary. Abernathy was with him on the camera boat, when Cameron let out a startled cry of "What the hell is *that*?"

Along the *Keldysh*'s port side, sea spray and humidity had pasted scores and scores of the colored squares to the ship's white-painted hull. Fortunately, they had been made with watercolors, which would wash away and dissolve through the night; but presently they were dripping pigment, ruining Cameron's shot. Abernathy conducted a quick mental assessment to see if the mosaic of tissue-paper squares pointed in a pattern toward cabin number 5513, my cabin, but the wind had apparently scattered them in random directions before they became stuck against the hull.

Charlie got lucky this time, Abernathy thought, and kept the secret behind the colored squares to himself.

Dolphins had attended our arrival. At night they stayed with us, racing around the ship. Deep-ocean explorer Ralph White told us to keep our eyes open for one of nature's rarities. He called them the "lightning dolphins."

The greatest migration on Earth occurs during every diurnal cycle of the seas. Each night, bioluminescent predators and prey ascend from a zone so thick with life that it scatters sonar signals and is therefore called the *deep scattering layer*. Normally, ships do not stand stationary in the middle of the Atlantic, allowing people to look down from the fantail into clouds of sparkling creatures drifting and feeding—among them, a tiny squid species that leaves behind a cigar-shaped cloud of glowing ink whenever it jets away from a predator. Every time a squid or a fish touched a comb jelly or other bioluminescent animal, the creature gave off a greenish-yellow flash of distress.

On some nights—such as our first night above the *Titanic*—the "biolumes" were like giant swarms of underwater lightning bugs that usually kept their lights off. Collectively, they were millions of tiny pixels spread near the sea surface—waiting (no one really knew why) to flash their presence at the slightest disturbance. Thousands upon thousands of them were flashing all at once as the dolphins swam through them. The pixel flashes gave the thoroughly beautiful illusion of being racing streamers of lightning, shaped like pods of dolphins.

White delighted in pointing out that for all we thought we knew about the deep frontier, there was so much more we did not know. He told us that down there where the *Titanic* had fallen, "there are all sorts of large animals that no one has ever seen." He had been up close to some of them, but never as personal as he alternately wished for and dreaded (any thoughts about an encounter of the "here-be-monsters" kind only added spice to the danger of White's dreams and ours).

"I've seen giant puffs of dust," he explained, "larger than the submersible—much larger. Something big just left Dodge City as we were moving along the bottom and our lights approached. So, there *are* some really big animals down there. We've seen them. Fortunately, they haven't seen us yet."

It's strange to be thinking about what might have evolved in a world that knows no sun, while planning to explore the planet's ultimate haunted mansion, the *Titanic*, and to be thinking too about the rapid evolution of the machines we use to explore the deep range. In 1985, the first robot to perform a reconnaissance of the *Titanic*, named Argo, could scarcely be called more than a sled for equipment that, by the standard of the time, had been "miniaturized."

Exploring the wreck site then was like trying to navigate a New York City street with a camera attached to a wrecking ball, dangled on two and a half miles of cable from a helicopter in the wind—and Argo was over ten feet long. Weeks later, during Expedition Argo-Rise, we flew Argo over the hydrothermal spreading centers of the Galapagos Rift (along the East Pacific Rise). Although the Argo control van looked and felt like the bridge of a spacecraft—with racks of multiview picture tubes and VHS videotape recorders—we knew that this was but the first seedling of future-tech, and that if our civilization survived, we would look back upon Argo as a primitive relic. Thus did we live to see the future become history. By 2001, we had robots much smaller than Argo—just small enough to fit through *Titanic* passenger Molly Brown's stateroom window and explore the interior of the wreck freely. Robots still on the drawing board would be even smaller, no wider than toasters, and small enough to now commonly be called "bots."

Cameron and his brothers were able to shrink and evolve these machines year by year before our eyes, with plenty of hard-lesson glitches along the way. The equipment took on biological overtones, rendering the whole mission profile like evolution itself: chaos with feedback.

On day one of the expedition, Jim Cameron announced that submersible assignments would depend on mastering the bots. Every spare moment, we began running virtual bots through virtual rooms (in which we could select the states of ceiling, wall panel, and pipe deterioration). After a while, one really did get a sense of becoming a pair of telepresent eyes trying to seek out passenger Edith Russell's stateroom and the passageway to the Turkish baths.

We were told to expect the camera eyes in the *Titanic*'s interior to become next of kin to an out-of-body experience, with occasional jolts of reality whenever we looked out the viewport of the *Mir* submersible and saw the lights of the bots moving busily to and fro behind the *Titanic*'s portholes, like little spirits. Look away from the portholes and back again to the screens, we were told, and you will have become, again, the spirit on the other side of the hull, roaming along corridors and into staterooms.

Cameron had given a curious name to this kind of real-time telepresence, the sense that one inhabits a machine that is deep within the wreck and not part of oneself, yet at the same time it is somehow part of the self. He dubbed this the "avatar effect."

Fifteen years earlier, all of this technology was the substance of pure science fiction. Even being here in 2001, aboard a Russian ship, was like something out of an Arthur C. Clarke novel. The *Keldysh* and the two *Mir*s were built during the Cold War—a spasm in history that probably qualified as the greatest waste of human brain power since advertising and chess. Ocean explorer Robert Ballard's deep submergence machines were, like the *Mir*s, funded to serve Cold War purposes.

Within that same time frame, at Brookhaven National Laboratory, physicist James Powell had formed brainstorming sessions devoted to the design of Valkyrie rockets (antihydrogen propulsion feasibility studies), and nuclear melt-through probes to explore seas hidden under the ice of Jupiter's moon Europa and Saturn's moon Titan. These sessions became, for Powell, welcome breaks from the Strategic Defense Initiative (then popularly known as Ronald Reagan's "Star Wars" program). Along the way, Senator Spark Matsunaga had invited our brainstorming team to join his Space Cooperation Initiative.

Microbiologist Johnston and I had agreed to name some of the equipment we would be planting on and around the *Titanic* after the late Senator Matsunaga and his Russian counterpart, Roald Sagdeev. Together they had proposed that their two adversarial nations should work together toward a joint space rescue capability, perhaps even an international space station, and a joint exploration of the deep ocean (a prelude, perhaps, to Europa). They believed that by working together and learning to survive together, all alone in the cold and the dark, adversaries might discover their common humanity and in at least some small way diminish what Matsunaga and Sagdeev feared most: the possibility of annihilation by nuclear weapons, humanity's Pandora.

It was all turning out a little different from what Matsunaga and Sagdeev had anticipated, and much of it had occurred a lot faster than any of us dreamed possible. Yet, here we were, with the old "duck and cover" nightmares and fears of global nuclear winter a thing of the past. Civilization had earned its complacency the hard way. For nearly a decade, now, the world had been breathing a collective sigh of relief— and yet, although Johnston and I were working together with Russian scientists and engineers aboard the *Keldysh*, there still existed a thin, residual membrane of the Cold War standing between us.

The membrane would eventually break—it would be gone in an instant and gone seemingly forever—but not for another three weeks.

Cameron had shown Johnston and Abernathy the bronze plaque he made, questioning whether he should place it on the bottom, somewhere near the *Titanic*'s stern. It was not the calling-card type of plaque left on the bridge by so many prior expeditions, naming an institution, a society, or some dot-com millionaire on an expensive submersible camping trip, memorializing the date of each dive. It was only a simple, nameless, and timeless plaque, and on it these words appeared: "The 1500 souls lost here still speak, reminding us always that the unthinkable can happen, but for our vigilance, humility, and compassion."

5

Trinity

At a quarter past midnight, most passengers seemed to think they had all the time in the world, but not a certain Japanese efficiency expert.

On the stern, Masabumi Hosono had managed to navigate around the officer who was blocking the path to his own second-class quarters and the lifeboats beyond. When he returned to his cabin, Hosono grabbed the wallet with his identification papers and his ticket, vowing not to repeat the mistake of stepping out on the deck without the proper papers. This time, he pulled a woolen blanket from his bed, but he forgot to grab a shirt before he hurried out. He also left behind his watch, his glasses, and a wealth of gold coins representing many different countries.

Despite Hosono's attention to carrying the proper papers, his race against the rising water to the imagined safety of the boat deck was blocked once again, this time by a crewman who ordered him to remain behind and below the second-class promenade, ostensibly because the boat deck was for first-class passengers only.

As crowds began to gather on the increasingly cold upper decks, the first class congregated near the center of the ship—between the third smokestack and the two wing bridges. This was a stretch of deck space along which twelve lifeboats and rafts were available to them. The second-class passengers—those who, unlike Hosono, easily reached the promenade space just behind the third smokestack—had immediate access to eight lifeboats. The third-class passengers, along with many of the firemen and coal trimmers, who came up from below, were segregated on the two well decks in front of and behind the boat deck, where they milled about, generally following orders and awaiting permission to proceed toward the boats. They expressed various degrees of confidence and skepticism about the repeated insistence of the crewmen that there was no cause for worry.

Violet Jessop believed she saw the lights of another ship on the horizon—a savior that stood agonizingly near yet did not move.

A little after 12:15, as the water rose halfway toward the two-story ceiling of the racquetball court, Jessop descended to her cabin and folded her nightgown, putting it neatly into a drawer. She began tidying up the rest of the room—for despite Annie Robinson's description of the floating mailbags in a front compartment, the linen rooms and the Turkish baths nearby were still perfectly dry and apparently safe, even though abandoned.

The ship seemed to Jessop to be as steady as rock-solid land, so she continued folding clothing—until her friend Stanley, a bedroom steward, stopped at her door, glaring at her as though she had just joked during a eulogy.

"My God!" he swore, grabbing her by the arm. "Don't you realize that this ship will sink?"

Suddenly there seemed nothing else to say, except perhaps to ask what to wear. "I brought no warm coat," Jessop complained. "It's springtime. Who thinks of coats to meet icebergs?"

Agitatedly, Stanley grabbed the first spring outfit he saw hanging in her closet that appeared to provide some multilayered protection from the cold.

"No, Stan, that won't do," Jessop said. The outfit's multilayering was the result of ornate flowery frills. "That's no rig for a shipwreck," she protested—trying to joke, trying to say that the outfit was more appropriate for the Easter parade, trying to distract herself from crying.

"You'll need a hat," Stanley said, in what Jessop was not yet prepared to accept as a last gesture of fatherly advice. He withdrew a hat from one of her boxes—it was even more ornate than the dress.

"No, Stan—you would not wish me to go up in that, even for precautionary measures." She borrowed one of Robinson's scarves, stepped out into the corridor, and locked the door. Stan escorted Jessop to the

E-deck landing of the grand stairway, motioned for her to leave, then stood back and did not follow.

"Stan, come up soon yourself, won't you?" she asked. Two flights up, she looked down and waved to him. He did not move, "but rather stood," Jessop would write later. "He was standing with his arms clasped behind him in the corner where he usually kept his evening watch. He suddenly looked very tired."

Even as the sea reached the racquetball court ceiling between 12:20 and 12:30, it seemed difficult for people to decide whether to joke about canceling a 7:30 a.m. racquetball court reservation (as Colonel Gracie did) or scurry back toward higher ground (as racquetball pro Frederick Wright did) or whether to fret about what to wear on the boat deck (as Jessop did) or remain on the lower decks stoically facing death (as Stan did).

One who had no doubts about how to behave was Maude Slocomb, the head masseuse of the Turkish baths. She, like Jessop, had transferred from the *Olympic*. Much like Juliette Laroche, Slocomb boarded the ship with trepidation, haunted by dreams of the *Titanic* plunging down into the cold Atlantic. Unlike Jessop, she expressed not the slightest hesitation about what to wear this night. She had boarded at Southampton carrying a heavy military overcoat with plenty of pockets— which were normally absent in women's wear but were valued by Slocomb because in an emergency she could carry a cigarette lighter, plenty of food, drinking flasks, and anything else that might become useful in a lifeboat.

Slocomb was not the only person to feel an odd sense of having dreamed of or lived through this night before. Aboard the train to Southampton, she had sat next to racquetball pro Wright—who, in what appeared to be an uncharacteristic moment of self-pity, snuggled up to her and confided his premonition about their approach to something terrible, saying, "I've never felt worse about taking a ship."

Four days into the voyage, Slocomb's early unease seemed anticlimactic, if not downright silly. The only incidents were more annoying than alarming and should normally have disappeared into history, utterly forgotten. She had found the Turkish baths a shambles. The mahogany trim and decorative tile walls were properly stained, gilded, and grouted but had never been cleaned. The floors were covered with filth. Liquor bottles and half-eaten sandwiches were in every bureau drawer.

Oh, well, Slocomb told herself; the finishers were, after all, Belfast men. But they had cost her much business through the early part of the voyage, during which she and another attendant had cleaned the floors and the couches and polished the wood and the tiles to the perfection in which they were now presented—and which no one from her century was ever to see again. Yet being seen in the next century was never in the plan.

The room and its exotic furnishings were expected to last only about thirty years, the maximum anticipated service life of even a superliner like the *Titanic*. It was planned obsolescence: by 1942, the ship's designers had expected the Edwardian, Victorian, and Arabic-Oriental styles to be dismissed as "Grandma's architecture," just as they expected newer, larger versions of the automobile engine down in the number one cargo hold to replace coal-fired boilers. According to plan, sometime around 1945 (and probably sooner, but certainly no later), the *Titanic*'s Turkish baths would be dismantled along with the rest of the ship's decorative trim and furnishings, to be passed along at fire-sale prices to British hotels and pubs, while the ship's hull, ribs, and engines would be recycled as scrap iron.

Nature had a different plan. Iron- and sulfur-metabolizing organisms called rusticles would inevitably become a living reef throughout the ship, a nesting place for the actual creation of life, as though Brahma, the creator god of the Hindu triad, were being made manifest in the deep range. The sea that was swallowing and destroying the *Titanic* (Shiva) was also a paradoxical preserver (Vishnu), as though at least two members of the triad were conspiring to keep the walls of the Turkish baths standing and gleaming far beyond the liner's 1940s expiration date. Instead of vanishing, the colorful porcelain tiles from Asia were to survive unfaded and unbroken a century later, much as Slocomb had last seen them when she applied her cups of polish.

During the next half hour, as gently as the sea had seeped into the racquetball court, so too would it flow into the Turkish baths. Somehow, the entire room was fated to survive, as though it were in a cocoon, through the approximately forty-mile-per-hour impact with the bed of the Atlantic. Once oxygen-consuming microbes surrendered the room to anaerobic bacteria, woodwork and traces of fabric might last for centuries, or at least as long as the steel decks managed to stand.

Even after the last rib of steel dissolved, the tiles themselves were all but guaranteed to endure beneath a bed of rusticle dust (the residue of a microbial reef). Covered with a silica-based, hard-fired glaze whose tight crystalline structure was as near to indestructible as anything fashioned by human hands, the tiles would continue to resist dissolution long after Mount Vesuvius reburied Pompeii's mosaics and would probably even outlive Egypt's pyramids. Deep in the sunless abyss, beneath the detritus and decay products of another fifty million years of bellowing creatures, the *Titanic* itself was destined to become little more than rusticle-encased fossils sandwiched between layers of siltstone. Even then, the beautifully decorated tiles of the Turkish baths would survive, probably as the final recognizable feature of the *Titanic*, perhaps preserving in the glaze itself a fingerprint smudge from a man or a woman who painted one of the tiles—or, on a tile surface, in a latent trace of chemical polish, a print from the hand of the last person to touch it: Maude Slocomb.

On that final Sunday night in 1912, during the hours leading up to the impact, mail clerk Iago Smith told Slocomb he was leaving the *Titanic* after it returned from New York. He had a girlfriend in Plymouth, England, with whom he wanted to spend the rest of his life. Smith explained that he was unhappy that those in charge kept lighting more boilers and pushing the engines up to higher and higher revolutions despite the risks.

"I don't like it," Smith said. "Sloky, I smell ice."

"Don't be silly," Slocomb answered. "You can't *smell* ice."

When she felt the crash at 11:40, on a Sunday night—when the line between life and death often depended on decisions made during the first half hour—Slocomb realized that the odor of eroded land probably *could* be smelled in glacial ice after all and that the nightmare she had experienced back home and had finally shrugged off was becoming quite real. She grabbed her army coat and filled the pockets with her survival gear and went straightaway to the boat deck.

Another who moved quickly toward the top deck was passenger Celiney Yasbeck. She did not have much cause for denial or even hesitation. The impact in her region of the ship almost threw her out of bed. Third-class quarters in the bow were reserved almost entirely for male passengers, except that all of the Lebanese passengers, men and women alike, were also quartered there.

Celiney was the fifteen-year-old bride of Fraza Yasbeck, who had begun building a chain of shoe stores with his brothers in Pennsylvania. During a time in which women often died before the age of fifty, a twenty-year-old unmarried woman was considered a "spinster," and wealthy British families threw coming-out parties for their sixteen-year-old daughters to announce that they were ready to marry. In 1912, girls typically married between the ages of sixteen and seventeen—and most marriages, whether among the rich or the poor, were arranged between the two families.

Although the Yasbeck marriage was arranged in accordance with custom, Celiney, whose Arabic interpreter for the White Star Line would later recall her as "the poignantly beautiful one," described her marriage of fifty days as "a love match."

She and Fraza knew at once that the ship had been hit hard. The noise of the impact was tremendous. Their room was most likely located on the starboard side of F deck, behind the number 1 cargo hatch region, where the impact was strong enough to literally throw fireman John William Thompson from his bunk. The Yasbecks could have been residing as low as G deck, just forward of the number 2 cargo hatch, where what were originally designed to be third-class open berths for men were remodeled to accommodate tiny subdivided cabins. This was the general region from which crewmen like Charles Hendrickson and passengers like Daniel Buckley were able to immediately begin seeking the cause of the interior earthquake and assess the damage.

Fraza had decided from the start not to take any chances. The rumble on the lower decks at the front of the bow had been too great and too alarming. Like Hendrickson and Buckley, he did not wait for official news or instructions to come down from above; rather, he went on a fact-finding mission of his own, and Celiney went with him. The path down the spiral stairs, toward the foremost boiler room, was already underwater within the first three minutes, just as Hendrickson and Samuel Hemming had found it. Fraza wanted to personally assess the damage in the boiler rooms, but the only way now open to him, to get a view of what were in essence the lungs and circulatory system of the ship, was to proceed along F and E decks toward the roof hatches over the boiler casings.

The newlyweds, still in their bedclothes, peered down into one of the front boiler rooms—probably boiler room number 5—and saw the crew at the bottom of a long ladder "trying to repair parts of the ship."

The Yasbecks rushed forward again to their cabin, grabbed life jackets, and climbed hurriedly toward the bow section's well deck. Then, in an unexpected moment of second-guessing that in later years would be compared to Lot's wife looking back at Sodom, they reversed course and attempted a journey back to the cabin, where they had left seven hundred dollars in savings (more than twenty-eight thousand dollars today) and a dowry of gold and jewelry valued at a thousand dollars (more than forty thousand dollars today).

Judging by what he saw under Hemming's hatch and in a front boiler room, Fraza was not necessarily surprised to find the return route blocked. The Yasbecks' room was simply gone, and the narrow maze of corridors leading to it had slid completely beneath the flood. It occurred to Celiney that they might never be saved, and she stopped on the stairs at the edge of an indoor lake and began to pray.

Fraza was a "God helps those who help themselves" sort of man. He had no intention of standing on the stairs praying until the Atlantic Ocean lapped at their shoes. Grabbing his wife by the hand, he led her to Charles Lightoller's side of the boat deck, where a lifeboat hung only half filled with passengers and where Lightoller was interpreting the skipper's instruction "women and children first" as "women and children only."

Celiney gestured frantically at all of the empty seats in the lifeboat and begged Fraza not to send her away alone. He stepped onto one of the wooden seats and swept her into his arms, kissing her as though he feared that it was their last embrace—which, in fact, it was. Two men dressed in what Celiney took to be police officers' clothing grabbed her husband away and pushed him onto the boat deck while two crewmen in the lifeboat pulled Celiney to the floor. One of the officers on deck forced Fraza away from the scene at gunpoint, and Celiney began struggling and crying and demanded that the crew free her to join Fraza on the sinking ship.

"Shh," one of the men restraining her said. "It's okay," he lied, "your husband will get away on another boat and join you afterwards."

Celiney did not believe him, and she would lament forty-three years later, in a letter to historian Walter Lord, how the half-empty boat was lowered "so fast from the *Titanic* that I couldn't jump off to be with my husband."

"Why are they lowering the boat only half full?" she wondered.

Boat 6 was the first one to leave on the port side, finally touching down on the water at about 12:55 a.m. It had a carrying capacity of sixty-five, but only twenty-eight people were aboard.

On the other side of the ship, boat 7 had reached the water about ten minutes earlier, carrying twenty-eight people and passenger Margaret Hayes's black Pomeranian dog, wrapped in warm blankets.

At 12:45 as boat 7 touched down, and just before boat 6 began lowering along the port side, and the first distress rocket went up, something inside the ship seemed to give way with a hollow thud and a surge, and an initial list toward the iceberg damage along the starboard side began shifting suddenly to the port side. During the seconds that followed, thousands of tons of water started to shift in the same direction. Aboard boat 6, Molly Brown saw a great gush bursting suddenly through an open porthole on what she believed to be D deck, although it was more likely the next deck below, E.

In the same chamber where the tires of passenger William Carter's Renault Town Car were now slowly collapsing beneath fifty feet of water pressure, the *Titanic* had already claimed its first human victims nearly an hour before.

Fireman George Kemish was certain that the kindly stowaways living in the cargo hold must have died within the first three minutes after impact. There the water had come in fast enough to inflate and billow upward the number 1 cargo hatch's interior canvas deck covers. The men did not have a chance. Kemish knew them as young, penniless, ship-hopping adventurers, and he would regret in later years that he never did learn their names.

"Stowing away in those days was quite easy," Kemish wrote in June 1955. "No one knew who the stowaways were. Apparently they had no relatives or friends. That type is to be seen in most big ports. Never [listed as] missing, because they are never known—just world wanderers. They were always welcomed by us because—[in exchange for our keeping their secret]—they would keep our quarters clean."

Edith (Rosenbaum) Russell's stateroom, A-11, was still high and dry, more than four decks above the feeding frenzy of tiny grazers and predators being suctioned into the cargo holds, the firemen's quarters, and the racquetball court. After surviving the *Titanic*, the famed and previously timid fashion reporter would become addicted to action and adventure. By the time World War I broke out, she was to become not just the first female war correspondent but also one of the very first war correspondents, literally living in the trenches.

However, during the first hour of April 15, 1912, Russell behaved not much different from Jessop. Russell returned to her stateroom repeatedly, giving in to the human tendency of shifting to a nesting urge in times of great stress—a natural default setting that often makes one attend to absurd details during a crisis. The impact with the iceberg had caught her just entering her stateroom. It seemed to Russell to have begun far forward in the bow and then to have rushed toward room A-11 (which was located on the starboard promenade deck, beneath the first smokestack).

The impact arrived as a series of distinct shocks. Nearly 250 feet forward, the same crash that almost bounced Celiney Yasbeck out of bed came to Russell as "a slight jar—[with a] second one quickly following, a little stronger—and then a third: a sort of *bang*, violent enough to make it necessary for me to cling to my bedpost."

She saw the top of the iceberg—gray and monstrous, passing the promenade windows—and the floor of her room had started listing barely a minute later toward the starboard side. Just as quickly, she began to feel sick. Russell had been looking forward to arriving early in New York, on Tuesday night instead of on Wednesday. Now she had seen the effect of firing up more boilers and pushing the propellers to seventy-five revolutions per minute.

At first, as the lifeboats were swung out on their davits, the officers had told Russell that they were lowering the boats merely as a precaution: "Only a matter of rules and regulations. There is no danger whatsoever. You'll be back aboard before breakfast."

The idea of leaving a comfortable ship to row around in the cold for a few hours and come back for breakfast seemed inexplicable to Russell. Either the idea was as asinine as it sounded or the crewmen were not being quite so truthful as they seemed.

Russell locked her windows, her bureau drawers, and her trunks in two staterooms as she tidied up. In A-11, she filled her cup near the dressing mirror with whiskey, which she drank while putting her clothes away. She emptied the cup, then filled it again; then, while she was vacillating between denying danger and actually believing she was in danger, something so distracted her that she left the room with her last large shot of nerve-calming whiskey forgotten in its cup holder.

Years later, when various news organizations would write about Russell's escape from the *Titanic*, they would invariably mention the item that she did *not* leave behind in A-11: a little toy pig she had carried with her onto the boat deck.

"As for my saving a musical toy pig," she wrote in 1956, "there has been so much silly-ass talk about that pig that it's time somebody tells the world what it's all about." The recipient of this letter was Walter Lord, and even though Russell and the historian would later become such close friends that she would actually bequeath the toy pig to him in her will, her initial contact was a harsh criticism of Lord's book, *A Night to Remember*, in which the historian had described her escape with the toy.

"It's just unfortunate that I cannot correct this very unpleasant impression of me," Russell wrote, "that in a time of such great danger, I would have been so frivolous [that I would] walk around carrying a musical toy pig with me. The pig—which is a mascot [of good luck] in France, was given to me after a motorcar accident in which everyone was killed except me. I promised my mother to keep [the pig] as a mascot with me in time of danger."

As the *Titanic* began developing into another of her many encounters with disaster—"always fatal to others"—Russell believed that she had to keep her promise never to leave the pig behind.

The fashion reporter wondered how her life had come to another disaster in the first place. Like Juliette Laroche, Russell had boarded with the impression that there was something monstrous about the ship—like a sleeping kraken waiting to awaken and break its chains. Like Laroche, Russell memorialized her trepidation in a letter on *Titanic* stationery, posted after the ship left Paris:

> My Dear Mr. Shaw—In length [the *Titanic*] would reach from the corner of the Rue de la Paix to about the Rue de Rivoli. Everything imaginable: swimming pool, Turkish Bath, gymnasium, squash court, cafes, tea gardens, smoking rooms, and bedrooms larger than in an average Paris hotel. It is a monster, and I can't say I like it. . . . I am going to take my very much needed rest on this trip, but I cannot get over my feeling of depression and my premonition of trouble. How I wish it were over!

A century later, most people would remember the name of Russell's "monster," but few would be able to name its older twin. If all had gone according to expectation, more people would remember the *Olympic* than the *Titanic*. The *Olympic*'s maiden voyage had received all the photographic news coverage, all the movie newsreel attention. A reason that so relatively few pictures existed of the *Titanic*'s first days arose from the simple fact that it was never good to be the second of anything. Even the grander staterooms, the glass-enclosed promenade deck, and all of the boasts that it was the largest ship in the world were seen as transparent publicity stunts. The *Titanic* was many tons heavier than the *Olympic*, but it was longer only on account of a few extra inches of steel added to the prow. By the time the clock touched 12:45 on the morning of Monday, April 15, even calling this ship "almost" unsinkable had deteriorated into a grand and meaningless boast.

Almost directly beneath Russell's stateroom, down near the keel, a critical limit had been reached. The steel bulkhead separating boiler room number 5 from boiler room number 6 was on the verge of becoming the first falling domino in an unstoppable cascade effect. The bulkhead was designed to withstand a maximum water pressure of 19.6 pounds per square inch. About the time Molly Brown saw water bursting out through an open porthole near E deck, the water pressure at the bottom of the bulkhead—now being exerted by flooding corridors five to ten feet higher than boiler room number 5's dam—was 22 to 24 pounds per square inch. Across a width of ninety-two feet, this meant that more than 145 tons of water pressure was seeking a weak spot along the lower foot of the bulkhead, trying to bulldoze an opening through it.

In the end, the barrier was functioning beyond its design standards; it might actually have continued to resist the various abuses of the night had the coal fire reported by Fred Barrett not warped and dented and, to one degree or another, diminished the flexibility of the steel at the base of the dam. In addition to this improbable event was the even more improbable circumstance of the iceberg's final kick to the lower starboard hull, which occurred along the base of the wall to which the embrittled steel barrier was attached, and this opened up holes on either side of it. Surely the final blow compressed the bulkhead itself between the two holes, rendering the last two or three feet of iceberg damage in boiler room number 5 the cruelest wounds of all.

If not for either the warping and stiffening of the barrier by a coal fire or for the final stab from the iceberg reaching barely a human arm's length past the wall, the *Titanic* might have floated another hour or two, and perhaps longer.

Shortly after the 11:40 p.m. impact, Barrett had closed the empty coal bunker's steel door, thus allowing the chamber adjacent to the damaged bulkhead to slowly fill through the single hole caused by one of the iceberg's final stabs. This prolonged the life of the bulkhead by more or less equalizing the water pressure on both sides, until 12:45 to 12:50 a.m.

In boiler room number 5, Barrett's attention was drawn suddenly to a knocking noise; then he saw a great wave of green foaming water tearing through a space between the boilers. The whole *Titanic* immediately began losing buoyancy in this compartment, as though air were being let out of a giant balloon. This was probably the cause of the shift that sent water spilling toward the port side and out an open porthole near Molly Brown and Celiney Yasbeck in boat 6. The volume of air compressed upward by the breach—and especially from the moment that boiler room number 5's rooftop escape hatch was opened on E deck—was proportional to the amount of water Barrett saw surging into the chamber.

Like the air surge that Hendrickson and Hemming had observed pushing up a tarpaulin and a hatch cover near the front cargo hold, this burst of air possessed the power to displace—a power that, if it had been confined primarily (during the first few seconds) between the floor and the ceiling of E deck, should have contributed to the sloshing movement, from starboard to port, of any water that had been pooling in the corridors nearby. The addition of a jetting effect to the slosh was consistent with the sudden gush from a porthole near boat 6.

Barrett scarcely had time to swim to an escape ladder and pull himself up through one of the roof hatches that the Yasbecks had peered down into nearly an hour before. There was little doubt in Barrett's mind that he had been witness to the bulkhead itself bursting. The great surge of water probably began with a rupture in the relatively thin steel that enclosed the flooded coal bunker—which the single firehose-like puncture had taken all of an hour to fill to the breaking point, slowly, in the manner of a swimming pool being filled by a garden hose. The coal bunker burst would have taken just three or four seconds to empty the bunker of its water, after which the only source of continued flooding should have remained the hoselike spray from the bunker's sole opening to the sea—which was not the sort of leak from which Barrett or anyone else would have been forced to flee. What came into boiler room number 5 was much worse.

During the minutes leading up to the burst, engineer Herbert Harvey had asked Barrett to help him lift a manhole cover that gave access to the pump valves inside one of the double-hulled bottom's forty-four watertight compartments. Shortly before the preflood knocking sound drew Barrett's attention, another engineer, Jonathan Shepherd, was hurrying across the deck to a piece of equipment that he never did reach. Not knowing that a manhole cover had been lifted, he tripped into the hole and fractured his leg. Barrett, Harvey, and Kemish lifted Shepherd from the hole and laid him down near boiler room number 5's pump valves.

When Jim Cameron finally succeeded in guiding one of his bots past the fallen steam pipes and other debris along a hallway called Scotland Road (the long E-deck corridor), marine engineer and historian Parks Stephenson noticed that one of the rooftop escape trunks from either boiler room number 5 or number 6 was open, with the escape ladder below the lid still visible. Of the two possible boiler rooms lying beneath the opening, more likely this was an escape hatch from number 5. The abandonment of the next chamber forward, number 6, had been a relatively orderly event. Although steel doors were closing off the floor level between the compartments very shortly after impact, water entered boiler room number 6 as a wide and fairly steady spray rather than as a boiler-submerging gush that developed quickly into sustained, riverlike rapids. The last men out of number 6 would most likely have sealed the hatches, in accordance with the regulations. Barrett and Kemish had left number 5 in a hurry, knowing that two of their companions, Shepherd and Harvey, were still below and had at least some chance, no matter how small, of reaching the ladder and pulling themselves up through the escape trunk, as long as no one added the extra handicap of closing the lid on them.

Since the men were running and then climbing for their lives, the release of the equalizing head of water in the coal bunker must have been followed in quick succession by a rupture at the bottom of the fire-damaged wall—a rupture that the flooding bunker had been helping to prevent. A breach in boiler room number 5's dam no broader than a sidewalk square and no higher than a man's knee, with a fifty- to fifty-five-foot head of water pressing back and downward from boiler room number 6, became all that was necessary to produce a horrifying, continuous gush.

With all of the coal having been removed from the starboard front bunker of boiler room number 5—and with the rapid loss of buoyancy in number 5 pulling the bow down deeper—a natural tendency for the rising flood in number 5 would be to shift toward the coal-heavy port side, causing the entire ship to begin shifting in the same direction.

Barrett and Kemish managed to escape the broken dam by a margin of seconds, before the flood developed into deep and deadly rapids and began shifting the *Titanic*'s list from starboard to port. When they looked down from the ceiling hatch, there was no sign of engineers Harvey or Shepherd.

6

Of Nature, Not above It

AUGUST 20, 2001
RUSSIAN RESEARCH VESSEL *KELDYSH*
EXPEDITION *TITANIC XIII*

The lessons of what happened that night cannot be forgotten here.

From the beginning, Anatoly Sagalevich (our director of submersible operations) and Jim Cameron were ever vigilant for anything that could possibly go wrong with our new array of great machines. In addition to our two bots, there was a one-ton photo-recon robot named Medusa, designed to follow and film the submersibles while providing floodlighting so intense that the *Titanic* would stand out in the darkness like a Ken Marschall painting come to life.

During a briefing on the procedures to be followed if something should go wrong with Medusa and the *Mir*s at the same time, Bill Paxton, the actor who was to become the narrator for Cameron's IMAX/ Disney documentary, was looking increasingly worried about actually climbing into one of the *Mir*s. Paxton began spending more and more time on the top deck, nervously and almost obsessively sketching everything he saw. In only a few weeks, he would begin evolving, with fascinating rapidity, into a good artist.

A conference about the survivability of a rapid ascent in the *Mir*, in which the submersible might actually tumble the crew compartment like a clothes dryer all the way up, had left the actor a little pale.

"Oh, stop worrying," Big Lew Abernathy said. "If a man's gotta die, what better way to die than advancing our knowledge of science and history?"

The comment left me grinning and nodding in agreement. Paxton looked at us both as though we had lost our minds. He began rattling off some other choices of how to die, some of which even sounded somewhat pleasant; but Abernathy had not really been asking a multiple-choice question.

AUGUST 21, 2001

Artist-historian Ken Marschall and I unintentionally managed to put a heightened sense of trepidation into poor Bill Paxton with a simple discussion of perspective. I had always referred to the depth of water from the surface to the submerged *Titanic* as being ten World Trade Center twin tower lengths. Marschall pointed out what this meant in terms of artistic perspective. If the waters of the North Atlantic could somehow be made as transparent as air, then at our "ten Twin Towers" altitude, if we looked over the side of the *Keldysh*, the 450-foot-long bow section of the *Titanic* would appear as tiny as one's own fingernail viewed at arm's length.

Paxton did not believe it possible that anything could give him a sense of acrophobia, or fear of heights, over open water. "Impossible," he said—but there it was. Fortunately, his sense of wonder remained intact (helped along by a nightly rereading of his favorite childhood novel, the illustrated edition of Jules Verne's *20,000 Leagues under the Sea*). There were plenty of discoveries being made to keep his love of mystery alive. Lori Johnston displayed her film footage from the previous month's reconnaissance of the World War II ship *Bismarck*.

Compared with what could be seen in photos taken during Robert Ballard's expedition to the German warship a decade earlier, there had been a surge in the growth of rusticles—mostly bacterial-based organisms whose interior structures were so specialized that if they had been built from nucleated cells (instead of being built from archaea, a score of different bacterial species, and at least two species of deep-ocean fungi), we would have said that, like sponges, they belonged to the field of zoology.

Johnston had come up with a fascinating new puzzle: Why this explosive growth on the *Bismarck*—which had previously been almost rusticle-free? In a very short time, it had become almost as densely draped in rusticles as the *Titanic*, when it was discovered in 1985. Was it possible that the *Titanic* had been lying on the bottom in almost pristine condition for decades until the rusticles reached a sort of biological flash point? Or was something on the bed of the Atlantic changing, causing recent accelerated rusticle growth at two wreck sites hundreds of miles apart?

Georgyj Vinogradov and the other Russian biologists corroborated the observation that something interesting was happening here. During a 1996 French-American-Canadian expedition, we had charted a greater than 75 percent increase in the number of brittle stars and sea cucumbers (both cousins of the starfish) living outside the *Titanic*'s debris field, compared with the population density of these same bottom-dwelling echinoderms recorded during Ballard's 1986 expedition. Since 1991, Vinogradov and his colleagues (people who were literally writing the books on deep-ocean wildlife) had been watching the area for miles around the *Titanic*, while it transformed into the deep-ocean equivalent a forest from what in the 1980s had seemed to be a biological desert.

Flowerlike crinoids and sea squirts were growing anywhere their stems could find anchorage, including atop rocks dropped by passing icebergs and on lumps of coal from the *Titanic*. Unusually long-legged, bright red hermit crabs were on the march, often using, as a protective helmet, the shell of an unidentified snail species whose defensive exoskeleton appeared to be made mostly of rubber. A calcium-secreting worm thrived on all solid surfaces, from the occasional boulder to the *Titanic*'s rusticles.

Red krill were drifting about—not swarming, as they do in upper waters. They appeared to be solitary hunters and scavengers. A previously unknown organism was building nests on the seabed from tiny, individually selected black pebbles (selected from an environment in which the majority of the pebbles being dropped by icebergs were white quartz). The pebbles were bound together with a silklike twine into inchlong hollow tubes. Evidently, the web spinners abandoned the protective stony tubes as they grew, building successively larger shelters up to four inches long. And just as evidently, the black pebbles were chosen because they made the tubes harder to see, notwithstanding our presumption that the world of the *Titanic* and its web spinners lacked any light source significant enough to make such selection necessary.

No one had yet found one of the pebble tubes with the creature that built it still inside. They resembled the stony shelters of freshwater caddis-fly larvae, but despite their apparent familiarity, as far as we knew, no insect had ever conquered the deep sea, so we were looking at the home of something no one had seen yet.

A one-liter jar full of surface-layer sediment (adding up to about a quart) from our sunless abyss, collected nearly two miles north of the *Titanic*, contained almost two thousand shrimplike arthropods of several species—all of them smaller than garden variety ants, many of them barely larger than grains of sand. Unsegmented worms dominated the samples, uncounted new species—fistfuls of them sometimes residing in just a few liters of surface-layer mud. Cicada-sized, spindly red octopi roved about in the company of a black bioluminescent species of fish that appeared to be all mouth, with a huge eye on either side of its jaws. The fish was eerily intimidating even if it was only two inches long.

In general, twelve liters (just over twelve quarts) of mud scraped from the top inch of the deep-ocean plain—whether gathered near the *Titanic* or ten kilometers (slightly more than six miles) away—yielded for us nearly a liter of worms, arthropods, and hard-shelled limpets. Collectively they represented up to several hundred species. The mud around the *Titanic* was roiling with at least as much life as mud from the floor of the Amazon rain forest; and this count did not even get near the microbial base of the food chain, which we suspected was growing under the influence of increasing levels of deep-ocean "snow." Something appeared to be causing more nutrients to drift down from the deep scattering layer, more than a mile above the *Titanic*.

No one could say with any degree of certainty what was causing the increased nutrient throughput. All that could be said for sure was that a measurable change was taking place. Our latest rusticle samples showed marked growth spurts during the last seven cycles of ring deposition—an actual doubling of growth rates. This was consistent with other indications that something had been happening that was indeed quite different from a prior record of relatively lifeless deep ocean plains, as memorialized in thick clays just a few inches beneath Vinogradov's mud samples.

At a guess, overfishing—to such an extent that more than 90 percent of the North Atlantic cod were gone and swordfish boats were being required from about 1990 to hunt farther and farther east—was removing so many predators from the equation that the deep scattering layer was undergoing a population surge. We wondered if something else, by the hand of humans, was bringing about the change, or maybe what we were seeing was the result of some as yet undiscovered natural cycle, perhaps amplified by the spread of civilization.

Vinogradov agreed that the *Titanic*'s rusticles seemed to have begun growing at a biologically explosive rate. During only a decade, the thin steel decking at the rear part of the bow section had been metabolized by the invader (whose growth also depended on biological nutrients in the water)—to the point of total disintegration. The decks once covered the rear boilers like a garment, but rusticles had now stripped them away, making the front half of boiler room number 2 visible for the first time.

The *Titanic* was presently a very different ship from the one that Ballard had first landed on in 1986, different even from the ship Vinogradov had first seen in 1991. The starboard boat deck, from just behind the second smokestack all the way forward to the grand stairway entrance, almost to boat 5's location, had collapsed down into the promenade deck. The entire gymnasium was falling with it. Alongside the cavity where the first smokestack once stood, the roof and the starboard wall of Captain Smith's quarters were devoured, revealing the skipper's rusticle-encroached bathtub.

Ten years earlier, our submersibles would have landed on a completely level steel deck outside the captain's still-intact quarters. Now the deck was rippled, resembling swells at sea, frozen in midroll. Fortunately, our multi-ton submersibles, once submerged, became undersea blimps, flying at close to zero buoyancy, touching down with barely more negative buoyancy than an overfed cat. These days, if a mass equal to one of the *Titanic*'s own lifeboats were placed on the starboard boat deck, it would most likely fall through to the deck below and continue falling. The rusticles had done their work. The steel was now a house of cards, accelerating toward total collapse.

When Ballard first photographed the uppermost rail on the *Titanic*'s point bow in 1986, the railing itself still appeared almost new, with only an occasional rusticle bud breaking out here and there. In 1991, rusticle growths enclosed the entire head of the rail's stem, and Georgyj Vinogradov photographed a delicate gorgonarian colony flowering atop the rusticle consortium.

A relative of the hydra, "Georgyj's gorgon" was named after the trinity of mythological monstrous sisters that included Medusa. The flowerlike growth was really a colony of branching "snakeheads." Each head sent forth its own set of branches: eight poisonous tentacles surrounding a mouth.

Under the gorgon's trunk, as the rusticle consortium grew in strength, absorbing organic debris from the water and metabolizing iron, zinc, and sulfur while converting more and more of the *Titanic*'s mass into its own shell-plating and DNA, so too grew the gorgon.

By 2001, the rusticle reef was growing out horizontally from the front rail, tracing the direction of the prevailing currents and sending forth slender shrublike branches of its own. During this same time, Vinogradov's gorgon (identified as *Chrysogorgia agassizi*) had been growing steadily at one centimeter (almost half an inch) per year. The species was previously known to grow on rocky bottoms and atop old telegraph cables, at depths generally no greater than the deep scattering layer, where minute planktonic animals were widely available. Despite a long-presumed relative scarcity of prey, Vinogradov's *Titanic* gorgon was sprouting more heads per branch, compared to its upper-water cousins (two or three polyps, versus only one or two), and it was growing four times faster.

Notwithstanding all we once thought we knew about the lack of food in this world without a sun, there was much more life in the so-called deserts of the deep than had been anticipated, and the *Titanic* was becoming a good place to be a filter feeder. The rusticle reef and the gorgon told us so; they drove home again explorer Ralph White's mantra: for all we know, there is so much more we don't know.

For those who looked with a parallax view into the crumbling triumph of civilization against nature, the corpse of the *Titanic*, though fascinatingly ugly from one angle, could be mournfully beautiful from another. Like the Colosseum—which in eighteenth-century paintings was overgrown by hanging gardens of wildflowers—even the most ordinary railings of the *Titanic* were a curious blend of natural and man-made lines. As the thirteenth expedition progressed, and bots Jake and Elwood penetrated into stateroom after stateroom, revealing that most of the plastered walls and ceilings had fallen away, bot-eye views became, on multiple laptop screens, a gallery exhibition of life aboard the *Titanic* during the last days and during the subsequent decades of a lost world.

In rusticle-draped rooms reminiscent of Luray Caverns, instead of seeing stalagmites sticking up from the floor, we beheld row after row of stateroom bedposts with their original Edwardian carvings, softened by bacterial erosion into hauntingly artistic shapes. Passenger Henry Sleeper Harper's porthole was still open, just as he had last seen it, but it was the bedposts that caught my eye. One of the eroded wooden posts seemed to have a veiled female head precariously balanced at the top. I was reminded immediately of a chapel carved into a corner of an old east European salt mine, where the moist exhalations from centuries of congregations had similarly reworked the salt-carved statues of saints into impressive new sculptures of the sort Picasso might have made. Looking at the bacterially hewn bedpost sculptures, I decided that one of them did indeed resemble a Picassoesque Madonna and child.

Even as holes opened up on the boat deck and even as the *Titanic*'s ceilings and bulkheads became more rusticle stalactite than steel plate, the ship did not merely lie in state in its orange shroud. It was evolving into a living work of art.

Everywhere we looked, microbiologist Roy Cullimore's "old lady, elegant lady" was alive. The steel decking above boiler room number 2 was now part of the rusticle reef's skeletal and circulatory system. The boiler room was newly exposed, as if by a surgeon's scalpel, allowing us to peer into the compartment where George Kemish had been standing during the very first rumblings of iron against ice. Rat-tailed fish patrolled the boilers at the aftermost part of the bow section—"like the sentries to hell," Paxton remarked.

7

The Cascade Point

The critical turning point was 12:45 on Monday morning, April 15. Up to that moment, as the forward E-deck portholes came down almost level with the sea surface, the ship was actually approaching a chancy sort of balance with the twelve square feet of breaches inflicted by the collision. Although the state of equilibrium was tenuous, the rising water levels inside the punctured compartments were slowing to a halt, and the sea within had come almost level with the new waterline outside the ship.

Each boiler room could be sealed off at the roof by closing the casing hatches, which were somewhat like bottle caps. In theory, this feature added to the ship's invincibility. In practice, the true power of water lay in its mass. A road flooded only one foot deep with water moving at only three miles per hour could easily carry away a one-ton car. This meant that just one bathtub full of water (or its equivalent volume and mass), pressing against a car at three miles per hour, could push the car completely off a road. The volume of water working against the interior dam that separated boiler room number 5 from the flooded compartments in the bow was many times greater than car-displacing bathtub volumes and roads flooded one-foot deep.

THE EXAMINATION

According to naval architect Edward Wilding, the bulkhead should normally have been able to resist a level of water pressing down upon it from significantly higher than E deck before reaching either the bending or the breaking strength of the steel—which was half an inch thick at the base of the dam and one-third inch thick at the top.

"Any height at all [of water]," Wilding explained to examiner Clement Edwards, "will produce a certain amount of bending. The steel is flexible."

Edwards asked, "Assuming the water was up to fifty-five feet, with the flexibility of the steel, have you any idea to what extent it would cause a bend?" He was talking, of course, about a bulkhead already dented and made less flexible by a coal fire. "There would be a certain point reached by the bend," the examiner continued. "Which [do you think], might cause a displacement of the rivets?"

The dam in boiler room number 5 was the tipping point at which the sinking could either be slowed or be dramatically quickened. Wilding insisted that the rivets, according to his math, would not give way until the forces exerted against them reached seven-eighths the break strength of the steel. He added that the height of water above the dam was "nothing like enough to do that."

"Nothing like?" asked Edwards.

"Nothing like," Wilding insisted.

Edwards continued to press the question, wanting to understand whether it had been possible for the water to create a bend in the wall of riveted steel plates sufficient to cause displacement of the rivets and, in such a manner, indirectly trigger the springing of steel plates along some part of the dam.

"No," Wilding insisted again; then, after several seconds of reflection, the shipbuilder came back with a question of his own: "Do you mean to push [the rivets] out or to make them slightly loose in the hole?"

"I mean to make them slightly loose in the hole to begin with, and then to cause a movement of the plates or a movement of the [plate supports, or] stiffeners."

Wilding acknowledged that loosening the rivets would occur much earlier than their actual popping or being pushed out.

"And the moment [that] a loosening [is] begun," Edwards pressed, "there might be an accelerated process of displacement?"

"No, I think not," Wilding replied.

"You think not?" Edwards asked.

"I think not," Wilding insisted, adding that even if the rivets could put up only seven-eighths the resistance of the steel plates, then according to calculations based on almost identical bulkheads, tested in tanks filled with water, the *Titanic*'s boiler room number 5 bulkhead should have held back the sea even with more than a hundred feet of water pressing down upon it.

The examiner saw that this defender of the ship's builders seemed either to not be grasping or to be evading the core of the question. Wilding's calculations did not take into account the many random processes that began converging against the critical bulkhead after half past midnight, as the angle of the deck increased toward the bow and started shifting slowly toward the port side, and as the equivalent mass of several truck convoys of water, moving generally toward the stern, shifted at the whim of the flooded decks on the other side of the dam.

Edwards began to express skepticism about Wilding's math; in particular he questioned the shipbuilder's conclusion that the critical bulkhead could have held back more than twice the depth of water for which it had been designed.

Wilding finally admitted, regarding the critical bulkhead's *really* being able to hold back more than a hundred feet of water pressure, that this conclusion was "only in general terms."

"That is where your [test] tank is perfectly still and the water is quite passive?" Edwards wondered aloud. "And if there were a swaying movement, *that* would make a very great difference to the power of the water and the pressure of the water on the bulkhead, would it not?"

"It would undoubtedly make some difference," Wilding said, "and that is why the strength of the bulkhead is so much in excess of the height."

"Do you not think," Edwards asked, considering the recent example of the *Titanic*, "that it might be very advisable, instead of relying upon mere calculations, to get bulkheads [more] practically tested under actual water conditions?"

The question clearly irritated the architect, and he replied as a headmaster might reply to an unruly schoolboy, "I think I told you that the results were known to me of bulkheads which had been tested, and they agreed with the calculation."

Edwards did not take the dressing down quietly. "That is not quite an answer to my question," he said, stressing again that the tests and calculations were based on water sitting perfectly still in a tank and not on real-world conditions representing "as near as may be approximated, the actual conditions which these bulkheads are built to resist."

The commissioner now interrupted, on Wilding's behalf, "Sometimes they are in a storm, you know."

"Yes," said Edwards.

"Are you to get a storm?" the commissioner sniped, "for the purpose of your test?"

Edwards conceded that he appeared to be on the verge of getting a storm, right there in the hearing room; and the commissioner cut Edwards's whole line of questioning short.

Human law was capable of silencing an inconvenient line of questioning and turning it into instant resolution. Nature's laws resisted such resolution, and under such laws, the *Titanic*, like Earth itself, could only abide. The test of Wilding's bulkhead calculations, under conditions of nonpassive, shifting masses of water, was already being applied by the time Fraza Yasbeck led his beloved Celiney toward boat 6.

The Yasbecks had traveled from the forecastle and the forward well deck to the relative safety of the portside boat deck without facing the sorts of obstacles that Masabumi Hosono encountered at the stern. A few minutes behind them, twenty-one-year-old Irish immigrant Daniel Buckley—who, like the Yasbecks, had returned below to find the entire third-class section gliding down beneath the flood—now discovered the path from his quarters to the boat deck guarded by sailors.

On the starboard side of the well deck, the gate at the top of the stairs behind the cargo cranes would remain locked throughout the bow section's final plunge, throughout deck-flattening bottom impact and a tsunami-like down-blast from the column of water that followed the wreck to the bottom. The barrier would still be telling its story, even after a century of rusticle assault.

The gate was little more than waist high. Although it was not an impressive barrier, according to Buckley there was a moment after midnight during which men identifiable to him only as "sailors" lined up at the top of the gate and stated with authority that the steerage passengers were to remain down below, either in their cabins or on the well deck.

Buckley knew that there was precious little left of "down below." He had seen the disappearance of the cabins. Others had seen it, too, so it seemed to them that the crew had contrived a plan to keep them down in the forecastle and on the well deck to be drowned like rats in a cage. Buckley joined a group of men who rushed the gate—a rush that began when a steerage passenger was thrown down the steel steps by one of the sailors, as an example to anyone else who attempted to climb up to the boat deck. The man stood up again and made himself an example of another kind. He ran up the steps and over the gate, with an enraged crowd scrambling up behind him in support. The sailors fled as the leader of the charge vowed that if he could find the man who threw him down the stairs, he would pay him back, an eye for an eye and a tooth for a tooth and then some, by throwing him overboard.

Buckley recalled the gate being broken during the onslaught, but for the gate to still be closed when submersibles flew over it a century later meant either that Buckley misremembered what was in fact a mass exodus *over* the barrier or that crewmen came back to fix and relock the gate.

During the American inquiry, Senator William Alden Smith asked Buckley if the breakout through (or over) the gate was the only opportunity that third-class passengers from the well deck had for getting away in lifeboats with passengers from second class and first class. Buckley affirmed that this was indeed the case, because after the assault on the gate, the steerage passengers could not be kept down on the well deck any longer, and the classes on the boat deck became "all mixed."

The British inquiry gave no such insights, because neither Buckley nor any other third-class survivor was seated for testimony.

At the stern, Japanese efficiency expert Hosono, like Buckley, refused to take no for an answer and barged past the crew member who had tried to keep him below. Swedish passenger Anna Turja and several of her friends from the stern made a similar, lifesaving decision to break out from the lower decks, refusing to listen to the commands of a crewman who ordered them to stay below in third class. Hosono and Turja had been shocked but not entirely surprised to discover lifeboats swung out all along the top deck with their covers off. The first clustering of passengers around the aft boats seemed a curious mixture of order and chaos.

Neither Turja nor Hosono knew anything yet about the mathematical discrepancies between naval architect Wilding's calculations of bulkhead resistance and the real-world effects of water in motion, nor did they know of the discrepancy between the total maximum seating of 1,180 in the lifeboats and the more than 2,200 passengers and crew aboard the ship.

• • •

At approximately 12:45 a.m., almost up to the point at which Wilding's miscalculation made itself known in boiler room number 5, Fifth Officer Harold G. Lowe was asleep in his quarters on the port side of the boat deck. His room was located near the first smokestack, several decks above the critical boiler room number 5 bulkhead. He had been forgotten by the rest of the crew; the work of waking the passengers and swinging the lifeboats out on their davits had begun without him.

It was the sounds of disorder that accompanied the cranking out of boat 4 outside his window—and probably the sudden loud arrival of "Buckley's brigade" from the well deck—that finally woke him. Stepping outside his cabin, Lowe found women in the officers' quarters with life jackets strapped over their clothing.

He could feel beneath his feet that something was terribly wrong with the ship, as though it were slowly tipping toward the bow, about ten degrees down. He knew this, in spite of (or rather, because of) the paradox of leveling. The *Titanic* had been constructed with a natural curvature of the decks, from the bow and stern downward toward the middle of the ship. Under normal circumstances, the deck in Lowe's cabin slanted upward toward the forecastle. The uncanny leveling out was no less alarming than the dead engines. By the time Lowe had gotten out of bed, the initial listing toward the iceberg damage on the starboard side had also shifted to almost level. Directly underfoot, vast quantities of water were moving toward the port side.

Dressing quickly and crossing over to the starboard side, the fifth officer assisted in the lowering of boat 5, which reached the water about the same time as the boat carrying Molly Brown and Celiney Yasbeck. Lowe now carried with him a loaded revolver, under the premise "You never know when you will need it."

The first distress rocket burst a hundred feet or more above the *Titanic*'s decks at about 12:45 a.m. At this time, mystery writer Jacques Futrelle arrived on the port side. This was also around the time that Molly Brown, descending into boat 6 along the port side, observed water suddenly exploding out of an open porthole near the waterline. Within this same time frame, the dam in boiler room number 5 broke and engineer Herbert Harvey, evidently unable to help engineer John Shepherd quickly enough to safety with his broken leg, died with him.

Lily Futrelle felt something strange happening beneath her feet. "I had no sooner reached the deck than she [the *Titanic*] began to list to port," Mrs. Futrelle recalled.

Within ten or fifteen minutes, the porthole through which Molly Brown saw water rushing out would be carried down by both the shifting mass of water (indicated by the gush itself) and by the rapid and catastrophic loss of buoyancy in boiler room number 5. The increasing list to port was sure to pull the gushing porthole beneath the ocean surface, reversing the outflow to an inflow.

This was not the only opening now threatening to quicken the pace of the sinking.

On the starboard side, directly above boiler room number 6, publisher Henry Sleeper Harper had been awakened by the 11:40 p.m. impact. He ran to the nearest bedroom porthole and looked out to see what was happening. As reported in an April 1912 edition of his own magazine, *Harper's Weekly*, he watched the iceberg racing toward the stern and into the dark only a few feet from the starboard hull, "crumbling as it went." He could never have seen such details by looking through a closed porthole; only, as he said he had, by looking out of the porthole.

Almost a century later, When the mini-robot Jake maneuvered into Harpers's stateroom, D-33, its lights revealed—beyond the wreckage of a wooden dresser that had spilled out Harper's bowler hat—the port-hole nearest his bed: wide open, in a manner consistent with Harper's description of how he witnessed the iceberg's passage. The dimensions of the porthole were twenty-four by nineteen inches. It was mounted on a pivot; so it would forever remain anyone's guess what the original angle of the opening had been when the ocean reached D deck, for the journey to the bottom, with water rushing along the hull and the effects associated with the final crash into deep-ocean mud, must surely have changed the angle. At minimum, even if partly closed and even if no other openings of this sort existed, the Harper port at some point added two square feet to the original surface area of the damage (which had begun at only twelve square feet).

Three starboard D-deck portholes near the Harper stateroom were also open. Opposite the Harpers, on this same deck, the port side of the bow section displayed four additional open portholes plus an open gangway door. The D-deck portholes alone constituted a surface area approximately equal to the initial iceberg damage and were capable of doubling the rate of the ship's sinking.

In 2001, historian and artist Ken Marschall began a count of porthole openings that would eventually combine the photographic results of more than twenty years of expeditions, all the way through 2010. Along the port side, Marschall counted 132 portholes that were located in regions of the hull not ruptured, bent, or otherwise deformed by the final crash on the abyssal plain. Only in uncrumpled areas could people's intent be guessed at; of the 132 portholes, including a porthole under the front of the well deck, 18 percent appeared to be open.

On the starboard side, 17 percent of 114 C- and D-deck portholes appeared to have been left open. C deck hardly mattered, for by the time the D-deck openings were submerged, the cascade effect must have been gathering such momentum that any openings above, along C deck, were reduced to mere redundancy.

From E deck down through F deck, no determination could be made regarding the porthole accelerants, because the ports were of a different design: they swung upward and had to be "dogged" (or latched) closed with locking pins. The portholes of the Chambers staterooms (E-5 and E-7), into which ice had fallen during the 11:40 impact, had an open port of this either "propped open or dogged shut" style. The only determination possible, in this case, was from the Chamberses' own testimony.

Marschall concluded that once the bow section broke away and began plunging toward the bottom, any open E-deck and F-deck portholes would probably have swung shut and possibly "only appeared 'closed' today from the outside. So we'll never know how many of the E and F deck ports were undogged [not locked with a pin]—unless someone wants to take the time and expense of manually pushing on each and every port [with a submersible's robot arm] to see if it pushes inward, open."

The portside door at the front of the long E-deck corridor known as Scotland Road appeared at first glance to have been opened by someone (which would have made it a major, early source of flooding), but it was located in a region where the bow section had been bent like tin foil during bottom impact and must have popped open like a cork, for the doorway's inner safety gate was still drawn shut and secured. Evidently, the Scotland Road door remained closed throughout the sinking and did not contribute to the *Titanic*'s acceleration toward its final plunge.

Above the damaged Scotland Road door, the portside first-class door on D deck told a different story. Although it had fallen off its hinges by 1996, it was still hanging open against the hull when Bob Ballard performed his first reconnaissance dives ten years earlier. Because the door was located in a region where there was no discernible hull deformation, with its inner gate clearly drawn open, Marschall believed it doubtful that the door could have been knocked open during the crash on the plain. The door's eight locking pins should have kept it secure, just like the next steel door immediately behind it.

In this instance, Marschall's bets were on someone "having opened it during the sinking." He explained, "Considering the bow-down angle and the [development of a] list to port, one can imagine how that heavy door must have swung open with a vengeance the instant its last [locking pin] was released." These steel "shell doors" were expected to be opened and handled only in calm ports with the ship standing level. "But surely," Marschall decided, "with the bow angling down and tipping toward the port side—once that heavy door flew out of their hands, I would imagine all bets were off. I'm guessing that closing the door again (pulling it back 'uphill') would take far more manpower than was available."

About 160 feet away from the open shell door, under the front of the well deck, the foremost open D-deck porthole was located on the port side of the third-class men's open recreation area and smoking room. Sometime before 1:20 a.m., and perhaps within only fifteen or twenty minutes of the boiler room number 5 flood, this porthole would have become the first open one *above* E deck to slide beneath the ocean surface (not very far behind the probable E-deck porthole observed from Brown's and the Yasbecks' lifeboat as gushing water).

Fourteen inches in diameter, this single recreation-room porthole was able to add approximately 10 percent to the total surface area of openings made by the iceberg. All by itself, the rapid flooding of the third-class open space on the port side would further increase the ship's list to port. The tilt was bound to keep Harper's large first-class porthole on the starboard side (in room D-33) above water for a while longer, but his stateroom and his belongings were by then enjoying only a brief respite. Even under a design plan by which the deck spaces curved from the center of the ship upward toward the bow, in a manner that had made the floor beneath Fifth Officer Lowe's feet feel peculiarly level in spite of the fact that the *Titanic* was settling by the bow, by the time Lowe awoke, the line of portholes along the front of D deck was already shifting from parallel with the sea surface to a slight downward slant.

Probably within ten minutes of the recreation-room flood, the open porthole near stateroom D-20 was pulled below the surface, quickening the rate of the water's climb toward Elizabeth Lines's stateroom, a little farther back on the port side (at D-28); at this point, the lower boundary of the gangway door, forty-five feet behind Lines's cabin, was poised to become the biggest opening of all.

By the time the sea began flowing one foot deep across the threshold, the door, which was four and a half feet wide and six feet high, became an open wound equivalent to one-third of the iceberg's accumulated stabs. Only minutes later, once the water streaming through the door had reached a height of three feet, the total iceberg damage would have been effectively doubled by this single door, even if no other openings (including the front portholes) had existed. A few minutes after that, the damage was tripled. This single opening was capable of pulling the entire *Titanic* down by the port side. This final fatal hemorrhage probably began about 1:30 a.m.

Shortly afterward, the bow section's well deck was drawn down by the port side and began to flood—exposing many square feet more to the sea through its hatches and doors. Along D deck, water entering through the gangway door found quick passage down to E deck through stairwells and began moving along Scotland Road, as far back as the second smokestack.

Scotland Road ran nearly the whole length of first and second class, along E deck's port side. The pressure thus building against the front bulkhead of boiler room number 4 (behind the already flooded boiler room number 5) was immense. This was not a static head of water building against an interior dam; rather, it was water inside an increasingly unstable ship prone to powerful shifts and sways. As the *Titanic* shifted, water in already flooded compartments was driven by the same law of inertia that forces passengers in a car slightly forward or backward whenever the driver applies the brakes or the accelerator. Even a small inertial push was potentially fatal to a wall of steel already being pressed to its breaking point.

The boiler room number 5 bulkhead had ruptured under scarcely fifty feet of water. By 2 a.m., the water pressing against the base of the boiler room number 4 dam was sure to reach eighty feet, with a significantly lesser but nonetheless major head of water pressing down on the thin metal of the boiler room roof and its closed hatches. The chamber was doomed to a slow squeeze toward its bursting point, from both forward and above—and even from below, from which came another source of flooding, as early as the 11:40 crash.

Before the first distress rocket left the deck at about 12:45 a.m., before engineers Shepherd and Harvey were drowned by the boiler room number 5 breach, and before Celiney Yasbeck was held by force from leaving a lifeboat to rejoin her husband on the deck, Thomas

Patrick Dillon, the coal trimmer who had been assigned to clean the gear under the giant reciprocating engines when the impact occurred—and who (being located far aft) was among the last to feel the jolt from crumbling ice—saw how another line in the epitaph of the ship was going to be written.

Immediately after the crunching sounds passed, Dillon saw engineers running to their stations, readying the pumps and valves. Chief engineer Joseph Bell then ordered Dillon forward with several other men to open the watertight doors—which had been closed from the bridge by William Murdoch. Dillon's team was instructed to run pump hoses forward, because the most powerful pumps on the *Titanic* were located aft of boiler room number 4. Dillon would live to tell British investigators that his orders were to crank up and secure the watertight doors as far forward as he could go. His team was also asked to make sure that the men in boiler room number 2 kept the steam pressure up for the electric generators. The doors were opened all the way forward to boiler room number 4. They were still open when the chief engineer ordered Dillon and most of the younger men up to the top deck with life jackets, about fifteen minutes after Shepherd and Harvey had died on the other side of boiler room number 4's bulkhead.

THE EXAMINATION

"If Dillon's evidence is correct," examiner Edwards said to naval architect Wilding, "could he account for the watertight doors being kept open up to a point when it seemed water was about to start entering boiler room [number] four?"

Wilding explained that he could see no reason the watertight doors should not have been kept open—"provided there was no need to close them."

Seemingly perplexed by Wilding's answer, Edwards phrased his question another way: "What point in the filling of the fore compartments do you suggest would represent a need for closing the watertight doors between [boiler room numbers] four and three?"

"Whenever water began to come into number four in a serious volume," Wilding replied.

"Not until then?"

"Not until then," Wilding insisted. "It would be of no value until then; and the reason for [not closing the doors until] water begins to come in—and in a serious volume—[is that before the water actually does reach that point, it's] necessary to take steps to check its flow."

"It would not be necessary to close those watertight doors until such time as it might represent the ship being in a state where the whole thing was hopeless?"

"Quite," Wilding said, not entirely grasping, even after the fact, how hopelessly time-critical the situation had become.

Shortly after Dillon had been sent away to the upper decks, the sea was climbing up to, and then into, the open gangway door on D deck's port side, ultimately putting more than 230 tons of pressure against the lower foot of boiler room number 4's dam. If the bow dipped or tilted perceptibly, the motion of water in and above the flooded boiler room number 5 could easily increase the force against the bulkhead by a multiple of two or three. Although the boiler room number 4 dam was not embrittled by fire and side-kicked by ice and could surely stand longer than the bulkhead that had preceded it in boiler room number 5, the fall was nonetheless inevitable.

Not very long after 1:15 a.m., the port side's open gangway door was bound to start angling the bow down like the minute hand of a large clock that had broken and was picking up speed—and which was connected to a time bomb. When finally the surge came through boiler room number 4's front wall—or through the rooftop casing or both— there would be no time to close the boiler room number 3 bulkhead (especially if it had been propped up by a wooden brace to allow a pump hose to be run through).

Even worse, the shared ducting with the second smokestack would assist in the overflow of water from boiler room number 4 to boiler room number 3, regardless of whether the number 4 compartment could be quickly sealed. Possibly, the boiler room number 2 bulkhead was also about to be rendered unclosable by the ferocity of the flood waiting to break through boiler room numbers 4 and 3. No one would ever know. The door to number 2 would never survive the breaking of the *Titanic*'s spine. Only the door at the rear end of the reciprocating engine room, as revealed by the robot Jake in 2001, would show any signs of having been closed in time. If boiler room number 4's forward bulkhead and the doors lifted behind it were the bomb's detonators, then D deck's open gangway door was the timing device.

By his own testimony, Second Officer Charles Lightoller appeared to be the man who set the device in motion. He continued to believe that the newer lifeboats could buckle if filled on the decks to their maximum carrying capacity of sixty-five or seventy people; he continued to believe that the ropes could not bear the weight of fully filled boats. Lightoller decided that the safest plan was to send the lifeboats down on the ropes with only a minimum of passengers, have the half-empty boats row to the gangway doors, and then send additional passengers down to them on "pilot ladders" and "Jacob's ladders," lowered from the doors. The plan made sense in principle, but in practice it came apart quickly.

Captain Smith called out to the first boats through his megaphone—ordering them to come back to the ship's side and be ready to take more passengers down through the gangway doors; inexplicably, their crews disobeyed, rowing away as though their minds had suddenly been illuminated by something more frightening than quartermaster George Rowe's distress rockets and they were now trying to get away from the *Titanic* with all possible haste.

Harper and his entourage got away in boat 3 about the same time that Rowe's third rocket went up, near 1 a.m. Forty people and Harper's prize Pekinese dog, Sun Yat Sen, were launched aboard a boat designed to hold up to seventy.

The tilt toward the port side evidently increased by the time boat 3 had descended along the starboard side. Harper noticed that before the ropes could finally be loosened, the lines were leaning his lifeboat inward from its normal vertical alignment with the starboard hull until the side of the boat actually bumped and grated against the wall of rivets and steel.

The D deck porthole in the third-class recreation room—and within this same general time frame, D deck's portside gangway door—had begun probing the cascade point.

Lightoller, in accordance with his plan to load half-filled lifeboats *after* they touched down on the sea, had sent a boatswain and six other men below with orders to open gangway doors on both D deck and E deck. None of them was ever seen again, and Lightoller never received confirmation that the order had been carried out. An analysis of the actual ruins of the *Titanic* indicates that only one door was successfully opened.

It was plain that other officers understood Lightoller's plan and intended to abide. Passenger Norman Chambers, a mechanical engineer, would report that as boat 5 reached the water, Third Officer Herbert Pitman was under instructions to stay near the starboard side and prepare to take additional passengers down through an open gangway door. Chambers was certain that the starboard doors remained closed—all of them. This observation was consistent with physical evidence that only a single portside door was intentionally opened, almost certainly by the men Lightoller had sent below. It was also consistent with the disappearance of Lightoller's boatswain and his entire team.

If the portside D-deck door was indeed open about the time the first or second rocket went up—which was about the same time Molly Brown saw water bursting suddenly through an open porthole near boat 6 and minutes before Harper's boat began grating against the starboard hull (as the third rocket went up)—then a tilt to port that started with the boiler room number 5 collapse intensified during the flooding of the third-class recreation space, beneath the bow section's well deck.

Under such conditions, once the steel door had been opened, not even seven men possessed enough strength to pull it closed again, "uphill." Their most likely reflex, once they saw water rising perilously close to the door, would have been to keep trying, even if the odds seemed impossible, right up to the moment the water began surging over the door's baseboards. Within seconds, the tilt to port must have begun worsening even further, and by the time the rush of seawater was up to the men's knees, even wading would have become difficult—and running away impossible.

This was also within a time frame approximately ten minutes after boiler room number 5 gave up its buoyancy, meaning that the D-deck doorway and the portside corridor leading fore and aft of it ranked high among the last places on Earth that any seaman still taking in air and in his right mind wanted to be. There was no mystery in the question of why Lightoller never saw the boatswain or his men again—or about any of the other questions put to him regarding open gangway doors.

8

∽

Everything Was against Us

THE EXAMINATION

On May 21, 1912, Solicitor General Sir J. Simon asked Second Officer Charles Lightoller the following question: If the *Titanic* was already down by the head, would it not have been unwise to open a door in the front part of a ship that was sinking by the bow?

Lightoller said he had not particularly noticed that the ship was tending to go down by the head when he gave the order for doors to be opened.

"Of course, you know now that the water was rising up to E deck?"

"Yes," Lightoller replied. "Of course it was."

"It appears to me," the solicitor general said, "that you would be very unlikely to order the forward gangway door to be opened. You might get the head of the ship so deep in the water that you would ship water through that gangway door."

"Of course, my lord, I did not take [it] into consideration at that time. There was no time to take all these particulars into mind. In the first place, at the time, I did not think the ship was going down."

• • •

At approximately the time he ordered boat 6 away and Celiney Yasbeck screamed out for her husband, Lightoller found a gauge by which to measure what was actually happening to his ship. He ran forward and took a quick look down the narrow emergency stairway behind the portside wing bridge, which descended as far as D deck. He was shocked to find water on the floor of D deck. After the next lifeboat was sent away, he looked down and saw that the sea had climbed higher into the front compartments.

"Frankly," Lightoller told an interviewer on November 1, 1936, "I'm never likely to forget the sight of that cold, greenish water creeping step by step up that stairway. Some of the lights were shining down on the water—and others, already submerged, were giving it a sort of ghastly transparency. But for my purpose, I could tell by that staircase measurement exactly what was happening; how far down she'd gone and how quickly she was going."

The second officer would be unable to recall exactly when he realized that time was running out, but sometime before he prepared to assist with the launch of boat 10, shortly after 1:10 a.m., he began ordering more people into the lifeboats, despite his belief that a fully loaded boat might break. By then the list to port was growing so pronounced that the gap between the boat-deck rails and the lifeboats themselves was widening to three feet.

Boat 10 was eventually filled with fifty-five people, but Lightoller continued to abide by his rule of allowing only women and children into the boats, and he was inclined to tighten even that rule when it suited him. He believed that passengers from the third class had no right to be on the boat deck, whether they were men, women, or children. Lightoller's definition of *women* did not include Violet Jessop, Annie Robinson, or the other stewardesses of the *Titanic*. His definition of *children* ended when any ten- or thirteen-year-old boy seemed either to have entered puberty or to be on the verge of it, therefore making him old enough to be a man.

Under Lightoller's rules, when Fifth Officer Harold Lowe found a boy among the women in boat 14, he forced him out. Although the child was hardly more than a schoolboy, Lowe drew his revolver and said, "I give you just ten seconds to get back on that ship before I blow your brains out."

By the time a second child was barred from a boat, Colonel John Jacob Astor, then known as the richest man in the world, had seen enough of Lightoller's rules. A boy of about twelve was declared old enough to be a man and told he could not enter a lifeboat with his mother. The mother, of course, would not enter without her child, and anyone looking on who understood the escalating series of events unfolding beneath the boat deck would have known that this was a sentence of death for both mother and child.

Colonel Astor was among those who knew from the captain what was about to happen to everyone. Grabbing a hat—by one Astor family account, a girl's hat; by another account, his own—he covered the boy's head and declared, "He's a child now!" However illogical the Astor declaration might have seemed, it was powerful enough to intimidate Lightoller into letting the boy enter the boat with his mother.

Even as Lightroller's gauge at the stairwell revealed the water to be crawling up the steps with steadily increasing speed, his actions continued to create bottlenecks at the portside lifeboat stations. An insistence on separating wives from their husbands and mothers from their young boys caused heart-wrenching delays. His occasional retreats into denial of what his stairwell gauge was showing him caused further, fatal delays—in a race against time that his order to open gangway doors had already accelerated.

When passengers asked, "Why are you getting the boats out?" he had assured them and himself that the launchings were merely a precaution.

"Very likely you'll all be taken aboard the *Titanic* again at daylight," Lightoller insisted. He seemed to believe, even then, that it might somehow turn out that way. But everything was against them, Lightoller would tell Lord Bigham Mercey's commission. Had the sea not been as flat as a tabletop, with not a ripple or a breeze, they would have seen a glow at the base of the iceberg even on a night such as this without a moon. No one in Lightoller's time knew yet about the phosphorescent sea life that migrated more than seven-tenths of a mile underwater during the day and returned to the surface every night. All anyone knew was that every night, the strange oceanic lights came on, and the slightest disturbance of the ocean surface made them flash.

"Therefore," Lightoller explained, "at any time when there is a slight breeze, you will always see at nighttime a phosphorescent line around a berg." Even the slightest ocean swell, he added, causes the same effect, "showing a phosphorescent glow."

The oars of the lifeboats were enough to reveal the effect that Lightoller said should normally have alerted First Officer Murdoch and the crow's nest lookouts. Henry Sleeper Harper found the sea lights so bright that he almost imagined he had seen a sliver of moonlight reflected onto the water: "And at every stroke of the oars great glares of greenish-yellow phosphorescent light would swirl aft from the blades and drip in globules like fire from the oars as they swung forward. The phosphorescence was so brilliant that it almost dazzled us at first."

In the same vicinity—as surely as the *Titanic*'s poolroom and Turkish baths were now alive with swirling lights—these same organisms would have revealed the iceberg at least a quarter to half a mile ahead of the collision point, if only there had been a breeze or a swell.

Lightoller also told the investigators that at 10 p.m. he was under instructions to keep a sharp lookout for ice; yet he had no apprehension about the continual firing up of more boilers to push the steam engines up to twenty-two knots. He and the rest of the officers had an ambition to see what the ship's maximum speed would eventually be as it steamed full ahead on a moonless night through waters darker than a mineshaft, into an ice field that he and the captain had already discussed for twenty-five minutes.

"Everything was against us," Lightoller insisted.

9

❦

Stalking the Nightmare

AUGUST 23, 2001
RUSSIAN RESEARCH VESSEL *KELDYSH*
EXPEDITION *TITANIC XIII*

John-David Cameron, Jim Cameron's brother, was one of those Marines whose unit followed the old Greek philosophy of developing, to the men's maximum potential, both the mind and the body. One requirement of his unit had been IQ scores that belonged up in lights on a movie marquee. Naturally, John-David was one of the men who understood our new generation of bot probes down to the smallest fiber-optic spool and plastic clip. In his spare time, while watching the deep scattering layer come up to the *Keldysh*'s fantail after sunset, he liked to kick back with beers rigged to either freeze in the bottle or foam all over a friend's hand, arguing about where theoretical physicist Stephen Hawking might have gone wrong with the idea that information could never pass through the cosmic singularity (the Big Bounce) and where Stephen Jay Gould appeared to be taking the Butterfly Effect (an idea in chaos theory) and contingency theory (a behavioral theory) too seriously.

"And of course," he'd be glad to tell you, "[physicist Werner] Heisenberg might have been here."

John-David Cameron's Internet link to the expedition (a predecessor of YouTube) and the Cameron brothers' bot company were not given names like Earthship and Dark Matter, respectively, for nothing.

With historian Don Lynch, we had been reviewing Walter Lord's careful matching of the *Titanic*'s passengers and crew members with their staterooms. Because many prospective passengers (including Lord William Pirrie and his friends) canceled their plans for the maiden voyage, there had been many opportunities for passengers to change and upgrade their rooms once they boarded—which, in fact, many wrote of having done. Thanks to Walter Lord's decades of correspondence with survivors and his analysis of their family memoirs, when our bots ventured into a stateroom, we now had a very good idea whose room we were visiting.

Lynch would eventually become heir to Lord as the historian who knew more about the *Titanic*'s passengers than anyone alive. In the years leading up to our expedition, Lynch and I had disagreed often about the details of the ship's last voyage. Now that Lord had allowed me to produce multiple copies of his entire history of correspondence, Lynch and I still disagreed on many points, but at least he finally understood the firsthand eyewitness accounts from which some of those disagreements had originated.

More often than not, the side-by-side addition of Lynch's documents and his recollections of conversations with survivors revealed that his interpretations were correct. More and more, we came to appreciate the old cliché of how three witnesses to an accident could give three entirely different accounts of what happened. The paradox was multiplied when the memories were told and retold over many years. Memories kept bottled up inside and not spoken about for several decades tended, when finally spoken or written about for the first time, to more closely match the British and American inquiry testimonies. Memories repeated over and over by survivors from the very beginning tended to pick up mutations along the way.

As an example, Lynch pointed out to me how the little black bulldog spoken about so eloquently by passenger Eva Hart in later years did not exist in her earlier accounts; nor did many other details she gave, some of which became self-contradictory as the decades passed. It seemed that constant replay through numerous retellings could be damaging to memory and to historical reality.

We began to wonder what percentage of our collective human history might be illusion, brought about quite innocently by the mutation of memory. Aboard the *Titanic* alone, some famous examples were emerging. In her May 31, 1964, interview with Lord, Renee Harris recalled different details about her last card games aboard the *Titanic* from those she had written in an earlier family memoir. By 1964, she had begun relating clear recollections of being invited to a poker game in one of the two B-deck suites with its own private promenade sundeck.

Lynch did not think this possible, for Harris was identifying the Cardeza suite (B-51, B-53, and B-56—which, along with parts of *Titanic* owner Bruce Ismay's suite, was replicated as the Cal Suite in Jim Cameron's film, *Titanic*). Lynch strongly suspected that the game of poker recalled by Harris fifty-two years later must actually have taken place on another private promenade, on another ship, probably years after the disaster—having subsequently been composited into Harris's memory of that last Sunday afternoon aboard the *Titanic*.

Lynch's reason for such suspicion was that the Cardezas were, to put it as politely as he could, "rather snobbish." During an era in which racial prejudice, including anti-Semitism, was perfectly acceptable— war correspondent Edith Russell had been required to Anglicize her Jewish-sounding name (Rosenbaum) in order to be successfully published—the Cardezas were fashionably prejudiced against Jews and would have shunned the Harrises, who were also Jewish.

Most of the individuals aboard the microcosm called the *Titanic* simply behaved as people trapped by their time. The norms of the time were such that Fifth Officer Harold Lowe could be perfectly open, without fear of rebuke, about having attempted to keep nonwhites out of boat 14. He was remembered more for bringing the boat into the midst of survivors and floating wreckage after the *Titanic* had sunk and rescuing nearly thirty people. Lynch was quick to point out that there would have been one fewer in boat 14 had a child and a woman working the oars not dissuaded Lowe from abandoning a survivor he found clinging to a wooden door, after the fifth officer saw that the man was not white.

Lynch personally knew one of the young women who stayed aboard boat 14 at least up to the point at which Lowe off-loaded most of the passengers onto other lifeboats so he could return to the site of the sinking in search of anyone who might still be alive. The woman told Lynch that the one horror from which the lifeboat passengers could never fully recover was hearing the call of a familiar voice here and there in the dark, then rowing toward the caller only to hear the voice weaken and die out before they arrived. Lynch said this happened to them repeatedly. Like the emerging picture of often inhumane treatment aboard the *Titanic*, which had once been called the "ship of dreams," Lynch's oral history of the silenced voices was traumatic, and the trauma tended to reassert itself in surprising ways.

During a free hour in our mission, Lori Johnston, Bill Paxton, and Big Lew Abernathy invited me to go out through a gangway door with them aboard the Zodiac to enjoy a once-in-a-lifetime event: swimming in water two and a half miles deep. Before I could step through the door, it occurred to me that the missing boatswain and his team must have opened the *Titanic*'s shell door when a similarly quiet sea was similarly close to their feet. Distracted, I lost my footing and my glasses fell off overboard.

"Zodiac transfers to and from the ship are a good way to break an arm," John-David Cameron warned, while my spare set of glasses headed down to Medusa and the *Mir*s.

"Gee, thanks," I said, and asked, "Can you tell me of any other good ways to break an arm?"

"You want to stop and think about this," said the Marine. "You've waited fifteen years for a chance to get down to the stern. If you break an arm, you can't dive."

Nothing more needed to be said. I stayed aboard at the shell door and watched my friends swim in water that during the past few hours had become dead calm (what we had come to call "*Titanic* calm"). Suddenly I could think only about the freezing water of that April night eighty-nine years before—and the people in the water, with the *Titanic* gone.

As the others prepared to come back aboard, Abernathy asked Paxton if he had ever played hide-and-seek in a graveyard. Paxton said no—and Abernathy told him, "Look around."

Paxton said later that his mind was taken instantly back in time to Lynch's story about the women with Fifth Officer Lowe, trying to find those voices in the dark. He very quickly came back aboard. They all came back, shivering—and certainly not from swimming in the North Atlantic on a summer afternoon.

AUGUST 24, 2001

Late at night, after Johnston and I discovered the cyclic (and possibly annual) layer of tree ring–like growth bands in our first and second sets of rusticle samples brought up by the *Mir-2*, I went to bed with a copy of Arthur Clarke's *Rendezvous with Rama*. It had been a full day of new discoveries, including clear indications that some of the microbes in the rusticle consortium came from hundreds of miles away in the east, at the volcanic vent zones. Microbial cysts must have been drifting along the bottom for centuries until one by one they washed up against a friendly substrate named the *Titanic*. Sooner or later, we would have to journey to the vents themselves, looking for the origin of the *Titanic*'s rusticle reef.

Alienness—that's what the rusticles were: glimpses of how multicellular, tissue-based life might have gotten its start on Earth, or perhaps also as far away as the subsurface seas of Jupiter's moons Europa and Ganymede or Saturn's moons Enceladus and Titan. Alienness; utter alienness.

The questions answered this day, each answer springing open the door to ten new questions, left us in a wonderful state of information overload—and tired.

I did not get far beyond the top of page 2 in Clarke's *Rama* adventure before I dozed off. And at the very top of that page, Clarke had written about the approach of a dazzling fireball: "At 0946 GMT on the morning of September 11 . . . "

Coincidence. All is coincidence. Or so we scientists like to say.

More often than not, the idea that a coincidence was an omen or of some other prophetic significance existed in the eye of the beholder only and not in reality. Attributing foresight through hindsight was a way of meddling, and meddling usually turned out to be a way of causing trouble.

During this final week of August, as a sample of iron from boat 8's railing came up and the rusticle roots revealed a shared yet poorly understood circulatory system, Abernathy marveled over the latest live images from the *Medusa* showing rusticles hanging from walls of riveted steel like stalactites, and exclaimed, "There must be millions of them!" Johnston corrected him, "Not *them*, Lew. *It*. They're all one organism." A consortial life-form, new to science, was converting the 460-foot length of the *Titanic*'s bow into one of the largest "creatures" on Earth.

A second source of iron substrate with its roots intact came up in the form of a davit bitt, also recovered from the approximate location of boat 8, near the place where Violet Jessop's old friend Jock Hume had joined his fellow band members, trying to calm the crowds with music.

These two rusticle bases were the only samples raised from the *Titanic* for study this year, with the understanding that after the organisms were removed for dissection and preservation, the davit bitt and the rail section were to be returned to the *Titanic*'s portside boat deck.

The rusticles were, in their own right, fascinating enough to create their own field of study. Whatever cycles (annual or otherwise) were involved in the rusticles' growth rings, the rings themselves had more than doubled in thickness during the past seven cycles, which was consistent with the unusually rapid growth rate of Georgyj Vinogradov's gorgon and the apparently explosive increase in the rusticle-based deterioration of the *Titanic*. The recent identification of rusticlelike fossils in Australia, dating back approximately 2.5 billion years, added spicier seasonings to our bio-archaeological dreams, turning them into an analogy of what the multicellular origins of plants and animals might have looked like and turning our quest into the sincerest form of ancestor worship. Science was telling us that we might have begun as clay and iron-oxide–rich mud around the bacteria-smeared hydrothermal springs of the sea, much as the biblical book of Genesis said we were: born of mud and dust.

Although we were by now thinking a little more kindly about mud and bacterial slimes, Johnston and I did not mention Genesis to the Russians; we presumed that they must have been as troubled as American atheists by the *Apollo 8* crew's reading from Genesis thirty-three years earlier. Yet something else happened with our rusticle samples—which, with the aid of such meddling as the calculation of odds against coincidence, could be bound in the meddlings of hindsight and (rightly or wrongly) interpreted as echoing Clarke's fire in the sky.

The davit bitt had pieces of rope still dangling from it. The railing, when Abernathy first brought it out of the sample basket, had broken into the shape of a cross. Someone had gasped at this, as though it were a kind of omen. The rail was merely crosshatched metal; "so, naturally it could break into the shape of a cross," I wrote later. I'd have been impressed if the metal had broken into the far less probable shape of a fish or a Star of David. The davit bitt, when viewed from a certain angle, was also cross-shaped, and the length of rope draped over both arms of it had brought an even louder and more unexpected gasp—this time from one of the Russian scientists.

She said, "Two were hung on their crosses with rope . . . on that hill, that day. Three were crucified on that hill. A third cross is coming. And it will be big. Terrible big."

"Imagine no religion," John Lennon had sung. I mentioned to Ken Marschall that the Russians had tried that experiment, and what the Russian scientist just said seemed to me the strangest of observations, coming as it did from a person from a country in which the entire population had been raised atheist.

Marschall told me to walk with him to the top decks and to look at something I had seen many times, then to look again and really see it for the first time. At the top of what we sometimes called the *Keldysh*'s grand stairway, couches and armchairs were set about a meeting table. On one wall was mounted a stained-glass window, an abstract splash of color not very different from many similar examples of 1970s and 1980s architectural perks. It blended practically undetected into the background—and, according to Marschall, that might have been the whole point. He ran his finger down one line of colored curves and shapes and asked, "What do you see?"

"My God," I said.

"That's exactly what the artist must have been trying to say," Ken said.

Hidden on a ship once commanded by the KGB—hidden in open view, for those who had eyes to see—were the Madonna and child.

"Who would have thought it?" I said to Abernathy. "Glass cutting as a subversive activity."

Abernathy, who was a restaurateur as well as a deep-ocean explorer, spent many of his free moments in the ship's galley with the Russians. "As the wise man goeth the fool," he told me. "You have been out here for weeks with the Russians, and *still* you have no idea what it means to be Russian."

SEPTEMBER 1, 2001

Paxton was convinced he would never have any idea what sort of creature left a big puff of swirling mud behind as it fled ahead of the *Mir-1*'s floodlights during its approach to boiler room number 2. His initial suspicion of a large octopus left him thoroughly "creeped out."

"I felt a presence," he said, "as [though] it were still lurking somewhere along the starboard hull, beyond the range of our lights."

"Don't worry," I said, and I told him about one of my mentors, Ed Coher, who had conducted a histological analysis on a large octopus body part that washed up on a Florida beach. Though the results remained inconclusive, some size estimates for the full creature outclassed the largest squid pieces found in the stomachs of sperm whales. "What you're afraid of, Bill, I wouldn't worry about meeting it on your next dive," I assured him. "The occi that Doc Coher described is probably not hiding in or around the *Titanic*, because the *Titanic* just isn't a big enough playground."

In a log entry, I wrote, "Out here we [are] coming up with a lot of 'I-don't-knows.' What kind of animal is a flashing Milk Dud, really?

What was that large, poly-nose-like thing flying like a bat out of hell from behind the *Titanic*'s boilers? We're never afraid of not having answers; it's running out of questions [that] we should fear most. Being confused ('What the hell is that?') means some explorer is having a good day."

The "flashing Milk Duds" and the presence of large-eyed fish near the wreck were powerful indicators that there existed bottom-dwelling creatures who used bioluminescent organs as defensive and/or predatory stun weapons. Video of cruises through the *Titanic*'s debris field often revealed the puff trails of animals fleeing ahead of the submersibles' lamps or a tripod fish sitting light-stunned on its stiltlike fins.

I had a picture in my mind of creatures never seen before, swimming away from us the moment our lights began shining over the rim of a mound or a dune. I told Anatoly Sagalevich that one thing I really wanted to try was to move along the bottom with our lights completely off, then turn them on with our cameras running "and see who is around."

The Russian word *nyet* is designed to somehow mean much more than "no." Sagalevich explained that here and there, new boulders were appearing on the bottom, boulders not on the previous year's maps of the debris, because these boulders were being dropped randomly by icebergs each winter and spring.

"It's easy to get killed by an iceberg down here," Sagalevich said sternly. One did not even have to crash the ports of the crew compartment into a boulder directly. Any part capable of imploding—an external camera, a lamp—would do the killing. At the *Titanic*'s depth, and at six thousand pounds per square inch, a crushed lamp would implode faster than the speed of sound, creating a shock wave that could implode the other lamps, the cameras, and the crew compartment—all within less time than was required for a shout to travel the length of a New York City bus.

SEPTEMBER 6, 2001

The new questions seemed endless. We always knew that opal, like amber, was an organic gemstone. Some of the finest opals were actually found on, in, or even *as* fossils. They usually formed in bacterially generated fossil beds. Some of the rusticles from the boat 8 davit bitt had formed thin layers of interior opal, absorbing silica either from seawater or from slowly dissolving pieces of the *Titanic*'s glass, or from some combination of both.

Inside the bow section, our robots were revealing that much more wood survived than anyone had anticipated—especially in the wake of Robert Ballard's fifteen-year-old theory that the same wood-boring mollusks and bacterial mats that were responsible for the disappearance of the *Titanic*'s deck wood had also devoured the entire grand stairway. But the decorative carved wood of the reception areas surrounding the stairway was still standing—a little eroded and in need of repair, but otherwise remarkably intact. The oak arches were still there, and furniture—broken but still identifiable—lay everywhere, half buried in rusticle dust.

The delicate wood trim above the D-deck passenger-entrance gangways looked almost new, and so did the stacks of plates in a fractured sideboard that had crashed to the floor near an entrance vestibule.

Although wooden doors and ornate vestibules that once bracketed the grand stairway were intact, the stairway itself—which once descended from the boat deck all the way down to where Violet Jessop had last seen her friend Stan—had disappeared without leaving behind any trace of its brass and iron railings. Had the wood been eaten, the railings should have been piled at the bottom of the landing, nearly a full deck high. The eaten stairway scenario was also contradicted by the discovery of a great many structures surrounding the stairwell and made from the same type of oak, which had somehow escaped uneaten.

Instead of being piled at the bottom of the great hole where the grand stairway and the crystal dome had once stood, the brass and wrought-iron stairway railings appeared to have started their journey to the bottom, up to a third of a mile behind the bow section's final landing place. Fixtures consistent with the heavy stairway decorations were found scattered throughout the field of debris that surrounded the severed stern's crash site. It looked as though the multideck tower of solid oak had broken free and floated out through the crystal dome, pulling apart as the bow section disappeared beneath it, dropping bits of railing the way a melting and crumbling iceberg drops pebbles and boulders.

Inside the bow section, the bot probes continued to find surviving wooden structures from the periphery of the stairwell all the way forward to Edith Russell's stateroom, where wood still framed her unbroken mirror. Walter Lord had said that his friend Edith kept filling her water glass with whiskey before she left her room for the last time. As the room filled with water, Russell's drinking glass never floated out of the little rack to the right of her mirror. The glass was undoubtedly weighted down with its last fill-up of whiskey. In the end, though, according to Russell's diary, she had proceeded to pack most of her belongings neatly into the closets and drawers before she abandoned ship (just as they can be seen today). Something must have compelled her to give up this activity and to hurry away so abruptly that she left her last drink forgotten.

In the direction that Russell fled, the mahogany of the first-class reception room was now home to a snakelike white and lavender "worm" with phosphorescent "portholes" along its sides. *Worm* hardly describes the mysterious beast. It had dug a complex network of burrows, weaving in and out of mahogany flowerpot frames and decorative mahogany baseboards and up the main supports of the stained-glass windows. Vinogradov saw features that reminded us both of echinoderms (sea cucumbers), yet the "worms" were at the same time unlike an echinoderm. We could not even fit the animal into a phylum; we did not know of a creature that somehow made its home in mahogany, a substance that until April 1912 did not even exist in the deep-ocean environment in which it had evolved.

Perplexed, Vinogradov and I began calling D deck's stained-glass reception area "the lair of the white worm."

10

Points of Departure

Two decades after the *Titanic* fell to the bed of the Atlantic, Second Officer Charles Lightoller would still be trying to explain away everything that went wrong that night with the standard lament of "Here again we were up against it."

If nothing else, confusion was certainly against the ship, and confusion continued to hold dominion over virtually every aspect of the night. Fifth Officer Harold Lowe being left asleep in his quarters was not the only example of a person being forgotten while the senior officers came to terms with the unthinkable. After the two men in the crow's nest called out their warning to the bridge, they remained in their perch, several stories up along the foremast. They remained even after the *Titanic* stopped, moved forward at six knots, stopped again, hissed venting steam from its idle boilers, and began to sag into the sea by the bow. At midnight, when their two regularly scheduled replacements for the midnight to 2 a.m. shift—George Hogg and Alfred Evans—climbed up to relieve Frederick Fleet and Reginald Lee, the sea had already swallowed all of G deck in the first four compartments.

Sometime between 12:20 a.m. and the launch of the first distress rocket, as water reached the ceiling of the racquetball court and all of the third-class quarters on the forward part of F deck disappeared, Hogg pulled back the light-blocking tarps from the rear of the crow's nest. He saw lifeboats swung out on both sides of the bridge and people swarming about with life jackets tied over their coats. The lookout lifted the phone and called the bridge, but no one was answering. Clearly, there was no further point in standing watch for icebergs on a ship that was no longer moving and did not seem likely to move again.

Hogg and Evans climbed down a ladder inside the foremast and walked back along the forecastle roof, which at that moment was within less than an hour of becoming an island, isolated by the coming flood on the well deck.

Hogg arrived at boat 6 just as Lightoller's team was preparing it for launch and not very long before Celiney Yasbeck would be wrestled to the floor to prevent her from rejoining her husband on the deck. A boatswain ordered Hogg to bring out a Jacob's ladder from the supply room; when he returned with the ladder, expecting to be told that it should be unfurled over the side of the ship, he was instead told by the boatswain merely to drop it on the deck. Evidently, a plan to lower a ladder from the boat deck so boat 6 could pick up more passengers had changed while Hogg went in search of the ladder. By then, boat 6 had been lowered more than fifty feet to the water and was rowing away.

The lookout never did learn the boatswain's name, and he never saw him again. It is almost certain that no one did. Within the time frame of Hogg's search for the Jacob's ladder, Lightoller was deciding that instead of lowering a ladder from the frightening height of the boat deck, he would send a boatswain and six assistants down to the gangway doors. They were specifically assigned to lower Jacob's ladders and pilot ladders from points nearer the water's surface, through the side doors, but instead the men simply disappeared into history.

Violet Jessop and Annie Robinson stood on the port side as the distress rockets went up. Stewardesses were barred from the boats on the forward part of the port side, but as they headed toward the boats in the rear, First Officer William Murdoch crossed over from the starboard side to assist with the launchings. He was more efficient at getting the lifeboats loaded, because he avoided the Lightoller injunctions against stewardesses and young boys and eliminated the delays caused by women unwilling to leave without their husbands by urging couples to enter a lifeboat together if there was room.

As Jessop and Robinson stood looking around, shipbuilder Thomas Andrews appeared on deck with a steward and began throwing wooden doors, deck chairs, and anything else that might be assembled into makeshift rafts over the side of the boat deck. Robinson could not suppress the thought of "Oh no, not again." Just as Jessop had been unwilling to talk about the crash of the *Olympic*, Robinson too did not mention that this was her second shipwreck. She had been aboard the *Lake Champlain* when it struck an iceberg a few years before.

They were approaching boat 16 when Jessop heard music coming from the forward half of the boat deck, near the Marconi shack and boat 8. She had seen Jock Hume passing by with his musical instrument twenty or thirty minutes before, looking rather pale and remarking, "Just going to give them a tune to cheer things up a bit."

Jessop heard mostly cheery ragtime music, interspersed with Irving Berlin. "Alexander's Ragtime Band" was soon followed by what she swore to be a first attempt at "Nearer My God to Thee," which broke off into cheery ragtime again.

Surely it's all a dream, Jessop thought, as she watched Murdoch trying to persuade a small group of immigrants to enter a boat. The newest arrivals on the boat deck seemed to be speaking Russian, and the first officer could not make himself understood.

"Give a good example and get in," Murdoch said, and Jessop realized later a language barrier was the reason that she and Robinson survived: they served as examples for the Russian women to follow. Murdoch helped Jessop across the wide portside gap into a boat, bidding her good-bye and good luck. He then tossed her a baby wrapped in a blanket.

"Look after that, will you?" Murdoch said of the child, then ordered the boat lowered away. It creaked as its davit heads occasionally jammed against ropes that were a little too new, trying to slide through freshly varnished pulleys that had never been used. What Jessop remembered most about the descent was how dark it suddenly seemed after the boat passed below the bright lights of the promenade deck into the realm of the hull's black-painted steel. Darkness was followed by a sudden flood of light from a row of E-deck portholes, followed by another blackout. She was at once both fascinated and chilled by how the portholes night-blinded her and intensified the blackness of the ocean. Another flare of porthole rows was followed by the next blackout of steel plates, then (as her eyes began to adjust) the next porthole flare, and finally the touchdown on water calmer and blacker than an oil pool, until oars stirred the "biolumes" to life.

Another person saved by Murdoch was sauce chef George Harris. When the iceberg passed by, he was taking a cigarette break on the promenade deck outside the French café. Harris was among the few aboard who knew that a ship made of iron could not possibly be called unsinkable, so he assisted chief baker Charles Joughin in what was initially a mission to load biscuits and drinking water into the lifeboats. The mission had gradually evolved. Joughin assembled a handful of his kitchen staff to follow him down to third-class quarters in the stern and to usher women and children up to the boat deck.

Some of the crew had apparently arrived at arbitrary decisions to stand between third class and the boat deck; but on this night even a pastry chef was recognized as having some sort of authority in the rescue operation, especially if he seemed to be acting as though he were in charge. The kind of man who stood in the way of Masabumi Hosono and Daniel Buckley proved no obstacle to Joughin's mission. However, the women whom Joughin and Harris encountered below were reluctant to leave their husbands, so Joughin contrived a more aggressive plan. He and his team began snatching children out of their mothers' arms and running up the steps, knowing that the women would follow them. Then they formed a sort of bucket brigade at the lifeboats, literally "chucking" children into the boats and pushing their screaming mothers in after them.

Sometime between the loss of boiler room number 5 and the final fatal buildup of pressure against boiler room number 4 Harris and Joughin could plainly see that there was not enough lifeboat space left for even half of the people still aboard. The ship's surgeons, William O'Loughlin and John Simpson, in a conversation that seemed amazingly matter-of-fact in hindsight, advised that the ship would kill them quickly and relatively painlessly if, after the boats were away, they stayed indoors near the stern—which would presumably be the fastest part going down during the final plunge.

O'Loughlin recommended that each of them should help wherever he could, in any way that he could, while making certain to take a hefty supply of whiskey from the pantry and, after the last lifeboats were gone, drinking himself unconscious inside the stern so as not to feel the final crushing pressures that would surely prove deadly during the first thirty seconds of descent.

Shortly afterward, Joughin began drinking his "medicine." Harris, the sauce chef, sought out an expensive red wine, but his advance toward painless oblivion was interrupted by a woman wandering below the decks with two children.

"Leave the children with me," Harris commanded. "And get as many rugs as you can find to cover them and yourself when you meet me on deck."

By the time the woman arrived, Harris had already passed one of the children into boat 11. He held the other child while a crewman helped their mother into the boat with the heavy bundle of rugs she had yanked from the floor somewhere nearby in first class.

"You go into the boat with that other child," Murdoch instructed Harris.

"So I have to thank Officer Murdoch for my escape," Harris wrote thirty-four years later, adding that he ended up living what he would call a charmed life: "I am seventy-five years of age and was torpedoed four times in the last war—also a prisoner [of war] in Singapore and Hong Kong." The sauce chef added that when he finally retired from the sea to the peace and quiet of New Zealand, he arrived just in time for the Napier earthquake.

"Child, things are very bad," Dr. O'Loughlin told one of the stewardesses. He prescribed the same "medicine" he had offered the sauce chef and the baker, warning that the mail rooms and the cargo holds were gone and that soon, if not already, the poolroom and the Turkish baths would be, too.

Maude Slocomb's friend, assistant steward Joseph Wheat, had closed off several extra bulkhead doors near the Turkish baths on F deck when, about 12:45 a.m., he noticed water starting to flow down from E deck past the roof of boiler room number 5's casing and into the bath chambers. The doors he closed seemed to be keeping the flood from coming directly back along the corridor, but Wheat understood immediately that the sea had mounted the deck above and was spilling down the stairs—first as a stream, then quickly developing into a minor waterfall. Realizing that F deck and E deck must suddenly have carried him well below the sea surface, he did not wait to see the waterfall gather itself into frothing rapids. He raced the sea to the top decks.

About 1 a.m., someone tried to offer masseuse Slocomb a little dog to take care of, but she refused it. The crowd around her began to jostle and became more confused, and as Murdoch urged them, "Be British," and a strange man thrust a baby into Slocomb's arms and walked away, Wheat emerged from below and shouted, "Come on, Sloky, get in here!"

Wheat pushed Slocomb and the baby toward boat 11, insisting that there was not a minute to lose. He stepped onto a boat seat to steady Slocomb with the baby as she climbed in, and Murdoch told him to stay with her and the child in the boat.

• • •

This was turning out—not quite unexpectedly—to be too special a night for Joseph Holland Loring. Only six days earlier, he had scrawled a note in his account book and left it with his sister in France before boarding the *Titanic*, recording what his family would always regard as evidence of a premonition: "In case anything should happen to me, I wish all I own to be given to my wife as I know she will do her best for our children."

The note was dated April 9, 1912. It listed in his accounts a sum of $564,000 (more than $22 million in 2011 dollars).

Loring boarded the *Titanic* with his friend George Rheims, who had just become his brother-in-law by eloping with Loring's sister. The rest of the family had considered Rheims below their station in life, and only Loring seemed to be on the newlyweds' side. It must have occurred to Loring that he should not have been here at all on this special and all too interesting night. The only reason he came to be standing on the *Titanic*'s slanting decks was that he had set off at his sister's urging with her husband to plead her case with their father in New York.

Rheims and Loring shared neighboring staterooms on the starboard side of B deck, where the 11:40 p.m. impact had arrived as "a strong shock and a noise like steam escaping from machinery; really terrifying."

Loring pulled a heavy coat from his closet, met Rheims in the corridor, then climbed the grand stairway with him to the top deck, where they saw the iceberg. This was probably the same iceberg observed by able seaman Joseph Scarrott—the second iceberg the *Titanic* came upon, just three or four minutes after impact with the first. Loring had remarked even at this early stage about his certainty that everything they saw would soon sink and about his expectation that they would not survive among the icebergs.

Rheims promised not to leave Loring's side, and in the end he did not—until the ship began to leave them.

The fifth day of the voyage would have been of major importance to young Alfred Rush even if nothing at all had happened to the *Titanic*. April 14 was his sixteenth birthday. Up to that day, he and nine-year-old Frankie Goldsmith and the other boys in third class had played leapfrog over the stern's brass-topped bollards, held competitions for who could shout the loudest echo into the ventilator shafts, climbed the rear cargo cranes, and explored all the way down to the escape hatches for peeks at the world's largest reciprocating steam engines, which stood four stories tall, like giant mechanical sphinxes.

As the day began, never guessing that the *Titanic* had seen its last sunrise, that it was about to disappear into legend and become one of the pyramids of the deep, Rush—who was so short for his age that the other boys had nicknamed him Runtie—celebrated his birthday by wearing his first pair of long trousers. In accordance with British tradition, a boy always wore short pants before the age of sixteen. Long pants were a way of proclaiming that on this day he had become a man.

Rush was voyaging to America to meet his parents, who had gone ahead of him nearly two years before to establish a successful business. The Goldsmiths promised to look after him during the crossing, and they were among the lucky families from third class who chanced upon a path to the top deck free of closed gates, belligerent crewmen, or other obstacles.

Shortly after boiler room number 5 burst and Wheat had escaped from the submergence of the Turkish baths, the Goldsmiths and young Rush emerged on the starboard side, about the same time that a canvas-sided collapsible boat called C was being swung out on the davits. Boat 1 had already departed from this set of davits at about 1 a.m. with only twelve people aboard. This was the foremost set of starboard davits, and with the slant of the decks steadily increasing toward the bow and most of the rear lifeboats still being lowered, many people were leaving the front deck for what they believed to be the safety of higher ground. When the Goldsmiths reached boat C, the deck near the starboard wing bridge was still sparsely populated, with no hint of the chaos that would soon follow the emptying of the rear davits.

Had Rush emerged on the port side to confront Lightoller's rules, he would automatically have been declared old enough to be a man, and even nine-year-old Frankie Goldsmith might have faced the deadly Lightoller injunction. Under the rules that Murdoch had laid down before he headed uphill to assist with the launching of the rear boats, women and children were to board first, accompanied by their men if any vacant seats remained.

Frank Goldsmith Sr. was instructed to wait on deck until boat C was ready for launch, while Emily Goldsmith, Frankie's mother, and her son were ushered in. Rush was also ushered toward a seat. Perhaps trying to live above the taunts he had endured over his short stature, even though he could easily have passed as a child about Frankie's age, Rush stepped back and joined Mr. Goldsmith.

"I am a man," he declared, and before Emily could convince him otherwise, with a final *no*, the boy disappeared into a crowd of men ascending suddenly from inside the ship—some displaying expressions of panic and wearing wet clothing.

Meanwhile, Bruce Ismay, the ship's owner, approached, eyeing boat C as one of his last chances to escape alive. This would turn out to be his final management decision: to save himself, knowing that women and children remained aboard, knowing that there were now too few lifeboats to accommodate even a substantial number of them, and that it was his earlier management decision to override Andrews's design for more lifeboats that had created this shortage. Knowing all of this, Ismay ducked quietly into boat C: false authority, Ismay was—the boy was ten of him.

Henry Harper's boat had been launched ahead of boat C, fifteen to twenty minutes after the boiler room number 5 collapse and about the time the first wave of stokers came running up from below. Even amid this earliest precursor to crowding and panic, Harper found room for his dog and his manservant from Alexandria, Egypt, who had been eager to cross with him on the *Titanic* "to see the country all the crazy Americans come from."

In his report for *Harper's Weekly*, Henry Harper mentioned in passing that about the time he and the Egyptian "dragoman" made themselves "quite at home" in boat 3, "four or five stokers or some such men came along and jumped into the boat at the forward end. The sailor who seemed to be in charge laughed a little."

The sailor allowed the jumpers to take seats, and according to Harper, the men did not seem to him to have behaved improperly under the circumstances—an observation that he doubtless hoped would reflect favorably upon himself.

Just as boat 3 reached the halfway point in its descent, an Australian had hailed the crew to stop lowering so he could climb down on the ropes. The crew obeyed, the Australian slid down through open air to the boat, and he was later acknowledged for his bravery.

Harper's boat had touched down on water about 1 a.m. Frankie Goldsmith and his mother saw the last of Alfred Rush about 1:30 a.m., while an atmosphere of general calm still prevailed around boat C for at least a little while longer.

Between these two events, efficiency expert Hosono arrived on the rear boat deck, where he found the forward tilt of the ship so extreme that it became difficult for him to maintain his balance. The curve of the deck had been designed to make the superliner more structurally immune to the stresses of rising and falling against ocean swells, and it made the bow section's upturn toward the prow seem (by illusion) to become initially more level as the front decks slanted nearer the sea. This design had an equal and opposite effect at the stern, however: it exaggerated the tilt forward and heightened people's level of alarm.

To Hosono, the tilt of the deck seemed impossibly extreme, and he saw sailors in the vicinity of boat 10—Fifth Officer Lowe among them—threatening men at gunpoint as the distress rockets continued to burst overhead, roughly every five minutes.

Chief baker Joughin seemed to be acting with greater desperation than even Lowe—grabbing children and throwing them so forcefully into boat 10 that he seemed not to care whether he broke their bones. First Officer Murdoch arrived on the scene, seeming just as desperate. The list to port had grown so great that Murdoch was forced to half pull, half hurl women across the gap between the boat deck and the lifeboats.

There was certainly good reason for Murdoch's sense of desperation. He knew from the beginning that he was seeing the unlikely science fiction of a "penny dreadful" Morgan Robertson novel catching up with the realities of technological hubris; he understood that he might live just long enough to see a dystopian fantasy become history. Joughin knew all this and more.

The chief baker's quarters on E deck were located on the port side, just in front of the upper casing for the giant reciprocating steam engines, behind the third smokestack. At 1:20 a.m., his porthole was already descending below the sea surface, and the imbalance that would soon be raising the three manganese-bronze propellers out of the water must already have begun to produce increasing strain on the hull. As the bow section continued to angle down, the rising stern kept the center of rotation located between the second and third smokestacks—with the fulcrum of the sea surface running almost directly through Joughin's cabin. This was, in fact, the area where, at about 2:17 a.m., the *Titanic*'s spine was going to shatter.

At approximately 1:20 a.m., Joughin returned to his cabin to continue following "doctor's orders." He drank, preparing himself for the *Titanic*'s final plunge—which he realized, to his horror, might be sneaking up on him a bit faster than anyone had anticipated. There was water in his room—only enough to cover his ankles if he stood in the deepest part of the cabin's portside tilt—but clearly, water was seeping down into his room from somewhere. He headed uphill against the list, up to the pantry on the starboard side, seeking out something a bit stronger to drink before he returned to the boat deck. Then, within those few minutes, Joughin heard what sounded to him like the first harbinger of the cracking and breaking of the ship, like the first tremors of tectonic pressure being released during the buildup toward a major earthquake. Joughin ran through the third-class section on his way toward the top deck and boat 10, snatching up more children and forcing their mothers to chase him.

At 1:27 a.m., the *Titanic*'s two Marconi operators sent out a desperate update hauntingly consistent with what Joughin was seeing and hearing: "*Titanic* calling CQD. Engine room flooding." The first signs of metal fatigue appeared to have already begun manifesting as actual stress fractures, from at least as high as Joughin's E deck cabin and possibly far enough down to become the first telltale leaks in the reciprocating engine rooms or the rearmost boiler room.

At boat 10, Hosono probably read everything he needed to know in Joughin's face. "I tried to prepare myself for the last moment with no agitation, making up my mind not to leave anything disgraceful as a Japanese," he would write to his wife, on the *Titanic* stationery he had kept in his pocket while leaving all of his gold currency behind.

An officer in charge called out that there was room for at least two more people, and he invited two sailors and a steward named William Burke to jump across the portside gap into boat 10. When a man next to Hosono jumped in, Hosono reflexively followed his example.

Boat 10 went down on the water with fifty-five people aboard, about fifty of whom could be crowded into and around the wide seats, with the rest obliged to either stand up in freezing air or hunker down on the floor under the seats. Burke would report to American investigators that after reaching the water, he found two men crowded underfoot.

"One, apparently, was a Japanese," Burke said. "I put him at an oar. The other appeared to be an Italian. I tried to speak to him but he said, 'Armenian.'"

The Armenian's last name was Krekorian, and he was evidently Neshan Krekorian, the man whose cabin had been close enough to the waterline to reveal the stars being eclipsed by icebergs on the horizon about forty minutes before one of the shadows loomed directly ahead of the *Titanic*'s prow.

In his 1913 book, *The Truth about the Titanic*, Colonel Archibald Gracie listed the Armenian passenger as someone who had jumped from A deck into the boat (more or less heroically, like the Australian who slid down the rope into Harper's boat). Gracie listed the Japanese jumper in the same boat as "a stowaway," a designation that carried with it, by sheer definition, the stigma of having allegedly entered the boat by illegitimate or even cowardly means.

Gracie's listings reflected the groundswell of thought from the time in which he was raised. Against this backdrop, passages that would clearly be seen as pompous a century later were never expected to be read that way by Gracie's own generation. Thus his description of what happened on the decks that night tended to diverge in two directions: Anglo-Saxons behaved bravely (whether jumpers or not), and certain nationalities and non-Anglo-Saxons behaved dishonorably (whether jumpers or not).

"The coolness, courage, and sense of duty that I here witnessed," wrote Gracie, "made me thankful to God and proud of my Anglo-Saxon race that gave this perfect and superb exhibition of self-control at this hour of severest trial."

Gracie listed an Italian in boat 14 and a Frenchman in boat 4 as stowaways—the latter evidently because he arrived very drunk at boat 4's side after swimming with two other men as the bow submerged beneath their feet. In boat D, a Swede, an Englishman, and an American made, in Gracie's eyes, legitimate jumps from the deck, whereas a "steerage foreigner" named Joseph Duquemin was listed as a stowaway. Aboard boat C, Gracie classified four "Chinamen or Filipinos," but not Ismay, as "stowaways."

British schoolteacher Lawrence Beesley jumped from B deck into boat 13 as it was being lowered. He came away from the *Titanic* with a book deal and was quoted favorably by Gracie. The colonel did list one "Japanese" man in Beesley's boat without commenting or drawing further attention to the man's case. Actually, the man was a Chinese sailor, and according to Millvina Dean (as related by her mother, who was a passenger), the women in boat 13 were "so disgusted" to find a nonwhite in the boat while their husbands remained on the decks above that in a near riot they threatened to throw him overboard in an impromptu oceanic lynching. Each woman later justified her own behavior by accusing the man of having acted ignobly to save his own life.

Jumping into boat 10, Hosono was trading death by freezing or drowning for a special kind of hell. He did not yet know that condemnation, firing, and decades of shame lay ahead of him. Although he was initially falsely accused of being the man the would-be murderesses of boat 13 had targeted, being able to demonstrate that he was in boat 10 would serve Hosono no better. Any apologies that might have been whispered quickly devolved into fresh accusations.

In the same boat with Hosono were Juliette Laroche and her two girls, Louise and Simonne. Joseph Laroche had pocketed all of his family's valuables, including cash and a pouch of jewels, intending to give them to Juliette. As they neared the lifeboat, however, something happened about which Juliette would never speak, and Joseph was separated from her before he could pass along his life's savings. She began her descent on boat 10's falls with two fatherless daughters, pregnant and penniless, without even the memory of a parting kiss from her husband.

Forward of the Laroches and Hosono, boat 4 was among the next to begin its descent, twenty to thirty minutes after Joughin heard the grinding or cracking sounds below the decks and water had begun entering just behind the third smokestack.

Anyone in the Laroche and Hosono boat, looking toward the bow, would have been able to see what Emily Ryerson would soon be reporting in her affidavit to the American inquiry. The forecastle was now a submerging island, separated from the superstructure of the bridge by a turbulent strait that only a short time before had been the well deck. The distance from the foremost part of the boat deck to the sea was only about twenty feet on the port side because of the increasing list. According to Ryerson, everyone could plainly see the forgotten C-deck portholes: "open, and the water rushing in, and the decks still lighted."

When boat 10 reached the water and was rowed off a dozen feet, Hosono looked back and observed that the distress rockets were still flying up and detonating, but his most lasting memory of those first moments on the water would be of the children in his boat suddenly wailing and shrieking.

Aboard boat 6, the last glimpse Celiney Yasbeck caught of her husband revealed him to be running toward the starboard side of the ship. She held out hope that he was no longer on the sloping decks and had made it into one of the starboard lifeboats, for it had not yet occurred to those in boat 6 that the reason for Lightoller's increasingly fierce "women and children only" rule and the reason so many people were still milling about under the deck lights was that by now there existed only about four hundred spaces in the remaining lifeboats, and there were more than eighteen hundred people still aboard.

As Yasbeck watched, as the flood entering the forward portholes and the submerged D-deck shell door made the original damage inflicted by the iceberg negligible by comparison, and as the slope of the decks progressed with awful perceptibility, the people began yelling and crying. Yasbeck did not know that eighty-seven women in third class (49 percent) and fifty-four of the children (64 percent) were about to be lost, compared with four women and one child from first class.

In the same lifeboat with Yasbeck, first-class passenger Marjorie Newell was mystified about how, at a time such as this, the band played on—Irving Berlin tunes, one after another, came sharp and crisp across the water. "We were very privileged," Newell would recall. At twenty-two, she and her father had just completed a tour of Egypt and the Holy Land and had boarded the *Titanic* in Cherbourg, France. "There was always something really odd about first-class passengers. They had different ways. They never looked over to third class, not even in the worst of moments. They were apart."

Despite the clarity of the approaching horror, Newell maintained her complacency; she was not nearly as aware as fifteen-year-old Yasbeck of how easily life could turn all so clearly too hard. Not until Newell heard the screams did she begin to understand that something might have gone seriously wrong with the *Titanic*.

"How ironic," she would tell history at age 102. "How ironic: My father felt he was safer [on the ship] than we were in the boat." Only later, after her father had walked away from the portside boat deck, would it occur to Newell that humanity had pushed nature too far and that before her eyes, nature was pushing back.

The inequity of it began to gnaw at her and would continue to do so for the rest of her life. Those who were the most innocent of the hubris committed that night seemed condemned to be punished the hardest for it. In the lower rear quarters of third class, aft of the fourth smokestack, the little portholes along E deck and F deck went dark, and Newell would forever wonder about the passengers behind those portholes who must have been trying to find their way out.

Whether the dousing of the lights was a result of circuits shorting from the leaks Joughin discovered, from an adjustment made by the engineers in an attempt to conserve power for the Marconi apparatus and other life-saving equipment, or from localized electrical surge and burnout effects, there was little light for the two hundred or more third-class passengers who had been delayed—and kept mostly uninformed below deck—until most of the lifeboats were already descending from their davits.

"In first class, you had all the light you wanted," Newell observed. "In the darkness, the passengers in third class could not find their way out. They couldn't see anything at all. The women and children were trapped in the dark. They [must have been] screaming. It was the single, most callous, inhumane act."

11

The Geometry of Shadows

SEPTEMBER 2001
RUSSIAN RESEARCH VESSEL *KELDYSH*
EXPEDITION *TITANIC XIII*

Had he lived to see it, Isaac Asimov would have loved our 2001 expedition, especially during the planning stages for the rescue of our little robot Elwood, after it became trapped among the chandeliers, above the mahogany and the white worms. According to plan, my dive to the virtually unexplored stern section was to be followed by a detour to the bow section one-third of a mile away so we could plant new equipment to enable history's first rescue of one robot by another.

We almost did make history. Jake's video of little Elwood's battery burn-up revealed gas bubbles, ranging from a quarter of an inch to more than an inch wide, being ejected toward the ceiling. The surrounding water pressure was nearly six thousand pounds per square inch. The bubbles were probably hydrogen, mostly. If that same burn-out had occurred at the surface, the smaller bubbles would have instantly expanded larger than cantaloupes, and the larger ones would have released enough gas to fill refrigerators. The very same explosion at or near the surface, with Elwood caged in the submersible's bot bay, could easily have made a bit too much history.

A further review of the Jake footage revealed a small section of the grand stairway still intact down near E deck: several wooden steps, fifteen feet across, with the metal railings evidently having been lifted away with the rest of the structure. Near the end, the five stories of oak must have developed tremendous positive buoyancy, most likely departing the *Titanic* in a single mighty burst through the crystal dome. A section of metal framing consistent with the top of the dome lay almost a third of a mile behind the bow section, near the stern section's crash site (although it might also have come from a shorter yet otherwise nearly identical rear stairway). In the bow section, fragments of the front stairway's dome had evidently slid off the emerging wood pile and fallen to the bottom of the empty stair-well, landing not very far from its single segment of intact wooden steps.

The destruction in and around the great stairwell was immense, and the clear impression, based on the evidence coming in through our gallery of bot-eye views, was that most of the destruction occurred during the final minutes at the surface and during the first seconds of contact with the bottom.

When the bow section crashed onto the deep-ocean prairie at approximately forty miles per hour, the slipstream of water that trailed down behind it burst down the stairwell without meeting any resistance at all: a strip of bulkhead from the boat deck was swept back as though steel sheeting were merely a flag of cloth rippling in the wind. The flag of steel was raked down the stairwell, through the promenade deck and B deck, meeting none of the obstacles that would have blocked such raking had the stairway been standing in the well.

The force of impact was so great that it was difficult to imagine medicine jars surviving unbroken in their racks in the crew infirmary, or Edith Russell's mirror standing unbroken. This second crash of the night, combined with a slipstream that obeyed the law of inertia and continued speeding toward the bed of the Atlantic even after the *Titanic* had stopped, pushed in the steel roof of the officers' quarters, the reception areas, and both sides of the gymnasium—and pressed sheet metal bulkheads outward. Both wing bridges were peeled away from the bridge itself, as though their metal frames were slabs of warm taffy caught in an explosion emanating from the center line of the ship.

On the well deck, all of the railings were blown outward from the center and fell to either side of the bow; only the vertical steel walls between the rails survived, each bent outward, away from the center. The foremast lay across the well deck during the down-blast;

it was bent downward toward the deck, suffering a series of fractures behind the crow's nest that by 2012, aided by rusticle buds taking root within the fractures, would cause the entire mast to sag and break. As the ship's width narrowed toward the front of the fore-castle, the rails suffered a proportionally decreased bending out, until the forepeak rail on which Georgyj Vinogradov's gorgon grew stood with no bends at all.

Near the great open well that had been the grand stairway, the combined forces of the crash and the down-blast had pressed B deck down upon C deck and bowed out, like rows of bent knees, every verti-cal steel column that had bracketed the stairwell at C deck.

The down-blast effect, born of inertia, punched down to E deck and then burst out laterally indoors—where the portion of the inertial fist that punched aft must have found its way blocked by an opposing fist of water being forced from the tail end of the bow section, where decks already massively weakened by the breakaway of the stern compressed like an accordion. At the rear end of the broken bow, the down-blasting and stacking of the decks one upon another over boiler rooms number 2 and 3 added a complex series of interior surges and colliding eddies that tore some tables, beds, and chairs to splinters while leaving others intact. Metal-framed chandeliers showed signs of having been dented by speed-slung furnishings. Wooden beams went crashing through the walls of forward cabins, and the surge that went with them blew down the remaining wall supports. Yet amid such devastation, the forces of destruction had occasionally collided and diverged or simply died.

The stems of palm trees still stood undisturbed in mahogany flow-erpot holders, and Russell's cup never moved. The bot Jake squeezed through the crushed flooring beneath C deck, through a narrow grotto so thick with rusticle stalactites that we were reminded at once of a beautiful limestone cavern—until a wall of unbroken leaded glass and mahogany loomed out of the dark and we saw a type of rat-tailed fish we had never encountered before, almost as translucent as frosted glass; in one corner among the wooden eaves, there was an animal that Vino-gradov and I could only tentatively classify as a new variety of cuttlefish. It's huge "wings" made it look like a semitransparent undersea bat, as graceful as a manta ray.

The other rooms were no less intriguing. The best guesses about who had occupied a given stateroom followed a partial list recovered from the body of a steward named Herbert Cave, and this had been known ever since as the Cave list. By the 1920s, young Walter Lord's interest in the *Titanic* had grown so large that he convinced his parents to make one of their Atlantic crossings with him aboard the *Titanic*'s sister ship, the *Olympic*, and by age fourteen (in 1931) he had already written his first draft of *A Night to Remember.*

Lord also started arranging his first meetings with survivors, and he began discovering from firsthand interviews and from letters provided by the families that there was a tendency for people to change their accommodations once they actually boarded the ship. Russell, for example, had decided to rent a second, inboard stateroom, simply for the purpose of storing all of her luggage nearby. The official, pre-sailing list could not be taken as the last word on who had occupied the beds.

Most of the corridors had lost their walls and were sometimes outlined only by an occasional closed door standing in its frame. As Jake prowled the corridors, we continued uncovering evidence that the mystery of the final room assignments was far from completely resolved. Room D-31 had been officially assigned to two individuals who had canceled their plans to board the *Titanic* and whose room was believed until now to have been unoccupied during the voyage.

Yet the wooden drawer at the bottom of the shaving and washing sink had spilled out a set of brushes, combs, and a pair of eyeglasses. There was luggage in the room, buried amid the *Titanic*'s increasingly familiar paradox of preservation existing side by side with destruction. The mirror had cracked, but the mattress was still on the bed, underneath a fold-down bunk that had crashed upon it. A chair nearby was crushed but still recognizable, whereas the dresser drawers behind it remained closed and undamaged.

About ten minutes after Elwood's battery melted, Jake had flown over a service cart that appeared to have rolled and crashed behind the elevators. It was broken wide open, somehow with its dishes and teacups intact. As we reviewed the video, Ken Marschall and I began to wish we knew the secret of Edwardian packing.

Then, out of nowhere—the deep, impersonal nowhere—came a reminder of when and where we were really probing. Jake pointed a finger of light at something I had at least half expected to see ever since microbiologist Roy Cullimore and I investigated what had come aboard the *Ocean Voyager* during the 1996 expedition. A rusticle-embedded soup tureen, found in a field of down-blasted ejecta from the stern section's port side, had been attached to a pocket of organic material that caught us by surprise—much as the amount of wood standing almost perfectly intact inside the *Titanic* now seemed surprising to most people who had never sailed aboard the *Ocean Voyager* and the *Nadir* with the submersible vessel *Nautile*.

Shreds of clothing came up with the tureen, having fared no worse than the mattress fibers inside cabin D-31. Then, in the tureen's mixture of mud and rusticle reef fragments, Cullimore and I had found two pieces of bone—one of them large enough to be easily identifiable as a lamb bone. Strangest of all, we discovered that bacterial threads from the rusticle encrustations had enclosed and preserved bits of tendon still attached to the bone.

On August 17, 1996, I had written in my *Ocean Voyager* log that the presence of even a single animal bone should have prepared our minds for the idea that we would eventually encounter human remains. According to all of the textbooks, bones should have long ago decomposed into their calcium-deficient surroundings, but evidently this was just another self-perpetuating textbook dogma based on too little actual data.

At the beginning of the 1996 expedition, Cullimore and I had found calcium-absorbing and -secreting mollusks living on the iron-oxide shells of the *Titanic*'s rusticles. "We now know that [throughout the wreck site] bones might still exist," I wrote in the log. "The game we thought we were playing is not the game at all."

Five years later, Jake swept a beam across an object that made it suddenly seem wrong to have wanted to equip the bot with claspers so we could capture some of the strange *Alice in Wonderland*–like wildlife that inhabited the grotto of the white worms.

The floor of the reception area was covered with fallen rusticle stalactites and a powdering of deep-ocean dust, so shapes were softened by rusticle encrustations and the shadows could easily play tricks on the eyes. Near one wall, the layer of fallen plaster and rusticle debris was knee-deep; near another, it was only ankle-deep. There in the shallows, I saw something, and I cried out for historian Don Lynch to run the tape back and freeze the frame. I knew almost to a certainty that I had just seen the left side of a human skull, half sunk in dust, and in perfect profile. Producer John Bruno came up behind us as Lynch slowly ran the tape backward and forward, trying to deny that it could be what I thought it was, trying to insist that it was a trick of the lighting played by the geometry of shadows.

Naturally, this part of the ship was a likely place for such a discovery. Near the end, as the last lifeboats began lowering away, the light and the warmth of the grand stairway and its surrounding lounge areas would have become attractive shelters. When the ship started to take its final plunge and as the stairway suddenly broke free, many people would have fled into and been trapped in the adjoining corridors and reception areas. Scores of them must have been swept into and around the grotto and its halls when the bow section crashed two and a half miles down; then their bodies would have faced the same down-blast and random shock-cocooning (preservation in the midst of destruction) effects as the reception area doors and the vestibule wood.

Lynch ran the tape back again repeatedly, and I pointed out the brow ridge and the profile of a cheekbone. Bruno saw it too and agreed. Lynch and Marschall let the video continue running forward after that and decided not to let it run backward again.

"It's a whole roller coaster of emotions out here," I wrote later to Mary and other family members. "Every emotion imaginable. One moment we hear Ken [Marschall] getting all excited because he never knew the *Titanic* had electric fans in the reception area. The next [moment], I had to go away and be alone—I was in tears."

Two notes were written on Styrofoam coffee cups, to be shrunk down to shot-glass size by the pressures two and a half miles down, outside the *Mir-2* submersible:

Dear Mary, I'm sending Charlie down to the stern tomorrow because he's finally reached the stage where he can be more annoying up here than down there.

—Jim Cameron

To my Mary: With love, from 10 Twin Tower lengths down—at the world's ultimate haunted mansion.

—Charlie

DIVE 7
MIR PREDIVE CHECKLIST
OBSERVER 1, RIGHT SEAT

Upon entering:

Power up DVcam decks.

Check focus and iris on 3 fixed cameras (iris should be wide open).

Insert new tapes in all 3 decks. Hit record and confirm roll on all.

Set digital timer for 2 hours, 50 minutes.

Confirm to sub crew that you are ready for Observer 2 to enter.

Put on your audio headset, and prepare Observer 2's headset.

Confirm audio inputs are working.

12:06 p.m. Begin descent at 2.5 feet per second.

12:08 p.m. Water becomes a deep blue.

12:12 p.m. Deep violet outside. Robot arm outside our viewport is in silhouette.

12:13 p.m. Violet fading to black—quickly.

12:14 p.m. All black now. Depth 178 meters.

12:15 p.m. Should soon be in Deep Scattering Layer—upper daytime limit.

12:16 p.m. Seeing first bioluminescent flashes. Depth 261 meters.

12:26 p.m. Deep Scattering Layer quite thick [meaning at least 3 or 4 organisms, 2 centimeters or more in length, per cubic meter]. We're riding through cloud-tops of deep-ocean snow.

12:30 p.m. Deep Scattering Layer [DSL] thins out between 700–800 meters.

12:32 p.m. DSL thickens again at 800 meters.

12:35 p.m. DSL thinning, but still with us at 872 meters.

12:37 p.m. At 900 meters, occasional large "jelly" [up to fist-sized], with small red shrimp inside [being digested, or parasitic]. Most DSL organisms 3 millimeter diameter or less. 99% of them unidentified invertebrates [we are descending past them too quickly for a close look at everything]. Occasional fish trying to ride away from our wake.

12:43 p.m. DSL thinning considerably. Depth 1,130 meters.

12:50 p.m. DSL thickens again [equal to or greater than 3 or 4 organisms, 2 (centimeters) or more in length, per cubic meter] at 1,295 meters, then thins out at 1,335 meters. Thick cloud deck of invertebrates at 1,415 meters. Observe large fish (10 cm long) swimming vigorously under our wake—needle-shaped and fluorescing.

12:55 p.m. DSL ends at approx[imately] 1,500 meters—then thickens [into a whole new cloud deck of life] at 1,545 meters. Seems as if DSL is going to be with us all the way, [shifting between] thick and thin. Lantern fish at 1,795 meters.

1:07 p.m. Thick and thin, multideck DSL continues. Almost once per minute, we pass through a layer and see a species of translucent fish, about 4 cm long, with its lights on.

1:15 p.m. Still encountering decks of DSL. Have just passed 2,000 meters. *Mir-1* 1,000 meters below us. Lori calls down from the *Keldysh*: Medusa is positioned 10 meters from [the *Titanic's*] stern, traveling NW [northwest], 5 meters off bottom.

1:30 p.m. Depth 2,520 meters. DSL has thinned out to mere, deep-ocean snow of seemingly dead biological particles. DSL gone.

1:38 p.m. Depth 2,789 meters. No DSL.

1:45 p.m. We are completely below DSL. Contact from *MIR-1*. They have reached bottom.

1:57 p.m. Depth 3,200 meters. Lifeless outside. Mostly microscopic, dead drift matter from above.

2:24 p.m. Depth 3,780 meters. Lifeless [still, during the] past 500 meters. Descending to 3,820 meters. We are at altitude 38 meters. The view from High Gate [approach to landing]: Greeted by a rat-tailed fish. Starfish and sea cucumbers occupying almost every square meter. And a few things not yet in the books. An invertebrate tumbleweed (echinoderm?) blows by.

2:50 p.m. Flying over flooring from inside *Titanic*. Railing. Sheets of thin metal in a pile. Encountering eject[ed material] from engine room—approaching stern from starboard side.

A huge section of steel framing arched down toward us, over the edge of the stern—twisted in a manner consistent with the stern section having crashed into the bottom even more forcefully than the bow section, at perhaps nearly twice the bow's speed. Marine archaeologist John Broadwater (who had been investigating the wreck of the *Mir's* remote ancestor, the *Hunley*) noticed that a very troubled expression seemed to have crossed my face.

During our first moments under the arch of steel, I felt physically ill. The arch seemed somehow to remind me of a mass of twisted steel I had seen hanging over me in this same configuration once before—yet I knew I had never seen the like. I thought of all the people who had struggled above me and who were probably brought down to the bottom behind imploding walls of steel. As nausea and headache began to take over and as I wondered if oxygen and carbon monoxide levels in the sub had gone out of balance, my thoughts turned inexplicably to Mary's friend, Captain Paddy Brown. That's what you get for going two days without sleep and skipping breakfast before climbing into the sub, I told myself. Ghosts of the imagination.

A handful of nuts and raisins seemed to bring me around. Yet even our flight over the center of the stern did not lessen my sense of foreboding—actually, something stronger than mere foreboding—adding at least one more to the list of "every emotion imaginable" being felt out here. Gone was the elation of passing through the living cloud decks of the deep scattering layer. The landscape over which we hovered, in which solid steel hull sections and deck plates had down-blasted and surged out until the terrain resembled an explosion in a taffy factory, did indeed seem to trigger every emotion imaginable, including one that could no more be described in words than it could be described in a color one had never seen before.

It was not a pleasant emotion, either. I could never have imagined that after so many years of wanting to investigate the mysteries of the stern I could feel something that would make me want to leave just as the most rarely visited part of the ship began to give up its secrets.

The shaft wing to which the starboard propeller was attached had been pulled four decks high from the bottom of the stern, all the way above the rear cargo hold. The cargo hold itself was probably squashed flat, occupying the very same space as the two decks that had lain below it.

The *Titanic*'s severed stern section appeared to have struck bottom somewhere between a thirty- and a forty-five-degree angle—tail first, hammering its rudder deep into the earth. The rudder was turned all the way to the port side and had likely swung into this position and stayed there from very near the surface all the way down. Acting as the leading edge, it would have kept the stern in a tight, clockwise spiral until the moment of impact. Everything we saw was consistent with a strange, high-velocity spiral to the bottom.

Yet for some unimaginable reason even the thrill of discovery could not keep my thoughts from turning to Mary's friend Captain Brown—a man with whom I'd spoken only twice, on the phone. I tried to shrug off what Big Lew Abernathy had called "playing hide-and-seek in a graveyard," and what Lori Johnston had called, after her dive, "a sense of quiet voices." I was almost militantly agnostic, so I stowed away any further thoughts of Captain Brown in favor of the present reality.

Every prior map of the *Titanic*'s stern section was wrong. When the aftermost portion of the stern embedded itself, the front portion continued turning clockwise around a center of rotation located (and suddenly mud-locked) near the propellers. The rotation must have continued for approximately one second—long enough to break the stern's back and to split the deck plates—straight across the well deck, just behind the anchor cranes. The clockwise rotation continued about twenty degrees before the down-blast struck, with all the force of a tsunami striking a skyscraper at almost ninety feet per second (sixty miles per hour).

For up to one second before the down-blast squashed the front end of the stern like an insect, the entire front half of the portside hull was dragged as it crashed down level with the bottom. The dragging motion pulled the wall of steel sharply to starboard, thirty feet or more—stretching and smearing it out of shape like a slab of warm taffy and thrusting a huge wedge from the double-hulled bottom out through its side.

Farther back, behind the point where the well deck snapped and almost as far back as quartermaster George Rowe's post on the (now missing) after-bridge, the down-blast splayed out both sides of the hull—what was left of it—and compressed the central decks one upon another.

According to Anatoly Sagalevich, the stacking had been intensified during the past decade because of rusticle activity, which helped gravity to finish what the down-blast had started. There was no hope of sending Jake into the ship's hospital or seeking out the Laroche, Hosono, or Mellinger quarters. No deck in that region any longer stood more than a foot tall.

Between the aftermost part of the stern and the reciprocating engines at the front end, the combined height of all the decks was now generally no more than twelve to fifteen feet.

Sculpturally, the stern was such a masterwork of twisted agony that I was overcome by a totally unexpected sense that we did not belong here and should leave. Once again, emotions crept in, causing abrupt shifts from scientist mode to the stubborn reality that we were exploring the place where the majority of the *Titanic's* people had died. Then, barely more than an hour after we arrived, the command to leave the stern came upon us—from our machines.

At 4:12 p.m., Johnston reported from mission control with news of an electrical problem: "Do not have control over Medusa." Electrical problems were also reported from the *Mir-1*; then, in the *Mir-2*, we started to lose external lighting and were suddenly down to half of our battery power. Jim Cameron canceled our planned bot exploration inside the heart of the *Titanic* (the reciprocating engine room) and said that we would move across the debris field to the bow section, using whatever power remained in the *Mirs* to make preparations for the next day's rescue of Elwood.

As we departed the stern, we suddenly regained full power and control—both the *Mir* submersibles and the Medusa robot were in perfect health again—for what developed into the longest dive, thus far, of the entire expedition. We did not surface until shortly before midnight, *Titanic* time [within the Newfoundland time zone].

After we were back aboard the *Keldysh*, I ate a hearty meal, but I could not sleep. I prepared the davit bitt and the boat 8 railing for their return to the boat deck the next day, and in my sleep-deprived state, I wrote a letter to Mary Leung and the children, trying to describe what I later characterized as "the shriek in the night."

I explained how, as we flew over the part of the stern where chief baker Charles Joughin had eventually made one of history's most impossible escapes and where hundreds of others were either swept off into freezing waters or carried to the bottom, there were moments during which I had to look away and close my eyes, despite years of waiting to actually see the stern.

Of all the oddest things I could think of, in trying to describe how it had felt to be there, I recalled the pre-expedition train rides I had taken with Mary to the stopover point at the World Trade Center, en route to her office in New Jersey. I reminded her of the fright I had felt when we first met and I learned that she was living literally in the shadow of the Twin Towers. I reminded her of how, from the moment they were built, those towers had filled me with a strange mixture of fascination and dread. "The stern," I said, "was something like that."

Only someone who constantly viewed even Manhattan through archaeological eyes—who saw how graffiti in a flooded subway station should, along with the cave paintings of Spain, last twenty thousand years or more while everything above disappeared—would have had thoughts wandering (quite naturally) in the direction my own thoughts wandered that night. Given the more than six billion people on the planet, someone from New York was bound, just by coincidence, to be an archaeological thinker having just surfaced from the ruins of the *Titanic*, looking westward toward New York.

The only thing I could think about writing that could just barely provide a comparison to what it had felt like during my hour at the stern was to recall what I had said some four years earlier as we looked toward the two towers from the South Street Seaport. "When I let my imagination run with it, I see [those] tall buildings gone one day, and then I imagine someone having tried to . . . replace them. And [another generation who never knew the towers as they had stood] would think it right [the new skyline]. But to anyone from our own time, it would be apparent immediately that the skyline was all wrong.

"And what am I trying to do now?" I asked Mary. "Trying to describe an indescribable emotion? [But] sometimes you can . . . destroy mystery and beauty by trying to put it into words when the proper words don't exist yet; so you make do with the ones that already exist, and they turn out to be inadequate beyond measure."

I realized that it was now nearly 3 a.m., that I had not slept for three days, and that I was probably not making very much sense.

Vinogradov came into the bio lab and was surprised to find me still awake. Then he admitted that as exhausting as days like this could be, not many people were likely to sleep after exploring the wildlife of the deep scattering layer, the *Titanic*'s bow, and the *Titanic*'s stern—all in one day. Today had been one of the greatest days of my life, certainly the single greatest day of my career. My brain was in a wonderful state of sensory overload, with enough having been seen and learned to keep me busy for a decade.

Still my thoughts returned, without any good reason of which I was consciously aware, to Mary's friend Captain Brown. Neither Vinogradov nor I would have guessed that a particularly bad cold (or a summer flu) had altered Mary's schedule and was about to keep her out of harm's way or that an unexpected career change was about to send my cousin Donna in the very same direction as Captain Brown. It was 3 a.m. Both Paddy Brown and Donna had only a few hours left to live.

Paddy was captain of Ladder 3 at the New York City fire department, or FDNY. Donna worked for Marsh and McLennan, near the top of the World Trade Center's North Tower. Though safe, Mary would be close enough to see how death came to Paddy and Donna. Devastatingly close.

It was 3 a.m. *Titanic* time, September 11, 2001. As a child I had dreamed of descending where my idol William Beebe (codesigner of the world's first deep-diving bathysphere) had gone: into the realm of the ever black and strange fish. In reality, I had just gone beyond Beebe and exceeded my greatest childhood dreams. Who would have believed that the greatest of days and the worst of days could be the same day?

12

How Much Does Darkness Weigh?

At the expedition's start, a journalist friend named Rip MacKenzie had put forth a question that, once relayed through Arthur C. Clarke's laptop, was e-mailed around the world to a hundred scientists and theologians, quickly generating more than a thousand pages. The question was deceptively simple and direct: "How much does darkness weigh?"

Some respondents wrote about the three tons of water that pressed in against every square inch of the *Mir*'s hull, down in the sunless abyss into which the *Titanic* had fallen. Others wrote about the mass of a single photon against the immensity of space and time. Still others spoke about the emerging case for the existence of dark matter—incapable of interacting with the force of electromagnetism, and therefore unable to reflect or absorb light or even to form atoms as we know them, yet somehow making itself known through gravitation and dark energy. As much as 95 percent of the mass in the universe appears to be made of something unseen and unknown—and the rest, only 5 percent, consists of the atoms and energy of stars and planets.

"Darkness is only the product of our own senses, and challenges us simply because it is a mirror of our own limitations," wrote microbiologist Roy Cullimore, more philosophically than most. "If we could see into shadows and feel the contents, then it would have a relative value and would not be viewed as a shadow."

From Sri Lanka, Father Mervyn Fernando, a student of Pierre Teilhard de Chardin's works, provided an altogether different and perhaps even prophetic answer. Being a Catholic who often sounded more Buddhist than Christian, Father Fernando saw human intelligence, and perhaps sentience elsewhere in the universe, all originating in whatever universal singularity (or cosmic black hole) preceded the Big Bang. To him, from the dust of the first dying stars and the binding properties of the carbon atom, intelligent life became "only the final product, the apex of this vast process across billions of years." He viewed sentient life and the development of civilizations—the light at the end of the evolutionary process—as the point at which the universe started to become conscious of itself, of once dark and lifeless carbon trying to understand itself.

Humans are not only conscious, Fernando observed, but also the only creatures who know that we are conscious. He saw the future of human consciousness as a progression toward increasingly higher levels of interconnectivity. To the Sri Lankan theologian, the library at Alexandria and the earliest printing presses were but the first baby steps toward binding our species into a single global membrane of human thought. Electronic communication via telegraph and telephone were a next step—the global web, another. As early as the 1980s (with the aid of a local knight), Fernando's Subhodi teaching center and orphanage became one of the first places in the country connected to satellite uplinks and an astronomical observatory.

If sentient beings were living nearly ninety light-years away on one of the worlds circling the star HD 70642, and if they possessed a sufficiently sensitive radio telescope, the electronic shrieks of CQD and SOS from the *Titanic* would have just then been reaching them, as virtually a lone voice from wilderness Earth, crying out from one of 1912's most powerful wireless telegraphs. "One of our civilization's very first birth cries to the universe," the priest observed, "actually came from the *Titanic*."

By 2001, our robots were broadcasting close-up views of the *Titanic*'s interior across a whole interconnected world and into classrooms. Father Fernando saw in this the dawning reality of Teilhard de Chardin's Omega Point, the emergence of a global superconsciousness that might ultimately shine out against the darkness. "But this was not a development without peril," he warned.

"Though Teilhard [might] proclaim that the age of nations is past," Fernando said, "the task before us, if we would not perish, is to shake off our ancient prejudices, [for] there are strong resistances in the form of pulls towards breakup and fragmentation. The growing unity of [humanity] on the globe suffers a thousand violences and antagonisms, hostilities and wars, hot and cold, that prevail so painfully in the world today."

At 3:30 a.m. *Titanic* time, on September 11, 2001, I had still not gone to sleep. In my restlessness, I wrote my own answer to MacKenzie's question, "How much does darkness weigh?"

"It is the emotion for which there are no words," I said, referring to actually being in the presence of "the old girl," the *Titanic*. "It is the color with no name."

I realized that it might take the rest of my life to explain what I had felt a few hours earlier at the stern and what I was still feeling two and a half miles above, in the lab—a feeling for which there did indeed seem to be no words but that transforms the heart.

Hours earlier, Johnston had studied the expression on my face and asked, "You heard them, didn't you?"

"Heard what?"

"The quiet voices."

"I don't know," I replied.

All I did know was my sense that from those first moments at the *Titanic*'s stern, I was headed on a new journey, like a creature about to be reborn—in pain. It was not an epiphany. It was not a moment of understanding. In fact, it was quite the opposite of understanding.

I found myself turning more and more, during that last night of the old world, toward MacKenzie's question, and to what Fernando had tried to teach me about the hope of light against the darkness.

To save our civilization, the priest insisted, we must never use violence in fighting for our cause or our principles, and we must not even fight for ourselves. The last great hope of civilization, he believed, was in the human ability to sacrifice one's own best interests by putting the other person first.

Two and a half miles underfoot, given a Ken Marschall perspective in which the *Titanic*'s bow section, seen from up here, was no larger than a fingernail on one's hand held out at arm's length, the entire spectrum of human behavior had been played out in microcosm. Even in that overromanticized Gilded Age of pride and ignorance, lights had shone out against the darkness. For every Bruce Ismay on the deck, there had to be a Charles Joughin or an Alfred Rush. There *had* to be.

13

The 46th Psalm

In boat C, Ismay's boat, forty-year-old Shaneene Abi-Saab Wahabe, like the other Lebanese women huddled with her, had seen America as a beacon of freedom from religious persecution. She would not have been in the boat at all if her cousin Gerios and the other men had not physically lifted her and thrown her in, along with at least three other women. Amid the scuffle, an officer had fired shots into the air, ending the dropping of third-class women into a boat in which twenty empty seats could still plainly be seen.

Like the other women of boat C, Wahabe knew she would never see her husband again. Her adult son was also lost, but neither her husband nor her son were about to become casualties of the *Titanic*. Both had died recently from common infections. Living by a creed of never giving up, no matter what cross life forced her to bear, and determined to begin again, she would soon arrive in the United States under the temporary care of New York's Hebrew Immigrant Aid Society.

On the sidewalks of New York, street vendors of the early twentieth century were selling increasingly popular ice cream treats served in glass cups. Wahabe would never touch the stuff—at least, not the way it was being served. The lessons of her own recent family history ran too deep. The cone-shaped cups, after being licked clean by customers, were rinsed hastily in what often appeared to be dirty water, then reused, customer to customer. Wahabe knew that there had to be a better, more hygienic way, such as serving the ice cream in a single-use, sweet pastry cone.

Soon, as the Ismay family's fortune waned and the *Titanic* began melting into the bed of the Atlantic, the obscure middle-aged survivor from boat C would establish the Joy Cone Company. By word of mouth and then by newspaper ads and the wire services, Joy Cone would spread, entering the twenty-first century as the world's largest ice cream cone manufacturer.

David Vartanian bore a different sort of cross, having lost more family members to the approach of World War I than to infection. He had booked a third-class cabin aboard the *Titanic* and was traveling to America ahead of his wife, Mary, hoping to build a new beginning and then to bring his life's one true love as quickly as possible out of their increasingly dangerous homeland. Putting his entire life's savings into the trip, he seemed to have stepped out of the winds of war into Armageddon at sea.

Corralled below the decks in the stern, Vartanian and the other steerage men found their path upward to the boat deck blocked by a gate. Days later, passenger Eugene Daly would report to Dr. Frank Blackmar of the rescue ship *Carpathia* that steerage men trying to ascend the stairs were beaten back by members of the crew, and he saw two passengers (whom he derisively referred to as "dagos") shot.

"But the yelling and screaming above," Vartanian's daughter Rose would tell historian Philip Dattilo in 1999, "drove several of the men to tear the gate down." In the final half hour, some of the gate crashers had weapons in their hands, but their escape route was only an illusion. All of the lifeboats appeared to be in the process of casting away or were already gone, and Vartanian found himself trapped with hundreds of other frightened souls on the stern's well deck.

Anna Sjoblom was a third-class passenger en route to join her father at a logging camp in the Pacific Northwest. She too found the stairways to the upper decks closed against the third class, and it seemed to her that the crew really did not care whether the foreign immigrants lived or died. Fortunately, a Swedish friend of hers discovered an unguarded emergency stairway leading to the higher decks, and they were able to sneak up through the banquet halls and toward the lifeboats.

By then, hundreds of feet of empty lifeboat ropes were strewn along the boat deck. There were only two or three boats left on the davits, and they were already mostly filled and in the early stages of lowering and casting away.

"I tried to get into one boat and was pushed back," Sjoblom would report bitterly. Women and children first, indeed. It was her eighteenth birthday. The desperation she saw at this point in the foundering of the ship was increasing to such a level that under the Lightoller protocol, even a girl who had just turned eighteen that day could be barred from the lifeboats. She watched in a state of detached disbelief as a Swedish couple and their five children kissed one another and then leaped together over the side, never to be seen again.

After this, Sjoblom forced her way onto one of the last boats going down, shortly before Lawrence Beesley made his book deal–generating leap into the stern of the same boat. During the leap, he crashed down on Sjoblom's head and nearly crushed her neck. But this was not the cruelest thing she saw or felt before boat 13 reached the water.

"I remember watching a little boy about thirteen years old whose parent had gone off in one of the lifeboats," she would write later. "He slipped into a boat and was thrown back on deck by a sailor. He crept into another boat, and again [the sailors] threw him back to the deck. The third time he slid down into the bottom of a boat and was saved."

Both horrified and strangely transfixed—"fascinated," wrote Violet Jessop—"my eyes never left the ship, as if by looking I could have kept [the *Titanic*] afloat. I reflected that [only] four days ago I had wished to see her from afar, to be able to admire her under way; now there she was—my *Titanic* . . . her splendid lines [standing] against the night, every light twinkling. I started unconsciously to count the decks by the rows of lights [forward]. One, two, three, four, five; then again—one, two, three, four. I stopped. Surely I had miscounted."

Jessop counted them again more carefully, gently hushing the whimpering baby that William Murdoch had tossed into her arms. "No," she realized. She had made no mistake. "There were only four decks now," Jessop would recall. She started her count again. Only three decks now.

"No," she told herself, trying not to imagine the people she had just left—who would be warm and alive, as she and the baby were, for only a little while longer. Jessop tried to busy herself with the baby; but she could not refrain from looking up again. Only two decks now.

From the same vantage point, Lily Futrelle, the wife of mystery writer Jacques Futrelle, watched the ship's bow burying itself deeper and deeper into a dead calm sea. As she stared, the calm began to unravel. The strait of water between the forecastle and the superstructure of the bridge grew increasingly turbulent. Then the submergence of the forecastle and the rise of the propellers became a clear and present irritant to the biolumes. In death, the *Titanic* was creating exactly the sort of flashing display that would have illuminated the base of the iceberg and saved the ship from this fate.

"We could see the last of the two collapsible [rafts, on davits] putting away from the steamer," Futrelle would write. "The water by this time was so close to the upper deck that it was hardly necessary to lower the raft. I tried to shut my eyes but I could not. There was a horrible fascination about it. The ocean was aflame with the glowing phosphorous, which looked like a million little spirits of light dancing their way to the horizon."

Charlotte Collier had known from the start that the ship was in a desperate situation, but she lingered on the deck with her husband and her daughter near boat 14, as Charles Joughin and Murdoch tossed children across the portside gap and persuaded their mothers to follow and as Harold Lowe forced a schoolboy out of the same boat at gunpoint.

Eight-year-old Marjorie Collier cried and begged Lowe not to shoot the boy. Marjorie thought she had seen enough horrors for one night, beginning with the stoker who had come running onto the deck with all five fingers severed from one hand and the blood running shockingly bright against the black coal dust that carpeted his face and clothes. The stoker had assured her father, Harvey Collier, that the ship would sink. Despite his obvious state of physical distress, Murdoch commanded the fingerless man and his fellow stokers to stand back from the boat and allow passengers to be loaded aboard.

"How many unhappy men were shut off in that way I do not know," Charlotte would write a month later. "But Mr. Murdoch was probably right." To Charlotte, Murdoch was "a bulldog of a man who would not be afraid of anything. This proved to be true. He kept order to the last, and died at his post. They say he shot himself. I do not know."

Joughin, Lowe, or one of the other men assisting Murdoch grabbed little Marjorie from Charlotte's arms and flung her into boat 14. Before Charlotte had time to react, a crewman grabbed her by an arm, yelling, "You too! Take a seat in that boat or it will be too late." Charlotte tried to cling to her husband, but he broke her grip on him as a second man threw both arms around her waist and dragged her down toward her daughter and the boat.

"Go, Lotty," Harvey shouted, as Lowe jumped in and took command of the lowering. "For God's sake, be brave and go!"

Charlotte obeyed and stayed in boat 14; on a seat plank nearby, Madeline Mellinger clung to the side of her mother's coat.

After Lowe unhooked the ropes and the boat had rowed off a short distance, Charlotte saw an iceberg looming into view, staying close to the *Titanic* like a faithful dog. She at first believed it must be the same berg that had caused the present calamity; then she realized that this "dog" belonged to a very large pack. Two more mountains of ice drifted out of the starlight toward her. When she looked away from the bergs, the *Titanic* suddenly appeared to be both horrible and beautiful at the same time, somehow taking on the qualities of "an enormous glowworm."

Charlotte watched, hoping to recognize her husband's face up there near the davits, but all she could distinguish were shadowy groups of human figures on every deck. "They were," she would recall, "standing with arms crossed upon their chests and with lowered heads. I am sure that they were in prayer. On the boat deck that I had just left, perhaps fifty men had come together. In the midst of them was a tall figure. This man had climbed upon a coil of rope [or other chair-high object] so that he was raised far above the rest. His hands were stretched out as if he were pronouncing a blessing."

Moment by moment, the *Titanic* (which now added belches of foam and black smoke to the stirring of the biolumes) was transforming into a vision that was simultaneously volcanic and biblical—with mountains carried into the midst of the sea, the waters thereof being troubled, and the works of humanity broken and melting into the earth.

More than two hundred feet nearer than Charlotte Collier and Madeline Mellinger, boat 2 was in trouble. Fourth Officer Joseph Boxhall—the navigator whose 11:40 p.m. walk toward the bridge would forever memorialize the scant seconds between the warning bells and the impact—discovered that the lifeboat was being drawn closer to the ship, despite the best efforts of his rowers. Boxhall's initial plan to find an open gangway door and take at least three more people down Jacob's ladders into boat 2 was being thwarted as much by a growing sense of time running out as by an inability to find the now submerged D-deck shell door—or any other open door. He would recall for the American examiners that the developing suction, against which he now ordered the crew and the passengers to row in full retreat, was strongest while the broad flat regions of the forecastle and the well deck were slowly gliding down.

As the forecastle and other major deck structures finally relinquished their grip on the surface and slipped underwater, they created powerful eddies accompanied by sudden gulps, by the hollow thuds of imploding compartments, and by the wholesale release of trapped air. Aroused by the developing maelstrom, Lily Futrelle's million bioluminescent points of light blazed even more strongly to life. The people of boat 14 beheld, in the boundary layer of turbulence that completely enveloped the ship's submerged head, a far brighter pixelation effect than had ever been created by a mere pod of lightning dolphins. Little Marjorie Collier and her mother looked down and could see, near the place where Georgyj Vinogradov's gorgon would take root, the image of the *Titanic's* prow, as clearly as one could see a pebble in a pond on a sunny day.

Between 2:00 and 2:05 a.m., just about forty minutes after the last distress rocket showered white flares over the bridge, the sea was up to Daniel Buckley's closed gate at the top of the bow section's well-deck stairs. The foremast stood out of the water like a lone sequoia tree, tilting over toward the port side.

B deck and most of the superstructure from Buckley's gate up to the bridge were still above water, but with every boat except the last collapsible having cast off from the davits, Joe Loring and George Rheims knew that the final horror would soon be approaching from the direction of the mast.

Loring took his brother-in-law's hands in his own and said, "George, if you survive, look after my babies."

Rheims promised that if he lived, Loring would not have to worry about his family. He then told Loring to wait for a minute while he ran down two decks to his stateroom on B deck, which was still standing high and dry under the starboard side of the first smokestack. Expecting for himself nothing except death and wishing only that the one object in the world most precious to him would be found clutched close to his body, Rheims stayed in his room just long enough to pull his wife's picture from its frame and stuff it under his clothes. As he bolted up the grand stairway, the water was rising at least to the top of the stairway's D deck and onto C deck, but the greater mass of the oaken tower was still pressing down on the E deck landing with just enough force to keep the entire structure stable—for at least a few minutes longer.

When he rejoined his brother-in-law on the starboard boat deck, Rheims seemed to have developed a sense that their best chance for survival would be to jump over the side and swim as fast as they could toward one of the departing lifeboats. He understood that during a leap into the water from a height of two or three stories, the cork-filled and loose-fitting shoulder-strapped life jackets, which appeared to have been perfectly designed to parachute upward upon impact, would transform instantly into hangmen's nooses. Under "man overboard" conditions, the life jackets seemed to be a means of committing suicide by hanging oneself to avoid drowning.

Evidently, Rheims did not consider freezing to death. All he wanted to consider was how a faster, more streamlined swim toward the lifeboats might increase his chances, if only slightly, of reaching one of the boats alive, before they rowed too far away. Decreasing the weight he had to carry would shave critical seconds off his swim time, so he dropped his gold-filled money belt to the deck next to his life jacket, along with the heavy warm coat he had put on earlier. He shed his shoes and his long pants (along with the increased drag force inherent in pockets), keeping only his wife's photo tucked under the strap of his undershorts. Loring followed his example, stripping down to his shirt and undershorts and throwing his clothes to the boat deck.

The best bet they had, Rheims decided, was to walk down *toward* the approaching danger, jump from as low a height as possible into the water, and swim like Olympic competitors toward the nearest lifeboat. Loring hesitated, openly questioning his own swimming ability and looking pleadingly in the direction opposite the descending bow, toward the rising stern and the illusory safety of higher ground.

"There," Loring said. "We should go all the way up to the rear of the ship."

"That would be sure death, and you should come with me," Rheims insisted, as the water drew nearer the front of the boat deck and the white-painted sides of the lifeboats receded deeper into the night.

On the same side of the boat deck, Jack Thayer, the seventeen-year-old whose open C-deck porthole must by now be contributing to the accelerating rate of the *Titanic's* sinking, was having essentially the same argument as the two men who had stripped themselves nearly naked outside the grand stairway entrance.

Thayer briefly debated with a friend whether they should attempt to fight their way toward the last boat on the front davits or slide down one of the ropes dangling from the nearest set of davits and swim after one of the partly filled lifeboats, which they could both plainly see reflected in the *Titanic's* lights. The chances of actually seeing the lifeboats (much less reaching them) were diminishing fast, as the electric lights began fading from whitish-yellow to red and from red toward a ruddy brown glow. Thayer's friend dissuaded him from jumping—at least for a little while. Indecisiveness maintained a powerful and often contagious grip on people.

The ship itself had been behaving with a sort of mechanical indecision since about the time the last rocket had detonated. For a few minutes—probably as the Harper stateroom and other open C-deck ports dunked under along the starboard side—the *Titanic* seemed to have come gradually out of its list to port and developed a slight list to starboard. Soon, however, something along Scotland Road must have given way, like an arterial wall rupturing, and allowed a new, deep interior hemorrhage to bring the list to port into full control again.

By the time water had mounted the grand stairway's C deck and commenced its climb toward the next landing, the increasing pressure on the wooden tower to float free must already have begun generating loud, visible, and undeniably frightening stress fractures along the perimeter of the stairwell.

Thayer was suddenly aware of a large crowd surging onto the front of the boat deck, shortly before Purser McElroy fired two warning shots into the air. Along with the commotion of the crowd, jostling backward from the gunshots, came a series of loud noises from inside the ship. The noises, which made Thayer think of bulkheads snapping, seemed to be herding even greater masses of people onto the deck.

When first-class passenger Hugh Woolner saw Officer Murdoch fire two warning shots into the air, he decided with his friend Bjornstrom Steffansen that running to the port side and jumping overboard might be the better part of valor. They reached boat D along with Joseph Duquemin, who was eventually branded a "steerage foreigner stowaway" by Colonel Archibald Gracie.

On the starboard side, Colonel Gracie was working with First Officer Murdoch at the boat 1 davits, helping to crank the davit heads inboard again in the hope of being able to launch one of the collapsible boats, stowed upside down on the roof behind a cat's cradle of smokestack stays. A century later, the front davit would still be standing guard in its final, cranked-in position.

Somewhere amid the cranking in of davits and the jostling and the increasing confusions of the night, Second Officer Lightoller fired off a warning shot from the roof to prevent a rush by "steerage passengers."

During the last minutes before the ship tilted into position for the final plunge, collapsible boat A came crashing down from the roof, perfectly horizontal. On the way down, it broke most of the oars someone had leaned against the side of the officers' quarters, meaning to give the boat a smooth incline down to the deck. Gracie gave up any thoughts of trying to get away in the collapsible. Too many people were crowding around, so he decided to leave boat A to Murdoch, climb uphill toward the stern, and take his chances with what would surely be the last part of the ship going down.

During his ascent along the starboard boat deck, Gracie passed seventeen-year-old apprentice chef John Collins running downhill toward boat A with a baby in his arms and the mother trotting behind with a second child. Of this small group, only Collins would ever be seen again.

Murdoch continued to struggle with his team to pull boat A over the side on the davits, hoping to save the women standing nearby and to somehow keep a hundred people from swamping an emergency raft built to hold, at most, only sixty passengers. None of the women or children who stood near boat A's davits at this moment lived to tell what happened next, but in an evidently desperate bid to save them, Murdoch was required to fire more warning shots—which would escalate quickly into something worse.

Tennis champion Richard Norris Williams II was standing with his father outside the perimeter of the boat A crowd just before the final shots rang out. Richard's father had insisted, despite all of the signs before his eyes, that the *Titanic*'s design principle of compartmentalization would allow the ship to settle only so far into the water and then stop sinking. Not until Captain Smith sent a crewman running and shoving a path uphill from the wheelhouse, and they saw water sweeping across the floor of the bridge from its port side, did the elder Williams express a sense of fear and begin running uphill, toward the stern. Richard followed. As he turned, the sounds of gunfire erupted behind him. He quickened his pace, choosing not to look back.

The electric lights continued to dim until they were barely, if at all, brighter than embers and coals in a campfire, but most people's eyes adapted, to one degree or another. The *Titanic*'s lamps no longer drowned out the starlight. The stars themselves now stood out in the night like grains of bright dust as, uphill, the distant deckhouses and people gradually became vaguely outlined shapes.

Against this backbone of encroaching black, passenger Eugene Daly was near enough to the side of boat A to see what Richard Norris Williams II had heard. An officer was attempting to save the women behind him in the collapsible raft—first with warning shots into the air, then by pointing his revolver at a group of men and threatening to shoot if they dared rush toward the raft, and finally by actually shooting two of them. The crowd scrambled toward the stern, and there followed a third gunshot. When Daly looked back, he saw the officer himself lying on the deck. Passenger Carl Olof Jansen could not tell whether any passengers had been shot, but he glanced to one side just in time to see the officer in charge of boat A's launch putting the revolver to his own head and pulling the trigger.

Rheims witnessed the shooting of at least one passenger by a discharge from an officer's revolver, and while everyone around the mostly naked Rheims either fled or stood in shock, providing the people in boat A with just a few seconds more in which to attempt a safe launch, Rheims saw the officer give a military salute and shoot himself.

Moments later, boat A's davits began to slip beneath the surface, its ropes pulling the boat down with them in a sudden upsurge of icy black water that washed everyone who had been standing behind Murdoch out of the boat. Seconds after that, Rheims too went under, and he never did see his brother-in-law Joe Loring again.

Apprentice chef Collins did not get near enough to boat A to even attempt saving the mother and children he was escorting toward Murdoch. As boat A went under, he was struck by a wall of water glutted with people and debris. It taught him the incomparable horror of having a child torn out of one's arms.

Deep below, the bulkhead at the front of boiler room number 4 had resisted twice the height of water that broke the damaged bulkhead between boiler room numbers 5 and 6. The dam had by now taken all the pressure it could hold.

The rupture—the probable cause of the boat-deck wave—occurred about 2:10 a.m. Once boiler room number 4 was filled, the final stage in the cascade effect took command of the night. The boilers in room numbers 4 and 3 shared all of their vents, joined in an upside-down branching pattern, inside the second smokestack. Once boiler room number 4 collapsed and overflowed, water spilled over the branch at the E-deck junction into the boilers in the next compartment back, and out the boilers' mouths.

If the watertight doors had by then been used to seal the bulkhead between boiler room numbers 3 and 4, the doors were, against the multiple geysers in boiler room number 3, as ineffective as valves against a major arterial rip. The only event that could now slow the bleeding toward the stern, albeit only slightly, was the tendency of water that had already pooled behind the second funnel to rush forward as the bow section suddenly angled down more steeply.

Thayer had heard what sounded and felt to him like a deep interior thud, a seemingly explosive force muffled by many intervening decks. The thud and the wave were consistent with the implosion of an entire boiler room, manifested as a sudden loss of buoyancy that pitched the deck down toward the flooded chambers of the bow, initially to an angle of about fifteen degrees.

Thayer also believed, during this final phase of the sinking, that the list to port briefly began to even out—intensifying the strength and volume of water being drawn onto the starboard deck. The wave gave Thayer the false impression of a ship that had suddenly started moving forward, and from above him came a rumbling roar that gave him the further and all too realistic impression of "standing under a steel railway bridge while an express train passes overhead, mingled with the noise of a pressed steel factory and wholesale breakage of china."

Not very far from where he stood, the breaking of glass and steel overhead would have been precisely the sounds guaranteed to accompany the grand stairway's breaking free, coming apart, and beginning to push upward through the crystal dome.

When Thayer finally leaped over the starboard side, the sea was almost level with the roof of the bridge and the crow's nest. Water was only seconds away from the base of the first smokestack. Watching from boat D, quartermaster Arthur Bright noticed that even though the lights along the stern were still blazing, the windows, portholes, and deck lamps had all but faded from existence in the front half of the ship, leaving Thayer with little more than shadows by which to interpret what he saw happening between the first and second smokestacks.

From at least as far back as the third smokestack, the *Titanic* seemed to be surrounded by a glare that stood out in the night as though the stern were coming alive with St. Elmo's fire tinted red. The contrast between the heavenly glow aft and the shadows it threw across the forward part of the ship stopped Thayer from swimming away and held him transfixed to the spot. The piercing cold of the water had suddenly lost its power to shock or frighten him.

He was now more fascinated than afraid. The *Titanic* had been transforming before his eyes into a horror, yet it was now also, paradoxically, spellbinding. Thayer could no more look away from the ship than he could turn from the stare of a cobra.

As boat A tore free from its davits and popped to the surface, the rumble and roar of parting steel, breaking glass, and cracking wood became louder and more distinct. In the shadowy front of the ship, between the first two smokestacks, Thayer believed he saw the superstructure break. Something buckled and blew upward near the first smokestack. A huge dark shape seemed to be rising on its haunches, like a volcanic island trying to be born. What Thayer probably witnessed was the emergence of the grand stairway.

Thayer's friend Richard Williams was still moving uphill along the boat deck with his father, having managed to slow the elder Williams's panicked pace, just before the ship began its sudden lurch downward and swept them up in a wave. "I turned toward the bow," Williams would write later. "I saw nothing but water with a mast sticking out of it. I don't remember the shock of the cold water. I only remember thinking, 'suction,' and my efforts to swim in the direction of the starboard rail to get away from the ship."

Before he could move more than five breaststrokes from the starboard boat deck, Williams believed he felt the deck rushing forward and rising up beneath him. What he believed was all a matter of relative perspective. What he actually felt was a rush of water and debris carrying him backward and dropping him onto the deck somewhere behind the second or third smokestack.

Williams and his father were suddenly able to stand—suddenly high and dry. He would later record, "My father was not more than twelve or fifteen feet away from me."

Underfoot, the flood within the ship was forcing bursts of trapped air up to the surface along with great masses of cracked oak. Every grain of coal dust that had clung inside the vents from the first four chambers of boilers appeared to be breaking loose—either to be jetted out through the tops of the stacks or to be sent gurgling up through the intake vents at their bases. The dust and the black mist spread out horizontally in distinct layers over the sea, breaking the glare from astern into eerie red streamers of light and shadow.

One of the two forward smokestacks buckled at its base and leaned suddenly to one side just as Richard Williams recognized his father among the shadows and began moving toward him.

At precisely that moment, Williams would record for historians, "I saw one of the four great funnels come crashing down on top of him. Just for one instant, I stood there transfixed—not because it had only missed me by a few feet; curiously enough not because it had killed my father, for whom I had more than a normal feeling of love and attachment; but there I was transfixed, wondering at the enormous size of this funnel, still belching smoke."

14

∾

The Truth about William Murdoch

SEPTEMBER 2001
RUSSIAN RESEARCH VESSEL *KELDYSH*
EXPEDITION *TITANIC XIII*

During an April 1962 lunch with Walter Lord, Richard Norris Williams II said that he had more of a grandstand view than he'd have wanted of the *Titanic*'s last minutes. Finally, he struck out swimming, kicking off his shoes and trying to shed his thick overcoat to gain speed, and he came to believe that he had traveled nearly a mile from the starboard side.

Yet when he turned around, he saw that for all his efforts, he had actually put no more than a hundred feet between himself and the monster. Despite the horror and the peril, he could not help feeling that the *Titanic* was a majestic sight. The bow continued to angle down, seeming to pivot around a center of rotation behind the place where the second smokestack had been. For every one degree down that the bow angled, the glowing stern angled up one degree, raising the golden propellers into the air, the equivalent of nearly four city blocks away.

Eventually, Williams saw a large, shadowy figure up ahead: collapsible boat A, with its canvas sides torn. Others approached the floating shadow. They kicked and fought to climb aboard. Williams was among the stronger ones. He managed to scramble inside with Carl Olof Jansen and George Rheims, both of whom had been rather closer to boat A minutes earlier, when it was filled with women and children and Williams had heard the crack of a revolver shot.

Among the people who scrambled aboard the risen wreck of the last boat, there seemed to be a certain historic significance in the fact that the three who reported those final minutes of pandemonium and gunfire at the forward davits—Williams, Jansen, and Rheims—were able to prove their proximity to the event by actually being found aboard boat A. A fourth witness, Eugene Daly, was found aboard the upside-down wreck of boat B, and he too had been near William Murdoch in the end.

Walter Lord and I believed it most significant that the Daly and Rheims accounts were memorialized in letters to wives and sisters before the rescue ship *Carpathia* landed in New York; these were not sensationalistic newspaper reports based on hearsay. The witnesses were consistent in their stories about an officer who shot men attempting to lead a rush on the last starboard lifeboat and who afterward demonstrated that he would not take a space of his own in the boat by shooting himself. It seemed to Lord most revealing of all that the Daly letter was penned by a third-class passenger—"describing exactly the same incident" yet coming from a man who would not have personally known the first-class passenger, Rheims. Partly as a result of our narrow focus on the last three minutes of Murdoch's life—a focus that continued through the 1996 expedition—Jim Cameron had incorporated the Rheims and Daly accounts into his 1997 film, *Titanic*. The evidence was historically sound, but it told only a small part of the story—and in such manner that I had committed a grievous wrong against Murdoch.

Shortly before the thirteenth *Titanic* expedition, historian Paul Quinn completed the much overdue and much required homework of following, through an exhaustive study of the British and American *Titanic* inquiries of 1912, Murdoch's movements throughout the night. The first officer was seen front and starboard, launching boats and making sure they were filled to capacity, and he was also seen rear and starboard and rear and portside doing the same thing.

In contrast to the injunctions that separated women from their adolescent sons and their husbands, creating the heartbreaking gridlock that John Astor had tried to stop, and that caused Celiney Yasbeck's boat to be lowered hurriedly and half empty, Murdoch made repeated efforts to fill the boats and prevent gridlock by any means necessary. Charles Joughin and a small crew of cooks and stewards helped Murdoch to literally hurl women and children into the boats—along with the husbands and fathers.

Jim Cameron and Don Lynch were impressed with the Quinn analysis of Murdoch's efficiency, especially compared to the half-empty boats launched from the front port side under the Lightoller/Lowe injunctions. "And here's Murdoch," Cameron said, reviewing dive video of the boat A davit head. "Here's Murdoch, getting the boats in the water as quick as he can, shoving men in, women, children—first class, third class—he didn't care. Almost two-thirds of everyone who [got away in the boats and] survived had Murdoch to thank for it." And I should have known better had I looked deeper.

In 1995, Susanne Stormer published her biography of First Officer William Murdoch. The *Titanic* was not Murdoch's first encounter with disaster, and he had a history of holding up selflessly in the worst of times, putting the many others aboard a ship ahead of himself without regard for the personal consequences.

Nine years before the *Titanic*, Murdoch was second officer aboard the White Star Line's *Arabic*. Charles Lightoller was on the bridge when Murdoch and one of the *Arabic*'s lookouts sighted the light of another vessel, ahead on the port side. Murdoch ran onto the bridge just as the chief officer commanded the bow to be turned hard to the starboard side, but Murdoch saw, looming out of the dark, the expanding dimensions of a much larger sailing vessel than had originally been presumed. So he countermanded the order. Simultaneously, he pushed a quartermaster away from the ship's wheel and took the helm himself.

"According to Lightoller," Stormer wrote, "everyone on the bridge was looking for a safe place, because the sailing ship came closer and closer—and there was the danger of the yards crashing on the bridge of the *Arabic*—while Murdoch stood at the helm, completely cool, and not moving the wheel or even himself an inch." The *Arabic* missed the other vessel by what witnesses on the bridge called "a very close thing," but there was general agreement that Murdoch had prevented the White Star Line's newest ship from smashing its bow straight into a multimasted sailing ship.

In spite of his direct disobedience of a senior officer (which in those days was next of kin to mutiny), Murdoch was only temporarily transferred to a less prestigious ship, the *Celtic*. It was clear that management appreciated the significance of Murdoch's lifesaving action. They saw in him a man who, even if he feared responsibility, did not shirk it. He was quick to react and could be counted on to handle himself very well when havoc threatened.

Only in the last few sentences of her book did Stormer focus on Murdoch's last three minutes of life. "He had to fight a personal fight," she wrote. "He had to suppress his will to stay alive. He had to go down with the *Titanic* like countless other people, among them many old shipmates and friends. Murdoch had been senior officer of the watch when the collision occurred, and his desperate maneuver to avoid an accident [had] failed. With this, he had a part of the responsibility, and this meant he had to stay with the ship. There was no other way and there was no escape for him. If hell really did exist, Murdoch must have gone right through it during the last two hours and forty minutes of the *Titanic*."

And so, on a September evening in 2001, I crouched inside the steel shell of the *Mir-2*, looking out across time to a cold April night, toward the cranked-in davit where Murdoch had made his stand. Everything marine archaeologist John Broadwater, pilot Victor Nescheta, and I were doing was (from Murdoch's point in time) far beyond the science fiction of Jules Verne.

From Murdoch's point in time, we of the *Keldysh* were living and breathing somewhere between fantasy and the shape of things to come, descending in contraptions of steel, Plexiglas, and blazing light. Lifting off from the boat deck and landing on the roof of the officers' quarters, we watched the *Mir-1* dispatch the robot Jake, which glided down into the grand stairwell. Viewed through imaginations that lived in two time frames, Jake seemed to pass with contemptuous indifference through spaces once occupied by people, on its way to more important concerns in the reception rooms and the rusticle caverns.

It was dinnertime aboard the *Keldysh* when we came to rest on a ragged patch of deck where hermit crabs now roamed toward the grand stairway crater. In my mind's eye, the specter of Murdoch was still out there, eighty-nine years earlier, doing whatever was necessary, as the deck began to slip away, to give the women at his back a few seconds more to get the ropes undone and push themselves away in the last lifeboat. There were, at that moment, barely more than fifty seats at Murdoch's back for fifteen hundred people still aboard.

In this replay of history, the decks still seemed alive as I turned away from the viewport and penned a promise on the title page of Stormer's book.

SEPTEMBER 10, 2001
ON BOARD RMS *TITANIC*

To First Officer William Murdoch:

A wise archaeologist named Trude Dothan once told me that we (we who stroll through the cellars of time) are the biggest storytellers in the world—that we have become speakers for the dead; simply that. Nothing more. Nothing less. But we are more than that, and I believe [my friends] and I have done you wrong, William McMaster Murdoch—done you wrong by focusing on the last [three] minutes of your life without realizing that [nearly] 75% of the people who got away from this place owed their lives to you. I, especially [committed a wrong against you]—for I painted less than half of your face and asked the world to guess from that the measure of the whole man. [Someday,] I will correct this picture. Trude was wrong. [Archaeology] is not so simple as telling stories about the dead. We must keep a faith with the dead—and I've a faith to keep with you, Mr. Murdoch.

Your friend, in time. C. R. P.

Earlier that day, during our flight over the port side of the stern, the terrain below lay so flattened and distorted that we found it difficult to distinguish between the launch points of boats 14 and 16. What we could discern and what we did understand was that some ten meters (almost 11 yards) below us, at the top of a portside wall of steel that was now stretched out almost perfectly horizontal across the sea floor, Annie Robinson, Violet Jessop, and the baby thrown into Violet's arms had been among the many who were saved by Murdock's actions.

From a vantage point equivalent to two or three city blocks away, in boat 16, it seemed to Jessop that the ship was taking "a sudden lurch forward," an inevitable illusion created by the dipping of the bow, the simultaneous rising of the stern, and the wave running back along the boat deck. The sudden motion gave the liner the false appearance that it had come alive again and was driving ahead, trying (unsuccessfully) to shunt great quantities of seawater off to the starboard and port sides. Before Jessop could even begin to interpret the illusion, one of the smokestacks toppled off as though it had been nothing more than a huge cardboard model, "falling into the water with a fearful roar."

Sauce chef George Harris, another person saved by Murdoch, sat in boat 11 with Maude Slocomb, who tried to comfort the baby someone had put into her arms, but Slocomb's nerves were becoming increasingly frayed by the dying ship and by the constant ringing of an alarm clock some woman had judged important enough to bring aboard the lifeboat.

"Shut it off!" Slocomb hollered, adding, "You old bitch."

The woman was neither old nor a bitch, and the alarm clock was not an alarm clock. Boat 11 had more children aboard than most of the others, and Edith Russell was sitting on the gunwale, winding the tail of her musical toy pig, playing the *Maxixe* and trying to keep the children's attention diverted from the ship.

A mile away, in boat 13, nine-week-old Millvina Dean had started to cry when her bare feet were exposed from beneath the blanket in which she had been wrapped. Ellen Phillips, the daughter of Kate Phillips and Henry Morley ("the Marshalls") was almost nine months away from being born on the night her mother took her turn among the women who cradled and comforted baby Millvina.

Unlike Millvina, Ellen was destined for a life of neglect by a mother who was to become increasingly unbalanced and (in the best of times) distant. For Ellen, the saddest cut of all was to learn one day that Millvina was cradled and cared for by "Mrs. Marshall"—and by almost every other woman in boat 13. Ellen would eventually grow up to resent the tiniest *Titanic* survivor, unable to understand how her mother treated a stranger's child, however briefly, like her own adored infant but then treated her own daughter like a stranger.

15

To Dream on the Ship
of Sorrows

SEPTEMBER 11, 2001
RUSSIAN RESEARCH VESSEL *KELDYSH*
EXPEDITION *TITANIC XIII*

Sometime between the post–dive 7 debriefing and Georgyj Vinogradov's
3 a.m. visit to the bio lab, another one of the Russian biologists found
me at work on something that, puzzling though it might have seemed,
I simply thought should be done.

I was carefully cleaning what had by now come to be called the two
Titanic crosses: the boat 8 railing and the davit bitt. Days earlier, Lori
Johnston and I had stripped them completely of their rusticle roots, and
I was carefully cleaning and oiling the two crosses for their return to
the portside boat deck. Wherever the metal allowed it, I tried to make
their surfaces appear shiny and new.

The other Russian scientist, like Vinogradov, thought I should be
in my cabin resting; he added that there was no apparent "use or purpose" for what I was doing.

"Why this?" he asked.

I did not know why. I said that I simply wanted to return something to the *Titanic* in better condition than we found it. He nodded and said that he understood.

There was no way of guessing, between 2 and 3 a.m., the weight of time and coincidence in the heft of a rope from the boat 8 davit bitt as I draped it around the shoulders of its cross. There was no way of knowing that in just a few days, journalist Rip MacKenzie would be e-mailing me photographs of a Franciscan chaplain standing with a group of firefighters and recovery workers beneath a steel cross (with a sheet of aluminum down-blasted over one shoulder to resemble a shroudlike piece of cloth), atop a place that would briefly be called Ground Zero Hill.

Recalling what a Russian scientist had said many days earlier about two *Titanic* crosses and a third cross coming, MacKenzie captioned the photo, "Here's your third cross."

About 3:30 a.m. *Titanic* time, I stepped out of the lab onto the portside deck and looked up at the stars. In the past few nights there seemed to have been more bright meteors than usual, including the occasional smoke trailer and spark thrower.

Either one found boredom out here or one found peace. For me, the middle of the ocean was incomparable peace.

Under the meteor shower, as the line of shadow that bisected Turkey and Egypt retreated toward us from the east, my cousin Donna Clarke was still peacefully asleep in New York City. She had shared some tears with our Aunt Hannah earlier that night, a bit worried (in a superstitious sense) that her thirties were almost at an end. Donna "knew" from childhood that she would not see age forty.

Donna's sister, Sharon, was autistic and, like many in our family, did not always follow a regular pattern of sleep. Sharon's thoughts this night were mainly about the classes she would be taking, one by one, toward her bachelor's degree in journalism. When we were children, we communicated through sand castles that grew to become cities as well as through drawings—entire homemade comic books of drawings. In 2001, Sharon had an eerie picture in her head of Donna sitting on a hand-hewn wooden bench, laughing and at peace with my mother, who had passed away from leukemia just hours before the 1993 bombing of the World Trade Center.

Captain Paddy Brown often went to sleep about this time. To his friends he was known as "brother, student, teacher, Sensei, Marine." In New York he fought what he called "the little *red* devil"—sometimes with such ferocious bravery that on many a day the Fire Department of

New York's battalion leaders were unsure whether to pin a medal on him or bust him down a rank or two.

In the end, they assigned Paddy to the firehouse on 13th Street. He hammered together a heavy teak bench, placed it on the sidewalk in front of the firehouse, and decided, "There's no better place to be than with 3 Truck."

Like most in his profession, Paddy was required to be part chemist, part structural engineer, and part psychologist. For a while, he had competed for command of the city's amphibious unit, Rescue 1, because he was just crazy enough for the job and was also "part fish."

Few people had followed Robert Ballard's first submersible landings on the *Titanic* with greater intensity. Paddy was not merely curious about rusticles, hydrothermal vents, and the idea that the robots of the deep might be pointing the path to finding similar life under the ice of Saturn's moons Enceladus or Titan; he *understood* the wilderness into which science and technology were struggling to open new doors. He was also, as one close friend phrased it, "the only person I have ever encountered who could be profound by saying 'kinda' and 'sorta' and 'you know?'" The robots Argo and Jake were the actual ancestors of deep space probes, and that was "really kinda cool" in Paddy's universe.

A friend had described him as "bouncing with excitement" one day as he showed off the new thermal imaging equipment that allowed him to peer through dense smoke and, for the first time, to actually see the red devil. "I never knew this was so dangerous!" he said, and laughed.

On that last night, as the line of daylight crept toward the *Keldysh* and New York, there were now enough moments for Paddy to look back on and call, "Kinda beautiful, you know?" He had recently helped fellow Ladder 3 firefighter Jeff Giordano carry a young woman out of a 13th Street fire. They tried twice to resuscitate her, but she remained flatlined each time.

"Keep going," Paddy commanded, and they tried again. And again. And again.

"And then Paddy saw it," his friend explained later. "That most beautiful sight—the light of life coming back into Jessica Rubenstein's eyes."

"I just keep seeing those eyes," Paddy would often say.

For years to come, I would just keep seeing the unusually clear and calm, meteor-filled predawn sky of September 11, 2001. At 3:30 a.m. *Titanic* time, it was just past 2 a.m. in New York. In only a few hours, Paddy would be performing his yoga and meditation exercises before getting into his daily fight with his coffee machine. The very same man who knew how to tweak the new infrared sensing equipment, who could perform undersea rescues, and who had made a point of learning exactly how to secure the emergency thrusters if the president's helicopter should crash could not get his coffee machine or his cell phone to work. He kept a more reliable landline Mickey Mouse phone at his desk.

The question "How much does darkness weigh?" led to an e-mail conference that spread almost from pole to pole, and Rip MacKenzie, Roy Cullimore, and I had eventually come around to addressing humanity's dark half. One day, someone asked, "If you were God, how would you set up justice in the universe, in terms of life after death?" If one was permitted to speculate on the subject of justice in the universe, then the idea that our present existence was merely the most recent cusp within an infinite (and possibly identical) series of cosmic expansions and contractions held a certain poetic attraction.

Justice, for me, would be for every person to live the lives of everyone else whose lives they had touched. "Mother Teresa is eventually on the enlightened, receiving end of the lives she has touched," I explained, "and especially those who were transformed by her to spread forth into the lives of others two simple commandments of mercy and kindness."

I did believe that in a just universe, the truly evil mind, which throughout life drew a malicious joy from the infliction of misfortune upon others, would, during the moments between dying and death, stretch time to its outermost limits and create its own eternal punishment. In such a universe, I wrote, Timothy McVeigh, the architect of the Oklahoma City bombing, after experiencing the suffering of his victims, might be reborn somewhere in the world every few seconds, fully sentient of his fate, as a cockroach about to be stepped on. "Would it really be enough for him to experience the last moments of pain he inflicted on every man, woman, and child he murdered?" I asked Cullimore and MacKenzie.

My just universe gave Cullimore the shivers. He warned that I needed to be more careful, because "Evil has a way of worming its way into the hearts of good people, turning them toward the furies of anger and vengeance." He emphasized that the good were evil's golden ships.

Sometime after 3:30 a.m., I went to sleep, not very long before the bot team and the camera team started to work. I woke up about 7:30 a.m.

to dead calm seas and beautiful blue skies. The *Mir* meeting was at 8 a.m. sharp.

In Maine, Mohamed Atta and Abdulaziz al Omari lifted off in Portland's nineteen-seat Beech 1900 to fly to their connection at Boston's Logan Airport. Both carried plain shoulder bags. To deflect attention, their hair was cropped short and they were clean-shaven.

Atta's primer, or last manifesto, read, "Remember that which you were told earlier. God says that when you are surrounded by several nonbelievers, you must sit quietly and remember that God will make victory possible for you in the end. . . . Don't give the impression of being confused, instead be strong and happy with confidence because you are engaged in work that pleases God."

The primer was far removed from what Islam's founding prophet taught, just as the murderous Jim Jones and the burning Ku Klux Klan crosses were far removed from everything Jesus had tried to teach. As daylight crept nearer, the plotters hid themselves and blessed themselves in the shadow of the ancient enemy: humanity's dark, reptilian core, which, as always, held commerce in depths of evil most people could hardly guess at.

At daybreak, three days with a very bad summer cold had changed Mary Leung's usual route to work, via the World Trade Center. Before what would normally have been the morning's quick, jump-start coffee break, two women from Mary's office would be fatally burned by a jet engine crashing down near them, trailing a quarter-mile slipstream of blazing fuel.

At 9:30 a.m. *Titanic* time, the *Mir* meeting was over. The launch of the *Mir-1* toward the rescue of our bot Elwood was scheduled for 10:30 a.m., with the *Mir-2* to follow an hour later. History's first rescue of one robot by another was being eagerly awaited in science classrooms around the world. As an added bonus to this bright and beautiful day, the International Space Station, also with an American and Russian crew, would be passing overhead and making e-mail contact.

Lori Johnston and Lew Abernathy were planning another swim in two and a half miles of water, and this time I would join them, once the second *Mir* was away.

An hour and a half behind *Titanic* time, in New York, Paddy Brown arrived at 3 Truck's engine bay and wrote, "0800 Capt Brown RFD [reporting for duty]" in the journal.

Half an hour earlier, at 7:30 a.m., American Airlines Flight 11 had prepared to take its position on the Logan Airport runway in Boston. The California-bound Boeing 767 was specifically outfitted with extended-range fuel tanks, for a total capacity of twenty-four thousand gallons. Aboard was Paige Farley-Hackel.

Farley-Hackel was a spiritual adviser and family counselor who had achieved some fame in California with a radio show titled *Spiritually Speaking*. Before traveling to the East Coast with her best friend, Ruth McCourt, and McCourt's four-year-old daughter, Juliana (who was also Farley-Hackel's goddaughter), Farley-Hackel sent twelve unusual letters to people she counseled, saying, "You're doing well. We've accomplished everything we need to accomplish together."

Farley-Hackel's letters, according to her mother, Marjorie, had caused some recipients to wonder if she were recently diagnosed with a serious illness; Marjorie assured (then and later) that her daughter did not know anything was going to happen to her. "She had no premonition, just a sense that it was time for them to move on."

"I'm just like a butterfly, Mom," Farley-Hackel had said. "So even if anything ever should happen to me, and you see butterflies around, just imagine it's me."

After the 9/11 attacks, Marjorie planted flowers that were known to attract butterflies. They brought a measure of comfort and closeness, the always present butterflies in "Paige's garden."

Just before 8 a.m. in the New York and Boston time zone, while *Mir-1* was sealed and prepared for hoisting from its bay on a crane, Farley-Hackel could have looked across the runway from her plane to United Airlines Flight 175, where her friend McCourt was on board with Juliana.

Juliana was a "miracle baby." McCourt had been told it was unlikely that she and her husband would ever be able to have a child. But Juliana was conceived and born perfectly healthy and cheerful.

So far, this had been a morning of what were supposed to be only brief good-byes. McCourt's husband was being delayed in Boston by a new series of business commitments, and he had kissed his wife and his daughter good-bye at the airport. For Juliana's sake, McCourt and Farley-Hackel had taken some of the sting out of the little girl's missing Daddy by promising a visit to Disneyland after they arrived on the West Coast. Then Farley-Hackel had said good-bye and boarded a separate plane in order to take advantage of a frequent-flyer upgrade. The two women planned to meet again at the airport in Los Angeles.

At 7:58 a.m., two minutes before Paddy Brown signed in, and while *Mir-1* prepared to hit water, Flight 11 was accelerating down a Logan Airport runway. It was airborne at 7:59 a.m. Flight 175 followed at 8:14, and lifted off at 8:15.

On this morning, the temporary separation, brought about by a frequent-flyer upgrade, meant that Paige Farley-Hackel would die within the same one-fiftieth of a second as my cousin Donna in the North Tower and nearly seventeen minutes before Ruth McCourt and her little girl, Juliana.

About the time that Flight 175 became airborne, Lori Johnston emerged from the communications shack, and we made sure that the two *Titanic* crosses were secure in the *Mir-2*'s specimen basket. The *Mir-1* was now set for launch in forty-five minutes. The *Mir-2* would follow an hour later, and then we would take our two-and-a-half-mile swim. The swim was planned as a sort of decompression break for Johnston, who had spent a particularly long shift in the communications shack, monitoring my dive the day before.

I had volunteered to "take the coms" (the communications desk) after the *Mir*s were on their way down and give Johnston a long-overdue break. In addition to monitoring my dive, our endless debates about such arcane matters as precisely where, in rusticle biology, a line could be drawn between geochemical structure and truly biological structures, were bound to be tiring even for übergeeks.

I did not feel tired, but I must have been, for I did a rather dumb thing, I can say in hindsight. Scientists collect samples; scientists do not leave them behind. During the last three minutes, before it was time for us to depart the *Mir* bay, I ran back to the lab and filled a cloth bag with our reference samples of rope and microsamples of "bio-wedged" wrought-iron railing—all of them—and placed the bag in the "return to *Titanic*" tray.

"No," Johnston said, but she and Abernathy both saw that my eyes were full of tears. I did not know why. Johnston asked me again about hearing the silent voices, and I did not answer.

We put the bag in the tray with the crosses and sent it down.

16

Falling Stars

On the 98th floor of the World Trade Center's North Tower, my cousin Donna was, through a random swerve of history, so recently transferred from a much smaller building to the target area of the attack that she wondered if she would ever get accustomed to the view. Her office faced west, overlooking the Hudson River. On a clear day such as this, had she been looking toward Newark Liberty International Airport, Donna should have been able to see United Airlines Flight 93 taking off at 8:42 a.m., headed for San Francisco but targeted for hijacking (it is believed, to crash into the U.S. Capitol in Washington, D.C.), and bound for legend in the largely unknown farmlands of Shanksville, Pennsylvania.

United 93 was nearly a quarter mile below the upper floors of the Twin Towers, at the moment it lifted off the runway in Newark, New Jersey. At the same moment, Flight 11 was barely more than four minutes away from a direct impact into the offices of Marsh & McLennan, at 8:46:40 a.m. No cell phone calls were ever to be heard from any Marsh & McLennan shock cocoons (places that remain eerily undamaged in the midst of explosive events). Death in those offices was universal, instantaneous, and painless. In time, I would be able to live with that.

• • •

Ruth McCourt's brother, Ron Clifford, was about to become one of that day's Charles Joughins. Along with equities trader Welles Crowther and a patent attorney named Paul Hoffman (and many whose heroic actions might be recorded by history, but not their names), Clifford immediately joined the rescue effort. He would always imagine his sister, during those last minutes of Flight 175, showing nothing except strength for little Juliana, speaking soothingly and cradling the four-year-old's head against her chest as the smoke trail from the North Tower and then the undamaged South Tower came sweeping into view.

At the moment that his sister and his niece died, Clifford was propping up a burn victim from the first impact, guiding the woman through the lobby of the Marriott Hotel. The hotel was located directly between the feet of the two towers. Clifford had been about to enter the open spaces of the South Tower's ground floor when the crash of Flight 175 rocked the Marriott to its foundations, as if the building had been located between the prongs of a giant tuning fork.

A firefighter took hold of the burn victim and began guiding her away. A minute later, Clifford was headed back where he had seen other injured people, but he paused to seek out a phone, knowing that all of this must be breaking news on major networks and that his mother would be worried. He wanted to let her know he was safe.

Despite the escalating confusion, Clifford found a working phone. He called his mother and said, "There's been a plane crash and an explosion, Mom, but I'm safe."

His mother did not reply; she just remained wordlessly breathing on the other end of the line.

"Mom?"

Clifford realized from the continuing silence that his mother was focusing on what both of them already knew: Ruth and Juliana were on a plane. But, no, he thought. It couldn't be *that* bad.

"Mom? Where's Ruth?"

McCourt and her daughter had been seated in the back of Flight 175. Ruth McCourt was a very religious woman, and when her husband returned home, he discovered that the precious medallion she had kept near the bed—blessed by the pope, with the name and the date of their wedding in Rome engraved on the back—was missing. Before leaving, she had placed the medallion in her wallet, which continued traveling northward after the impact, somehow shock-cocooned. Weeks later, the medallion would be found perfectly unharmed within its cocoon of folded leather.

Looking east across the river from Paine Webber's Weehawken offices, Mary Leung was thinking of her old friend Paddy Brown. She knew that he had probably gone right into the thick of things. When the second plane shot through the South Tower, she thought of her friends who were now at the *Titanic*, and the steadily increasing levels of horror felt so unreal to her that for a moment it was possible to convince herself that this was simply a nightmare (far too vivid) from which she could not wake up—or that she was somehow standing outside the event, watching special effects from an ultra-high-definition movie.

She pleaded to herself, "Come on, Jim. Stop this. Yell, 'Cut!'"

At 10:40 a.m. *Titanic* time, the *Mir-1* had just launched.

We on the *Keldysh*, along with the winter team in Antarctica and the two Russians and one American who were building the core of the International Space Station, ranked among the world's most isolated islands of humanity. Although we had the ability to receive information straight from the space station, the Pentagon, and the Centers for Disease Control, by the end of the day, the only satellite news link we would be able to tap into was MSNBC; the link would be weak and the images fuzzy.

Between the *Mir* launches, I was heading toward my cabin to grab my bathing suit for the two-and-a-half-mile swim when our assistant director, Kristie Sills, told me what was happening. I was scheduled to take the coms and monitor the *Mir*s immediately after the swim was filmed. I skipped the swim and climbed the stairs to the *Mir* lab a few minutes early. There was nothing else to do. I took my post.

On the bridge of the *Keldysh*, the Russians did not know yet what to do about the messages that started arriving. The first one was logged at 12:10 p.m. *Titanic* time, transmitted at 10:40 a.m. eastern daylight time (EDT), just twelve minutes after the North Tower had collapsed.

Prior to the expedition, Mary had been given a direct fax line to the bridge, via satellite uplink, just in case we encountered an emergency at sea. Mary's message read, "Terrorist attack on World Trade Center. Both buildings are gone. Pentagon attacked. I can't find Mom. She exercises down there and the whole area has been closed since early this morning."

The *Titanic* is launched on April 10, 1912, from the dock at Southampton on its first and last voyage.

William Murdoch and Charles Lightoller at a portside gangway door during the *Titanic*'s brief stop to pick up additional passengers at Queenstown, Ireland. Most of the crew standing behind them did not survive.

The bend in the base of the foremast shows the forces that were operating when the *Titanic*'s bow section broke away from the stern and began its 2.5-mile fall, during what evidently began as a steep, nose-down plunge.

Stewardess Violet Jessop serving as a nurse aboard the *Titanic*'s sister ship, the *Britannic*, shortly before she became a double survivor.

The Turkish baths on the *Titanic*.

Almost all of the wood trim and other organic furnishings in Captain Smith's quarters have disappeared, leaving behind only a bathtub and other plumbing fixtures. In the lower left corner of the photo, rusticle branches are growing up from the edge of the captain's bath.

By 2001, the prow of the *Titanic* was completely enclosed by a living rusticle reef. Georgyj Vinogradov's "gorgon" can be seen growing like a flower mounted on the stem and anchored to the reef. Like the rusticles, the gorgons were recording a recent history of perplexing growth surges—literally a sea change.

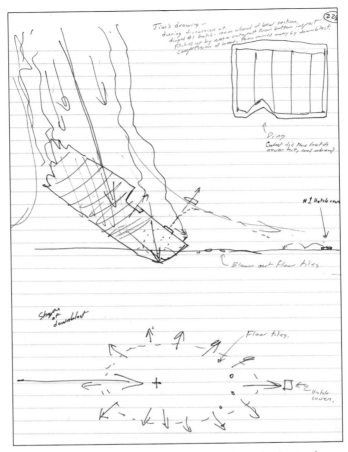

Field notes by James Cameron and myself from the September segments of the 2001 expedition, illustrating the column-collapse, down-blast, and surge-cloud effects explaining how objects from the middle of the *Titanic*'s bow section ended up being carried in front of the bow.

Though it resembles a rose, this tunicate, living on the rusticle reef that covers the *Titanic*'s prow, is closely related to ancestral vertebrates. Like a Venus flytrap, this organism closes whenever a small animal ventures too near. The stem was sprouting secondary colonies of Vinogradov's Gorgon when it was photographed in 2003.

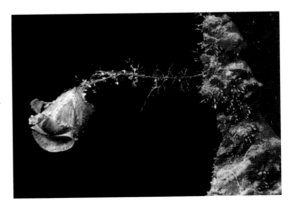

In August 2001,
Mir-1 surfaces
from one of
Expedition *Titanic*
XIII's first dives.

Aboard the *Keldysh*
in September 2001,
James Cameron
presides over a dive-
planning session, with
a properly scaled *Mir*
submersible at center.

At 7:30 a.m., New York time, on September 11, 2001, the two rusticle substrates brought up for study were being returned by *Mir-1* to their original location near boat 8. After the first sample broke into the shape of a cross and a cross-shaped davit bit came up with a section of rope draped over its arms, a Russian scientist eerily lamented that the objects were a bad omen and that a third cross would soon be seen.

While inch-thick steel was disappearing year by year before our eyes, newspapers and other delicate organic materials often exhibited greater survival power. Howard Irwin's racing sheets from Australia were still readable after more than eighty years under the sea. During the 1996 expedition, after a child's shirt was found, a moratorium was declared against landings near a burst point in the stern.

One of the strangest organisms observed inside the *Titanic* was the mahogany-dwelling "white worm," discovered in 2001. This animal, notable for the rows of glowing portholes on its sides, was finally identified as a sea cucumber, a cousin of the common starfish, in 2005, when one of them was seen resting on a pantry shelf. These photos were taken by Jim Cameron.

Rusticle flowers growing up through the floor of the *Titanic*'s Turkish baths were photographed by Jim Cameron moments before the mini-bot Gilligan flamed out a battery and became a permanent resident of the lost liner.

Daniel Buckley's gate still remains locked against third-class passengers even though the foremast came crashing down to one side of it and the rusticle reef has been metabolizing its iron.

Across the officers' quarters and along the more than 450-foot-long bow section of the *Titanic*, the rusticle reef that is slowly creating an unusual blend of natural and man-made patterns is turning the *Titanic* into one of the largest organisms on Earth.

The polymathic explorer Carl Spencer made his first dive in the *Mir* to the *Titanic* only a short time before his death aboard the nearly identical sister ship, *Britannic*.

Close-up view of a rusticle stalactite living on the *Titanic*'s number 8 boat railing near the spot where the band played. Note the calcium-absorbing and secreting invertebrates colonizing the rusticle's outer shell.

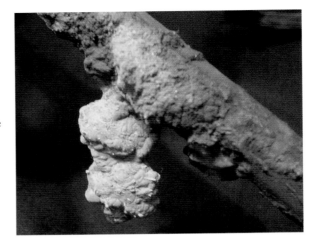

Upon impact with the seabed, the *Titanic*'s prow was buried almost up to the base of its anchors. By 2003, rusticle branches had grown from the anchors down to the sea floor. The depth to which the prow is embedded can be appreciated by comparison of this same anchor, seen high above the water line, in the 1912 photo of the *Titanic* leaving Southampton on page 1 of this photo insert.

The wholesale disintegration of the *Titanic*'s iron and sulfur is shown quite dramatically in this photo of the rusticle reef hanging down from the crow's nest region of the foremast in 2003, as the hollow steel mast began to split and sag toward collapse.

A surviving picket of rails along the *Titanic*'s bow section serves as an example of how the rusticle reef often branches out laterally in the currents, maximizing surface area in the manner of a tree. The reef supports rich filter-feeding populations of anemones, gorgonarians, and tunicates, all of which are visible in this 2003 photo.

Under a mysteriously accelerating surge of rusticle growth, decks have begun collapsing ("pancaking" down) one upon another, as in 2003 images recorded by Lori Johnston, showing decks that were still standing seventeen years earlier, when the Ballard team first surveyed the *Titanic*.

Young Walter Lord (top photo, left), author of *A Night to Remember*, with a family friend on the *Titanic*'s twin, *Olympic*, in July 1926. A 1912 photo (right) taken by Father Frank Browne from almost the same angle, in the same location aboard the *Titanic*, demonstrates how nearly identical the two ships were.

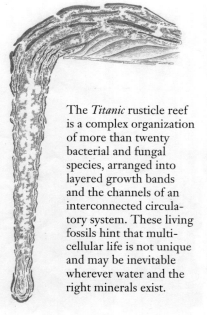

The *Titanic* rusticle reef is a complex organization of more than twenty bacterial and fungal species, arranged into layered growth bands and the channels of an interconnected circulatory system. These living fossils hint that multicellular life is not unique and may be inevitable wherever water and the right minerals exist.

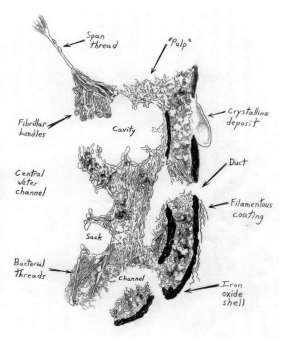

Span thread

"Pulp"

Fibrillar bundles

Cavity

crystalline deposit

Central water channel

Duct

Filamentous coating

Sack

Bacterial threads

Channel

Iron oxide shell

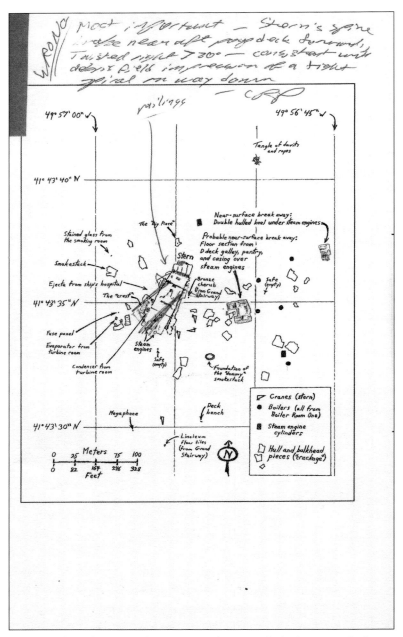

This map from the September 10, 2001, dive records the location of rails blasted off the stern upon bottom impact and the important discovery that prior maps were wrong. Red markings record verification of a lateral breaking of the stern section, indicating that it was falling in a tight spiral at the moment it hit the seabed.

The growth of the rusticle reef and the deterioration of the *Titanic* is seen in the years 1985, 2001, 2040, and 2080.

Rusticle streamers on the port side of the *Titanic*'s prow reveal an interesting pattern of rooting, expansion, and branching.

• • •

Lori Johnston stepped into the *Mir* lab, insisting that she take over my position at the coms. "Too much is happening, and you've got to be tired," she said.

I replied that staying at the coms and keeping my mind focused on the job might be what would preserve my sanity at this kind of time. "I can't do anything about what's happening to friends and family in New York except worry myself sick over them," I said. "But we've got friends down there [in the *Mir*s], who need looking after."

Johnston understood immediately. I did not know yet that the Russians were checking their records and had already confirmed that there were two of us aboard who had family in New York. I was the only one receiving faxes about people who were missing, and no one on the bridge seemed to be sure when or what to tell me.

"Anything I can do to help?" Johnston asked.

All I could think of saying was "Just get me a hunk of meat from the galley, a thermos of coffee, and a bag of Skittles—and I'll be okay."

The communications log was recorded in naval time: By 12:38 hours, I recorded a delay in the descent of the *Mir-2*, which had resurfaced shortly after its 11:30 launch for adjustment of a cord problem. During relaunch, a little extra flotation was vented, speeding descent from two feet per second to three feet per second, to avoid the *Mir-1*'s having to spend an inordinate amount of time waiting on the bottom for the arrival of the *Mir-2*. This created a unique arrangement: at 12:39 hours, both of the *Mir*s were descending together at two thousand meters (one and a quarter miles), each within view of the other.

Marine John-David Cameron and I began discussing what to tell his brother and the others in the *Mir*s. We knew the Russians had already exchanged communications with their *Mir* pilots about the attacks on New York and Washington. Nonetheless, they were continuing their descent toward Elwood.

I did not believe anything good could come from me or John-David telling the rest of the *Mir* divers what was happening. There was little doubt in my mind that this was the last dive anyone would be making to the *Titanic* for a very long time. It seemed sensible that we should rescue the bot, return the rusticle roots (the two crosses) to where we had found them, and collect more samples of an organism living nearby that was already opening up new avenues in cancer research.

"The deep ocean pharmacy," I said. "Are we going to let terrorism stop the dive—and win a victory over *that*?" John-David had, for perhaps all of two seconds (and no more), been thinking of aborting the dive.

At 12:45 hours, *Titanic* time, John-David took the coms and called down the news to the *Mir-1* and the *Mir-2*. He told them of a terrorist attack and the closing down of airspace over North America. Jim Cameron asked how bad it really was, and John-David gave him the rest in code, leaving Ken Marschall completely puzzled.

"What's 'loveshack protocol?'" Marschall asked. He received no answer.

The Russians knew the answer. Most of them were fans of American music, so naturally they immediately recognized the term *love shack*—the title of a song by the B-52s, a band named after the long-range strategic bomber. The term meant many things, including the fact that certain types of scientists were now protectorates of the military and that if necessary, their families must be under immediate preparedness for evacuation to safe locations.

None of us was certain, at this moment, who was behind the attacks. On the bridge, and in a sealed-off section deep in front of the bow, the Russians were literally praying that none of their close allies were involved. "Loveshack protocol" meant only one thing to them: in a few hours, or perhaps within only minutes, the United States would be at war with someone.

Suddenly there were Russian officers we had never seen before, emerging from that mysterious forbidden zone in the bow. They were most conspicuous in wearing a darker, different cut of uniform than the men in command of the bridge—as well as by the fact that one of them was among the most shockingly beautiful women I had ever seen.

The *Mir*s were down to twenty-one hundred meters (one and a third miles) at 12:45 hours, when John-David gave Jim the code and left the abort–no abort decision to him and Anatoly Sagalevich.

At 12:50 hours, I recorded in the communications log, "*Mir-1*—they will continue with mission."

At 12:57 hours, I wrote, "*Mir-1*—2,700 m depth."

At 13:01 hours, I recorded, in the margin of the communications log (based on what we knew of an attack that was said to have commenced at approximately 9 a.m. EDT): "It happened 9 a.m. NY Time, 10:30 a.m. our time—2.5 hours ago—feels like a year. I dream of hurling our species to the stars. 'Man plans' [my mother used to say], 'God laughs.'"

• • •

We received an e-mail from the International Space Station (ISS). Like us, they were a Russian and American crew: Vladimir Dezhurov, Mikhail Turin, and Frank Culbertson. They moved toward a viewport as the ISS passed within view of the eastern United States. The smoke plume was now the most conspicuous man-made object visible from space. They told us it was reaching almost a hundred kilometers (sixty-two miles) out to sea, pointing straight at us. It was a very short message, but one line gave me a terrible chill of gooseflesh (along with something that felt strangely like guilt) because I had written it somewhere before: "Tears just do not flow the same way in microgravity."

The *Mir*s reached three thousand meters (almost two miles). The clock touched 13:13 hours.

Almost as quickly as they appeared, the unfamiliar Russian officers returned again to the hidden portions of the *Keldysh*'s bow. We never did see them again, but it soon became clear that decisions were being made about the Americans aboard. We would not have our communication links to the *Mir*s for very much longer.

13:20 hours. "*MIR-1*, *MIR-2*, at same depth with visual contact."

13:40 hours. "*MIR-1*—contact garbled. *MIR-2* is on ground at 13:40."

13:55 hours. "*MIR-1* tells *MIR-2* to replace rusticle roots [the two *Titanic* crosses]. Kenny [Marschall] and Don [Lynch] in *MIR-2* confirm they are doing that now. Then, rendezvous."

14:00 hours. "Switching coms to *Koresh* [to Lev in support boat, just relaunched]. All silent in *MIR* Nav[igation] Lab/Com[munications] Shack."

14:25 hours. "[Intercept] faint signal. Silent."

15:04 hours. "*Koresh* at comm[unications]. Nav Lab all quiet."

15:15 hours. "No grid coordinates for *MIR-1*, *MIR-2*; they are apparently [if running by schedule] on bow, in position for Elwood rescue operation."

16:05 hours. "*Koresh* still at com[s]."

16:25 hours. "All quiet, still."

16:40 hours. "All quiet."

Later, one of the Russians took me to *Keldysh* Mission Control and tried to link me by satellite to Mary and my father. The officer apologized for taking our coms, explaining that they "had to receive, officially, the word from Moscow, that we were not at war with each other."

"It's okay," I explained. "History teaches us that you Russians have earned your pessimism the hard way. Maybe now, we learn as well."

I explained that part of the Pellegrino clan ended up in New York because they had migrated to Russia more than a hundred years earlier and then converted to Judaism about the time that Joseph Stalin started persecuting the Jews.

"Always trying for the Darwin Award, right—your family?"

I nodded, and then we tried to contact New York.

We could not get through to Mary. But e-mails started running sporadically between the *Keldysh* and the East Coast, and I gradually heard that the children were with my father and that Mary was okay, except for what she had seen and for being stuck in New Jersey. Mary knew that Paddy Brown must have been "in it, and that he was gone." Mary's mother had called in. My cousin Donna, like Brown, was still officially listed as missing.

The kids were all right, except that one member of the family had insisted that there should be no celebration whatsoever for my daughter Amber's birthday. My dad decided he was not going to give the terrorists one more victory, no matter how small—least of all over a little girl: "This year, more than any other, she needs a birthday cake, with candles and a song."

I later learned from Amber's teacher how all of the students' parents had left their jobs and arrived at the school, one by one, as the attacks progressed, and silently took their children away from class until only one child remained: a girl whose parents still worked where they had first met—at the World Trade Center.

Time began to lose meaning. Suddenly the sun was setting and the *Mir*s were on their way home to us.

Soon I received an e-mail from Tom Dettweiler, Bob Ballard's science officer from Expedition Argo-RISE and the first *Titanic* expeditions. He was supposed to have been in the Pentagon but had been called away for an eye examination that probably saved his life. Dett-weiler wrote:

> We are waiting to hear of the impact here in D.C. The wing of the Pentagon which was attacked is the wing [where] most of the guys we work with on a daily basis were housed, but no information has been released yet. We know we lost friends and colleagues. I was supposed to be there for a meeting, but because of an eye problem I had to post-pone. But then there are thousands of stories like this. I was gone for several months on a Navy op which carried a high degree of risk. We just got home, and now some of those guys I was at sea with are prob-ably dead, killed where they thought they were now safe. My best to you and the crew out there. Please say hi to Jim for me and give him my best wishes for a safe and successful mission as well as for yourself. I will be talking to you when I get back.

Tom had put his finger on the impossible disconnect. Everything was backward.

In the submersibles, we always accepted a certain degree of inher-ent danger. We accepted the idea that something might happen down there, at three tons per square inch of pressure. We accepted that we might not return to daylight. But we also got used to the idea that our families and our friends were safe at home or at work. What I had never considered was the possibility that something might happen to them and not to us. Backward—everything.

In April 1912, people had gathered around the White Star Line offices in Lower Manhattan. Names were being posted with agoniz-ing slowness and uncertainty. The people waited for the complete and definitive list of those lost and saved at the *Titanic* to come through the increasingly crowded and confused lines of wireless communica-tions. They had swarmed before an office whose site had become a Radio Shack electronics store; now it was buried in a shroud of dust and paper, where it had stood, until this day, literally in the shadow of the Twin Towers. And nearly nine decades after the crash of the *Titanic*, here we were, above the liner's grave, waiting for damaged communications systems to provide news of the lost and the saved in Lower Manhattan.

Long after the subs were in their bays for the night, I walked out onto the fantail to watch the "biolumes." But the brightest lights this night seemed to be in the sky: whole swarms of shooting stars, often two at once. I knew we were beyond the time of the annual

Perseid meteor shower; yet the sky was ablaze with meteors every few seconds.

I recalled Mahala Douglass's account of having watched, from this very same place eighty-nine years earlier, in boat 2, the aurora borealis rising over the *Titanic*'s grave as a backdrop for meteors—more meteors than she had recalled ever seeing before. She thought about a myth told to her by her mother: every time a shooting star appears, it signals the return of a soul to heaven.

There should have been thousands that night, but I'd been awake nearly four days straight, and I was not about to start keeping count of falling stars.

17

Movements of Fire and Ice

SEPTEMBER 12, 2001
RESEARCH VESSEL *KELDYSH*

Past is prologue, or so the poets say—prologue to the future.

I remember being astonished by row after row of unbroken stained- and frosted-glass windows inside the *Titanic*—astonished to the point of sometimes becoming misty-eyed. Ken Marschall and I both remarked that it looked like a chapel in there—driving home to us (as if we needed to learn it again and again) the lesson of hallowed ground, and perhaps too the growing awareness that we really did have a faith to keep with those who could no longer speak for themselves.

William Murdoch was among the most heartbreaking examples of this. From the first moments of impact, the first officer must surely have wished he had taken the same initiative that had resulted in his temporary demotion from the *Arabic* to the *Celtic* in 1903.

The race through ice that so mystified Antarctic explorer Ernest Shackleton during the British inquiry had its origins in a policy called "cracking on"—which had its own origins in profit margins arising from the intense competition among White Star, Hamburg-America, and the other shipping lines. Ships were to run at full speed, "cracking on" and keeping to or ahead of schedule, even in darkness, mist, and ice.

The very clarity of the moonless, glass-smooth sea had set the stage for a lethal "cracking on," requiring only the convergence of one final event—which, however improbable, was sooner or later bound to occur, if enough ships played dice with the Labrador current. The greater probability was that the first iceberg sighted would be a tiny "growler" illuminated by the ship's lights and passing by on the port or starboard side (with the result that the ship would be slowed down). Even more probable, a tall, star-eclipsing shadow should have appeared on the port or starboard side (and again, the ship would be slowed down). The most improbable scenario of all was for the first sighting to be directly ahead and for the berg to be no taller than the boat deck— the perfect height at which to remain invisible from the crow's nest and the bridge until any response from the helm was reduced to near irrelevance.

Again and again, our thoughts returned to that moment, about 10 p.m., when Murdoch told lamp trimmer Samuel Hemming to shut out the last traces of light from the lamps in the forecastle so that he could more clearly see every star along the horizon from the bridge. He had specifically mentioned that the *Titanic* was heading into the vicinity of ice.

The day after we traveled over Hemming's hatch and landed just behind Murdoch's post at the starboard wing bridge, the events of September 11—and more than a decade of repercussions—were upon us. Here aboard the *Keldysh*, most of the American crew reflected on all of the warning signs around the world that had been ignored, each pointing toward the fires of September, like the warnings that had led up to the *Titanic*'s disaster. There had been one Marconigram after another, right up to the last message from wireless operator Cyril Evans, at 11 p.m. on Sunday night, April 14, 1912, warning that his ship, the *Californian*, had been stopped and surrounded by ice. People could be heard making the inevitable analogy, over and over: the 9/11 attacks were the first bump against the iceberg at 11:40 p.m., and we were now on a path into a downward spiral that could not be stopped. Jim Cameron, the Marines (John-David Cameron and Rich Robles), and I did not agree.

"Is it *really* 11:40 p.m.?" Jim asked. "Or is it a minute earlier?

"Is it 11:40, or 11:39?" he repeated, then answered, "We are all Murdoch now."

Murdoch was at the wing-bridge, and the iceberg was a minute away; the final alarm had not yet rung out from the crow's nest. The iceberg was looming ahead in the dark, cold and uncaring and still unseen—and massive.

"We can [as a civilization] drive straight toward it," Jim said. "We can try to [steer] around it. But the important thing to know is that we still have time. We can slam into reverse and still be sunk. We can ram head-on and sink, turn and sink. It may be that no matter what we do, we sink. But we've got [a little bit of breathing space], and we haven't really run up against our doom yet. We've got to try everything we can think of while there is still time to consider the alternative outcomes."

We had arrived during the Week of the Dead in the Chinese calendar, seeking only to probe history and science. At first, I viewed the *Titanic* as a revelatory microcosm from the past. Now I was beginning to see that what human beings did on and around the *Titanic* that night was as much about where we were going as how we had gotten here.

18

Frailty

Sooner or later it was bound to happen: the convergence of improbable events compounded by a series of improbable errors. Almost without exception, no single improbable error or event causes complex systems to fail, and that is the frightening part.

In 1995 a U.S. exploratory satellite, launched into the aurora borealis over the North Pole, dropped booster stages and probes of just the right size and in just the right sequence to give Russian radar the precise impression that a first-strike high-altitude missile had dropped multiple intercontinental reentry vehicles (resembling hydrogen bomb capsules), including the inevitable EMP (electromagnetic pulse) precursor weapon, which is meant to knock out Russian electronics. NASA's Jet Propulsion Laboratory had notified the Russian space agency far in advance of the launch, but no one had passed the word along from the space agency to the Russian military, and no one at NASA had requested confirmation that the word had been passed along.

Russian military analysts, watching what appeared to be the signature of an American MIRV, knew that their country might be crippled in a matter of minutes and then incinerated if they did not act quickly. Russian president Boris Yeltsin was informed and was shown the tracking data. He declined to order a counter nuclear strike. Yeltsin had been around long enough to know that complex systems, and especially chains of communication, failed. During this latter part of civilization's nuclear adolescence, an iceberg for all humanity was seen in a perfectly aligned trajectory, the deuterium-tipped weapons in the earth were the worst approximations of open portholes and shell doors, and a civilization's last bulkhead was primed for collapse. But the iceberg was seen and avoided—that time.

Practically the very last chance the *Titanic* had was a warning from the *Californian*, almost directly ahead and surrounded by ice. Wireless operator Jack Phillips had cut the *Californian*'s Marconi operator off, and he neither took the message nor passed it along to the bridge. The *Californian*'s Marconi operator—near exhaustion in the first place and obeying the *Titanic*'s order to "shut up" in the second place—shut down his wireless apparatus, went to sleep, and missed the distress calls that shortly followed.

The *Titanic* would have needed to cross the Atlantic for more than a century and perhaps for as long as a thousand years before the lining up of so many low-probability events became a mathematical inevitability. What the ship's builders and officers did not understand was that the odds of drawing two royal flushes in a row are the same in the first two hands of poker as in any two hands in the next two million. The maiden voyage was a lesson in risk assessment, demonstrating the frailty of civilization itself, written in microcosm.

In his 1936 account, Charles Lightoller wrote that during the very last minute leading up to the final plunge, he and several men working beside him were trying to push one of the collapsible boats off the roof of the officers' quarters and down to the port side deck when he heard the familiar voice of lamp trimmer Samuel Hemming. Lightoller had ordered Hemming away more than an hour earlier, in command of Molly Brown's and Celiney Yasbeck's boat 6. By now, the entire forward part of the ship had become too dark to recognize Hemming by anything other than his voice.

"Hello, is that you, Hemming?" Lightoller asked.

"Yes, sir."

"Why haven't you gone?"

With a perplexing tone of cheer and optimism, Hemming replied, "Oh, plenty of time yet, sir," seconds before a sudden surge of water reached the roof and sent him racing both the sea and the eruption of the grand stairway toward a safe jumping-off point, where he could swim toward boat 4. Evidently, Hemming decided that burying himself in work and denial could serve him only so much before it became necessary to admit that there really was not plenty of time after all.

Lightoller noticed that the crow's nest was descending to a point almost level with the sea when the roof of the bridge slipped under and sent Hemming racing aft. In that moment, the ship took a slight but definitely steeper plunge down toward the bow—"and the sea came rolling up in a wave."

Lightoller's description of the relative depths of the bridge and the crow's nest during the 2:10 a.m. surge was a key observation, setting in place a critical time marker for the sequence of the *Titanic*'s final plunge and providing the angle of the entire ship at this moment—as a line drawn through the base of the crow's nest and the submerging bridge.

Lightoller was now in water so cold that it stung like the tips of a thousand knives digging in at once. Stunned, he began swimming instinctively toward the abandoned crow's nest with the thought of hauling himself out of the freezing water and into what he soon realized was only the illusory safety of a cage riveted to the descending foremast.

Reminding himself about the futility of climbing aboard and clinging to anything attached to the *Titanic*'s bow, Lightoller turned right as the crow's nest gulped under. He tried to swim toward the starboard side of the now vanished well deck and forecastle, but something appeared to be dragging him down, making it increasingly difficult for the second officer to even keep his head above water. He thought of the heavy revolver still at his side, withdrew it, and dropped it down toward the well deck. The loss of weight did not seem to help very much.

Every stroke and kick away from the ship was canceled by a force drawing him two or three strokes back toward it and trying to pull him down. In what seemed almost no time at all, he was swimming over his starting point, the submerged bridge.

Behind the bridge, at the front of the first smokestack's base, a twenty-foot-wide air intake—which had been designed to face forward in the *Titanic*'s direction of motion (into the wind)—was now scooping down tons of rushing water instead of air. It scooped Lightoller down as well, holding him against a wire grating originally installed only to prevent airborne bits of paper, the occasional bird, or a wayward child about Alfred Rush's size from finding ingress.

Lightoller feared a failure of the grating; he, along with the tons of inrushing water, was far beyond anything for which the barrier had been designed. He imagined a sheer drop all the way down to the front boiler rooms, but by now the decks below had been flooding steadily for more than two hours, and only the upper two or three stories of the shaft were flooding, in a torrent not likely to have been capable of lasting more than a minute. Lightoller kicked and struggled but was dragged back again against the grating for what understandably seemed to him a very long time. A stall in the flow allowed a tremendous surge of air to blast up through the shaft, more or less "burping" the second officer to the surface.

A final inflow of water drew him down against another grating, abreast of the smokestack, about the time the two forward smokestacks began to cave in at their bases and fall. Again a burst of escaping air seemed to blow him free, "coughing" him up along the starboard side, next to the overturned boat B, which he and Hemming had launched from the port side and which had somehow come over with Lightoller to the starboard side, near one of the front funnels (possibly number 2, the funnel that fell to starboard and killed Richard Williams's father).

"Then the forward funnel fell down," Lightoller would tell Senator Smith. "It fell alongside the lifeboat," he would explain; it fell seemingly only inches clear of the boat and right among the people struggling in the water, between boat B and the submerged bridge.

"Injure any of them seriously?" Senator Smith asked, in what Lightoller supposed, under less tragic circumstances, would have been a question designed to provoke laughter.

One effect of the smokestack crashing down so near to the overturned boat was to generate a wave that washed over and pushed the raft, as Lightoller clung to one of its ropes a full 150 feet away from the sinking ship.

Jack Thayer was also in the water with Lightoller, near boat B, when a smokestack fell. He believed it was the second smokestack that fell toward him, while structures much farther back, including the last two smokestacks, continued to stand. Thayer would recall that the fall of the second smokestack was preceded by the loudest wrenching and tearing he had heard yet; the superstructure (the upper deck, the gymnasium, and the region around the grand stairway) became deformed before his eyes into large, dark shapes that seemed to "blow or buckle upward." The lights in front of the second smokestack were dead or dying by this time. What he probably saw was the approximately synchronous collapse of the first smokestack—off toward the port side—and the rise of the grand stairway amid the turbulence and gushes of air that blew Lightoller to the surface.

Eugene Daly, the passenger from third class who had witnessed shootings on the boat deck, was swept overboard, disoriented and in a state of disbelief. Like Lightoller, having spent part of the first two minutes of the *Titanic*'s final plunge with his head underwater, Daly would recall for Dr. Blackmar of the rescue ship *Capathia*, "Everything I touched seemed to be women's hair." Whenever his head broke the surface, he heard children crying. "Women screaming," he told the doctor, "and their hair in my face.

"My God," he lamented, "if I could only forget those hands and faces that I touched."

The only thing worse than the screaming and crying, the hair, and the hands and faces, was what Daly saw when he reached Lightoller's position at the overturned boat B. He looked back toward the *Titanic*'s starboard profile in bewilderment, trying to interpret what his eyes were seeing. Between the moment Daly entered the water and the moment he reached boat B, the second smokestack had fallen nearby, and the reinforced cylindrical rim at its base must have already begun descending with the *Titanic* like an express elevator. Daly looked back to see people swimming away from where the crystal dome and the second smokestack's base had been. He saw them dragged backward and sucked down into the two forward cavities.

By the time Lightoller climbed atop the upturned keel of boat B, the sea had already reached the compass tower and eaten the roof of the first-class lounge. The stern section was still alight like a giant glow-worm, its rudder and bronze propellers pivoting high above a center of mass located just in front of the third smokestack.

Almost two decades later, Lightoller would tell young Walter Lord that the people clinging to the high ground near and beyond the third smokestack started crying out to one another and to the sea. The bow had now completely submerged below him, and the rising stern was fifty yards away from boat B. He could hear some of the cries quite clearly. What Lightoller could never forget, he told the historian, were the cries of "I love you."

Almost eighty years after that, another emerging historian named Anthony El-Khouri, reading about Lightoller's words to Lord, felt a profound sadness for Lightoller. "It's even more upsetting when you consider that Lightoller was the one who forced couples apart that night," he wrote. "I wonder how it affected him, to hear people say that. I cannot imagine his sorrow, on the receiving end of a call like that."

Climbing atop the same piece of wreckage that was about to become Lightoller's command, Thayer looked back and discovered that there was still something violently entrancing and dreadfully beautiful about the monster. Boat B was fifty to sixty yards away when Thayer reached it, but a current seemed to be drawing the two men nearer the stern, which lifted at a slow and stately pace, "seemingly in no hurry," Thayer would write later. It amazed him that the rear funnel, leaning forward at an increasingly crazy angle, was still being held in place and did not fall.

Now, with its tip standing nearly two hundred feet overhead, the funnel held, but not all of the people did. Thayer saw them clinging in clusters of dozens and hundreds, "like swarming bees," only to begin jumping from the sides or sliding down the deck in pairs or singly—then increasingly in masses, as the angle steepened beyond twenty-five degrees (an angle at which standing became impossible, unless one happened to be clinging to a rail or a bollard).

Third-class passenger August Wennerstrom was amid the swarm that Thayer observed from boat B. Unable to maintain his balance, Wennerstrom slid all the way into the water. Shocked by a painfully cold sea and surprised not to have skidded into an obstruction and broken half the bones in his body, Wennerstrom swam forward, toward the place where the bow had been. He wanted only to put some distance between himself and the debris and the people spilling toward him from astern, like tons of coal down a chute. Somewhere among ascending planks, the descending compass tower, the avalanche from astern, and the bursts of air from below, an eddy brought him alongside the half-sunken wreck of boat A, which seemed, at that moment, to be bumping precariously against the curved hull of a capsized ship that turned out to be the last visible remnant of a collapsed and sinking forward funnel.

Within sight of Wennerstrom and boat A, George Rheims had managed to free himself from a mass of deck chairs entangled in ropes—more than three hundred feet of rope that had been unfurled onto the deck from each lifeboat lowered on the davits. Rheims hauled himself into the wreck of boat A in only his underwear and a thin shirt, then stood knee-deep in water that was 28 degrees Fahrenheit and looked around. He never saw his brother-in-law again.

Tennis star Richard Williams, whose father was most likely beneath the smokestack August Wennerstrom had watched descending beneath boat A, followed Wennerstrom and Rheims into boat A. They were joined by two women, evidently mother and daughter. Wennerstrom soon discovered that all sense of feeling was leaving his legs, and as a cold-induced delirium spread through him, he started reaching down obsessively into the water to make sure he still had legs. The delirium became contagious, and the other men began searching for their feet. The young girl who had climbed aboard died—whether from her injuries, the shocking cold, or a combination of both, there seemed no way of knowing. Then the mother gave up, and they were both dead, clutched in each other's arms.

Albert Moss had long ago accepted the fact that this was indeed turning out to be his second shipwreck in four months. The reality that the *Titanic* would be far worse than the sinking of the *Hebe* dawned a bit more slowly, and he did not completely accept it until he slid into the water and struck out in the general direction of Thayer and Lightoller, toward boat B.

Behind Moss, on the last funnel—which vented fumes from the kitchen stoves and other auxiliary equipment but had otherwise merely been added to give the ship a more powerful, streamlined appearance—equipment oiler Alfred White emerged through a door onto a small platform, on what was known to the crew as "the dummy funnel." White's journey was already among the rarest and most eventful of the night. About the time that coal trimmer Thomas Patrick Dillon was instructed to leave the engine room and save his own life, chief electrical engineer William Parr told White, "We are going to start one more engine," and he sent White to the main electrical switch box to assist with the switch-over.

The switch-over was probably accomplished by about 1:30 a.m. If water was entering through an extension of the crack chief baker Joughin had seen and heard developing on E deck about that same time, it had not reached White's region of the engine compartments when he made the switch-over. White would recall in a letter to Parr's brother-in-law that his team continued to work and to provide power for the generators, as though nothing was particularly out of the ordinary. They simply locked the collision out of conscious thought—"as if nothing had happened."

One of the enduring enigmas of the night would become the steam source for the generator engines mentioned by White. All of the boiler rooms, from number 6 all the way back to number 2, had been shut down, with most of their steam already vented by the time Parr sent White to the switch box. The only power that should have been available for the electric turbines was residual steam in the rear boilers.

When Jim Cameron filmed the exposed furnace end caps in the bow section's boiler room number 2, he found, as expected, that they did not crack under exposure to freezing water but bent slowly inward under increasing water pressure—in a manner consistent with boilers that had been emptied of steam, hot water, and coal and that had been dead cold for more than an hour.

Marine engineer Parks Stephenson, when he turned Cameron's high-definition cameras on the single-ended boilers that had spilled out of boiler room number 1, discovered that at least one of three furnace faces on each boiler was fractured and bent outward—suggestive of hot steel that cracked when cold water was first poured upon it, near the surface. Unlike boiler room number 2, he observed, the end caps on the single-ended boilers appeared normal, as though sudden cracking had pierced the thick steel and allowed water to enter and equalize the pressure before deeper waters could squeeze and deform the cylinder from the outside. "The fractured furnace fronts on the single-ended boilers, then [though exposed to essentially the same physical destruction as the boilers in boiler room number 2], might contradict our conventional wisdom that the boilers in boiler room number 1 were cold iron when the ship sank. If they were lit [and active] at the time boiler room number 1 was torn apart [along with the aft end of boiler room number 2], then they were either lit before the collision (which would contradict eyewitness testimony) or possibly brought up afterward with the intention of supplying service steam." White's instructions from Parr to start one more generator very late in the sinking would prove consistent with what Stephenson observed nearly a century later.

White continued to work closely with Parr and two other men, named Peter Sloan and Archie Frost, until the entire engineering team felt the ship angle down suddenly, as though the *Titanic* had started moving again, and lurch strongly enough to throw them off their feet.

Lightoller was probably beginning his swim toward the sinking crow's nest when Parr and Sloan decided that the equipment would continue functioning for as long as the *Titanic* lasted without needing any oiling or maintenance from White. "It looks like we'll be putting in a little extra time on this one," someone joked, and then Parr said, "Alfred, go up and see how things are going on, then come and tell us."

The slant of the deck had increased so quickly that White encountered difficulty simply in climbing up the turbine room ladder. Near the third-class quarters he found the path to the boat deck blocked by a closed gate. Passengers were gathered on the other side in prayer. He watched for a moment, trying to figure out what he should do, then decided that the only way to carry out Parr's request was to continue upward—and the only way up was through a ladder in the dummy funnel.

About the same time that Lightoller reached the overturned boat B, White threw open the doorway and looked down from the fourth smokestack. The first thing he noticed was that all of the lifeboats were gone and that the second funnel was sinking. He should never have been aware of the second funnel's condition, much less be able to see it, if in fact it was still standing. From a perspective halfway up the center-line of the fourth smokestack, the second one would have been blocked completely from view by the third. What White probably witnessed was the final crumpling and sinking, to starboard, of the second smoke-stack.

From the moment Robert Ballard's team began mapping the wreck site, there would be little doubt about what White believed he witnessed next. A crevice opened up below him, spanning port and starboard in an instant, between his perch and the third smokestack. The lights snapped off, then flicked on again, revealing to him what appeared to be a clean cut—"as if by a butcher's blade"—and reveal-ing to him also, by even the briefest return of the lights, that Parr and the other engineers were still working at their stations. "And so would I have been," White told himself, "if they had not sent me up."

His impression was that the front half of the ship was being cut loose. He saw people below, surging together as shadowy masses over the tops of deck structures or clinging in groups of twos and threes to ropes and davits. Disintegration was upon them all. The third funnel began to crash forward, and the fourth funnel—his funnel—crumpled at its base and swung suddenly back.

Chief baker Charles Joughin had continued to follow "doctor's orders" to drink himself unconscious after he saw the last lifeboat safely away on the davits. In the pantry of the Café Parisian, he again encountered old Dr. Will O'Loughlin, who likewise never expected to get through this night alive and seemed to be rummaging around for something with which to "fortify" himself. Joughin found whiskey. He never did learn what the doctor found.

In future decades, historian Walter Lord would come to regard Joughin as "sort of like the horse-and-carriage cab drivers of San Francisco" in the aftermath of the 1906 earthquake. A number of people who survived the quake, including Martha (Eustis) Stephenson of the *Titanic*, told the historian how the cab drivers, on their own initiative, had organized much of the rescue operation that safely evacuated people from the spreading fires, whereas those in positions of authority generally failed in their leadership abilities when havoc struck.

Here too, Lord observed, whereas the manager ducked into a lifeboat and the men in command of all but two of the lifeboats refused to row back to the *Titanic* and rescue people struggling in the water, Parr's crewmen stayed at their posts until survival became an impossibility; the ship's two doctors, architect Thomas Andrews, and Joughin also "came to the fore, helped people into the lifeboats, and refused seats for themselves even though they were offered space repeatedly."

Shortly before White ascended the dummy funnel, Joughin locked the bakery's iron pantry door and stuffed the heavy iron keys into his pocket alongside two cakes of hard tobacco. In later years he would look back with curiosity at what he had done and what he had chosen to save in his pockets during what he truly believed would be his final minutes of life. "It made no sense," he would say later. "But that was because God made the Irish perfect. And then he gave us whiskey."

In the end, after the work of warning and rescue was, for all practical purposes, finished, Joughin leaned against a pantry wall that was tilting more and more steeply toward the bow, and he used the increasing tilt to help him tip his last drink, "bottoms up." Then, without warning, the whole progression of the tilt appeared to be interrupted by a crash, as though the ship had just run into (and through) a giant brick wall, started to buckle, or both. Drunk as Joughin was, he could clearly distinguish the sound of large masses of iron parting and even cracking and granulating. Immediately, the sound was accompanied by hundreds of people stampeding toward the rear, as though trying to get away from something they had seen happening in front. The floor seemed no longer to be angling down toward a final plunge; it was instead being levered backward, to become an almost level floor again.

Joughin ran outside to see what was happening. He was surprised most of all to discover that there was still a ruddy orange glow of light by which to see—bright enough to read the dials on his watch, ticking just beyond a quarter past two. The growing herd of panic-driven humanity became so alarming to the baker that all he could think of was to steer clear of them and try to pull himself outboard along the starboard rail. This was when the *Titanic*'s severed stern section suddenly keeled over onto its port side and threw everybody downhill and away from the baker. Then, unbelievably, the base of the fourth smokestack crumpled, and the entire structure seemed about to follow after the sliding crowds, threatening to pull the stern even more forcefully over to port.

Looking backward in time, Walter Lord would conclude, "Charles Joughin possessed a marvelous sense of balance"—which even an attempt to drink himself into a painkilling stupor before the final plunge could not diminish. As everyone else slid down toward the port side and into the sea, Joughin hauled himself over the starboard rail and began alternately strolling and crab-walking along the actual side of the severed stern.

Thomas Patrick Dillon, who had been working deep below the third and fourth smokestacks, among the four-story reciprocating engines at 11:40 p.m., and who had assisted with the opening of watertight doors all the way forward to boiler room number 4, was by now completely disoriented. First, the *Titanic* seemed to have been taking the coal trimmer and everyone who stood near him on the stern section's well deck down into an accelerating, nose-first plunge. Then the deck seemed to have stalled and righted itself again, but before Dillon could exhale a sigh of relief or grab onto a slim hope that compartmentalization was going to work after all, the funnel on which Alfred White was perched lurched toward him.

From that moment onward, Dillon's whole world tilted irrationally, and he was dragged down beneath what he believed to be at least two fathoms (twelve feet) of water. When he surfaced and looked around, Dillon thought he was seeing the whole *Titanic* coming up again, but it was only the stern's starboard side rising near him. Then the front part of the wreck began to rattle and shift downward, hoisting the after-bridge and the propellers against a night sky. There were no longer any brightly lit masts and deck spaces, only starlight against stark blackness.

Swimming near Dillon, or clinging somewhere above him on the silhouette of the stern, Henry Sutehall Jr. must have been wondering, like Joe Loring, how he came to be anywhere near this disaster in the first place. A major victory in a contest of musical skills had allowed Sutehall and his friend Howard Irwin to complete the rest of their around-the-world adventure more or less "in style." Both men were musicians who had begun their journey in 1910, from Buffalo, New York.

Irwin, however, often fell prey to a tendency to get distracted at quick notice by one political movement or another. And so, typically, while Sutehall developed his musical skills and found his first true love in Australia, Irwin diverged north and, as his diaries recorded, became involved with the revolutionary leader whom Henry Sleeper Harper's dog was named after—Sun Yat Sen—giving whatever assistance he could to Chinese forces in the overthrow of the Manchu dynasty and ultimately the downfall of the last emperor.

Sutehall, meanwhile, won a sweepstakes in Australia. The money was more than enough for them to meet again in England and complete the trip homeward aboard the *Titanic*. More important, the winnings were enough for Sutehall to complete his musical training, then follow through with his plan to return to Australia, get married, and start a career as a successful concert violinist. After a brief stay in New York, he intended to travel back again across the Atlantic to take up a scholarship and an invitation to practice with the symphony orchestra.

Irwin, as was his nature, had become distracted again by the time he reached Durban, South Africa—this time by a young and charismatic lawyer from India who was hoping to reclaim his country from British rule, using the novel concept of peaceful resistance. His name was Mohandas Gandhi.

Even after Irwin and Sutehall met again in England, Irwin continued, according to his diary, to have an odd tendency to fumble his way through history, by chance to be in the middle of everything and to get away alive by the skin of his teeth. During their last night together in Southampton, Irwin had expressed reservations about heading home with Sutehall aboard the *Titanic*. What he really wanted to do was join his new Russian expatriate friends, led by a man named Vladimir Lenin, in a revolution to free the people Masabumi Hosono had seen so mistreated that many of them were rendered incapable of surviving the Siberian winters.

Not quite one week earlier, on the night of April 9, 1912, Irwin told Sutehall he was going out for a short walk to settle his mind on whether to continue to New York or detour with Lenin's forces in Russia. In the morning, Sutehall awoke to find Irwin missing—presumably either still walking about Southampton, trying to figure out which path to take, or having already made a decision to join the revolution and leave all of his belongings behind.

Sutehall clearly doubted the latter to be the case, so he closed Irwin's steamer trunk—full of sheet music, clothing, playing cards, and an assortment of precious items that included a boxed toy airplane, musical instruments, a carefully wrapped bundle of letters from a girl named Pearl Shuttle, and a diary. Sutehall then traveled to the dock with all of Irwin's treasures, saw them loaded with his own belongings into the *Titanic's* third-class luggage compartment, then boarded himself, probably expecting that Irwin would arrive at any moment. What Sutehall could not know, from then through the moment the ship began to come apart around him, was that someone had rendered his friend unconscious in a Southampton pub and that Irwin was presently serving as a forced-labor coal trimmer aboard a tramp steamer bound for Egypt.

Fireman George Kemish, who in the end had half slid down and half dropped down a dangling davit rope and was now swimming toward boat 9 amid what sounded to him like thousands of fans shouting together at a World Cup final, swam with such vigor as to overtake the rowers of boat 9. He was quite familiar with the source of a separate catastrophe that had simultaneously disrupted Irwin's life and diverted him from Kemish's fate.

"There was a shortage of labor," Kemish would record for future historians. "Very often, ashore [men] were invited to have a drink in the saloons, by strangers who eventually turned out to be employment agents. They were doped [or knocked out]—and they came to their senses well on their way to Buffalo, the Great Lakes, and other places where labor was short." This sort of activity was so widespread in 1912 that there was a common name for it: being shanghaied.

Lamp trimmer Hemming was probably wishing he had more of Irwin's "luck" as he and Dillon were plucked out of the water by boat 4, each so cold that he thought he might die. In the same boat, Martha Stephenson, who remembered the cab drivers coming to the forefront of the San Francisco rescue operation six years earlier, was equally impressed by the young quartermaster Walter Perkins. He ordered the occupants of boat 4 to row toward the *Titanic's* stern even as the majority of the passengers—including Stephenson herself—implored him to steer them away from the danger, especially after the air around the broken stern became filled with screams.

In boat 14, the men in charge tried to tell thirteen-year-old Madeline Mellinger that the people in the water were singing, but she knew they were screaming.

In boat 16, able seaman Ernest Archer estimated that they had rowed a quarter of a mile away when the *Titanic* broke. In the same boat, Lily Futrelle had watched the lights fade as a terrible creaking noise came to her across the sea, followed by what sounded like a tremendous, rattling explosion. Somehow, still alight, the stern rose into the sky.

In boat 2, able seaman Frank Osman could not keep his eyes away from the scene; he could not stop trying to figure out the physical mechanics and the causes of what he saw. Scarcely more than the equivalent of a city block away, Osman had watched the stern fall away, spilling heavy dark objects into what had to be either the bow section's disappearing after end, or a compact black cloud of disintegrating hull and deck sections. In the region of the breakup, everything appeared to be exploding apart, sometimes flying into the air and granulating down to fragments as small as lumps of coal.

Quartermaster Arthur Bright was also located only about three hundred feet away from the breakup. He watched the *Titanic*'s stern from the side opposite Osman, aboard boat D. He was certain of having just witnessed the stern section breaking away and settling back again on an almost even keel. What astonished him was how the stern's portside lights—after initially snapping off and leaving the *Titanic* all but invisible against the darkness—came on again. He could see them glowing through portholes and rows of windows.

"All the lights on the ship were not out then?" Senator Fletcher asked twelve days later.

"No," Bright replied. "It was only the after section, though, that was burning. The after part of the boat had her lights burning."

"After she broke in two?" Senator Jonathan Bourne asked.

Bright affirmed, "Until she went down in the water; yes sir."

More than a hundred feet nearer, and also from a portside perspective, in boat 4, oiler Thomas Ranger likewise believed that some of the ship's lights had stayed on after the breakaway. One of the last things he had noticed before being sent away from the engine rooms, only slightly ahead of Alfred White, was that the emergency light dynamo was still running under the dummy funnel. Ranger suspected that it might have continued running even after the stern leveled out and began to roll. Just abeam of the place where the fourth funnel had been, the smoking-room windows stayed alight—and some of the portholes continued to glow even after the severed stern tilted nearly vertical. They burned all the way to the rear, going out only gradually as the stern began its slow, stately descent.

The examiners who questioned Ranger and Bright could not understand how the emergency dynamo kept the electric lights burning in the smoking room and behind it, beyond a point in time at which water should have reached the dynamo or at least shorted out the fuses. Briefly, questions focused on how many oil-fueled lanterns Hemming had been handing around to Bright and others who were launching the *Titanic*'s lifeboats. It was reasonable to expect that those who stayed behind knew that the electricity would not last and therefore kept the oil lamps nearby. Toward the end, a great percentage of those lamps would have been concentrated in the stern, where most of the people were. Emergency oil lamps must have come increasingly into use as the electric lights gradually dimmed from yellow-white to a reddish-brown glow.

There were many possible sources for the "ghost lights" at the portholes. On a very cold night in which service steam through the pipes had been cut off for nearly two hours, the fireplaces in the first- and second-class smoking rooms were more likely to have been refueled than put out by people taking shelter indoors. The fireplaces would have spilled hot coals across the carpeted floors and against the wood-paneled walls as the stern moved through extraordinary angles.

Groups of people trapped below the decks, including a prayer group White observed during his climb toward the fourth smokestack, probably gathered around oil lamps as the electric lights variously winked out and dimmed. If even only some small percentage of those lamps slid forward and broke, oil fires should have been burning behind the portholes. Such fires, had they occurred, were likely barely distinguishable from the fading and sometimes flickering red glow of the electric lights as the power failed sector by sector up to the moment of breakup.

In boat 10, able seaman Edward Buley was no less puzzled than Ranger and Bright by the persistence of the portside lights. He knew that when the final plunge began, there must have been little if any steam left in the *Titanic*'s rear boilers—which he determined to be where the ship had broken apart. Yet Buley was certain of seeing lights still burning dimly from within the parted stern. He concurred with Ranger that they went out only gradually as the ship began to disappear.

Masabumi Hosono was also seated in boat 10, some two hundred feet away from the wreck. In a letter to his wife, he would describe having heard the cries from the decks above prior to the breakup. The entire ship had reached an angle he perceived to be in excess of forty-five degrees; after this, "extraordinary sounds" came to Hosono that seemed to him like four distinct explosions. He would never describe the details of what he saw afterward; indeed, until his death in 1939, the mention of the name *Titanic* would be forbidden in his home.

Compared to what Buley was to tell the world about Hosono, Colonel Archibald Gracie's wrongful listing of him as a boat 10 "stowaway" was generous. Describing Hosono and another foreigner who survived aboard boat 10 as "a couple of Japanese," Buley would swear before Senator Fletcher that they could never have entered the lifeboat unless they had sneaked in among the women—that is, "dressed up as women."

Although he was to live through the night, Hosono would never truly be allowed to live again. He would forever keep buried inside himself, unspoken, what able seaman Frank O. Evans, only a few seats away, saw unfolding before his (and everyone's) eyes. It was plain to Evans that the center of chaos was located somewhere just ahead of the fourth funnel. The third funnel had disappeared in a gush of granulating debris that seemed to include the tops of the first two reciprocating engines pitching forward from inside the *Titanic*. After only a few seconds, the last funnel had shown signs of weakening, and the entire stern section had begun to follow.

Many hundreds of people were still struggling on and in the stern. Joughin and White would be among the very last of them, if not *the* last, to leave the *Titanic* alive.

Once the severed stern attained its final, vertical position, seemingly as tall and straight as a twenty-story skyscraper, the tower's base spilled an unusual assortment of artifacts. The undersea hailstorm was a slice through the first-class dining areas and the quarters of the stewards who served the passengers; it continued through the quarters of the immigrants and the men who served the *Titanic*'s machines—heralding, as though for real, the "leisured class versus working class" fable of the Eloi and the Morlocks in H. G. Wells's *The Time Machine*.

From bottom to top, the artifacts included wrenches, ladders, and catwalks from the engine room, mattresses from third and second class, the steel door Joughin had locked before pocketing the pantry keys, Sutehall's carefully packed violin, and Irwin's trunk. There were cases of wine and Bass Ale, an electric dishwashing machine, a grand piano, Charlotte Cardeza's ninety-one pairs of gloves, a workman's toolbox, and necklaces with women's names spelled out in diamonds.

From boat 10, Juliette Laroche and Hosono watched silently as the tower on the sea began to descend, dousing its last lights one by one. At a radius of only two hundred feet, night-adjusted eyes could easily see stars rising above the knife-edge shadow of the six-story rudder—first by twos and threes, then by half dozens, then by scores of stars all at once.

The *Titanic*'s final, stubborn grip on the surface was loosening with increasing speed. Its towering silhouette diminished from being a partly lit skyscraper to being the shape of a large black rock on the ocean, then to being an outcrop of coral. Finally the stern was completely submerged, accelerating toward fifty knots or more into the realm of the white worm and the *Mir*s.

19

A Crevice in Time

SEPTEMBER 13, 2001
RUSSIAN RESEARCH VESSEL *KELDYSH*
EXPEDITION *TITANIC XIII*

As soon as the *Mir-1* and the *Mir-2* surfaced with the rescued bot, Elwood, we "pulled anchor" and began steaming directly toward St. Johns, Newfoundland. One of the sponsors of the expedition had declared that we must cease and desist from all further work, based on the premise that no one would be interested in the *Titanic* anymore.

Other matters quickly intervened to reverse that order, however. The first cause for change arose from the revelation that several key robotics people had been killed in the Pentagon on September 11, including members of Tom Dettweiler's team. In certain areas of science and engineering, the survivors were at the *Titanic*. The word came down to Mission Control from John-David Cameron: a plane would be approved for flight to St. Johns, to resupply us from California with any equipment we needed or desired, after which the standing order was simply, "Find something to keep yourselves busy at the *Titanic*. Go back to the *Titanic*, where it's safe."

The "pulling of anchor" had already canceled what was to have been the last dive of the *Titanic XIII* series, dedicated primarily to biology. A new organism, thriving on the prairies near the *Titanic*, had displayed for us a sophisticated immune system based on chemical defenses—with multiple disease-fighting potentials. If we could go back and complete the dive series—well, what choice was there? Because the *Titanic* had sunk where it did, there was a chance to turn something horrible toward the saving of more lives than were lost all those years ago.

In an e-mail to Arthur C. Clarke, I mentioned how, at first, when the Russians took our coms, I was reminded of a scene from his *2010: Odyssey II*, in which a developing international crisis on Earth caused the Russian-American crew of a space station to isolate themselves on opposite sides of the ship. I thought the same thing was about to happen to us.

Big Lew Abernathy told me right away that in recalling *2010*, I had underestimated the Russians. "There are no words in English to describe the pain that we Russians feel for you," said Sergey Kudriashov, the expedition's cameraman for Russian television.

When Anatoly Sagalevich finally came down from the bridge on September 12, bearing the fax from Mary, he produced the piece of paper only after he had learned from me that her mother was safe. He suddenly had tears running down to his chin. Throwing his arms around me, Sagalevich said something that fifteen years earlier I could never have imagined hearing from a former Cold Warrior: "We are all Americans now."

All of us agreed that no matter what acts of stupidity our two governments might commit in the future, on this little piece of planet Earth called the *Keldysh*, we were now and always would be family.

By the time we reached St. Johns, Newfoundland, we were receiving the first clear feeds of still photographs, revealing the stages of the Twin Towers collapsing. Photos from police helicopters showed the South Tower surge cloud moving westward over the water at substantial speed and still with substantial mass. The photos illustrated for us what had previously seemed inexplicable and perhaps even impossible: Pliny the Younger had described a pyroclastic surge cloud moving effortlessly over the face of the water during the AD 79 burial of Pompeii by Vesuvius, but for most of two thousand years, no one believed him.

I contacted Haraldur Sigurddson, a volcanologist who had sailed with me and Dettweiler during Robert Ballard's Argo-RISE expedition, in the fall and winter of 1985. While robotically mapping and filming the hydrothermal vent zones of the East Pacific Rise, we were able, in our spare time, to examine the first robotic reconnaissance photos and video of the *Titanic*, dating back to only a few weeks before. From the very start, it appeared that something had exploded over the very center of the *Titanic*, in the manner of a fluidlike, volcanic column of ash suddenly collapsing downward, under its own weight, upon a city.

In this case, the collapsing column was the slipstream of water trailing behind the *Titanic*. Inertia then kept the column punching down into the earth from the moment the *Titanic* stopped descending. "*Downblast*," I had called it. The column collapse and down-blast effect bulldozed vertical bulkheads outward from the center of the ship and also hurled outward, in a spreading surge cloud of deep-ocean sediment, broken railings, floor tiles, forks, and glass.

The concept of column collapse applied as much to Sigurddson's studies of the Mount Vesuvius surge clouds as it did to the *Titanic*—and vice versa. Each area of study fed back to the other (except that at the *Titanic*, one did not have to excavate a buried city over the course of decades to reconstruct what had happened; it was all laid out in pictures). Likewise, the first pictures from New York were showing us that volcano physics applied with spine-chilling fidelity to the collapse of the Twin Towers. This observation quickly began to redirect the focus of research as I prepared for our return to the *Titanic*.

Two millennia after the eruption of Vesuvius and the surge clouds in Pompeii, nearly a century after the *Titanic* and in a way no archaeologist could ever have anticipated, the fall of the Twin Towers pointed the way toward a new understanding—which might ultimately save lives in volcanic hot zones. If anything could drive home the message that the only way to survive a volcanic surge cloud was to obey the predictions of people like Sigurddson and not be anywhere near one when it formed, the physics of 9/11 pointed the way. The eruption that surged through Pompeii in AD 79 was a thousand times more powerful than a Hiroshima-level atomic bomb (roughly 10 percent the force of the Hiroshima bomb). The combined collapse force of the Twin Towers was 1.6 kilotons. The approximately 40-mile-per-hour column-collapse that impacted the *Titanic* bow section was minuscule compared to the towers, just as the 120-mile-per-hour World Trade Center column collapses were minuscule compared to Vesuvius, but each of them was full of new insights.

"When Charlie and I started to discuss the eruption of Vesuvius and the events of 9/11," Sigurddson told a friend, "both of us realized the very interesting features of this parallel: when the Towers came down, they looked just like a column-collapse, when an entire eruption column cascades down, just like [a column, from a fountain of] water—and it cascades down, then it spreads over the ground."

At the place in New York that was being called ground zero, the physics were nearly identical, but with two critical differences: witnesses and temperature. Because the *Titanic* was two and a half miles underwater, no one ever saw the ship's column collapse and down-blast effect in action. The evidence was etched in bent steel and across a blanket of ejected artifacts. Volcanic column collapses and pyroclastic flows (of air and hot dust) typically surged at more than four times the boiling point of water and killed every potential witness they touched. The collapse of the Twin Towers created crushing forces—up to six tons per square inch—but this falling debris cloud was not (in most places) nearly as hot as a volcanic column collapse. This allowed first-hand eyewitnesses to survive it, at close range (at least, until the Zadroga effect, also called Ground Zero lung disease, reached into their bodies and began to kill).

Sigurddson and I realized that there was an important study to be carried out in New York. A return to the *Titanic* would provide additional baseline information for that study. Conversely, the World Trade Center investigation would enhance our understanding of the *Titanic* and of Vesuvius, as well as giving us clues about what to expect from other volcanic hot spots. In New York, for the first time and from virtually every angle, every stage of the column-collapse, down-blast, and surge-cloud events had been recorded on film.

Even more important, there were surge-cloud survivors—and not just from outside the column-collapse event, but inside. One of FDNY captain Paul Mallery's men from Ladder 10, Engine 10, had actually been a shock-cocoon survivor. As we approached St. Johns, Newfoundland, I received word of fourteen people safely cocooned inside a six-story, twelve-foot-wide stairwell in the core of the North Tower. In addition to what forensic archaeology could teach, their stories would provide unprecedented data about the physics that pounded portions of the *Titanic* flat and guided pyroclastic density currents through Pompeii. With this information, we could begin to explain how a table remained set for lunch in the nearby ancient Roman town of Herculaneum while half of the mansion was carried away, how Edith Russell's cup remained in its fragile holder while so much else nearby was destroyed, and how a small number of people inside a vertical tsunami of debris and down-blasting air were shock-cocooned on 9/11 while so many others were killed.

Aboard the *Keldysh*, I told John-David Cameron of my plan. I had already completed my one scheduled dive for the expedition, and I was quite satisfied with my "day of magic in the ever-black." All I needed now was for someone to gather new information from a handful of key targets. In the debris field, chunks of steel ranging from toaster-size to table-size had rained down from what I called the liquefaction zone, located between the bow and the stern, and concentrated mostly below the boat deck, just ahead of the fourth funnel. There were areas I wanted the observers to film in more detail, to perhaps illuminate what happened in a similar liquefaction zone that appeared to have developed (first along the east side) as the South Tower sagged and then snapped suddenly eastward, before accelerating toward terminal velocity.

Up to this point, Big Lew Abernathy and the Russians had been helping to keep me enough at peace to at least try and get some sleep. Abernathy kept reminding me of United Airlines Flight 93 whenever I seemed to be getting too worried about the future.

"Remember Shanksville," he told me—repeatedly. "We'll all get through this. United 93. That's what we're made of." Not just Americans are made of this stuff, he emphasized. All humans were born with the capacity to put the other person first. "Remember Dr. O'Loughlin," the *Keldysh*'s surgeon said, offering me a Russian alcoholic concoction called a Sheila. "Drink heavily." I wasn't about to obey that order too often. After only two glasses of the Russian doctor's "medicine," I sent a very mushy letter to Mary—but I had mistakenly e-mailed it to Arthur C. Clarke instead, who wrote back, "Charlie, I love you too, but not in the same way."

John-David Cameron was more serious. He began giving me strange, clearly uneasy looks as I described for him the intended study of the WTC crater. He could easily see that my way of coping with the unthinkable was to bury myself in the science of it. He seemed concerned about my health. Initially, I thought his concern was for my emotional health.

"Look," I said, "there are maybe six other people in the world who really understand down-blast, and I'm the one in New York. Now, I'm told we've got Port Authority police officers, NYPD, and FDNY—all of whom were trained in telling you, 'At this minute, I was standing here, within two feet of this spot on the map; and this is where I ended up; and this is what I observed; and this is what I felt.' From what I'm hearing, we have more than two hundred such eyewitnesses—many of whom are willing to talk—and each of these is like having a 'black box' flight recorder."

"Don't go in there," John-David said. "In fact, I'd stay away from New York altogether, if I were you."

It was my physical health that worried him. According to a report he had received from the Centers for Disease Control, there would be additional casualties, in years to come, just from what was in the air. No one had ever before burned large quantities of aluminum and Teflon mixed with gasifying plastics, cartridge ink, liquid crystal sheets, and other random, flame-toxified substances—all of this in a "background radiation" of gypsum, alkaline dust, and enough asbestos to get half of Manhattan Island condemned if it were a building.

I only saw, in the study, a chance to save lives in volcanic hot zones, using what we could learn at the *Titanic* and at the crater.

I reminded John-David of Paddy Brown. He and Bill Paxton knew about Paddy being recategorized from "missing" to "lost" before I did. Somehow, about a quarter of the people in Hollywood seemed either to have known him or known of him, long before the 9/11 attacks. He sure did have a way of getting around.

"You know what they told me happened with Pat Brown when he entered the North Tower?" I said. "Another firefighter—a guy who seemed to have a very clear picture in his mind of what was really happening overhead—called out, 'Pat! Don't go up there!'

"And Paddy's reply was, 'Are you nuts? We've got a job to do!'"

Those were the words I would live by.

SEPTEMBER 19, 2001
RUSSIAN RESEARCH VESSEL *KELDYSH*
120 MILES FROM THE *TITANIC*

We received a drawing by fax from my daughter Amber's second-grade class at P.S. 26 in Queens. At a memorial service in the school auditorium, the children's chorus had chosen the song "My Heart Will Go On" from the film *Titanic*. How does one get the thought out of one's head of children singing that theme, for parents lost?

SEPTEMBER 21, 2001
RUSSIAN RESEARCH VESSEL *KELDYSH*

Jim Cameron discovered what is presently the only large piece of debris found forward of the bow section: the steel hatch cover that once stood on the forecastle, capping the number 1 cargo hold. He found it lying upside down, about seventy meters directly in front of the *Titanic*'s prow, with a V-shaped whack, or pucker, on one side.

The well-deck cranes and the pressed-back foremast were completely undamaged by blunt-force impacts, which meant that the steel lid had not lifted off near the surface and banged around the well deck during descent—which in turn meant that the same bending and compression of the bow section that blew down all of the steel-bolted tables in the firemen's mess and recreation room, all in the same direction, had popped the hatch like a cork during that same small fraction of a second. Flying straight up, the hatch cover could not have traveled very far, not much more than about ten feet before, almost instantly, the column collapse and the down-blast impacted the center of the bow and struck out laterally.

What began, ever so briefly, as a vertical ascent of the hatch cover would have been converted immediately into lateral motion as the cargo hatch, along with hundreds of floor tiles and personal items jetting out of the upper deck windows and trailing down in the slipstream, became part of a radial surge cloud. The single, V-shaped dent in the hatch cover was consistent with the diameter of the vertical steel post that supported the anchor crane on the tip of the bow, suggesting that the hatch collided with the post on the ship's prow, then continued straight ahead for nearly three hundred feet.

The strange journey of the number 1 cargo hatch cover conveyed some sense of the volcano physics we were beginning to explore. Yet the crash of the *Titanic*'s bow on the bed of the Atlantic, I reminded myself, involved only a fraction of the forces waiting to be studied in New York.

Ken Marschall's mapping of the buckling points near and around the bend of the well deck revealed that the rows of steel plates tended to ripple and warp, shattering only at the points where the aftermost part of the bow section tried to telescope forward under the well deck. At the very end of the bow section, where the decks had been stacked on one another by the down-blast, the starboard and port sides rippled outward more like thick slabs of rubber than like steel.

The stern deep-hammered itself into the earth at even greater velocity; there, just one cubic yard of water impacting an inch-thick sheet of steel was equivalent to a ton of water trying to burst through at more than fifty miles per hour. This happened to every square meter and yard of the stern section, and it was inflicted by an entire column of water thirty yards wide, more than sixty-five yards long, and at least a hundred yards tall. For at least one small part of a second, the action of steel sheeting and the slipstream of water that surrounded it and shot down upon it must have been indistinguishable.

Slabs of inch-thick steel were blasted off the stern and strewn up to seventy yards away by the surge clouds. They often resembled curled leaves, bent as much as ninety degrees back on themselves without breaking. When surrounded by and ejected by a sufficiently powerful column of down-blasting water, steel could act astonishingly like the water blast in which it was enveloped.

Although initial examination of the curled-leaf steel-plate fragments gave the appearance of having been warmed and then bent, the crystal structure, when viewed under a microscope, revealed that the curled pieces had undergone microcracking throughout, providing enormous surface areas for rusticles to take root. This explained why bent, highly stressed steel tended to sprout the most luxuriant rusticle formations.

Over a much wider area around the stern, scattered more than five hundred feet in every direction, were pieces of steel that broke away near the surface—many minutes before the surge clouds were formed—and which fluttered down like snowflakes and leaves, ranging in size from a few inches across to huge sections of the double-hulled bottom. Collectively, they told the story of utter disintegration as the lower half of the stern section, trying to fall level with the sea surface, crashed forward into the bow section and, for a second or two, sent the reciprocating engine room telescoping into the rear boiler room.

Above the steam engines, the entire deck of the galley and pantry broke free, joining a shower of bending and cracking parts—tens of thousands of parts—caught between two great forces that made everything in and around the junction of the break behave as if they were individual sand grains and pieces of seashell in a sand castle, brought down by a wave. Normally rigid structures rippled and shattered like walls of cinderblock and steel-reinforced concrete that, built upon seemingly solid sandy earth, resonated with the ground itself when a quake-generated process called liquefaction turned solid ground into a stormy sea.

During the breakaway of the *Titanic*'s stern, the area between the third and fourth smokestacks—and especially along the lower decks, within the junction of the break—was dominated by a process very similar to liquefaction. In that region, no individual piece of the *Titanic*, large or small, behaved any longer as though it had ever been part of anything else. Collectively, all of the pieces became separate elements in a fountain of debris. They afterward fell to the bottom in a spreading shower effect. Yet even within this shower, objects of the same density and grain size—the boilers were an example of this—sometimes tended to fall together and at the same speed.

SEPTEMBER 21, 2001

We had, from the navy, fresh comparative material from the wreck of the *Ehime Maru*, a steel-hulled Japanese fishing boat sunk in a collision with an American submarine on February 9, 2001. It fell to a depth of six hundred meters (just over a third of a mile), achieving a terminal velocity equivalent, at least, to the *Titanic*'s bow section.

Nine people, including four high school students, were trapped inside the *Ehime Maru* when it sank. As we set out for the *Titanic* again, a naval operation was placing straps under the 191-foot-long vessel, so it could be raised into shallower water.

Here is what has happened: Deck railings and vertical bulkheads that were not damaged during the collision with the surfacing submarine were bulldozed outward from the center of the ship—just as we had seen in the case of the *Titanic*'s bow and stern sections. The *Ehime Maru* impacted at an angle of at least ten degrees down-bubble, partly burying itself in deep-ocean sediment, almost exactly as the *Titanic* did. The rear portions of the hull (much in the manner of the *Titanic*'s bow section), buckled behind the point of sediment burial, with the sea floor acting like a knee, or a fulcrum, against which the keel was broken like a stick.

Water trapped between the sea floor and the *Ehime Maru*'s keel at the moment of impact ended up being jetted out through an impact crater, carving out a narrow canyon in the ocean sediment very reminiscent of the prominent canyon along the starboard side of the *Titanic*'s bow. The down-blast and surge-cloud effects that immediately followed the impact of the *Ehime Maru*'s column collapse uprooted railings and other deck structures and carried them out to a radius approximately equal to the ship's length—again, just as the *Titanic*'s surge clouds did.

SEPTEMBER 22, 2001
8 A.M.

Jim Cameron opened the production meeting by noting that not everyone in the room had arrived, in accordance with regulations, properly dressed.

"As I have said from day one," he announced, "everyone at these meetings who is scheduled for a dive is to arrive already in their *Mir* suits." A camera turned toward me, and Cameron asked, "Charlie! Where's your *Mir* suit?"

He got me—totally by surprise.

And for a reason I did not yet comprehend (and never would), it was about to turn out that I needed this dive. The last time, I surfaced into a world of horror. Now, although I missed my family more than words could describe, a part of me did not want to face the job that awaited me in New York. I did not want to see the World Trade Center crater, but I took comfort in the knowledge that Paddy Brown's words— "We've got a job to do"—would gird my spine.

Somehow, two and a half miles down in the everblack, I was about to come to peace with something, in preparation for the road ahead.

Big Lew Abernathy was making the dive with me. He put a hand on my shoulder and said, "Earth to Charlie: You have five minutes to pack your gack."

20

Dark Circle

Everything that was noble in humanity and everything that was reprehensible happened on and around the *Titanic*'s slanting decks. You could not escape it, looking out again across the rusticle garden that had spread from Murdoch's boat davit and extended its roots deep into the Ismay suite and across every square inch of the boat deck. One did not descend into this place without pausing, at some point, to wonder how, of all the lifeboats that were launched, only two came back looking for survivors. It might even have been said that everything civilization needed to know about its past, its future, and about the need for change could be found here.

Even the rusticle reef seemed eager to teach. It was the perfect organization of carbon atoms into iron-metabolizing symphonies written on DNA and performed by protein. Thinking about where we came from—more than three billion years ago in rusticle time—and where we (as a civilization and as a species) were going did not get more fantastic. Here was the realization, induced by a consortium of microbes, that DNA was not really the computer in our lives. We and the iron that coursed through our blood were merely the substances that DNA used. We scientists might have had it backward all along: DNA is the software, not the hardware.

"DNA does not care whether it lives in you or me or in a bacterium any more than the software cares which of the latest computer models it is inhabiting and controlling," I told a friend later. "The Earth has evolved the perfect parasite. If we disappear utterly, it will still be dreaming at the hydrothermal vents, waiting to pass down through the next chain reaction of diverging lineages. You are just one of the temporary masks that DNA wears. Men die, cattle die, termites die. All that truly lives on are bacteria (immortal fission)—and, perhaps, our deeds."

Alfred White suffered what future medicine would call *retrograde amnesia*, in which a sharp blow to the head temporarily prevents short-term memories from taking root. The effect on White was as though someone had reached inside his skull and erased all recollection of what happened from the moment of the blow backward in time to the minutes preceding the injury.

The young equipment oiler and apprentice engineer was able to remember everything that happened up to the second the ship started coming apart below him, just before he and the fourth smokestack began to fall. After that, his memory became blank, right up to the moment a hand reached down and pulled his semiconscious body into the damaged and half-sunk boat A.

The funnel on which he was perched had been built as lightweight as possible, held in place more by reinforced wires than by solid steel. When the deck to which the fourth funnel's front stays were anchored disintegrated and the rear stays pulled the funnel backward, the entire base of the structure became a crumple zone, probably allowing White to maintain his grip. As it fell back and to the port side, toward rising water, resistance from the cat's cradle of starboard stays conceivably allowed White to hold on until he had only a two-story drop to the water. A more violent and jarring breakaway of the fourth funnel would almost certainly have shaken him loose and sent him crashing onto the roof of a deckhouse, and there would have been no survivor's account by Alfred White.

Even so, survival was unlikely. The fourth funnel had landed White in the middle of a new danger—within a roughly three-hundred-foot-wide circle of nearly a thousand souls crying out in a unified, dismal moan that George Rheims would recall as "horrifying, mysterious, supernatural."

Rheims was also right in the thick of it. He had climbed into the wreck of boat A and was joined very quickly by about twenty other people. Though wearing nothing more commanding than undershorts and a thin shirt, he managed to take command of boat A. "What a horrible night that was!" he would write, adding that they had to push people back from the raft, which was loaded to the limit and could not stay afloat if everyone who swam toward it had been allowed aboard.

The people of boat A, according to tennis star Richard Williams, were fighting for life and scrambling, and they finally succeeded in paddling out of the area. Whatever they were using for paddles must also have been used in the fight to keep the swimmers away, and this probably explained why White's retrograde memory loss began at the side of boat A, fixing in time the moment of a blow to the head.

In the end, Charles Joughin was standing on or near the very top of the descending stern. Below, everything appeared to be simply black; not until the last few seconds could he make a clear determination of how near or far the water's surface actually was. Glowing red stern lights nearby—which he believed to be electric lamps rather than oil-fired lanterns—contributed to his night blindness. He could still read the dials on his pocket watch by the lights, which continued burning until the rounded, white-painted hull section on which he was standing disappeared underfoot. At that point—2:20 a.m.—the pastry chef put his watch in his back pocket, checked that his life jacket was securely tightened, and, as an ankle-deep wave washed over his shoes and a ghostly red porthole light slipped below, he stepped away into the Atlantic.

"And the water didn't suck you down as she [the ship] finally went under?" Walter Lord asked more than four decades later.

Joughin replied, "Didn't even get my head wet."

Like White and Rheims, Joughin had been deposited by the *Titanic* within an approximately three-hundred-foot circle of struggling people, each of whom felt the bite of paralyzing, 28-degree-Fahrenheit water as one might receive the repeated stings of a hundred scorpion fish—each, that is, except Joughin. In accordance with the orders of the ship's surgeon, he had consumed so much whiskey that he did not feel the stings at all, did not feel the sort of pain that put into most people's minds thoughts of "This cannot be endured. This cannot be survived. I'm going to die."

Joughin swam away from the people in the circle, the majority of whom would be unconscious and dying from hypothermia within twenty minutes. He never gave a thought to the possibility that he should soon freeze to death. Eventually, after a very long swim, he made it to Charles Lightoller's command on the overturned boat B. He kept swimming almost until sunrise and all the way into medical history: a man of average build who was to survive in the water longer than anyone else shaken loose from the *Titanic* that night.

In the next century, physicians and rescuers would know that the reason most hypothermia survivors had a tendency to die very shortly after being rescued was their obedience to their first instinct: to warm their frozen extremities. The fingers and the toes, the hands and the feet, and the arms and the legs lost heat and shut down in that order, but the reverse applies to warming the body: it has to be warmed gradually from the inside out. In 1912, no one knew that the torso should be warmed first and slowly, whereas the arms and the legs, the hands and the feet, and, last of all, the fingers and the toes should be left cold and warmed gradually only from the inside outward.

Under this rule, a rapid, supposedly even warming of the whole body at once invariably warmed the extremities first. Once warm blood from the fingers and the toes, the hands and the feet, and the arms and the legs rushed into the still cold body core, it would instantly stop the heart.

Perhaps the greatest medical mystery about Joughin was not how he swam away from the *Titanic* and survived without freezing to death but how he survived his own method for warming up.

In January 1956, Joughin's future shipmate, Captain J. J. Anderson, wrote about the plucky pastry chef's unorthodox solution (even by 1912 standards) for clearing the chill from his bones: "Joughin's initial treatment aboard the *Carpathia* was [to be] placed in a warm oven to thaw him out—or, as he expressed it, 'They popped me in an oven like one of me own pies.'"

Behind Joughin, as he swam away from the circle of death, August Wennerstrom, one of the Swedes who only two hours earlier had formed a taunting ring dance around a group of frightened Italians in the recreation room, could not understand how it had come to this. About the time that White was asked to help make a last attempt to service the ship with more electricity, Wennerstrom had stood smoking a cigar as the last boats were lowered to the sea. He was unable to feel sorrow or even fear, as though he were merely part of an audience watching "a wonderful, dramatic play."

Just before White and Joughin began their journey, Wennerstrom was standing with Edward Lindell and his wife, far astern on the boat deck, when the deck itself angled down suddenly, more than twenty degrees. They slid together downhill, trying to hold hands, all the way to the submerged bridge. They were among the very first people to climb into the swamped and battered wreck of boat A, which was dragged precariously over the top of a collapsed and sinking forward funnel, evidently still attached by a few steel wires and rolling half on and half off the boat deck.

Wennerstrom estimated that in the very end, boat A drifted within scarcely more than fifty feet of the severed stern's port side. There seemed to be a halo of light ringing the top of the structure; and in that light, Wennerstrom saw a man who must have clung to a joint along the front of the rudder after the stern section leveled out—then, still clinging, he was lifted with it. The Swede watched in amazement as the man, who was raised much higher out of the water than he must originally have intended to be, tried to lower himself from a height of more than fifteen stories down to the actual log line of the six-story, hundred-ton rudder.

After the stern and the rudder climber disappeared, so many swimmers clambered up one side of boat A that their sheer weight pulled it over and spilled almost everyone out. In the midst of the struggle, Wennerstrom was knocked unconscious, and only his life jacket prevented his head from going under.

"I recovered consciousness," he would live to write, "[but] how long I was away from the boat, I [did not] know. . . . When [finally] I came back to our boat, it was filled with water and all that held us up was the cork railing around the boat."

He fought his way back aboard with Edward Lindell, and they found Lindell's wife wounded alongside, without her life jacket. By now their fingers were paralyzed from the cold, and neither man had the strength or muscular control to pull her over the gunwale. Wennerstrom held onto her wrist until his fingers seemed to die, and he watched her disappear beneath the water while the cries around him diminished rapidly toward the last murmurs of life.

Wennerstrom turned toward Lindell, heartbroken and wanting to give some reason why he could not have held onto his wife a little while longer. What stopped him was the realization that Lindell's normally dark hair, had, like the hair of everyone else in boat A, sprouted tiny white ice crystals that sparkled in a billion points of back-scattered starlight. With the growth of the ice, Lindell seemed to have lost all sense of emotion, even about the loss of his wife.

Wennerstrom tried to make sense of what he saw: "His face had sunk in. His hair and mustache were gray. His eyes had changed. He just looked straight ahead, never made a move or [said] a word."

Lindell had probably been dead, by this time, for at least ten minutes.

Alfred White was now aboard boat A and still alive; so were George Rheims, Richard Williams, and David Vartanian, who had fled the warfare in his own country, only to be trapped in the lower decks by open warfare at the gates leading out of third class, and who had by some miracle made it to the open spaces of the stern just in time to become one of the hundreds of people Joughin saw spilled overboard.

"He swam through frozen bodies," Rose Vartanian, his daughter, would relate for historians. Soon after the stern disappeared, he found boat A. "But the people in the crowded lifeboat would not let him in. They would hit his hands with the oars and he would swim away a little, then come back. He kept doing that, but they would fend him off with the oars again."

"I will spare you the details, which were horrible," Rheims wrote to his wife. Nearly ninety years later, Jim Cameron would wonder if Rheims's statement was a veiled expression of remorse over having to beat the crowds of swimmers away with oars—meaning, in essence, that they had to kill people. Rose Vartanian's account provided some of the details that Rheims had chosen to spare his wife.

After most of the swimmers ceased moving and their corpses drifted off, a mother and daughter who had climbed aboard boat A died and were lowered together over the side. "Finally," Rose said, "they let him [her father] hang on to the side of the lifeboat. He kept kicking and kicking in the freezing water to keep the feeling in his legs." He also kicked to pull himself onto the side of the boat and to keep his chest and the rest of his body as high as possible out of the water. Rose would report that for the rest of his life, her father's legs were more of a "bluish color" than the hue of living flesh, and he always walked with a limp.

The strength of Vartanian's kicks and his grip on the gunwale inevitably began to weaken. By then, the passengers in boat A, according to Rose, "took turns holding his hands so that he wouldn't slip beneath [the water]." Rheims wrote of holding on to people clinging to the side. Eventually, after another died, and another, and then four others were lowered lifeless into the sea, "the people gave in," and someone pulled Vartanian aboard.

"Rosa" Abbott was the only woman still alive aboard boat A, but she was barely if at all conscious of her surroundings. Her two teenage sons, Rossmore and Eugene, had been torn from her arms as the *Titanic* went down—as if snatched away by a vengeful giant. Under Lightoller's protocol, sixteen-year-old Rossmore and fourteen-year-old Eugene were not allowed into a lifeboat. Abbott was told that she, but not the boys, could proceed to the boat deck, so she stayed on the stern's well deck with her sons. The men in boat A believed that everything would soon be right if they resisted the cold long enough for the first warming rays of sunlight to reach them. But Abbott knew already that she would never be right again.

Norwegian sailor Albert Moss reached the upturned keel of boat B about the time that August Wennerstrom was trying to find a gentle way of telling Edward Lindell that he had lost all feeling and control of his hand and had therefore lost his grip on Lindell's wife. Charles Lightoller was already standing on boat B with twenty to thirty people. Far from allowing Moss to pull the top of his body out of contact with the water and slow his rate of freezing, the people nearest the edge of the raft tried to push and kick him away.

Moss had a bit more experience with shipwrecks than Lightoller or anyone presently under his command. When the *Hebe* had sunk only a few months before, Albert Moss had made sure that everyone got away safely in lifeboats. He was not about to let someone push him or anyone else away from a lifeboat now. He swam to the opposite end of boat B and, by the light of the stars and the biolumes, was able to discern an empty space.

The flashes of bioluminescent sea creatures, disturbed by each stroke of Albert Moss's arms and each kick of his legs, probably illuminated his path in the water as though he were a lightning dolphin, because he was not quite near the empty space when he heard a crewman shout, "Phillip, shove him off! Shove him off!"

Lightoller countermanded the order, insisting that there was room for the newcomer. Indeed, his weight was needed on the open space to help balance the upturned boat. Moss pulled his shoulders, chest, and rump out of the sea, but he was obliged to sit with his swelling feet and legs dangling over the edge of the keel and in the heat-sapping water.

"If anyone tries to shove me off," Moss announced, "the person concerned will follow!"

A man near Moss died and was lowered over the side. As another died and was cast away, then another, the bubble of air that was keeping most of the upside-down hull above water lifted Albert's legs ever so slightly higher.

Huddled together with his crew in their wet clothes, Lightoller tried to keep boat B steady and afloat. "I made everyone face one way," Lightoller wrote later. "And then, as I felt the boat under our feet lurch to the sea, one way or the other, I corrected it by the order[s], 'lean to the right. Stand upright.' Or, 'Lean to the left,' as the case might be."

The murmurs of the dying continued, ever weaker but all so clearly too near. Somewhere in the dark, eighteen other lifeboats had rowed safely away from the *Titanic*—the first few of them at least half empty; collectively they held enough spare seats to accommodate everyone aboard boat B plus nearly five hundred others.

In boat 6, Celiney Yasbeck estimated that she was within about five minutes' rowing distance of the place where the *Titanic* had last been seen, near enough to have felt the impact of the ship's breakup, which had shaken the waters so fiercely that for several seconds she had believed the lifeboat would sink, too. She was near enough to see that several portside lights were burning until the stern disappeared, near enough to have heard individual screams. All of the women in boat 6 pointed out that there were fewer than thirty people aboard—there was room for another forty. They urged quartermaster Robert Hitchens to turn the tiller in the direction of the dying people, but he refused, insisting that their own boat would be overrun by the dying and swamped if it went near.

Boat 11 did not move near, either—even though Edith Russell knew it was already close enough to have felt the waves from the *Titanic*'s breaking. Those in command of boat 11 asked the women and children to cheer as loudly as they could when the first screams reached them—to cheer back at the dark spot where the *Titanic* had been. "Those cheers that you hear," one of them lied, "mean that they have all gotten into lifeboats and are saved." In later years, Russell would look back with disbelief on how she and the others fell for it—"that we actually cheered"—believing that the shouts in the night were cries of thanksgiving. Instead of rowing toward the swimmers, the crew of boat 11 rowed it farther away from the site of the sinking.

In boat 5, Third Officer Herbert Pitman knew what needed to be done, but his boat was filled with first-class passengers who operated under the belief that what they said was law.

THE EXAMINATION

"When she [the ship] went down," boat 5 passenger Karl Behr wrote, "Pitman ordered us to row back towards the wreck. There were hundreds in the water. We immediately turned around and commenced to row slowly back. Many of the passengers urged Officer Pitman not to go back into the crowds as they would swamp us. We rowed a short distance, however, before Pitman ordered us to cease rowing, and although it is hard to think of it, I believe he was wise in doing so."

Later, an incredulous Senator Smith asked Pitman about his actions and demanded answers. "Officer, you really turned this boat 5 around to go in the direction from which these cries came?"

"I did."

"And you were dissuaded from your purpose by your crew?"

"No, not crew," Pitman replied. "Passengers."

"[You] drifted on your oars?"

"We may have drifted along," said Pitman. "We simply lay there doing nothing."

"How many of these cries were there?" Senator Smith pressed. "Was it a chorus or was it—"

Pitman cut him off, saying, "I would rather you did not speak about that."

"I would like to know how you were impressed by it," the senator said, asking history to fathom how an officer ceded command to his passengers while listening to that awful chorus. Senator Smith conceded "that it is not a pleasant theme," then pressed again for Pitman to describe what he heard.

"Well," Pitman said, "I cannot very well describe it. I would rather you would not speak of it."

But the senator continued to speak of it. He continued to demand answers until Pitman told investigators about "a continual moan that lasted for what seemed about an hour."

"I ask you," said Smith, "if any woman in your boat appealed [for] you to return to the direction from which these cries came."

"No one," Pitman replied.

"You say that no woman passenger in your boat urged you to return?

"None."

Eighty-nine years later, during our 2001 expedition, historian Don Lynch believed he had begun to fathom at least one of the reasons so many first-class women in Pitman's boat—and in many other boats either drifting or rowing away from the circle of swimmers—were against rowing back. Many of them were locked into unhappy marriages, held in place by children, lack of their own money, and fear of shunning. Well into the 1950s, a divorced woman (but not the man) was considered so badly stained that were she Catholic, even her own brothers and sisters would be advised by the church to shun her and not even speak to her. Lynch believed that from the moment the lifeboats departed and the people looked back and understood that the *Titanic* might really be sinking, there emerged a small but significant and vocal percentage of women who saw widowhood as a quick and wholly respectable way to be rid of their husbands and keep the family jewels. In Pitman's case, especially, a crewman might have found himself surrounded by unhappy women for whom the worst of all possible outcomes would be rowing back toward the circle of death and finding their husbands alive.

Violet Jessop noticed that boat 16 was so fully loaded that its commander had almost no choice about moving. Boat 13 was another among the few that had no choice about going back. It had moved nearly a mile north and was surrounded by icebergs, and even if it happened to be located nearer the *Titanic*'s grave, boat 13 was filled above capacity with almost seventy people aboard. One of the passengers, Mary Hewlett, looked around and listened to the conversations and accents of her companions—mostly men of the unemployed class, she judged haughtily, as well as stokers, stewards, and cooks. Not all of the women shared Hewlett's attitude about the "inferior" classes or nationalities being saved, nor did they always (and perhaps not even often) wish their husbands conveniently disposed of by the *Titanic*.

Captain Arthur Rostron of the rescue ship *Carpathia* recorded, based on his discussions with survivors, how one of the last boats to cast off was so crowded that the crewman in charge refused entry to an especially powerful swimmer from the *Titanic*, who seized the forward gunwale. He was joined by a chorus of passengers yelling, "We are full. We are full! Don't let him in!"

Sitting on the boat's stern, clothed in nothing except a thin night-gown and frozen almost to the point of giving in to a hypothermic urge to sleep, yet knowing that the silent stranger clinging to the lifeboat's bow must be in an infinitely more life-threatening condition, a woman grieving her husband's death started a protest of her own and summoned the support of passengers sitting around her. The people at the stern prevailed over those at the bow, and the shadowy, half-conscious swimmer was hauled into the front of the boat. A lamp revealed that the haggard, hypothermic man whom the leader of the protest had helped to save was in fact the husband whose loss she had been grieving.

Of the ten or more boats that had plenty of extra space for rescues and so did have a choice about rowing back, all but two stood still. In the eight or more boats that stood still, the passengers and crew echoed the same fear: "We'll get swamped."

Boat 4 continued to linger just outside the place where the *Titanic's* stern, gulping and gently hissing, had gone under. Frank Prentice, one of the people plucked out of the water with Samuel Hemming and Thomas Patrick Dillon, felt that he was in "a pretty bad way," but he soon discovered that others were in considerably worse condition. Another man had fallen into such delirium that he wanted to dive out of the lifeboat and go for a swim; he had to be restrained. There was a fireman dead in the front of the boat.

By this time, first-class barber Augustus H. Weikman was standing safely inside boat A, after having paddled for a very long time on a bundle of wooden debris that surfaced near him—mostly deck chairs tied together with rope. During his last minutes near the bridge, the barber had been working alongside William Murdoch, trying desperately to secure and lift the raft's expandable canvas sides, when the deck broke into total pandemonium. For half an hour or more he had paddled his raft blindly until, by chance, he came upon the very same boat he had tried to launch.

Before able seaman Edward Buley descended with Masabumi Hosono and the Laroches in boat 10, he witnessed a frenzied attempt by the stewards and firemen to construct rafts on the aft end of the portside boat deck. They had evidently contrived a plan to send rafts of chairs and anything else that might keep their bodies above water over the side and then follow them down on ropes—or, alternatively, float off the deck as the water reached them. Buley did not think there was time enough to do either.

Once the final plunge began, the violent breakaway of the stern removed any margin of safety from a raft slide down the boat deck into advancing water. None of the raft builders would ever be seen again, but one of their rafts apparently survived, long enough for Weikman the barber to find it and save himself.

For a while, after Buley saw the stern break away from the boiler rooms and the coal bunkers and watched the after-part settle down again on an even keel, he and almost everyone else in boat 10 had held on to the hope that "the after-part would float altogether." The loss of that last hope, and the sudden sense of profound loneliness on the sea, was, Buley believed, what finally brought at least four of the portside boats together.

By 3:20 a.m., an hour after the submerging stern had stopped Joughin's watch and set him adrift, boats D, 4, 10, and 12 were converging. Fifth Officer Harold Lowe arrived in boat 14 and ordered the crews to lash the boats together. He then began distributing passengers from boat 14 into the less crowded members of the little fleet. While thirteen-year-old Madeline Mellinger and her mother climbed from Lowe's boat into boat 12, Lowe ordered Buley, quartermaster Arthur Bright, and other seamen into boat 14 to assist in a search-and-rescue operation.

In the dark, Lowe overlooked Charlotte Collier and her eight-year-old daughter, Marjorie. Charlotte had not suspected that she was leaving her stateroom for the last time that night, so she was dressed only in a nightgown and an overcoat, and little Marjorie wore only a White Star Line blanket over her nightgown. Both were too cold to attempt the transfer to another boat or to risk falling into icy water, so they remained huddled together and shivering, quietly hidden in the shadows of boat 14. They believed that the horrors of the sinking had ended with the vanishing of the stern and the fading of the screams; they believed they were merely escaping the cold as Lowe's men rowed them away from the other boats, but they were heading toward the worst horrors of all.

Lowe had been waiting, until now, for the cries and the moans to "thin out" before venturing in among the survivors. Tragically, he had miscalculated how long a person could survive. The individual calls and screams blended undetectably into a hauntingly steady moan, and the moan diminished into a series of faint murmurs. As finally he ventured into the circle, the sea became quiet—all quiet now.

Lowe's boat started grating up against what at first felt like clumps of ice or fragments of wreckage but which turned out to be hundreds of dead bodies floating in life jackets. They found one man still alive and pulled him aboard. Minutes later, the man died.

Two more were hauled into boat 14, but hypothermia had done its work with them, too. They could just barely be called survivors. In every direction, the lesson was being driven home: too much time had passed. Lowe's crew rowed deeper in among the bodies and among the masses of wooden wreckage until his electric torch revealed a man kneeling above the center of the deathscape, as though in prayer. He was one of the ship's storekeepers, and he was kneeling atop a large wooden structure that turned out to be a staircase. The storekeeper was the only person within the drifting circle of death who was still able to cry out for help. Boat 14 was only fifteen yards away from the man on the staircase, but the field of wreckage and bodies floating between the boat and the stairs was frustratingly dense.

"And I am sorry to say," able seaman Joseph Scarrott told examiner Butler Aspinall, "there were more bodies than there was wreckage. It took us a good half hour to get that distance to that man—to get through the bodies. We could not row the boat. We had to push them out of the way and force our boat up to this man. But we did not get close enough to get him right off—only just within the reach of an oar. We put out an oar on the forepart of the boat, and he got hold of it; he managed to hold on, and we got him into the boat."

Into the heart of the circle, Charlotte Collier probably kept her eight-year-old daughter's head buried in her shoulder, hiding the view from her. Neither of them ever spoke about what the crew had pushed aside while clearing a path toward, and then away from, the stairway. Charlotte would write later of "half fainting" within this same time frame of people being pulled out of the water, almost all of whom died soon afterward.

Somewhere among the wreckage, during Charlotte Collier's half faint, one of the men rowing away from the survivor's stairway and the frozen bodies caught Charlotte's hair in an oarlock and pulled out a huge clump by the roots. What happened next, still within the circle of bodies and wreckage, Charlotte and her daughter, Marjorie, would *not* keep to themselves, no matter how much the men of boat 14 wanted to recolor the event with a soothing coat of whitewash.

On April 25, 1912, steward George Crowe cheerfully described for the examiner Senator Bourne how, more than ninety minutes after the sinking, they picked up a storekeeper from the wreckage and he survived: "Yes, sir—also a Chinese or Japanese young fellow that we picked up on top of some of the wreckage." A month later, Charlotte told the rest of the story for *American Semi-Monthly Magazine*. "We saw a floating door," she wrote, and lying upon it, facedown, having lashed himself to its broken hinges with a rope, was a young Asian man.

The first turbulence of predawn appeared to be developing, and Charlotte Collier observed that the sea was beginning to wash over the man, bobbing the door up and down. He neither moved nor answered the calls from the lifeboat.

"What's the use?" Lowe said, according to the Collier report. "He's dead, likely, and if he isn't, there's others better worth saving than a Jap!"

Lowe turned the tiller away from the man on the raft, but someone must have observed signs of life in the glow of fifth officer Lowe's electric torch, for after some small amount of discussion and second-guessing, he changed his mind, turned the tiller around again, and hauled the young man, who was a Chinese sailor, aboard.

"After the rescue," Charlotte Collier wrote, all of her memories started to become "hazy." With cold sea spray beginning to lash her face, she thought she saw, in the shadows, other women rubbing the sailor's chest and chafing his hands and feet, although Charlotte was in fact the only woman aboard.

The last clear recollection the increasingly cold and seasick Charlotte Collier would have, before Lowe discovered the wreck of boat A, was of the Asian survivor suddenly speaking to them in his own tongue. "Then, seeing that we did not understand, he struggled to his feet, stretched his arms above his head, stamped his feet, and in five minutes or so had almost recovered his strength. One of the sailors near him was so tired that he could hardly pull his oar. The 'Japanese' bustled over, pushed him from his seat, took the oar, and worked like a hero until we were finally picked up."

Unlike Joughin's ill-considered strategy for overcoming hypothermia, the Chinese sailor's strategy—overcoming a cold body's normal resistance to exercise and warming up slowly from the body core outward—was a smart approach to survival.

"By Jove!" Collier watched Lowe exclaim. "I'm ashamed of what I said about the little blighter. I'd save the likes of him six times over if I got the chance!" In as much of a lesson as could be learned by a man trapped by his time, Lowe stopped speaking about the obligatory (and probably fictional) lower-class passenger sneaking aboard one of the last lifeboats dressed as a woman. Or, at least, he stopped identifying him as "a Japanese" and cursed him as "Italian" instead.

21

⌒

Explorers, Graves, and Lovers

AUGUST 17, 1996
FRENCH RESEARCH VESSEL *OCEAN VOYAGER*
EXPEDITION *TITANIC VIII*

The weight of stewardship, like the weight of a crown one did not want, grew heavier each passing year.

Robert Ballard's first robotic reconnaissance images of the debris field around the stern were grainy and often difficult to interpret despite cameras rated to four hundred thousand ASA that could see more than eight hundred feet through the dark. Geo-positioning by satellites (one of history's first applications of such technology) provided a 360-degree panoramic map of everything the robot Argo saw in 1985. By the time the Tulloch era (the artifact recovery era) of *Titanic* exploration began in 1987, leather suitcases and wood-framed steamer trunks that appeared to be lying perfectly intact on the bottom, but which must actually have been near the point of collapse, had occasionally caved in.

By 1996, explorers had learned that after the sealed trunks filled with water and drifted to the seabed in 1912, the oxygen in them must have been depleted quickly by deep-ocean microbes. The environment inside was thereafter dominated by reducing bacteria, which dissolved iron clasps and brass picture frames but left the pictures and the letters that were sometimes bundled near the disintegrated frames completely unharmed and still readable. Such biological cocoons were only transitory, however. Samples from the debris field had demonstrated beyond all serious dispute how, once a trunk's protective shell failed and oxygen-metabolizing microbes were given a friendly habitat, books and letters generally began to deteriorate, probably within a matter of weeks.

Had biology followed its normal course, uninterrupted, nowhere in all history would a talented young violinist named Henry Sutehall, or many among the hundreds of other anonymous figures Charles Joughin saw tossed and mauled by the descending stern, have stood much chance of being remembered, even by the scholars of the *Titanic* Historical Society and RMS *Titanic* Incorporated. Sutehall, Howard Irwin, and uncounted others would appear almost exclusively on lists naming those lost and occasionally on memorial plaques in cathedrals, their friends and loved ones yearning only for someone to remember: here was a life and not just a name. Despite such efforts, as the entire generation of the bereaved died off and as nature began in shadowy, silent secrecy to reconvert the *Titanic* to iron ore, of certain lives recorded only as names, there would be no remembrance forever, if nature had its way.

But time would have the final say. It always does.

Looking at the *Titanic*'s debris was like reading Ernest Hemingway's six-word short story: "For sale: Baby's shoes. Never used." There was so much more to each item than meets the eye, and together they told a much larger story than the mere sum of their parts.

So it was for the discovery of a soup tureen from the *Titanic* that landed in a strange place and became part of an archaeological nightmare. And so it was for a fragment from a child's shirt, and for Howard Irwin's steamer trunk.

The *Titanic*'s bow section hit the bottom at approximately thirty-five knots (in the range of forty miles per hour). The stern fell with a significantly smaller surface area facing into the water through which it passed—which, in essence, rendered it more streamlined. It therefore attained a higher terminal velocity, somewhere in the vicinity of fifty knots (approximately fifty-eight miles per hour). Water jetting out from the stern carved a noticeable crater, bordered by minicanyons.

Into and around these canyons of brutality fell twisted forks (their hollow silver handles imploded by water pressure), smashed cooking pots, bedsprings, medical tools, shards of hull and glass and coal, iron paperweights, tatters of clothing, and the contents of collapsed and exploded refrigerators. Most of these artifacts were carried along in a surge cloud that radiated away from the stern, exactly like a volcano-generated surge cloud. In much the same manner as a pyroclastic flow, dust from the cloud itself tended to settle on and entomb the objects that traveled with it.

Invariably, the most rapidly buried artifacts had been trapped inside the stern when it pounded down on the deep-ocean plain. They were jetted out by rupturing hull plates and decks that collapsed like an accordion being pressed closed in only a single second. During the next two hours of that April 15 morning, objects that fell out of the *Titanic*'s breakaway and liquefaction point, two and a half miles above, continued to arrive like a gentle fall of autumn leaves, often landing on top of the objects that had raced them to the bottom inside the stern.

A teacup landed softly on a boiler. A wooden crate of wine bottles slowly filled with water, sank, and settled near a crater; its pinewood casing and interior padding would be slowly eaten by microbes and scavenging invertebrates, leaving behind neatly stacked wine bottles. A silver soup tureen touched down upon a blanket of disrupted clay and silt that had already settled over ejected surge cloud debris.

No one would probably ever know how many human bodies became part of the ejecta-blanket—how many were actually carried down to the bottom inside the stern. During the final hour and a half before the stern broke away, almost everyone aboard was able to evacuate from the flooding bow, either into or atop the stern.

About the time that the very last lifeboats were being lowered, passenger Gus Cohen passed through the third-class general room, far back on C deck. It seemed to him that "everyone" was in the dining saloon, deep within the ship, saying prayers while the room and the after-bridge were lifted, according to Cohen, "very high above the water—abnormally high."

Alfred White had also reported seeing people gathered in prayer, deep within the ship, along his escape route up to the fourth funnel and within minutes of the stern's breakaway. He did not mention a specific deck, only that he was climbing upward through third class, which would indicate that he was looking aft along an E-deck corridor above the turbine engine casing. The Cohen and White accounts suggested to Bill MacQuitty and Walter Lord that as many as (but probably not much more than) three hundred people were trapped within the stern and were carried two and a half miles to the bottom.

Four decades passed, then two more and two more. Rusticle stalactites wedged twisted steel plates apart, intertwined their roots, shared
nutrients, touched the sea floor, projected out glacierlike from their
iron and sulfur sources, and, aided by their own swelling interior populations of "sulfur-loving" bacteria, bound grains of silt together in a
concretion bed (that is, a hardened concrete-like slab)—fossilizing
everything in their path. Little nuggets of white quartz gravel fell from
icebergs throughout each passing decade, landing on top of the bioconcretions and, like everything else, being fused to the rusticle bed. The
pebbles, fused atop the rusticles and sprinkled across every deck space,
were the youngest and uppermost stratum in an onion skin–like
sequence of archaeological time, pointing backward through history.

Many of the passengers trapped inside the broken-away stern
section—most of them holding rosaries, according to Cohen—died
squeezed together during the last minute against front walls turned impossibly into floors. Some were drowned in the turbine room. Others died
standing up, standing on the forward wall of the third-class general room.

Except where shock cocoons intervened, down-blast and jetting
effects stripped the dead naked, and in the next split second their bodies
were handled with the same reptilian indifference by which every bed
and every piece of medical equipment in the ship's hospital had been
shot out through the starboard side. Yet even in death and even after
more than two generations had passed them by, the people continued,
in their own archaeological time frames, to bear witness.

Microbiologist Roy Cullimore and I first met aboard the French
research vessel *Ocean Voyager,* during what became, for us, "the rusticle
park" expedition, *Titanic VIII.*

If not for a stubborn concretion glued to a soup tureen's base and a
dent around the tureen's upper rim, we would have been hard-pressed
to guess the silver bowl's age. It appeared to be brand new, as shiny as
the day the *Titanic* left the dock at Southampton.

Initially, the *Nautile* pilot thought the tureen was simply sitting on
the bottom, about a hundred feet from the stern section's starboard
hull, but a nine-inch-wide by six-inch-deep chunk of black, rusticle-
concreted sediment broke away from the seabed and clung to the bowl's
bottom. The pilot tried to shake the concretion loose with the *Nautile*'s
robot arm, but the fossil was glued solidly to the artifact.

Conservators are, by training, all about cleaning and restoring artifacts. They do not care about mud, rusticles, or fossils. After nearly two

hours of careful prying, one of the *Ocean Voyager*'s conservators finally managed to break the concretion free. She was about to throw it in the garbage, but three things drew my attention.

First, the concretion was part of a rusticle bed, unusually black and anoxic (lacking oxygen) and giving off the distinctive rotten-egg smell of sulfur. Second, one whole side of what we quickly came to call "the fossil" was a perfect, rock-hard mold of the soup tureen's base, including a mirror image of its stamp and manufacturing number. Third, screaming out for attention was a break-away cross-section through animal bone. Careful scraping away of concretion layers with dental tools revealed that the broken bone was surrounded by a mass of copper that had bubbled outward like Styrofoam, under an assault by reducing bacteria; it had bubbled out into a greenish, gold-flecked concretion within a concretion, more than an inch in diameter.

Two inches from the copper concretion, a brass screw and hook were excavated, inexplicably unassailed by the same microbes that had destroyed a different copper alloy less than a finger length away. Further scraping revealed a white enamel button and shreds of fiber.

I had hoped to preserve the fossil impression of the soup tureen's base; but we knew now that it was full of tiny artifacts and would have to be completely dissected. Most of the objects appeared to have little relation to one another, except for, at first glance, five buttons (each of a different style; two were evening-dress buttons made of gold). A fragment of dinnerware from first class lay next to a shard of blue-and-white-patterned china from third class. A stopper-shaped iron paperweight, only an inch and a half across, was pulled from the concretion. A piece of brownish-white fabric was freed: a shred of undergarment—sized, evidently, for a child—lay in the company of a dozen microfragments of bone and four larger fragments, two of them still connected by tendon.

The majority of the bone fragments appeared to be bovine. The largest of them certainly came from the kitchen area: a piece of cow bone, clearly butchered at one end. The two tendon-connected fragments also came from the ship's galley. The tendons appeared to have been preserved under a complex weave of bacterial threads. In front of Discovery Channel and CBS news cameras, we called them "chicken bones" and quickly closed them up in a water-filled specimen bag. We did not want to admit, even to ourselves, the marrow patterns we were seeing: distinctly nonavian. They were not cow bones; they were undeniably something smaller, yet mammalian.

When vertebrate zoologist Bill Schutt of the American Museum of Natural History examined photographs, conducted measurements, and confirmed that they were lamb bones, we breathed a collective sigh of relief. As it turned out, we were permitted to enjoy only a brief respite.

The presence of bones in materials ejected from the *Titanic*'s stern and deposited by surge clouds—even mere cow or lamb bones—told us that sooner or later we were bound to encounter human remains. Cullimore and I recommended to expedition leaders George Tulloch and Paul Henry Nargeolet that no more artifacts should be lifted from a hundred-foot radius of the soup tureen. Tulloch went a step further, recommending a moratorium on the ejected-materials zone: "Attempt no landings there."

Unwittingly, we had instigated a moratorium that interfered with the sampling plans of a marine engineer from Harland and Wolff (the company that built the *Titanic*). This was bound, sooner or later, to have a depressing effect on the politics of the expedition, although Cullimore and I and the French conservators were at first oblivious to the situation we had created. Prior to the moratorium, I had already alienated the Harland and Wolff advocate with discussions about the *Titanic*'s stern breaking away at the surface—which he considered to be "a patently false hypothesis."

There seemed to be a Harland and Wolff insistence that the *Titanic* had submerged in one piece with a great deal of air trapped in its food lockers, and that massive implosions in the galley area broke the ship in two about the time it reached a depth of about 800 feet. To say otherwise was taken as an affront to the company that built the *Titanic* and was met by an insistence that the ship could never have broken at the surface—an insistence that was on one occasion yelled in my face.

"No riveted ship ever broke in two at the surface!" the Harland and Wolff advocate hollered.

"The *Titanic* did," I said firmly. And the atmosphere that then settled upon the *Ocean Voyager* was only slightly less toxic than the one a friend of mine once created after being pulled over by a rural sheriff who shouted about no one ever having sped through that part of Georgia at thirty-five miles per hour, to which my friend replied, "Sherman did."

Closer examination of the concretion artifacts had already multiplied our troubles. The ring of expanded, ballooned-out copper we had found appeared to be a gold-covered band enclosing a bone that was perfectly consistent with the base of a human finger. The copper-bacteria "foam" had all but completely surrounded one side of the bone, and flecks of gold within the solidified mud suggested that we were looking at the bone-enclosing remnants of an inexpensive wedding band, of the sort that would have been worn by a lower-ranking crewman or a third-class passenger. Until that day, no one had really believed that bones could survive in or around the *Titanic*.

Like most every other clue from the stern, this was not the sort of discovery meant to warm the heart. There were good reasons, deep-rooted and instinctive, why most explorers avoided the stern. Even silver tureens and glittering flecks of gold evoked nightmares. The lifting of the soup tureen and its concretion had evidently broken off part of a finger. This meant that the rest of a wedding band, and the skeletal hand to which it had belonged, was still down there under the surge-cloud blanket.

Tulloch decided, even before Roy and I told him of our wishes, that the bone with the partial wedding band must be returned to the *Titanic* site on one of the very next dives.

The equipment being sent to probe the *Titanic* was a marvel; its imaging abilities were so sophisticated that the *Nautile* was able to send crystal-clear, wireless images of the two giant reciprocating engines to the surface, transmitted like a television picture, with lines of sonar signals instead of radio waves or cables.

After high-resolution sonar peered below the surface at the bow's buried head, a Harland and Wolff team concluded that the *Titanic* had been sunk by more iceberg damage than previously believed. But the conclusion was far from being the last word. Along the starboard side, a great horizontal separation of steel plates was indicated, all the way back to Frederick Barrett's boiler room number 5. The problem lay in too much of a good thing: there were so many prominent horizontal fissures in the starboard bow—which was the zone of contact with the iceberg but which was also a part of the ship that had crashed and plowed down into the sea floor—that if all of the damage were attributable to the iceberg, the *Titanic* should have disappeared before the first distress call could be sent out.

Paul Matthias of Polaris Imaging, and naval architect William Garzke, noted that although some of the damage was consistent with what Fred Barrett, George Beauchamp, and other survivors of the boiler rooms witnessed in the starboard bow (and bearing in mind that the original damage by the iceberg could have been enlarged by impact with the seabed, in such a manner that merely split seams broke wide open), our ability to separate iceberg damage from further damage inflicted by the crash might have become an intractable problem.

When Nargeolet and Matthias decided to scan the bow's portside hull as a controlled experiment (for the iceberg never reached the port side), they discovered that the forward port plates had separated in very much the same way as the starboard plates.

One of the Harland and Wolff advocates seemed to become particularly agitated by a discussion of these results—and especially by the emerging conclusion that Occam's razor was pointing toward bilateral damage to the front of the bow arising from a very forceful impact on the ocean floor.

Cullimore and I had by now decided to keep our interests focused on biology and to steer away from the politics of marine engineers. For us, the most exciting discoveries from the expedition lay in black mud, microbial slime, and rust. There were too many wonders right under our feet to allow petty human behaviors to distract us. Time was our most precious commodity, and there was none to spare for dueling egos.

Cullimore had already identified certain bacterialike organisms within the rusticles as having originated hundreds of miles away at the hydrothermal vents. We knew now that one day we would have to go to the vents, seeking the origin of the *Titanic*'s rusticles on and around metal-rich deposits in the volcanic springs of the deep.

We had expected to see oxygen-loving bacteria living above a layer of acidic, reducing bacteria. The former, covered by the latter, would have worked in the absence of oxygen by dissolving the *Titanic*'s steel, after which the top layer of the bacterial sandwich would merely have utilized whatever iron and sulfur happened to pass upward. I never imagined seeing complex rooting systems tapping down into cracks and seams in the metal, bio-wedging the steel apart, multiplying the rooting systems' surface areas, relative to volume, somewhat like ivy vines growing into a brick wall.

We expected (and this would have been fascinating enough) to find a two- or three-layer bacterial sandwich when we started dissecting intact rusticles. We were not expecting internal channels, fibrular bundles, external pores, and other complex structures that seemed next of kin to levels of tissue organization found in sponges or mosses and other members of the animal or plant kingdom.

As on any good day in the lab, each new finding raised more questions than it answered. Was this really a single "organism" or merely an intensely colonial association? Shouldn't we be asking the same question about every leaf and even about ourselves? Was this a "living fossil?" Was something like this already being evolved near Earth's hydrothermal vent zones, about three billion years ago, as the ancestor of us all, or was the phenomenon simply the result of relatively recent consortial arrangements?

Was it possible that much as cancer cells seemed to resemble portions of an orderly tissue structure that reverted to its ancestral "wild type" cell, viruses and other independently competing packages of DNA and RNA were telling us that multicellular life sheds pieces of itself the way a cat sheds hair? Was it possible to believe that in this case, the rusticles, rather than being ancestral, were an example of how nature was constantly laying down the foundations for a second genesis of multicellular life?

Cullimore was certain that he had already encountered "cousins" of the deep-ocean rusticles under the Canadian prairies and in water wells all over the world. "When they infest water wells, they are cursed and called 'iron bacteria,'" he wrote, "[because they form plugs] to stop the water flowing into the well. These iron bacteria form rusticle-like structures and appear to be closely related. Just one more example of how closely integrated nature is. If you were to go to a well in the middle of the Canadian prairies, you could trace the pathway of water, however torturous and indirect, leading to the RMS *Titanic*."

The only point on which no questions arose was that we needed to obtain more rusticles while they were attached "alive and well" to their iron substrate. Attempts to pull live rusticles from the *Titanic*'s railings were not working out very well. The submersible's robot arm was too powerful, and the rusticles tended to disintegrate at its slightest touch.

During a review of the *Nautile* video, we selected a piece of hull steel, about three feet across, that appeared to have been flung at stupendous speed from the impacting stern. It was twisted like a leaf caught in a great wind, and within the fold had grown a beautiful cavern of rusticle stalactites. The piece appeared to be lying in a region free of forks and other implements sticking halfway out of a blanket of black ejected material (this meant there was minimal possibility of repeating the soup-tureen scenario). It seemed a perfect candidate for the dual purpose of providing our biological samples and a hull cross-section for the marine engineers' metallurgy and forensics team.

The moment the "leaf" was landed on the deck of the *Ocean Voyager*, Cullimore and I must have seemed happier than squirt clams at high tide as we knelt down near our first large, fresh sample of rusticles still perfectly intact on their substrate.

"Do you see how these roots are interconnected?" Cullimore said, prying a rusticle base from the metal, revealing the branching network of "vessels" below.

"Like a circulatory system," I agreed. "And we've already seen cili-ated cells."

"Something like that," Cullimore said. "[Organized groupings of ciliated cells, as in a living sponge's circulatory system] must be at work. I don't think they depend on random currents alone for circula-tion."

I bent down to pull another root free but was interrupted by a firm hand on my shoulder. A Harland and Wolff engineer and one of his attendants were holding a diamond saw.

"We need to remove several inches from this for metallurgy," the engineer said.

"It's for your safety," his helper said. "You don't want flying parti-cles hitting your eyes, so we need you to leave the fantail and wait in the galley until we call you back."

The engineer acknowledged our concern about vibrations from the saw and our need for intact rusticles.

"It's okay," he assured us. "We'll leave the rusticles intact for you on the unsectioned, larger body of the steel."

"This is very important," Cullimore emphasized.

"I promise," the engineer replied.

Minutes later, one of the *Ocean Voyager*'s cooks came running into the galley to alert us that once we were out of sight, the engineer had begun sledgehammering all of our precious samples off the steel.

When we ran out onto the fantail, even the few large rusticles that had been hammered off intact were intentionally being smashed before our eyes. We were now at the end of the expedition and there would be no more opportunities in the schedule for the recovery of steel with an intact rusticle root system. Before we could stop the vandal, our entire sample had been reduced to whatever pieces we could rescue from a large green garbage pail or scramble after and retrieve before they were water-hosed overboard.

Tulloch and Nargeolet went down to the *Titanic* again with a special package in the sample tray. "Attempt no landings there," Tulloch had instructed, so they dropped the package without landing. It fell into the general area from which the soup tureen had been recovered. Inside were the copper-enclosed bone and several unidentified mammalian microshards. The dead continued to speak out.

The brownish-white strip of clothing was also returned, I under-stand. No one could be certain that it was actually worn that night, but whether it came from a drawer, a suitcase, or off a human being's back, it belonged to an unknown child of the *Titanic*.

All but one child survived in first class. All of the third-class families with three or more children died—all of them.

Of the Rice family in third class, only the cousins who had stayed ashore and immigrated to New York on later ships survived. A descendant from what remained of the family tree, Eugene Rice, would join the New York fire department, and on September 11, 2001, he was among the "38th Street Mutts" who emerged alive from the 9/11 attacks. During the spring of 2002, he volunteered for New York City's dirty-bomb protocol, for which the team members' instructions were to think only about the twenty thousand children downwind and to expect "secondary devices." In 2010, Rice was promoted to captain. A year later, some of the radioactive dust–removal methods he helped to develop in New York would be applied for the first time in Fukushima, Japan.

Ninety-nine years earlier, twenty-four-year-old Bertha Mulvihil knew the Rices and witnessed how the *Titanic* lineage of their family tree ended. Margaret Rice was seated on a bench, holding onto her three-year-old son Eugene while the other four children clutched at her skirt. The young widow was likely awaiting instructions, but no one who survived ever reported seeing the Rices again. Another family (evidently the Goodwins) was milling about near boat 10 just before Bertha Mulvihil climbed in. There were, Mulvihil said, "the father, the mother, and six children. The father was not permitted to leave the ship, but the mother and her six children could leave if she wished. The mother was weeping. She wouldn't go into the lifeboat and leave her husband to perish." This event evidently occurred very early in boat 10's loading, when there was plenty of room and before William Murdoch arrived on the scene and started breaking the Lightoller bottleneck by sending husbands away with wives and children.

"She wailed," Mulvihil said of the mother. "'I'll stay with my husband, then,' the woman cried. [Later], I saw her clinging to her husband and children just before I left the vessel. That was the last I ever saw of her. The whole family went down together."

Rosa Abbott knew the unthinkable horror of having gone under with the *Titanic* and survived while her children died. Yet despite the end of her every hope for the future, Abbott's heart went out to another family, the Sages.

"You ask if this is the Jacksonville [Florida] that the Sage family [was] coming to," Abbott wrote to Frankie Goldsmith's mother in

March 1914. "Yes, it is the same Jacksonville. I so often think of them—such a large, good family to be lost, every one. I often feel when I think of it that I shall lose my reason."

The Sage family sank with nine children, the youngest of them four years old. The body of eleven-year-old William Sage was recovered, indicating that the Sages, like the Rices and the Abbotts, had found a route to the top deck and were standing in open air when the stern broke away. Thus read the third-class census: The Anderson family sank with five children. The Goodwin family sank with six children. The Lefebre family sank with three children. The Skoog family sank with four children. The Pallsson family sank with four children. The Panula family sank with four children. The Ford family sank with three children.

Margaret Rice's body was found during the recovery operation. Her personal effects included a wedding ring, gold coinage valued at three British pounds, and a set of rosary beads. Rice and her five children were almost certainly separated by the currents, as inevitably as the sea separated Rice's friends the Goodwins. The oldest of the children likely survived up to a half hour after forty-year-old Charles Goodwin's watch stopped, but not nineteen-month-old Sidney Goodwin, who for ninety-nine years became a Halifax cemetery's "unknown child of the *Titanic*," until his DNA was identified in June 2011.

During a dive that preceded the soup-tureen incident and the moratorium, Tulloch, *Nautile* pilot Yann Houard and copilot Yves Potier came across a large steamer trunk in the debris. It was still wonderfully oxygen-starved on the inside, so its contents had not disintegrated.

Probing with the *Nautile*'s robotic hands revealed the steamer trunk to be so fragile that it appeared to be another of those rare and perplexing objects we were calling ghosts, because of their tendency to disappear. An increase in the velocity of undersea currents between dives or the first touch of the robotic arm often caused the "ghosts" to crumble into dust and spongy splinters.

The wood and wrought-iron lid of the steamer trunk collapsed into flakes and red dust the moment Potier reached out and tapped it with the robotic manipulator's fingers. The trunk's metal straps had been devoured from the inside during a rusticle-forming assault in which every milligram of iron seemed to have been mined out of the straps, leaving behind only the carbon and slag between the crystals, held loosely together by a bacterial biofilm (a layer of microorganisms and their secretions).

The entire top of the trunk avalanched down into a rectangular depression, as though the lid had been molded from cigarette ashes. Slowly, a cloud of ashes and "smoke" pulled apart, revealing the top shelf of the trunk's interior. The shelf was filled with objects: a leather pouch, its features softened by the fresh coating of dust; sections of wind instruments; and a penholder sticking up, glittering with bacteria-resistant gold.

Potier saw the unmistakable outline of intact paper in one corner. He understood immediately that the sudden disappearance of the protective oxygen-starved environment, which up to this moment had been barely maintained by the ghostly lid, exposed the paper to new populations of still poorly understood microbes. What he knew for certain was that the microbes would begin to work against the paper in a matter of months, weeks, or perhaps even hours.

Rotating the *Nautile* (and Tulloch's viewport) slightly away from the trunk to provide himself with a clearer line of sight to both the trunk and his sub's external manipulator arms, Potier lifted the paper pile, gently shook off the layer of debris, and called out his observations.

"George," he said, "there seems to be sheet music inside. I believe it's French. No! Wait. It's English, but it's a French composer."

"You're telling me that the contents are in such good shape that you can read the sheet music?" Tulloch asked.

"I'm telling you what I can see there," said Potier. "It's true. It's a musician's trunk."

At that moment, the *Titanic* became one of the few shipwrecks ever to yield up readable paper after so many decades. The Tulloch expedition's robot Robin had already found one of the *Titanic*'s mail rooms filled with bags—in a part of the ship where oxygen levels were relatively low and where all of the mail bags were sheathed in a protective layer of rusticle-related microbes that grew from the floor upward, completely covering the bags as they sent forth white, threadlike shoots that resembled a cross between an upside-down stalagmite and a ghostly white flower stem. For as long as the deck plates held up and the oxygen levels beneath the sheath remained too low for the Gorgonarians and their brethren to take root and throw open the gates to dissolution, the *Titanic*'s mail would be guarded by the crazy biofilm garden.

Somewhere between the writing rooms and the mail rooms—and probably at the bottom of the mail room stacks (because the clerks, during the time remaining to them after the collision, would have given priority to carrying away bags of registered mail to the imagined safety of the higher decks)—many of the letters written by passengers, crew, and officers during the first and last voyage of the *Titanic* were most likely still protected, near the bottom of the garden.

Although gold and silver had already been recovered in a leather satchel, the greatest treasures of all were the etchings of human fingers on sheets of pulped and pressed, rag-based paper. The musician's trunk told us so.

George Tulloch crawled to look over Potier's shoulder at the top level of the steamer trunk, below which lay objects that had not been seen in more than eight decades—just like the sheet music, only two feet in front of the port.

"How much of this do you want recovered?" Potier asked Tulloch.

"I want everything," Tulloch said. "This is a man's life."

"It's amazing how close we [might] have been to losing the story forever," wrote Barbara Shuttle. Her husband, Dave, was the descendant of a woman, Ann Elizabeth Shuttle, whose letters of motherly advice to Howard Irwin were preserved within the steamer trunk. "I'll forever be grateful to George for having the foresight to recover everything in Howard's trunk."

If a strong current had collapsed the trunk before the crew of the *Nautile* found it, no one would have known how Howard Irwin or Henry Sutehall had lived and had come to their association with the *Titanic*, or that one of them had ever lived at all.

Irwin, shanghaied onto a ship bound for Egypt, simply dropped off the face of the earth, insofar as Sutehall knew. Sutehall kept his friend's steamer trunk safely aboard the *Titanic*, and he either went down to the bed of the Atlantic with the stern or became one of the anonymous hundreds of people who were washed off the descending rear deck with Abbott, the Sages, and the Rices.

The reducing bacteria inside Irwin's trunk had destroyed the tiny iron wires that held a rubber band–powered toy airplane together, yet the strange micro-habitat had left the rubber band, the wooden propeller, and the paper on the wings unharmed. Aboard the *Nadir*, conservators opened Irwin's leather pouch of awls and chisels, very carefully, inside a water-filled tray. For a moment, the conservators thought they were looking at "ghosts" of the tools fading suddenly before their eyes. What they beheld turned out to be the bacteria that had extracted all the iron from the awls and chisels—with the carbon that had existed between the iron seams held together by bacterial threads that suddenly came apart. The metal tools disappeared utterly, leaving behind only the waterlogged but otherwise brand-new wooden handles.

Irwin's piccolo and two clarinets were intact, along with a deck of playing cards and a book in which he had recorded bets on dog races in Australia. Close examination revealed that Irwin was not a particularly honest young gambler. Some of the cards in his deck were marked—professionally.

Irwin's diary also survived, along with a carefully wrapped bundle of letters: three from Ann Elizabeth Shuttle and the rest from her daughter, Pearl. The paper fleshed out the story in a manner not possible from artifacts alone.

In his diary, Irwin had expressed a measure of shame about his own fiery temper and said he wished he could more faithfully follow the example of his friend Henry Sutehall. "Popular among his own set," Irwin wrote, "he was quite honest, unassuming, and upright. He did not drink, smoke, swear, or cast an evil eye upon the beautiful young ladies that crossed his path."

By his accounting of himself, Irwin seemed to be recording clues to the personality of a hard-core adventure seeker who would have run off to join the revolution of Gandhi as easily as of Lenin. He also provided clues to the sort of behavior that might have contributed to his being shanghaied—or to the fight he must have put up against being shanghaied—decades after the mystery of his disappearance had ceased to be remembered at all.

Irwin referred to himself as an "arrogant and aggressive" man who, unlike Sutehall, "would cuss and fight" and who would do so without a great deal of provocation.

On New Year's Day, 1910, Irwin and Sutehall had begun their journey from Buffalo, New York, to all parts of the United States. Neither of them possessed much money, but both were skilled musicians, leather craftsmen, and mechanics. In a world where more and more cars were being built every day, they were among the few skilled laborers who could bore and trim holes for internal-combustion engine cylinders and repair upholstery.

Pearl Shuttle was a young musician from Hamilton, Ontario, not very far from where Irwin's and Sutehall's around-the-world adventure began, in Buffalo. The twenty-two-year-old adventurer and the Ontario musician were clearly in love. A photograph revealed Pearl Shuttle to be a young woman of haunting beauty, although by the standard of her time, at age twenty, she was already considered a "spinster."

Seemingly as unconventional as Irwin and his friend Sutehall, Pearl traveled the country unescorted, as part of a vaudeville company, in which she always performed her cornet solo in a white dress. Pearl Shuttle's letters to Howard Irwin were postmarked from diverse places: Illinois, North Dakota, Wisconsin, Ontario, and Missouri.

Before Irwin departed for Australia, he and Pearl had managed to rendezvous for Christmas in 1910. This was the last time Pearl ever saw him.

Shortly afterward, Irwin learned a hard lesson in the need to keep secret his wanderlust. Usually, once Irwin and Sutehall arrived in a new city, one would find a job within hours and then, a few days later, would recommend the other to the new employer.

George Tulloch's son, Matt, discovered that the plan to finance their journey did not always work. Matt was one of the conservators working to restore and reveal the words of Howard Irwin's diary. The process was fascinating but slow. Some bug in the rusticle nest apparently loved sulfur and had been building a black sulfide patina between the pages. Nonetheless, Matt found in each newly revealed passage a sense of wonder that made him think of another Howard from Mr. Irwin's time: Few men since the day Egyptologist Howard Carter entered the tomb of Tutankhamun (a pharaoh better known as King Tut) had known moments such as this.

As the sulfur was cleared away, Matt noticed that there were several jobs Howard Irwin found that he did not keep for very long—evidently because he did not know when to keep quiet. "And there was one in particular that I recall," Matt said, "[of] which Howard Irwin wrote, 'Got fired today for giving notice.' And I think what happened was that he gave notice very shortly after he got the job. And so I think, probably, the employer got a little annoyed that he had such a good job and then didn't tell him he was going to be leaving so soon."

Meanwhile, letters from Pearl Shuttle began, like pieces of an archaeological jigsaw puzzle, to fill in some of the events unrecorded in Irwin's diary entries.

After their Christmas 1910 rendezvous, Howard Irwin and Pearl Shuttle wrote—each to the other—nearly every day, into February 1911. Then despite Irwin's desire to be more deserving of Pearl Shuttle by becoming more like his friend Henry Sutehall, his self-described temper and impatience got the better of him. As he did with his former employer, Irwin once again said too much.

While he freely wandered the world, Irwin became increasingly resentful of Pearl's travels. He had begun expressing insecurity about a man described in her letters as a brotherly musician named Albert. Irwin's letters clearly placed Pearl in the position of having to explain that she would never have mentioned her friend in the first place if she had been sneaking around. Subsequent letters were aimed at reassuring Irwin that she had been and would forever remain faithful to him.

By February 21, 1911, Irwin must have sent a particularly accusatory letter. On this day, Pearl wrote to explain that even though she loved him and would forever love him with all her heart, if he believed that he could not trust her and was insisting that she quit her career for no good cause, then she wished he would never correspond with her again. Pearl had a good sense of dignity, and she ceased writing to Irwin.

As the months progressed through the summer of 1911, Pearl's mother, Ann Elizabeth Shuttle, wrote to Irwin during his travels, bringing him the news that Pearl still loved him and that in spite of his absence and his stubborn nature, she had remained entirely faithful to him.

All of us who were reading and hearing of each new paragraph being freed from the sulfur, felt, ever more strongly, a sad kinship with the long-dead Egyptologist (Howard Carter) who had reconstructed the life of King Tut, another young man from another lost era. It was clear from Ann Shuttle's last letter, as the autumn of 1911 approached, that Pearl always expected Howard Irwin to mature into the man he aspired to become, and that he would afterward come back to her.

There the story from the vault of the abyss began to break off, dead-ending altogether just before April 10, 1912.

Archival research revealed that on March 14, 1916, the White Star Line awarded Henry Sutehall's father two hundred dollars (worth approximately eight thousand dollars in 2011) for the loss of his son aboard the *Titanic*. Irwin was also presumed dead, but even though a ticket had been purchased, no one ever did find a record of him actually boarding the *Titanic*, so the White Star Line probably did not consider awarding his family anything.

"Of course there would be no record of him," Matt Tulloch said. Throughout the 1996 expedition, the prevailing view (based on the deck of marked playing cards and Irwin's mention of having won a racing sweepstakes in Australia) was that he had most likely evolved into somewhat of a professional gambler. Not knowing yet about his being shanghaied, it was possible for us to imagine him as being one of the card sharps known to have infiltrated all classes on the ship, and we thought that he might have boarded the *Titanic* under a false identity.

The consensus view turned out to be false. After the Tullochs located Barb and Dave Shuttle, the message was driven home (again) how quickly everything we thought we knew about the *Titanic* and its people could be proved wrong.

Among the valuables left behind in Irwin's trunk were his wallet and travel papers. The wallet contained a card identifying him as a member of a fraternal club that still existed in 1996 and that had maintained records ever since 1910. What chilled the club's secretary, when Matt Tulloch visited, was that the Tullochs were not the only people who had been asking about Howard Irwin in recent years.

About 1990, an elderly woman had arrived, asking if the club had any letters on file about a man who had disappeared without a trace in April 1912. She was seeking any hints that Irwin might have been an undocumented passenger aboard the *Titanic*. The secretary could not recall the woman's name. He remembered only that she had asked if they had a record of their former member reaching Southampton in time for the maiden voyage.

Before the document search was completed, the woman, like Irwin, had disappeared without leaving any forwarding information. "Died of natural causes at advanced old age," the secretary believed. Our instant and enduring question was, "Could this have been Pearl Shuttle?"

In 1912, after being held captive on an Egypt-bound tramp steamer, Irwin was able to make a successful escape from Port Said. He wrote about his escape, and about Pearl Shuttle, in a new set of diary entries that were still being lovingly preserved by his descendants when Dave and Barb Shuttle introduced themselves to Matt Tulloch and the French conservators.

By the time he reached Lebanon, Irwin had learned that the *Titanic* was gone and that most of the third class had gone with it. For many months, he continued to hold out hope that his friend Henry Sutehall was still alive; but eventually he gave up hope for Henry, and he also supposed that Pearl Shuttle had by then given up hope on him and must surely be engaged or married.

Irwin knew that Sutehall's personality would have made him particularly vulnerable to following orders and staying below till the very end while the first-class men rowed away in lifeboats, sometimes with their dogs. It must have gnawed at Irwin's very soul that had he been there with his friend, he might have added at least some slim, street-smart hope of saving him.

Despite a tendency to run toward historic revolutions, Irwin seemed to have formed a resolve then to disappear anonymously into history.

He had no way of even guessing how the *Titanic* had broken apart; he certainly could not imagine that his steamer trunk was afterward cast free perfectly unharmed or that when it filled with water and fell to the bottom, its interior became the biological equivalent of a shock cocoon—much less that people would descend in machines unimagined in 1912 and find it. In her letters to Irwin, young Pearl, even as she too disappeared into history, had no way of knowing that she was writing history.

The man to whom Pearl had professed her undying love wandered alone, from country to country, in the aftermath of the *Titanic*, picking up one odd job after another and carrying out the work with none of his former enthusiasm. It was as though much of the life had drained out of Irwin's heart once he accepted that both Henry and Pearl were lost to him.

Not very far ahead of World War I, Irwin reached England. He was by then a homeless world wanderer who neither possessed nor cared to possess citizenship papers or money for passage to America. So he stowed away in the front cargo hold of the *Olympic*, becoming one of the nameless, penniless world travelers fireman George Kemish had described.

One day, Howard Irwin walked onto his parents' property, so broken that at first they did not recognize him. The Irwins had counted him among the *Titanic*'s dead; and they were nearly half right. The son who came home seemed to have lost his prior lust for life and to have aged two decades in barely more than three years.

Irwin had not heard from Pearl's mother in Ontario since several months before the *Titanic* went down. He knew that Ann Shuttle, like his own parents, must have accepted by now that he had died with Henry Sutehall. Having accepted the certainty that Pearl had long since given up on him, had healed from her grief, and was most likely starting a family of her own, he decided against opening up old wounds—which at best could only interfere with the course of her life. Irwin's way of finally proving his love was to let Pearl go, to let her continue believing he was dead, to let her be with another and never see her again.

Eventually, the wounds that almost killed Irwin's spirit scabbed over and became relatively unnoticed scars. Eventually, he loved again. Ivy Corristone stayed with him until death did part them in New Jersey in 1953. Irwin left behind, among his papers, several handwritten poems about his friend Sutehall. To Pearl Shuttle, in the autumn of his life, Howard Irwin penned a final poem, in which he envisioned her as by now having become a beautiful, matronly woman with children and grandchildren. In that very last poem, like the Australian thorn bird eloquently singing out the last of its life, Irwin reached out to Pearl—wherever she was, to step back if she could, just for a moment—to step back across time and touch, if she could, "the times of pure and innocent love . . . so many years earlier."

"Howard Irwin's treasures had resurfaced through the efforts of an expedition to the world's most famous wreck site," Barbara Shuttle wrote after meeting the Tullochs. "The story of a man who never sailed aboard the *Titanic* and the letters from a girl who loved him would shed light on a part of the great ship's history never before known."

Through the history of their own family, Dave and Barbara Shuttle were able to shed light on the identity of the elderly woman who visited the Boston fraternal club asking about Irwin, some seventy-eight years after the *Titanic* sank. The woman was definitely not Pearl.

Although Pearl Shuttle had continued to profess her love for Irwin until the end of her life, the reason her mother's letters broke off in the autumn of 1911 was that Pearl had become very ill after an outbreak of influenza swept through much of North America. In October, the sickness settled into her lungs, and on October 20, 1911, she died of pneumonia.

In 1913, Irwin had firmly resolved not to let Pearl know that he was alive. He never learned that in 1911, an unimaginably distraught Ann Shuttle had decided not to tell him that Pearl was dead. For Matt Tulloch, the unexpected story of Howard and Pearl had brought to life a tragedy hitherto unsuspected, through artifacts that allowed scientists and historians to reach across time "in direct association with someone."

The very concept of two world adventurers financing their travels mile by mile, country by country, had to be a rare occurrence all by itself, even without the introduction of doomed love. "When you hear about something like this," Matt Tulloch observed, "it just makes you wonder what other strange things were [happening]. It's probably not a far reach," he said, to suspect that this one revelatory tale from one randomly sampled steamer trunk could not possibly have represented "the strangest thing that was going on aboard the *Titanic*."

22

Terminal Velocity

SEPTEMBER 22, 2001
RUSSIAN RESEARCH VESSEL *KELDYSH*
EXPEDITION *TITANIC XIII*

I told Jim Cameron about the tiny red octopus with the extraordinarily thin arms that stayed with me, outside my viewport, for what seemed a very long time. Jim said it sounded to him like a species described down here only once before. I added that when I bent down to write some notes and looked up again to discover that my "friend" was gone, I suddenly felt the most profound sensation of loneliness I have ever known.

"Every once in a while, the sea tosses you a gift," Jim Cameron replied. "That was one of them."

While gliding over the sea floor, near the starboard anchor, we saw a broken octagonal floor tile—then more flooring, identical to flooring fragments seen strewn along the boat deck and in the reception areas. This material appeared to have been dislodged by the down-blast as it pounded down through the vacant grand stairway shaft and surged outward along the boat deck and the promenade deck.

Our bot, Jake, continued to reveal surprises around every corner. Venturing beyond the influence of currents reaching down through the cargo hold's shaft, the bot illuminated an environment that clearly became more anoxic. Crabs, deep-ocean corals, and anemones were suddenly absent. Beds in the crew infirmary and adjacent rooms were intact, along with undecayed but mauled and broken wooden furniture, yet a bedspread and a pillow tucked under a sheet were somehow unmoved by the mayhem of April 14–15, 1912. Jake glided in for closer views of what appeared to be long white rusticle-like growths sprouting in spiral shapes. The bot's thrusters broke the feathery rusticle "cousins" into flying strands of bacterial biofilm. Along one corridor, a microbial fog hung in a distinct, sheetlike layer, about a quarter of a meter (less than a foot) above the deck.

The bot revealed powerful forces at work that treacherous night in some of the foremost crew areas. Deck-mounted, iron-framed tables were all blown down in the direction opposite the one we would have expected, emphasizing the many random processes that came into play during the first seconds of contact with the bottom. The combined effects of rupturing hull sections, the column collapse, and the down-blast were a little more complicated and varied than we had believed. Water had been jetted and blocked and must have rebounded in multiple directions at once. Down-blast and other inertial effects were not a simple affair. For all of the evidence of destructive force, seen in every direction, this time the *Titanic* was, for me, becoming a strangely peaceful place—at least, until we ended up inside it.

As with most crises, more than one normally orderly event was required to go wrong and converge; and in our case, only one needed to go right and save us. So it began, at 4:40 p.m., a little more than six hours after we had left the surface.

A careful examination of the number 1 cargo hatch's rim had confirmed that it survived the sinking without the slightest damage. This meant that the huge dent in the number 1 cargo hatch cover occurred after it left the rim and surged forward, most likely as it rocketed past the anchor crane on the prow.

The secret to providing floodlighting into the cargo hatch for Jake was for us to trim the *Mir-2* a few degrees forward, because our lamps could not normally be aimed straight down. We pumped down to a slightly more negatively buoyant condition than usual and leaned partway into the shaft, during what could, at any moment, develop into a precarious balancing act on the rim. Pumping down to negative buoyancy consumed a fair percentage of battery power and required at least three minutes. Pumping up again consumed just as much time and power. When you were negative, you stayed that way for a while. This was not a time for mistakes.

Two decks below, we could see the little bot from the *Mir-1* moving among the steel columns. Our pilot, Victor Nischeta, invited Lew Abernathy to move toward the large central viewport and shoot clear photos of Jake in the pit, and without warning I heard the whir of engines above our heads (normally, within this thick shell of metal, one hears *nothing* of the engines)—and, that quickly, we were tipping forward, and my view of Jake was improved enormously because he was moving up toward us. No—correction: we were moving down toward Jake.

Abernathy had just slipped against the forward throttle, punching it to full speed. We were at negative buoyancy and going in on a trajectory that could not be broken by pumping up to positive buoyancy. The *Titanic* seemed to have an affinity for victimhood by mathematics. This time it was geometry.

To appreciate the math, one had to imagine the *Mir* as a football, perfectly shaped to make a lengthwise "swish," face-first, through a basketball hoop (the diameter of a circle equal to the width of the number 1 cargo hatch). The problem was that the football could never be backed out through the hoop, if it leveled out to any configuration other than pointy end first. If we crashed down near Jake, an uppercut punch from the deck below could level us out beneath the "basketball hoop" and preclude all thoughts of egress. The shape of the number 1 cargo hatch, combined with the worst possible angle and the full-ahead thrust, created the perfect mathematical combination for permanent residency on the *Titanic*.

Nischeta had seen incidents that required one *Mir* to pull the other *Mir* out of a tight corner—but nothing to compare with what happened during those first critical three seconds at the number 1 cargo hatch. The pilot knew that in this case, we would not be dealing with a crevasse in some frozen extrusion of lava trapping one of the helicopter-like landing skids. In this case, under the only cargo hatch rim that had been reinforced specifically to resist waves crashing over the bow, one submersible could easily get trapped trying to rescue the other—and, depending on our final location and angle, it might therefore be logical not to try.

As Jake and the inside of the *Titanic* loomed toward us—all of this unfolding within only three seconds—I glanced up toward the floodlights and realized that it might never come down to two days inside the

Titanic, waiting for hypothermia to wear us down. Our light booms weren't going to make it inside. If one of the thick bulbs struck the rim of the cargo hatch at just the right angle, with just the right amount of blunt force, the bulb would implode at several times the speed of sound. The resulting shock wave would herald a chain reaction of lamps imploding along the girder until it reached into the crew compartment and the cells in our bodies were reduced at supersonic speed to individual organelles and broken protein chains.

Nischeta was a very reserved, very quiet engineer and pilot. I never knew he could scream at my seven-year-old's pitch.

I did not hear what Abernathy said at that moment. The only words I whispered, as I watched Jake and the deck below tilting toward me at an irrational angle, were "This is one of those things that's bad, right?"

Then followed one of the most amazing acts of piloting I had ever seen or likely would ever see. In one fluid motion, Nischeta seized the controls, and the whir of engine noise coming down through the hull grew even fiercer. The only way I can describe how we survived is to say that there seems to be a unity of feeling between submersible pilots and their machines, very reminiscent of the empathy between experienced riders and their horses. It was as though Nischeta could feel the outer hull of the submersible as an extension of his own skin—as though he sensed within an inch or two the distance from the *Mir-2*'s skids and fiberglass skin to the nearest side of the number 1 cargo hatch rim and was therefore able to back us out, without hitting anything, in precisely the angle at which we had been going in. Full astern with some skilled maneuvering, and we were safe—once again on the rim, aiming our lamps down into the hold.

It occurred to me immediately that an action hauntingly similar to the one William Murdoch had called for (full astern) — an order argued by some historians to have hindered the *Titanic*'s steering and guaranteed that she would be on the bed of the Atlantic for us to explore—had, in this case, saved us.

The only damage done appeared to be Abernathy's avalanche of rusticle debris—most of which fell down upon Jake as a plume of red dust.

Jim Cameron continued maneuvering Jake down the foremost cargo hold, where George Kemish's stowaway housekeepers had lived and died near William Carter's Renault Town Car. Jake glided over intact wooden crates that had been jumbled into piles from the tilt, the plunge, and the crash. One crate had broken open, spilling out a pile of books. In another corner, a large piece of cargo was still tied with rope to the floor, and brass fixtures gleamed in the red fog banks, but no one could make a determination whether the battered object was a car. The fog of rusticle dust was too thick.

Cameron, whose sub was more than fifteen meters (about fifty feet) away on the other side of the foremast, must have suspected something, for he called over to us, mentioning the rusticle dust storm and asking how we were. Abernathy instructed Nischeta exactly what to say: "We just adjusted our position a little while ago to give you better lighting. We are fine. How are you?"

"New rule," I told Nischeta. "Every time Big Lew almost gets us killed, he owes each of us a beer."

23

❧

Laying the Music to Rest

On the bridge of the rescue ship *Carpathia*, Captain Arthur Rostron held out some small hope that he might find the *Titanic* still afloat. What all but dashed his hope was a series of messages received between 1:30 and 1:35 a.m. *Titanic* time, warning ominously that an "engine room" was being flooded; then, about 1:45 a.m., came a weak Morse code cry, "Full up to boilers." The only possible interpretation was that by 1:45, water was actively threatening all six boiler rooms. The sea could not have been reaching the engines and the boilers unless something inside the *Titanic* had gone terribly wrong with the watertight bulkheads as well as the hull and the ship was in position for its final plunge.

At about 2:10 a.m., the *Titanic*'s wireless shack had radioed out two V's in Morse code, each V consisting of three dots and a dash.

The *Olympic* had called out for a status update from its twin just minutes before the two V's. The *Titanic* seemed to be acknowledging the call but provided no further information, although the *Olympic*, the *Baltic*, and the *Frankfurt* continued calling the *Titanic*. One after another, the ships' wireless logs began recording, "All quiet now."

About 3 a.m., the *Carpathia* called out to the *Titanic*, advising it to stay alert for the *Carpathia*'s own rocket signals "if you are there." The logs of all the ships listening in recorded, "No reply."

• • •

As the first faint glimmers of dawn came over the horizon, a stiff wind came with them. The *Carpathia*'s prow was nosing around the side of an iceberg about the time that Fifth Officer Harold Lowe raised a sail and set off in search of lifeboats that were damaged and in need of help. He did not have to sail very far before he came upon boat A, with approximately twenty men and one woman still alive.

Headed in the same direction, Celiney Yasbeck's boat came upon the staircase. In the same lifeboat, Marjorie Newell observed decorative wood trim floating everywhere—"and what looked like an entire story of the grand staircase sticking out of the water, ten or twelve feet high."

The stairway on the ocean appeared to be surrounded by cakes of ice, which made sense to Marjorie, given that sunrise was plainly revealing several icebergs drifting nearby. What did not make sense to Marjorie, when she looked closer, was why it should be that the cakes of ice were all the same size. "Oh, no . . ."

Then she understood. The identical cakes of ice were really life jackets, scores and scores of lifejackets, enclosing the dead.

There was one more thing that did not make sense. The staircase was bigger than a lifeboat, yet there were dead people all around it. Had they all drifted to the wooden island *after* they died? How many had perished without ever noticing the island? Or had they all found it and scrambled for safety, sinking and tipping it repeatedly with their weight? There was a story behind the stairway and the bodies, but it would never be known.

Boat B appeared to have been left behind. Atop its overturned hull, Charles Lightoller and Albert Moss understood that they were all being kept above water only by the bubble of air beneath the keel. With increasing wind and the gradual development of ocean swells, the boat began to show threatening signs of tipping too far to one side or the other. All that was necessary to spill all of boat B's survivors into the sea again (including the recently arrived Charles Joughin), was for the tilt-and-burp effect to reduce, only fractionally, the volume of air underfoot.

Two more people, including the man Lightoller believed to be senior Marconi operator Jack Phillips, died and were lowered over the side. Lightoller commanded the rest to remain standing to follow his instructions for handling the swells: "Lean to the right. . . . Now, hold the middle. . . . Lean to the left . . ." Lightoller knew that inevitably they would weaken and miscoordinate their rocking motions with the sea, at which point they would all be sunk to their knees or spilled over the side, and the sea would probably finish them off in all of five minutes. Although it appeared that the time had come for even the most resilient soul to give up, Lightoller helped the survivors to keep a grip on their courage and to endure his precarious balancing act as long as a single drop of warm blood pulsed within them.

Their one chance at rescue almost backed away. Boat 12 was rowing toward the *Carpathia* with boat 4 in tow when the crewman in charge saw, in the distance, what he at first believed to be one of the *Titanic*'s funnels still afloat and decided that they should row away from it, especially after he heard what sounded like voices shouting. "Apparitions," he thought. "Ghosts of the *Titanic*." One of the boat B survivors, Jack Thayer, had no way of knowing that his mother was aboard a lifeboat that approached and then mysteriously began to withdraw.

Lightoller had concluded that the strange behavior of boat 12 simply meant that he and his crew were now so weakened by their ordeal that they were past the point of making their shouts heard. The thought of their shouts putting a superstitious dread into boat 12's commander did not occur to him as he reached into an ice-crusted pocket and withdrew his whistle.

"The piercing sound carried," Lightoller would survive to write, "and likewise [it] carried the information (for what it was worth) that it was an officer making the call."

As boat 12 pulled up alongside the wreck of boat B, Madeline Mellinger and her mother cleared a space for Lightoller. Thirteen-year-old Madeline was shocked at how frozen he appeared to be, clothed in nothing more substantial than a light navy suit with a seaman's sweater underneath. Two hours earlier, after he had taken charge of boat B, the clothing was soaking wet; now it was stiffened and crackling with ice.

Elizabeth Mellinger removed her cape and put it on Lightoller's shoulders, then rubbed his hands and arms and tried to restore circulation in his limbs. He seemed to recover his strength quickly. Though still appearing quite stiff, the officer stood up and took command of boat 12.

The usual command position in a lifeboat was at the tiller on the stern, but Lightoller gave his instructions from the bow to the superstitious seaman at the tiller. In this manner, they reached the *Carpathia*, where Madeline was lifted aboard on a sling, ahead of her mother. Lightoller saw that Elizabeth and everyone else went up to the warmth of the rescue ship ahead of him. Madeline watched him come up last, and then she discovered that she could not find her mother. While Joughin went to the ship's galley to have the chill removed from him in a warm oven, Elizabeth, who had left the *Titanic* in her bare feet, was taken to the *Carpathia's* infirmary for treatment of frostbite and for a level of hypothermia that had finally rendered her unconscious.

Madeline became the little girl mentioned in the newspapers, wandering from one deck to another crying out for her missing mother. Later in the day, the two were reunited. When Lightoller found them, he was so thankful to Madeline's frostbitten mother for putting her coat over his back and keeping him alive that he wanted to give her a sincere token of his appreciation.

"But I have nothing to give except this little tin whistle," he explained—the very same whistle with which he had summoned her lifeboat to his side.

Elizabeth cherished it till her death in 1962 at the age of ninety-one. In that year, sixty-three-year-old Madeline, in accordance with her mother's wishes, delivered the whistle to Walter Lord, the historian her family believed should inherit it for keeping the memory of that incredible night alive. The bond between the families was not to last, however.

"The whistle has a curious pitch," Lord told Madeline during a phone conversation, mentioning this only in passing.

"What do you mean?" Madeline asked.

"It's not the sort of sound I would have expected it to make," Lord replied. Sensing, then, that something was wrong on the other end of the line, he tried to explain further just how pleased he was to have Lightoller's whistle. "And, of course," he added, "the first thing I did was to blow it."

"Oh, *no*," Madeline said. "We had never blown the whistle, Mother or I—and in fact *no one* has—in all the years we owned it. And always, *always*, we believed Lightoller should have been the last one to do so."

"I did not know this," Walter tried to explain. Madeline did not speak to him for seven years.

Aboard the *Carpathia*, the arrival of seven hundred additional passengers put immediate and considerable stress on the food supplies. Linens were also suddenly scarce, and Juliette Laroche desperately needed towels to fashion into diapers for her two baby girls.

One of the earliest actions of the *Carpathia*'s crew was to start resegregating the passengers into their original, *Titanic*-based classes. A stewardess informed second-class passenger Laroche that there were no spare linens for her, so she devised and implemented her own covert plan to collect table linens during meals, sit on them, and leave with them when no one was looking.

Two women from first class soon heard about Laroche's plight and visited her, bearing gifts of extra clothing and linens. They were Madeline Astor and Edith Russell, both of whom had traveled with the Laroche family aboard the tender at Cherbourg.

Little Simonne liked the tall woman with the musical toy pig. Russell would continue to be friends with Juliette Laroche and her children in years to come. Laroche and her two girls clearly needed a certain amount of befriending even before they landed in New York, where religious leaders would soon be preaching from the pulpit against the sinners who brought God's judgment against the *Titanic* and the makers of mixed-race children. When anyone aboard the *Carpathia* asked about the racial makeup of the children, Russell would placate and shoo away the inquirers (especially those with the word *mulatto* on their tongues) by claiming that Laroche and her husband had just adopted two orphaned girls from China.

Passenger Kate Buss wrote from the *Carpathia* to a friend, "There are two of the finest little Jap[anese] baby girls, about three or four years old, who look like dolls running about." Buss's friend was the man to whom she had previously been engaged, and he now seemed a better bet to her than the "very agreeable" doctor who had gone down with the *Titanic.*

Any laughter Russell and Laroche might have shared while observing the ignorance of interlopers was short-lived. What few family valuables Joseph Laroche had managed to place safely in the pockets of Juliette's coat were soon stolen, along with the coat.

Long before the *Carpathia* reached New York, stories about the *Titanic*'s band, and the music it had played, were becoming the substance of legend. In Colne Cemetery, the marker above violinist Wallace Hartley's grave would bear the words *Propior Deo* ("Nearer to God"), a reference to the tune Violet Jessop thought she heard about the time the two V's went out from the Marconi shack: "Nearer My God to Thee." Author Helen Churchill Candee heard it, too: "And over [the hundreds that were left aboard] trembled the last strains of the orchestra's message—'Autumn,' first, and then 'Nearer My God to Thee.'"

In future years, many would consider the story of the song a myth. In some circles of historians and history enthusiasts, what the band played was to be hotly debated. Walter Lord was, for a time, swayed by Colonel Archibald Gracie's insistence that if "Nearer My God to Thee" had been played, he'd have regarded it as "a tactless warning of immediate death, and more likely to create a panic that our special efforts were directed towards avoiding."

A letter dated August 1, 1956, would tell Lord a different story, so convincing that a version of the hymn would be reproduced in Bill MacQuitty's film *A Night to Remember.*

Complete with sheet music, Roland Hind, an acquaintance of Wallace Hartley's cousin, a woman named C. Foulds, explained that Foulds was present at Hartley's funeral and was quite certain that Arthur Sullivan's 1872 hymn was used: "And," said Hind, "some people attended the [May 18, 1912] service who had been saved from the *Titanic* and who said that Sullivan's tune was the one played on the ship."

Hind also produced a copy of Elland Moody's April 1912 statement. He was a cellist who had sailed with Hartley twenty-two times aboard the *Mauritania.* "I recollect when chatting with him [Hartley] on one occasion," Moody said, "I asked, 'What would you do if you were on a ship that was sinking?'" They were on the *Mauritania* and actually out at sea when Moody asked this question, and Hartley replied, "I don't think I could do better than play, 'Oh God, Our Help in Ages Past,' or 'Nearer My God to Thee.'"

"When I speak of 'Nearer My God to Thee,'" Hind wrote, "I mean Sullivan's setting. That would be what the orchestra played on the sinking *Titanic.*"

Many of the survivors wanted to forget the music, and everything else about the night—all of it. Five months after giving testimony at the British inquiry, and on the six-month anniversary of the *Titanic's* sailing, Annie Robinson, Jessop's roommate, jumped overboard from a ship in Boston Harbor and drowned.

Lawrence Beesley would become known on Bill MacQuitty's set as the historical adviser who was constantly (and annoyingly) trying to insert himself into scenes. He confided that he believed that dwelling too much on the memories of "that night" had transformed the mental and physical health of many survivors—many (as MacQuitty believed) for the better, and many (as Beesley believed) for the worse.

Seventeen-year-old Jack Thayer would write one of the most detailed of all survivors' accounts for his family in 1940, just before his country and Masabumi Hosono's country went to war. In October 1944 Jack's son, Second Lieutenant Edward C. Thayer, a fighter pilot, was killed during the invasion of Japan's fortress islands. Six months later, Jack's mother died on the thirty-second anniversary of the *Titanic*'s sinking. Soon after, Jack himself was felled by a nervous breakdown and sudden bouts of amnesia; he drove away in his car, never to return.

Marjorie Collier's friend, twelve-year-old Bertha Watts, would grow up keeping the *Titanic* out of her thoughts. Seventy-three years after the sinking, when Robert Ballard's French-American team found the *Titanic* and a reporter from the *Toronto Sun* called for an opinion, Watts replied, "I don't give a damn."

24

A Fury Scorned

As the *Carpathia* left the western edge of the ice field, and the last four casualties of hypothermia were buried at sea, Kate Phillips ("Mrs. Marshall") must already have known she was pregnant, although her daughter would grow up convinced that she was a couple of weeks too young for her mother to know and must therefore have been conceived aboard the *Titanic*.

Nineteen-year-old Phillips was already a lost and aimless soul, certain only that she would never see San Francisco and was fated instead for a return to Worcester, England, branded as the destroyer of Henry Morley's family. Born of an extramarital affair, Phillips's child would, in the custom of the times, be branded a bastard.

Even as the first night aboard the *Carpathia* began to fall, Phillips's mind was racing in a loop, trying to find a way out. She was not the only survivor sailing toward scorn and fury. When Masabumi Hosono tried to sleep among other second-class survivors on the floor of the smoking room, he was shocked to see essentially every man in the room pointing fingers and mocking him. The abuse reached such an extreme that the Japanese efficiency expert walked out onto a damp, fog-shrouded deck and tried to sleep on a bench. In only a week, what had been a little more than a callous rumor until that first night away from the *Titanic*— that Hosono had entered a lifeboat dressed as a woman and that real women had tried to throw him overboard—would become a public accusation by Ed Buley at the American inquiry.

George Rheims would fare no better in the midst of a lost ship gestating into legend. Like all legends, the *Titanic* necessitated a search for villains. Even before the disaster, his father-in-law and his mother-in-law had refused to accept him. Their bitterness only intensified after they learned that Joe Loring had died on the *Titanic* while Rheims had survived.

In April 1987, Mrs. D. H. Patterson-Knight, the daughter of George Rheims, wrote to Walter Lord explaining that her grandfather—Joe Loring's father—had refused to ever speak with his own daughter again, because Loring would never have been aboard the *Titanic* in the first place had she not eloped with Rheims, and especially after his daughter had insisted on remaining married to Rheims.

"George Rheims was also said to have escaped in a woman's clothes," Patterson-Knight added. "When I was at the Mariners' museum at Norfolk, Virginia, in an area devoted to the *Titanic*, [I found that there] is a newspaper, listing among those saved, '*Mrs.*' George Rheims. It could have been a typographical error, though my family refused to give him the benefit of the doubt."

"What a fascinating letter," Lord replied. "I can understand your grandparents' bitterness but feel they were perhaps unjust toward Mr. Rheims—anyhow, as far as the *Titanic* was concerned. Many male survivors were labeled 'the man who got off [into a lifeboat] dressed as a woman,' but the appellation seems especially unfair in the case of George Rheims. He really had a harrowing time, and his account can be supported by several different sources. I have even found a man who remembered him in his underwear in boat A!

"This is not to complain," Lord continued. "It makes your letter and your background information all the more fascinating—(and intriguing, almost eerie)—and I am truly grateful to you."

By the early twenty-first century, a dozen theatrical and television films had been made about the *Titanic*. Jim Cameron's would be the first film to use the actual location of the ship on the seabed as a set. However, Bill MacQuitty's 1958 depiction of that cold April night, though filmed in black-and-white, was the first and last version to be produced by a man who, as a child, had stood with his father on the pier and watched the *Titanic* depart on her maiden voyage—and who grew up to sink it a second time on film.

A Night to Remember became the film that, as though by religious sacrament, was required viewing at the *Titanic* site during Cameron's 2001 expedition. It was also the last film to be made when scores of survivors were still alive and able to contribute details. This was also one of the best films that almost never got made. Bruce Ismay's family had attempted to stop production in every way legally imaginable, calling Lord and MacQuitty liars.

When Joseph Boxhall saw the first edits of the film, he clearly had tears in his eyes. The main thing MacQuitty wanted to know from him was, "Did we get it right?"

"Terribly right," Boxhall said, sobbing.

From the moment Edith Russell stepped onto MacQuitty's reconstruction of the *Titanic*'s boat deck, she was suddenly no longer her usual talkative self. With the exception of her occasional naps on his couch after Christmas dinner with the obligatory shot of dessert brandy, Russell would never again be known by the producer to go silent for so long.

"I can't believe it," Russell said at last, looking ahead with an expression like a war veteran's thousand-mile stare. "It was *here* that I stood."

25

Sleeping in Light

SEPTEMBER 24, 2001
RUSSIAN RESEARCH VESSEL *KELDYSH*
EXPEDITION *TITANIC XIII*

The stern turned out to be even more compressed between the reciprocating engines and the region above the propeller shafts than we knew. We had searched for ways inside, but Jake would never be able to fit between any two decks. Even if we could squeeze through, there was probably nothing to see. Almost everything inside appeared to have been squirted outside all those years ago. Along the starboard side, the contents of the hospital went straight out to starboard; so did pantry items and, two decks farther down, workmen's tools and a huge condenser from the turbine engine room. They were all ejected together.

The turbine room itself was clearly visible—not by way of robotic penetration into the stern but by nature of the decks having been compressed down upon that single engine with such violence that the tallest shape in the center of the stern is the engine's impression sticking up through multiple sheets of pressed (and steadily disintegrating) steel.

Jim Cameron's brother Mike said the twisted metal of the stern reminded him of the Bikini Island atomic test results. "It felt like death down there," he said. "All those people. Horrible, horrible death."

SEPTEMBER 25, 2001

The last *Mir* was on its way up from the expedition's last journey to 1912. The weather held off just long enough to give us four days straight of diving during a typically impossible time of the year for these waters.

The air pressure had been dropping steadily, and our meteorologist, Viola—who had an uncanny ability to feel and listen to the air after looking at the satellite printout and then provide a completely accurate weather forecast—said of the approaching storm, "Hurricane . . . is beautiful." We would have to leave soon.

Mike Cameron said that there were moments when it really did feel as though the *Mir* had the power to carry one's mind back to that horrible April night. He felt this especially at the stern, the presence of the people. He had felt a deep, instinctive part of himself looking out upon the violently misshapen metal of the stern and said to himself, "You don't belong here." Cameron interpreted this as an actual presence that projected itself toward him with a reassurance that no one would be hurt, but if the explorers stayed near the stern, it would be uncomfortable for them.

I did not believe in the motility of consciousness. I did not believe that some lingering resonance—a "soul," call it what you will—survives us and echoes downward along the stream of time.

Mike believed that some events were so large that they could not help but echo. Certain religions, he explained, seemed to be based on such echoes. Cameron's two brothers, Jim and John-David, held out some small possibility that the quantum universe allowed such echoes. It seemed to me that up to a third of the people with whom we were sailing believed in ghosts. I was a doubting Thomas, though, and I would probably have doubts even about the proof, if such proof existed.

"Still," I said to Lori Johnston, "I would love to encounter something I absolutely could not explain."

"There's an old saying about being very careful what you wish for," she warned, "because you just might get it."

SEPTEMBER 26, 2001

Even as we laid a wreath and left an approaching hurricane behind, the *Titanic* continued to bombard us with odd coincidences and haunting images.

Jim Cameron had told me of the white rainbow in 1995, and I had written about it in the supplemental log of the *Ocean Voyager* expedition:

"The 1995 [Cameron] expedition ended, for Jim, with an apparition the color of pearl. 'A white rainbow,' he had called it, as ominous and peaceful as it was mournfully beautiful. He was acutely aware that it had materialized during the final moments leading up to his departure, over the very part of the sea on which fifteen hundred people died—materialized amid white mist and sudden dead calm, as if someone were trying to bid him adieu." Six years later, it happened again.

Ken Marschall, Don Lynch, and I were below the decks, reviewing Jake footage in mission control when I glanced to the left, through a glass partition, and saw the television screens at producer Ed Marsh's workstation, each displaying the stern of the *Keldysh* and a white arch spanning the eastern horizon.

"I've never actually seen that footage," I called out to Marsh, then asked, "but why are we reviewing footage from 1995?"

"That's not 1995," Marsh said. "That's happening right now."

I ran up to the fantail and could scarcely believe it. Viola confirmed for me that this was a very rare atmospheric phenomenon, requiring a low-hanging fog of just the right density, with the sun burning through at a very low angle. She had seen the white rainbow only once before.

The talon of time, reaching out, I thought, and tried to shrug the thought away. The *Titanic* might never truly let us leave, especially now. During the September 22 dive, I had come to accept (though I was not at peace with) the hellscape I would soon encounter in New York. About four hundred feet from the surface, I remember rolling onto my back as we ascended toward the *Keldysh*, with eighty-nine years and the wreck of the *Titanic* behind me, receding farther with each passing second.

The human brain really is a time machine of sorts. Through sojourns of the imagination, time became elastic to us, and full of echoes. The white rainbow glittered in eight-minute-old sunshine. The sunlight of almost an hour and twenty minutes ago was just reaching Saturn and its moon Titan. It was 11:40 p.m., April 14, 1912, and the *Titanic* had just struck the iceberg. It was September 10, 2001, and William Murdoch's cranked-in boat davit was still standing before me on the starboard boat deck from eighty-nine years ago. It was late September 2001. It was 11:39 p.m., and our civilization had just glimpsed the iceberg. And whatever we were coming to, we were almost there.

26

Coming Home to Shock Cocoons

SEPTEMBER 29, 2001

All three of my children drew welcome home books for me. One of the twins drew a picture of Grandpa. Kelly-May drew pictures on four pages: a smiling family, houses, hearts, a tropical tree, a bowl, a rocket ship, and dinosaurs. Her sister Amber added the towers cracking and falling under an airplane.

As the threat of a war that was sure to stretch into the next decade projected itself toward us and as my cousin Donna's memorial service was scheduled, Donna's older sister, Sharon, retreated for a time into her autistic world. During my months at ground zero, there would be days when I envied Sharon her access to that private world.

• • •

The crater rim was strewn with objects and twisted shapes that could catch your attention and stop you dead in your tracks. In my case, the first sight that froze me in place was a mass of tangled beams from the North Tower, embedded in one of the Verizon building's lower ledges and arching down toward Vesey Street. I realized that I'd seen this awful geometry before, from precisely this angle: the shape of twisted ribs of steel arching down toward the *Mir-2* from the *Titanic*'s stern on the afternoon of September 10.

As with the *Titanic*, surge effects and shock cocoons were everywhere. FDNY captain Paul Mallery found it hard to believe that the greater part of his firehouse seemed to have been shock cocooned while a Greek Orthodox church nearby was carried away by the South Tower surge cloud, and the steel frame of the Deutsche Bank building across the street was cut in half. In the midst of a tsunami of dust and debris that started out at 120 miles per hour, slicing through steel and appearing to have turned everything it touched into dust, it seemed inexplicable to Mallery that more than two hundred injured evacuees from the South Tower were safely cocooned in his firehouse, so near to the core of the collapse.

The "miracle of Ten House" arose from a reinforced corner of the South Tower, which was pointed directly at Mallery's firehouse and acted somewhat like the prow of a ship cutting through a wave. At each floor, the "prow" needed only to survive and offer resistance for ¹⁄₂₀th of a second in order to put the firehouse safely behind the V-shaped wake of a diverging force.

The squat, nine-story building called WTC4 was also directly in line with the wake and absorbed a substantial proportion of the remaining force like a giant airbag. Outside the Ten-Ten House shock cocoon, nearly three blocks south along Washington Street, the surge cloud separated living muscle from bone.

Within the surge clouds of dust and debris that raced horizontally through the ancient Roman towns of Herculaneum and Pompeii in AD 79, the air flowed liquid, almost exactly like the surge that cratered the *Titanic*'s stern and spread out over the seabed. The superheated tsunami that swept through Herculaneum was eerie and provided only glimmers of understanding about how complex eddies and flows simultaneously converged and diverged, destroyed and preserved. In the

"Mansion of the Bicentenary," an offering of frankincense in a bowl on the second floor was shock-cocooned and flash-fossilized atop a small wooden altar while nearly half of the mansion burst apart and was flung out to sea. Such findings were strangely consistent with Edith Russell's cup and Paul Mallery's firehouse.

As the eruption column of Vesuvius collapsed and sent forth its first surge, the cloud entered the large arched boathouses of the Herculaneum marina with such paradoxical gentleness that here and there it might barely have riffled a child's hair. Were the dust and the air in which it traveled not heated to five times the boiling point of water, the people who took shelter under the arches would have survived within a shock cocoon. Instead, the cocoon fossilized whatever was left behind, faster than nerves could begin to register pain, exceeding even the speed of astonished thought.

The relatively cooler steam from vaporized flesh triggered a simultaneous implosion and drew contracting air and crystallizing dust inward against people's bones, freezing perfectly articulated skeletons within the shock cocoon and producing what archaeologists eventually came to call "the dead-alive effect." In one of the marina shelters, adults were seated in a circle, sharing food, while children slept in the center of their circle. The adults died in midswallow and midword. The children never stirred. The bones of one child, yet to be born, lay caged beneath his mother's ribs.

The column collapse and surge clouds of 9/11 were capricious. The same physics that swept half of a room away from Herculaneum's House of the Relief of Telephus, yet left a table setting intact on the other side of the same room, had killed two men instantly in the lowest level of the World Trade Center. Fifteen feet away from the two casualties was a shock cocoon that could have saved them. A broad section of steel-reinforced ceiling had survived. A table still stood intact beneath the intact ceiling, and chairs and lamps remained completely undisturbed in the midst of utter pulverization.

27

The Long Night of
Ellen Betty Phillips

When I sailed with Robert Ballard and Haraldur Sigurddson to the volcanic spreading centers of the East Pacific Rise in 1985, the first photographs and videos of the *Titanic* wreck site were brand new. At night, discussions about popped rivets and separated seams as the final cause of its sinking sometimes seemed irrelevant. The more we studied its watertight compartments and construction, the more we appreciated the *Titanic* as a beautiful machine, abused by people who drove it at psychopathic speed toward a fleet of icebergs on a moonless night.

From a certain point of view, the *Titanic* was the metaphor of a beautiful child born full of promise and then abused. In the dynamic by which the cycle of abuse continues through subsequent generations, Ellen Phillips, the baby born to Kate Phillips as Mrs. Marshall, would have to become a true survivor type—not only in the sense of surviving in the shadow of *Titanic*, but also surviving a mother driven insanely cruel by the *Titanic*.

Two decades after Ballard's Argo-RISE expedition, my daughter Amber would befriend a classmate who was surviving terrible emotional torture by a parent. Their teacher, it turned out, had survived such abuse herself. Amber and her friend and their teacher began what seemed to me insightful and instructive discussions about becoming a survivor type.

"As Amber told it," I wrote to Roy Cullimore, "each child comes into this world as a delicate piece of freshly blown glass. Usually a parent leaves a finger smudge on the glass, somewhere along the [child's] way to adulthood. Sometimes a parent leaves scratches. And sometimes a parent becomes a hammer and breaks the glass so that it can never be put back together again.

"I thought about it, and remembered what my mother had said about some of the cruel people around us, as I was growing up: 'The same hammer that breaks glass can also forge steel.' I guess what I need to tell the kids is that no one can do very much to change the behavior of the hammer. All we can determine is what our own reactions shall be. Are we really just glass? Or can we be steel?

"I know. I know," I told Cullimore. "The *Titanic* was steel. And look [at] what our beautiful little rusticles have done to her (to say nothing of a little frozen water)."

Kate Phillips "Marshall," penniless, pregnant, and scandalized, attempted to make a home for herself in the land to which she had been headed with Henry Morley Marshall. In 1912, even the child of an unmarried mother was reduced to *Scarlet Letter* status and cut off from many of the usual rights of being human. The social groundswell of the times could easily have driven people mad—which, in Kate Phillips's case, it did.

Phillips returned to her parents' home in Worcester, England, where Ellen was born on January 11, 1913. The birth certificate listed Phillips as the mother and, as was consistent with the custom of the time, left blank the space for the name of the father. As soon as Ellen was born, Kate fled the town, leaving her parents to raise the child.

In later years, Ellen would take the birth date as an indication that she was the youngest *Titanic* survivor, believing that she had actually been conceived aboard the ship on or about April 11, 1912. However, visible signs of pregnancy were the reason that Phillips had been rejected by a network of *Titanic*-aid volunteers in America, giving her no choice but to return home. Her departure from New York aboard the *Adriatic* on May 2, 1912, indicates that Ellen was most likely conceived about three weeks prior to the *Titanic*'s April 10 sailing. Phillips's discovery of a missed menstrual period would have been consistent with what by all accounts was a hastily arranged departure, attended by Henry Morley's brother and Phillips's parents—none of whom expected to see her again.

Although it seemed inordinately important to Ellen that she had been conceived aboard the *Titanic*, as "proved" by her birth date, pregnancies were much more likely to run two or three weeks early or late rather than to end exactly nine months after the date of conception. Given what happened throughout the rest of Ellen's life, most people would be able to understand why she eventually clung so desperately to the romantic notion that she had been conceived during the voyage itself, as the very last remnant of a father she loved dearly but never knew.

Ellen's first nine years were quite happy while her mother stayed away and allowed her to be raised by protective and kindly grandparents. Their house was located on the River Severn. "My earliest memory," Ellen wrote decades later, "is of sitting in the family punt [boat] while my grandfather strapped me in. 'We'll make sure you don't drown,' he would say. But I [didn't] know what he meant." Those first nine years with her grandparents were the happiest years—the last truly happy years—of Ellen's life.

One day each year, a strange woman started visiting "and smothered me with kisses," Ellen recalled. "But I didn't know her and I hated it." By then, her grandparents had moved to a new town and had started calling her Betty, instead of Ellen, to spare her the locals' gossip and stares.

In 1922, the strange woman arrived again, announced that she was Ellen's mother, told her that she had recently married, and—with legal documents in hand that allowed the transfer of not only the child but also monthly support payments from Henry Morley's brother—said that she was taking her away. Rather than being reunited with a loving mother, Ellen was ripped from the happy home in which her grandmother had delighted in designing and sewing her dresses and was thrown into a pit with a woman who could not look at her child without seeing a bitter reminder of the *Titanic*.

"Don't look at me like that!" Kate Phillips would often yell. "Your eyes! That's the way your father used to look at me—how he looked at me on that last night."

To all outward appearances, Phillips was a friendly and compassionate pillar of her new community. Inwardly, she had evolved into the sort of beast who would draw the curtains before the beatings began so the neighbors would not see. She made an exception to such secrecy with her parents, who were allowed to visit every August. Phillips would hit the child in front of them, as though daring them to say or do anything about it.

"The shock of the *Titanic* must have disturbed my mother's mind," Ellen would say in 2002. The Russians aboard the *Keldysh* were less understanding or forgiving of Phillips. Coming from a country whose people took their pessimism in stride, they judged that mental illness and drunkenness only brought out the real personality that hid behind one's everyday facade. In the Russian view, Ellen's mother must have been the sort of child who would have crushed a butterfly or kicked a puppy when she thought no one was watching.

"She used to cane me on the back of my legs as I walked upstairs," said Ellen, who in defiance of her mother began calling herself Betty, the name her grandparents gave her. "[I] had fleece-lined knickers down to the knees and the fluff [the sheep's wool] would stick to the cuts. I kept pulling at them, and one day my friend Elsie asked what the matter was."

Betty (as she insisted people now call her) broke down and told her friend for the first time what was happening at home. Her teachers had seen the wounds and had asked what caused them, but for too long a time for any child to bear, Betty kept the truth inside.

Elsie had a choice: take the easy path and keep the secret or take the brave path and tell someone. Elsie's mother then had to face the same choice. She went to the headmistress of the neighborhood school, who called Betty to her office.

"I cried," Betty recalled. "I was so worried about what my mother would do, but the headmistress said, 'She'll never touch you from this day.'"

Betty wished, then, more than anything, as she would wish or pray for the rest of her life, that she could be returned to her grandparents. But the law of favoring the natural (biological) parent no matter what prevailed. Betty's stepfather provided the court with a written guarantee that she would be looked after properly and that his wife would never harm her again.

"And she didn't," Betty recalled. Not physically, that is; at every opportunity, Phillips blamed Betty for ruining her life and attempted to convince her that she was ugly, stupid, and worthless.

Then one day Betty's stepfather left, and Betty was forced to care for her increasingly angry and bedridden mother.

"About that time," Betty recalled, "my mother gave me a diamond and sapphire necklace and a [leather] purse with a pair of room keys inside. I didn't realize their importance, because she could never speak to me about the *Titanic*. Years later, I was told by her sisters that my father gave her the necklace as a token of love just before she was ordered to get into lifeboat 13."

The whole story was as strange and almost as distressing to Betty as it had been for her mother. "She was cruel to me, her own child; yet [as Phillips's sisters told it], while she was being rescued from the *Titanic*, she cradled a baby, Millvina Dean, in the lifeboat."

Every night before Betty went to sleep, she would kiss the photograph of the father she never knew. Despite her love for him and for the last symbol of a love destroyed and a future derailed, by 1999 economic hardship forced Betty to sell the necklace, the purse, and the keys to a dealer of *Titanic* memorabilia, who made them available for exhibition in Freemantle, England.

Clearly taking advantage of the blue sapphire surrounded by diamonds and set in platinum—and of its outward similarity to the central prop in Jim Cameron's blockbuster film involving a necklace with a stone named the Heart of the Ocean, entwined around a story of forbidden love—a promoter evidently named Betty's previously unnamed necklace the Love of the Sea. According to Betty's friend John Hodges, the dealer gave her a pittance for the necklace—barely more than the weight value of a sapphire, small "old cut" diamonds, and platinum-gold alloy.

Hodges had come to know Betty through a shared sense of tragedy. He lost his son in 1998 and missed him beyond words. He and the boy had been planning to start a restaurant together, but after he died, "there did not seem a lot of point," Hodges said, so he began to immerse himself in the *Titanic*. When Hodges met Betty, the bond between them was instant. He too, had grown up without parents.

Hodges described Betty as "a grand old lady with a great sense of humor, and she has a very moving story. The only problem is that she insists on being the youngest survivor. I have had a chat with her on occasion stating that she has a great connection [with the ship]—and the story, with both [of] her parents on board the *Titanic*, and that she was born just nine months later." Hodges tried to advise his friend that her story should have been enough, without any necessity of challenging Millvina Dean for the title of who was the youngest *Titanic* survivor.

In his letters, Hodges referred to Dean as "an equally grand and humorous lady ('I never take ice in my drinks'), and equally strong-willed." He believed, like most observers, that Betty's fight for Dean's title went back to the story of how, even before boat 13 reached the

Carpathia, everyone including Phillips, wanted to touch the littlest *Titanic* victim.

The point at which Dean drew her own personal line in the sand was when British *Titanic* enthusiasts, ostensibly taking her side, circulated rumors that a DNA test had proved Betty to have been conceived by a man other than Henry Morley "Marshall" after the *Carpathia* reached New York and that she was therefore illegitimate by another man and not by Morley. "Poppycock," Dean said in defense of her adversary, to which she added scornfully, "There are no 'illegitimate' children." As late as 2001, Betty was still trying to get the DNA test that would finally put Morley's name in the blank space on her birth certificate.

When Hodges read a letter to Betty from one of the scientists who was headed out on the *Titanic XIII* expedition, she enjoyed very much the mention of a hope to send a robotic probe into the second-class quarters. "And when I mentioned her father, her eyes filled with tears," Hodges wrote. "I did ask which stateroom her parents would have shared, as they traveled under the name of Mr. and Mrs. Marshall (as shown on the passenger list), but she did not know."

She had been in contact with relatives of her father's for several years, but they repeatedly (and rudely) refused to allow a DNA test.

Betty's story, Hodges wrote, had "obviously upset one or two people [in] the British [*Titanic*] Society." The organization finally claimed that she (unlike Madeline Astor's unborn child), was not a survivor in any way, shape, or form. The word *fraud* was even bandied about, and she became the only *Titanic* survivor, or unborn child of a survivor, ever to have been expelled from a *Titanic* organization anywhere in the world on account of not having actually been aboard the *Titanic*. There was considerable mockery attached to the claim of having boarded the *Titanic* as a sperm and an egg and exited as a zygote.

Dean, who was nine weeks old when she survived the *Titanic* in boat 13, was, if anything, amused to be an honored member in a strange porthole-measuring and rivet-counting subculture of human beings who would be feuding into the twenty-first century over which of the *Titanic*'s children deserved the title of youngest survivor or even legitimate survivor.

John Jacob Astor VI, who was born four months after the sinking, was universally accepted as having been present, albeit as a borderline last-trimester fetus. Joseph Lemercier Laroche was younger still: a first-trimester fetus when his mother, Juliette, boarded the *Titanic*. He was born on December 17, 1912, and was considered an unborn passenger of the *Titanic*. Only in the case of Betty, born (as Ellen) three and a half weeks after the Laroche child and most likely conceived about three weeks before her parents boarded the *Titanic*, was the status of any "unborn survivor" questioned.

There was no question that Betty had lived her entire life in the shadow of the *Titanic*. Her dispute with British *Titanic* scholars over which of Boat 13's children—Betty or Millvina—was "really" the youngest survivor was but another demonstration of the never-ending resonance of odd coincidence and even odder psychology that seemed always to have surrounded the *Titanic*.

Human thinking and the laws of clubs and organizations could try to make either-or arguments; but nature rarely works within humanity's either-or fallacy. Dean was the youngest already-born, breathing, and actively vocalizing survivor the night the *Titanic* went down. Astor, Laroche, and Ellen (Betty) Phillips were also aboard the ship. Betty was the wreck's Schrödinger's cat scenario. To some historians, she was simultaneously there as the youngest *Titanic* survivor and simultaneously not.

By the spring of 2001, the combination of resurging interest in the lost liner and the scarcity of survivors had brought Betty invitations to attend numerous *Titanic* conventions, to address school groups, and to appear on talk shows.

And so it ended with debates about survivors and the ever present multigenerational scars of the unthinkable. In November 2005, Betty would die knowing that she deserved, to one degree or another, a rightful place in the roll call of *Titanic* survivors. After Betty passed away, Millvina Dean held the title of the youngest and—more significant—the *last* survivor, until May 2009, when, at the age of ninety-seven, she single-handedly carried the entire legend from the realm of living history into archaeological time frames.

28

The Thieving Magpies

Violet Jessop's friend and idol, shipbuilder Thomas Andrews, had designed the *Titanic* from the keel up to its mast wires, adding davits that were intended to pivot back from one stacked lifeboat to another, loading and releasing them like shotgun shells. Andrews's own notebooks made clear his intention to provide enough lifeboat space for every passenger and member of the crew, but the Board of Trade laws did not call for any more lifeboats on a large ship than on a small one.

To provide more deck space, the stacks of boats behind the multi-launch davits were eliminated, and the number of lifeboats was cut in half. The watertight compartments would prevent a flood within the ship from spreading, and in principle (and under the law), the safety of the compartments permitted the reduction of the number of lifeboats. Then, to provide larger luxury suites, the Turkish baths, and broader uninterrupted floor spaces, the height of several watertight compartments along the center of the ship had been lowered almost a full deck. Andrews was overruled at each vital turning point. This did not seem to matter, because the watertight compartments (even if reduced in height) had rendered the *Titanic* worthy of the title put to Edith Russell when she had become nervous and considered leaving the ship before it left Cherbourg: unsinkable.

During the same year that the *Titanic*'s davits were having their lifeboat capacity reduced by half, 146 young women were killed in Manhattan's Triangle Shirtwaist Factory fire. The investigators concluded that a reason for such high mortality was the scarcity of effective fire escape routes and "safe haven" fire towers within the building. Until the year 1968, the post–Triangle disaster fire codes eliminated the concept of fireproof technology and called for reinforced smoke-locked fire towers and enough stairwells, widely spaced throughout the diameter of a building, to allow escape for all occupants. The Verizon building, built in 1927 and rising thirty-two stories tall, withstood steel beams crashing through foot-thick reinforced concrete floors when the North Tower's column-collapse effect struck the earth at 120 miles per hour and sent forth a pyroclastic surge cloud that deposited a pile of debris a story deep at the Verizon building's south face.

More significant, after the Verizon workers entered the skyscraper and began jerry-rigging emergency communications lines—draping them out of windows and along West Street—there were more than enough fire escape systems still intact when, after four hours, word came through that building 7, next door, was "fully involved" in fire and might collapse. Afterward, one could only look with admiration upon the architect. He must have been out to challenge the staying power of the pyramids. Even after the east face of the Verizon building was torn open by building 7's column collapse at sixty miles per hour, enough of the structure remained operationally intact for volunteers to return up the fire stairs and continue stringing emergency communications lines out the west side windows.

The same regulations that kept the Verizon building humming while everything around it failed had governed the construction of the Empire State Building in 1931. An insulated, air-locked, fire tower stairwell ran, as a single vertical shaft, through the entire height of the building. Five concrete-reinforced stairwells ran all the way down to the sixth floor, where they were met by four additional stairwells leading down to the street.

The Twin Towers of the World Trade Center were a beautiful design that was abused. The two towers differed from their predecessor skyscrapers in deviating from a steel-cage design. Borrowing from nature, each tower had much of its structural support moved to the outer frame of the building, following the same basic blueprint as a stick of bamboo. An inner tube of interlocking steel followed the same principle. This design did not answer the question of why the towers fell but rather of why they stood long enough, against impossible punishment, to permit more than thirty thousand people to escape the danger zone. The fault lay in safety systems and in lessons forgotten.

Like Thomas Andrews, chief architect Minoru Yamasaki had put forth the right design. It was the magpies who, turning bamboo resilience and new concepts in fire-tight compartmentalization into complacency, began tampering with codes and regulations and contributed, in a single day, to the trapping of so many people above the fires that the loss of life would become comparable to two *Titanic* disasters.

A new system of lightweight trusses that bound each tower's inner and outer bamboo tubes was strong, but in the event of a fire, a web of steel sheets and wires heated and softened faster than a network of I-beams. Despite the inherent strength of the outer and inner bamboo structure, the trusses became one of several Achilles's heels. As with the critical bulkhead between boiler room numbers 5 and 6, the steel did not actually have to melt; weakening alone was the path to a lethal cascade effect.

The next fatal decision involved the World Trade Center's analogue to lifeboats. In 1968, the laws intended to guarantee fire escape systems for all occupants in a building were rewritten, and Yamasaki's design began to undergo further mutations.

Gone was the traditional fire tower of the Verizon building and the Empire State Building. The six widely spaced stairwells originally designed into each of the Twin Towers were reduced to three, all concentrated in the central cores, each enclosed in plasterboard instead of concrete.

Prior regulations had required fire exits on each floor to be "remote" from each other—"so that a single problem could not obstruct all the ways out," observed *New York Times* investigators Jim Dwyer and Kevin Flynn. "The new [1968] code amended that language in a small but significant way: when more than one exit was required, each now had to be [only] 'as remote from the others as is practicable.'"

The rentable square footage for offices and restaurants with wide-open spaces and world-class views was multiplied by eliminating a fire tower and widely separated, fire-resistant stairwells. Technically, all of the necessary laws and regulations were being obeyed to the letter as the final design for the Twin Towers was put into place. Just as the letter of the law had produced wide-open deck spaces and required the same lifeboat capacity for Captain Smith's *Titanic* as for Albert Moss's much smaller *Hebe*, the letter of the law required the same number of fire escape pathways for a quarter-mile-high city tower as for an apartment building only seven stories tall.

But then, this did not seem to matter, because new engineering methods had rendered the old codes of the Verizon building archaic. The worst fires imaginable could easily be contained until firefighting equipment put the flames out. Sprinkler systems and advances in the science of compartmentalization had rendered the buildings "fireproof."

29

Monsters Down There

World War I was called "the war to end all wars." Human nature being what it is, the number, naturally, came later.

The *Titanic*'s surviving sister ship, the *Olympic*, was ferrying troops to the eastern Mediterranean for the Gallipoli (Turkey) campaign by the time Violet Jessop became a nurse on the newer, nearly identical twin of the *Titanic* called the *Britannic*. There were differences, of course. A double hull now came up the sides, rendering the vessel a "ship within a ship." The interior watertight compartments had thicker, higher bulkheads. There were more lifeboats, but they were largely considered an extravagant precaution, because the most recent advances in compartmentalization had rendered the *Titanic*'s sister floatable in virtually any situation.

The protracted disaster at Gallipoli developed from April 25, 1915, through January 29, 1916. A young lord of the British Admiralty named Winston Churchill sent Australian and New Zealander soldiers into one of the worst killing fields since Gettysburg. Much as Charles Lightoller of the *Titanic* was yet to develop into a legendary hero of the Battle of Dunkirk in World War II, Churchill during the campaign in Turkey was, by every measure of both promise and blunder, the Admiralty's Lightoller.

In 1916, Albert Moss was headed for his third shipwreck, and David Vartanian, who had survived boat A's Armageddon at sea, was coming to terms with what sometimes seemed a worse ordeal: his comforters. Though well-meaning, perhaps, they advised him to give up and finally accept the certainty that his beloved wife, Mary, was now a casualty of the war that had spread like a horrible spasm through the Ottoman Empire and erased his hometown as though by a tsunami. David Vartanian firmly resolved never to give up, and so did Mary.

Mary Vartanian was still alive, but during the complete breakdown of communication that accompanied the start of the war, she was told only that the *Titanic* had sunk with almost every man from third class and she must accept that David was among the lost. Friends and relatives advised her to consider remarriage, but David and Mary each refused to count the other among the dead.

After years of seeking out every clue that could be filtered through the haze of war and rumor, the man who in the United States became known as "*Titanic* David," prospering and (in most people's minds) an eligible bachelor, remained faithful to a presumably dead woman. Then, one day—in a miracle, according to his comforters—he found Mary alive. He took her to their new home, where they had a daughter named Rose.

Meanwhile, Jessop sailed into "too much history" (as she put it) again. When she joined the *Britannic*, the thin interior bulkheads about which naval architect Edward Wilding had been so evasive at the British inquiry were thickened and provided with stronger bracing so that a bulkhead collapse between boiler rooms could never happen again.

Few people, anywhere or anytime, had more cause to utter the words "Oh, no, not again," than Jessop. She had completed her field medical training while the *Titanic*'s twin was being converted into the world's fastest and largest hospital ship but which was instead fated to become the largest ship sunk during World War I.

The heating problems that had compelled Jack Thayer, Norman Chambers, and so many others aboard the *Titanic* to open their portholes were evidently not addressed during the construction of the *Britannic*, beyond the installation of electric fans in every overheated cabin. All of the design improvements to strengthen the hull and the bulkheads and to prevent floods, which were meant to preclude a repeat of the iceberg scenario and the boiler room number 5 collapse, would be like using bandages to stop a heart attack if excessive boiler room heat, seeping and radiating into the decks above, could be relieved only by the wholesale opening of portholes.

Still, there were defenses in place to prevent the *Britannic* from becoming another *Titanic*. Captain Charles Bartlett had a reputation for being, if anything, overly cautious. He was also considered an added layer of protection for the *Britannic* because of his proven ability to detect the earthy smell of icebergs and because of his policy of taking long detours and being willing to arrive behind schedule to avoid ice fields.

Unfortunately, the precautions set in place for ice fields did not apply to minefields. The evidence of this was visible all along the hull's open ports in 1995, when Robert Ballard sent Ken Marschall down for a landing on the *Britannic*'s portside hull, aboard the nuclear-powered submersible *NR-1*.

Marschall's photos showed the windows of the firemen's galley and mess hall levered open. On November 21, 1916, just before the impact of a mine on the forward starboard side, just before the 8:15 a.m. flood, someone had chosen how far to open those windows. The open ports gave Marschall a connection with the people and with a leading accelerant in the tragedy.

After the ship shook, Jessop could feel, in the deck plates beneath her feet, that the *Britannic* appeared to be drawing in water even faster than the *Titanic* had, as though much more of the ship were open to the sea. It seemed that way because it was. Excessive heat within the ship's cabins, combined with the lingering odors of gangrene and death from the last rescue run as well as unseasonably calm and warm weather, had created a lapse of judgment in which the crew had left many of the forward portholes on E deck and F deck propped open. Captain Bartlett had allowed the airing-out of the ship, apparently without any troubling thoughts. After all, like Maude Slocomb's friend Iago Smith, Bartlett could smell ice.

During the first two minutes after the blast, water was already entering boiler room number 6, and the *Britannic* began listing down toward starboard just as the *Titanic* had done. Bartlett swung the bow toward the Greek Isle of Kea, about six miles away, and ordered the engines full ahead, hoping to beach his ship with plenty of time to spare.

Aboard the *NR-1*, Marschall could understand why Bartlett must have believed he had all the time in the world. The *Britannic*'s watertight compartments were stronger, and some of them came all the way up to B deck; it was a more rugged ship than the *Titanic*. Bartlett had only six miles to go, and its sister ship had floated for two hours and forty minutes. Yet, there the *Britannic* was, lying beneath the *NR-1* on its starboard side, brought down by open portholes, still with miles to go before it reached Kea.

Marschall saw only occasional blemishes on the rails, davits, and other deck structures. Entire deckhouses were remarkably intact, marred only by a slight fouling under tiny stands of sponges and other sedentary organisms. What was regarded as fouling from a deep-water archaeologist's perspective, however, was rare beauty to the Roy Cullimores and Lori Johnstons of Marschall's world—especially when a new variety of rusticle awaited discovery inside the *Britannic*'s bow.

The "icing on the cake," for Marschall, was to glide slowly aft along the portside propeller bossing, watching it protrude more and more winglike from the rest of the hull until "there it was: the massive, twenty-foot, nine-inch-diameter propeller itself."

The *Britannic* had not yet been steaming ten minutes toward the Isle of Kea and was only about three miles nearer to land when Jessop emerged onto the port side of the boat deck amid a crowd of officers and sailors. An officer looked at her in surprise, as though to ask, "What are you still doing here?"

The first lifeboats had already been filled and had launched on the new electric davits, carrying most of the nurses and the doctors. An officer instructed Jessop that she must take a seat in the next lifeboat on the davits, boat 4.

As she climbed in, a strange sound reached Jessop's ears. The front of the well deck was beginning to flood, and the increasing tilt to starboard was lifting the tip of the portside propeller out of the water. The moment it began breaking the surface, the decreased resistance offered by air (relative to water), caused it to spin faster. By the time someone called for boat 4 to stop lowering and for the bridge to stop the engines, it was already too late. The two previous boats, one after the other, were drawn directly into the violent churning, hundreds of feet back. "Though hands were lowering the boats," Jessop reported, "eyes were looking with unexpected horror at the debris and the red streaks all over the water." Jessop, became the sole survivor of her lifeboat. Boat 4 shot straight through the rising propellers and exploded into shreds of wood and flesh, somehow allowing Jessop to escape with only torn clothing and a dizzying blow to the head.

By the time World War II broke out and the first war had finally been named, Charles Lightoller had graduated beyond his own

Churchill-like Gallipoli campaign aboard the *Titanic* to become a hero of the Battle of Dunkirk, rescuing 131 British soldiers from the advancing Germans. His yacht, the *Sundowner*, returned across the English Channel so badly machine-gunned and shrapneled that it seemed unlikely it should have floated long enough to complete the rescue. "We've got our tails well up," Lightoller wrote to his brother-in-law several days afterward, "and we are going to win no matter when or how."

Fellow boat B survivor Albert Moss returned to sea about the same time. While his family remained trapped in Nazi-occupied Norway, Moss transported freight along the British coast. When a V-2 rocket fell onto the docks, obliterating a ship near Moss, his ship, the *Munin*, survived to deliver ammunition across the English Channel for the invasion forces in Normandy. Captain Moss returned to Norway as a survivor of German torpedoes, rogue storms, and Wernher von Braun's rockets, but after Walter Lord's book, *A Night to Remember*, was published in 1955, all anyone ever wanted to ask him about was the *Titanic*.

Throughout the same decades, Jessop did not speak of the *Titanic* at all. In June 1920, the *Olympic* had been revitalized from its wartime function as a troop carrier and returned to service as a luxury passenger ship, with even its third-class cabins (now renamed "tourist class") paneled and "spruced up." Jessop joined the last of the three sister ships as a stewardess, keeping her history on the other two ships a secret.

The passengers were by then very different. Immigration was no longer management's bread and butter. The U.S. Congress had instituted severe restrictions on immigration that reached from Ireland across southern and eastern Europe, across Lebanon and India and into China. In the wake of the congressional acts, new profit margins developed in the ferrying of immigrants who had prospered in the United States into international waters, where even some of the politicians who had actively supported the Prohibition amendment to the Constitution used the *Titanic*'s sister to circumvent the law. The *Olympic* became a drinking and bootlegging vessel.

Jessop's niece Margaret would remark, years later, that her aunt became a master at brewing a particularly fine-tasting (and potent) tangerine liqueur. Jessop had looked after a passenger in first class who was proud to call himself "the chief bootlegger of the United States." She and all of her staff became expert at helping the *Olympic*'s passengers to dodge U.S. Customs. Jessop told her niece about voyages that became parties on all decks and across all classes; she prided herself on eventually being able to smuggle passengers' little bottles of grain spirits undetected beneath her uniform skirt—a method topped only by "one ample-bosomed stewardess [who] found that she could carry off a quart of champagne in her 'balcony.'"

In July 1926, when nine-year-old Walter Lord's family needed to travel abroad, the boy convinced his parents to book passage on the *Olympic*. Already transfixed by what to most people of the period was an arcane subject, young Walter took photos for comparison with the *Titanic*, and managed to talk members of the crew into giving him tours that included a view of the engine room. Soon he would be writing captions for crayon illustrations of what would become the first rough draft of a book he would revise over and over between the wars.

Lord missed meeting Jessop by a matter of only a few months, during which time she stayed ashore before transferring to the Red Star Line. It did not seem to matter. Eventually, their two paths seemed almost bound to converge. They were both in love with the same ship, drawn forever into its mystique.

In 2006, John Chatterton and Richie Kohler, of the famous Shadow Divers unit, arrived at the *Britannic* with a few new team members: systems engineer Parks Stephenson, Ballard expedition veteran Bill Lange, and deep-ocean explorer Carl Spencer. Spencer and Stephenson shared an impish sense of humor, but it was always difficult to tell when Spencer was joking and when he was serious.

"There are monsters down there, John," Spencer announced to Chatterton one morning. As though behind a mask of full seriousness, he spoke about deep-ocean explorer Ralph White's giants of the deep. Then, with a more relaxed expression, he added, "I'm *not* kidding."

An hour and a half after they arrived and a hundred meters (about 328 feet) deeper, during an attempt to follow the firefighters' tunnel toward a comparative study of the *Britannic*'s failure points with the *Titanic*'s, Chatterton encountered what appeared to be a new variety of rusticle—dripping with hard spikes. The rusticle thorns scraped their suits and the hard plastic shells of their rebreathers as they moved, offering more resistance and seeming to have built much harder shells than *Titanic*'s rusticles had.

That evening, Chatterton became violently ill and started running a fever. Food poisoning was suspected—possibly even infection from a deep-sea microbe. Spencer knew that rusticle infections were not unheard of. He had formed a close friendship with microbiologists Lori Johnston and Roy Cullimore, who were always on the lookout for new and seemingly venomous sponges, fungi, and species that had been turning themselves into cave-water and deep-ocean pharmacies.

Only five years earlier, one of their colleagues had managed to infect his mouth with rusticles from the *Titanic*. An entire iron-metabolizing consortium seemed to have gained entry through a microcrack in a tooth filling—which rested above metal posts that descended all the way down through a root canal. Two years later, the filling collapsed, releasing an odor that the oral surgeon assigned to the case had never smelled before. The bacteria and fungi appeared to have expressed little "interest" in the tooth itself; they had converted the iron within the tooth (and most of the material immediately adjacent to the iron), into what the oral surgeon described as "cheese."

"I need a sample of that!" the scientist with the infected mouth had said. "I have to get a sample to Roy and Lori."

"You can forget that idea," the surgeon said. "I autoclaved [sterilized with superheated steam under high pressure] the damned thing. You're lucky I don't call the CDC. What were you thinking, walking around with the thing that ate the *Titanic* in your mouth?"

Unlike that scientist, Chatterton developed no new forms of tooth decay. The ship's surgeon simply confined him to forty-eight hours of rest and rehydration and made him cancel his next dive.

In 2008, Carl Spencer was working with Cullimore and Johnston on further miniaturizing their microbiology monitoring and tracking systems for robotic Mars missions. Spencer had recently been shortlisted for a slot in the European Space Agency's Mars exploration program.

Five years earlier, Cullimore and Johnston had begun placing test racks on and near the *Titanic* and the *Britannic*. The platforms bore plates of steel with various amounts of sulfur and—to simulate microcrack-generating bends in the *Titanic*'s steel—both twisted and untwisted plates.

Spencer had mentioned a rusticle growing inside the *Britannic* that seemed different from the rusticles growing more than two miles deeper at the *Titanic*. This had puzzled the microbiologists, but there was nothing more exciting to true seekers than a new puzzle to be solved.

Only days after a platform was placed atop the port side of the *Britannic*'s promenade deck, just behind the fourth window, cameras revealed evidence of rusticles already taking root on the platform's steel plates (called *coupons*). During his May 25, 2008, dive to the *Britannic*, Spencer sent the rusticle platform up to the surface for analysis after five years on the promenade. The results were not quite what anyone expected.

Cullimore's metabolic tracking system revealed that the chief instigator of the nearly 29 percent steel loss on the test platform involved at least five different types of bacteria working together in distinct layers of an almost perfectly familiar, rusticlelike consortium: (1) extremely active, acid-producing bacteria, (2) very active species that produced protective slime layers over the consortium, (3) moderately active iron-oxidizing bacteria, (4) moderately active nitrogen-metabolizing bacteria, and (5) a lower layer of bacteria that mined (or dissolved) iron in the absence of oxygen. No primitive, hydrothermal sulfur-loving bacteria were detected in the *Britannic*'s test platform, as had been detected in the *Titanic*'s rusticle reef; nor were photosynthetic algae signatures found on or in the *Britannic* platform.

Although it was only a preliminary result, the indications were perplexing. The *Britannic*'s rusticle consortium was very different from the one presently turning more and more of the *Titanic*'s inorganic hull and deck plates and deep-ocean nutrients into its own DNA and skeletal structure. The *Britannic* rusticles also appeared to be more aggressive. They quickly doubled the surface area available for the mining of iron by dissolving pathways into microfolds made in the steel during the rolling process of manufacture. They were experts at bio-wedging the folds open.

The *Titanic*'s test plates were losing an average of 1.7 percent of their iron per year. The *Titanic*'s rusticle shroud attacked bent or stressed steel almost twice as fast as it attacked unstressed steel, which was consistent with the much greater deterioration of the areas near and behind the down-blasted gymnasium and with the year-by-year collapse of the even more intensely ravaged stern section.

The *Britannic*'s test plates were losing approximately 5 percent of their iron per year, yet the *Britannic*'s rusticles did not exhibit a greater efficiency at attacking bent or stressed steel coupons—which seemed consistent with the randomly distributed rusticle hot spots on and in the *Britannic*.

No one knew how long the rusticles had been colonizing the *Britannic*. A recent invasion was implied, for if the 5 percent per year decay process of the nearly six-year-old platform was an accurate indicator of what had been happening to the *Britannic* all along—at a rate more than twice that of the *Titanic*—the entire structure should have collapsed into pieces of steel plates by 1960 and been converted into a molasseslike mass of iron ore studded with glass and porcelain artifacts long before Chatterton became infected. The implication was that something in the *Britannic*'s environment had been changing in the relatively recent past and that the *Britannic* itself would, within a decade or so, be subject to rather sudden collapse as its steel ribs weakened to such extent that they could no longer support the weight of the hull. Something was causing accelerated rusticle growth on the bottom of the Atlantic, and it appeared that something very similar was happening in the Mediterranean. Deep-water environments were undergoing recent and dramatic change, and some of the scientists were getting a little scared.

In May 2008, the microbiology team had recovered three rusticle test platforms from the *Titanic* and one from the *Britannic*, along with an emerging database from DKM *Bismarck*, DKM *U-166*, and several ships sunk during World War II in the Gulf of Mexico. The results were consistent with the warning of a sea change, first recorded in the *Titanic*'s rusticles.

Spencer was helping to expand the *Britannic*'s database. On May 25, 2008, he planted Cullimore's newer, improved General Underwater Coupon Corrosion Installation (GUCCI) platform. The sending up of the old platform and the planting of the new platform on the *Britannic*'s hull turned out to be two of the last things Spencer ever did.

After setting the GUCCI rack and two new bacterial etching experiments in place, Spencer still had a few minutes remaining to himself before he needed to begin the slow, carefully staged ascent to the support ship. Like Parks Stephenson, he was intrigued by the intact Marconi shack, but the extra minutes to explore its interior had not been available before.

He was, at that time, using a new rebreather system. As part of a pre-ascent safety check, Spencer was in the process of changing to a fresh set of tanks when something went terribly wrong near the Marconi shack. The new system gave him too strong a burst of oxygen—which, at that depth, sent him immediately into convulsions. Two safety divers tried to assist him by adjusting the mixture, but the convulsions only worsened, so a decision was made to propel him to the surface in an emergency ascent that would miss all of the scheduled decompression stops.

Preparations had already been made for a situation such as this. In this case, *contingency ascent* meant that were there not a hyperbaric chamber aboard the support ship, dissolved oxygen and other gases in

Spencer's blood would—within a minute of his reaching the surface and taking his first breaths—begin to expand like foam in a freshly opened bottle of beer, throughout every capillary in his body, from his big toe to his frontal lobes. As in the classic film *2001: A Space Odyssey* (in which an astronaut is thrust briefly into a vacuum), there was time to avoid boiling blood and the bends as long as the original high-pressure atmosphere he had been breathing was quickly restored.

Fortunately, the National Geographic support ship was equipped with a portable hyperbaric chamber, in which Spencer was immediately restored to an atmospheric pressure equivalent to what he had been breathing three hundred feet under the sea. The entire chamber was then flown by helicopter to the Athens naval hospital, but Spencer never regained consciousness, and there was no way to revive him.

It weighed heavily on Lori Johnston that Spencer had been placing hers and Roy Cullimore's equipment minutes before the accident occurred. "I have guilt and deep sorrow for Carl's loss," Johnston wrote to a friend. From the moment she had met Spencer, just before his first *Mir-2* dive to the *Titanic* in 2003, they had become fast and close friends and had begun plotting new scientific adventures on and under the high seas. Their next adventure quickly followed: the 2003 *Britannic* expedition, during which the first test platform was planted.

"Carl was the expedition leader," Johnston continued. "I spent two weeks bobbing around the Aegean while divers took experiments back and forth to the wreck. During that time, Carl took the time to learn what we were doing—which sparked his interest in bacteria and the power that they have, combining his love of diving with science.

"I thought," she wrote to her friends and to Spencer's family, "maybe if he hadn't had to get the experiment that day, things would have been different. We will never know." What she did know was a lasting habit: "I have gone innumerable times to call or e-mail Carl about the latest adventure, or news [of a new discovery], only to realize that he is gone. How do you say good-bye? It's a question I am unable to answer, or choose not to, for now at least."

30

Ghosts of the Abyss

In the large volcanic crater called Ground Zero, it wasn't just the collision, the collapse, and it's over. There was the aftermath. As Ellen Betty Phillips, Charles Joughin, and Jack Thayer were teaching us all along, the aftermath could be worse.

The mind is a monkey. Time and again, everything came back to a distinctly human way of coping with loss, to unnatural levels of stress, and to primal rage. Perhaps this explained the ghosts.

By coincidence, when I reached the *Titanic*'s stern on September 10, 2001, Mary's friend Paddy Brown was suddenly so much on my mind that it felt as though he were somehow present hours before he died. At home, he left behind a strangely resonant prayer: "When I am gone [exploring], release me, let me go. I have so many things to see and do. And if you need me call, and I will come. Though you can't see me or touch me, I'll be near."

The mind is a monkey, I kept telling myself—the reason we human beings sometimes see and feel things that are not actually there.

As the World Trade Center surge cloud and shock-cocoon studies came to a close and the rebuilding of Ground Zero began, all of the surviving veterans of Ten-Ten House were retiring or transferring to other firehouses. John Morabito was the sole survivor of the team that went into the North Tower that day. Morabito had survived in one of history's most inexplicable shock cocoons, with the forces diverting completely around him and even levitating him gently on a bed of dust, while people around him disintegrated before his eyes. Many of his fellow firefighters were leaving Ten-Ten House, because they had seen ghostly silhouettes and, occasionally, shockingly vivid images of their old friends appearing and vanishing throughout the building. Morabito was the only one who insisted on staying. "If something of them really has stayed behind," he said, "then I don't want them to be alone, and *I'm* staying. They were my friends. They were my brothers."

As the sixtieth anniversary of the Battle of Normandy approached—and as studies of rusticles and a new understanding of volcano physics that began with the *Titanic* were maturing—my father was fending off lung cancer. He had responded very well to the least invasive spectrum of drugs available, but with time, through a process of natural selection, a tiny minority of immunized cells had survived and begun to multiply. The only chemicals the immunized cells had not seen before were sure to leave Dad with no quality of life and might even kill him outright. He had decided to "let nature follow its course."

This was also a time in which, during planning discussions for the next *Titanic* expedition, I began talking about what people claimed they had seen in Ten-Ten House during the months after the towers fell. That's when, very quietly, a few people began talking about having felt or seen similar figments at the *Titanic*—and especially at the stern. I did not believe that the apparitions were real, but their cause was certainly something to think about.

In late May 2004, I had just finished a filming in the seventeenth-century BC volcanic surge cloud layers of Minoan Thera (more commonly known as the Greek isle of Santorini). Dad was not yet in his second phase of sickness. I was in the process of moving my office into his house for the duration. We were both expecting that he would have at least a couple of months more of reasonably good days.

On the morning of June 1, I had appointments scheduled in New York City. The Thera filming had left me about a week behind schedule, but I was planning to make my rounds and return in the evening.

"Why don't you stick around and we'll go out for lunch?" Dad suggested. He also wanted me to look at three new car models with him.

For a moment, I thought about all of the work I needed to catch up on. Then, within the same moment, I felt (or imagined I felt) two powerful hands shoving my shoulders forcefully from behind. Paddy

Brown—again. In the harsh language Brown would have used, I more felt than heard him calling me the worst kind of idiot and saying, "Forget your job. Your father is your job today!"

Perhaps my subconscious mind was able to detect a subtle change in my father's walk, in his breath, or in the way he spoke, and perhaps one's ever vigilant subconscious could put unnoticed clues together to arrive at a conclusion not ordinarily noticed (or wanting to be noticed) by conscious thought. Dad did not have as much time as we believed. I would never have consciously guessed that we had awakened to share the last breakfast of his life.

Perhaps the figment of Paddy Brown was merely my subconscious mind sending up an alarm bell of unfiltered thought, communicating an assessment that something had gone dramatically wrong during the night and that this could be my father's last day. "Perhaps," most of my family and several of Paddy's friends said, when I explained it to them this way. "And perhaps not."

One of Paddy's closest friends had explained that he carried a terrible burden—guilt, even—from Vietnam. We spoke at great length about what I thought (or imagined) Paddy tried to teach me at the *Titanic*'s stern; and she (his friend) agreed that whether or not something of Paddy actually had been present down there on September 10, 2001, his "message" saved me from an undeserved burden of guilt. Now it happened a second time.

It is strange to think that I still believe the event was simply a matter of improbable coincidence. I remind myself again and again that every hand is as improbable as a royal flush. And if there are nearly seven billion people on the planet, then even the most unlikely coincidences are bound to pile up around at least a few of us. It's certain to happen, given enough people. Everything else is illusion. Yet strangest of all is to think that if what happened at the stern in 2001 had not recurred in my father's kitchen in 2004 and changed the direction of my plans for the day, I'd have carried, for the rest of my life, an unfathomable guilt for missing that last wonderful day with my father.

I do not know for certain that a subconscious perception was sent up to the front of my brain as a warning wrapped in the memory of a firefighter I never really knew. Although I have to admit that the quantum universe and cosmology are teaching us every day that we do not yet have all the science, the "evidence" of personal experience is a non-reproducible result, and scientifically, it at best provides an insight into how human minds react to the level of stress known to have generated the old expression "There are no atheists in a foxhole."

All I can say, Paddy, is this: whether you were simply the memory of someone I wished I had known better, kept alive in some corner of the subconscious, or whether you were actually there, changing my direction that day, the words do not exist to express how much I thank you, Paddy Brown, wherever you are.

Sixty years earlier, my father was joining the fleet that would send him and the rest of the 82nd Engineer Battalion ashore at Normandy, on June 6, 1944. He was written down for a Purple Heart and apparently at least one other medal that he made me promise never to accept for him or allow the children to accept. I knew he had lost much of his hearing. I knew that when a truck came through during the final "mopping up" operation, he had run up to the vehicle seeking help for friends whose legs were blown off and who probably would not live through the night. There were no medals for them. Everyone who ran up to the truck was written down for a medal. It was simply the nature of bureaucracy.

By August 6, he was caught up in the battle of Vire in France, and the tattered remnants of his team were awarded the French Croix de Guerre—the only medal he allowed me to accept on his behalf, saying only, "We *earned* that one."

Somewhere between Vire, the Battle of the Bulge, and the liberation of Buchenwald, he was captured by the Germans and, according to my mother, had survived being buried alive, evidently in a mass grave from which he dug his way to the surface. Dad had been claustrophobic ever since. He once said there was no way he could imagine crawling inside one of the *Mir*s and dropping two and a half miles down through black water to the *Titanic*. "You're a braver man than I am," he said, to which I replied, "Are you nuts? You were on the beach at Normandy! No one was shooting at me in the *Mir*s."

On June 1, 2004, we had gone out to lunch together, looked under the hoods of three cars, and spent much of the afternoon talking about engines. In the evening, I drove to my office, put my clothes from the Thera expedition in the wash, then headed back to Dad's place with some fresh clothes, a stack of notebooks, and my laptop. Forty-five minutes to an hour before I returned, he had died from sudden heart failure. Although I knew that if I had arrived an hour earlier and been able to resuscitate him, I'd only have been saving him to begin suffering the most claustrophobic effects of advancing lung cancer in the weeks to come, that night was nevertheless the beginning of the inevitable, corrosive *if only*.

Although my father had actually said at lunch that he could not believe what the next couple of months would bring and had wished that an almost instantly fatal stroke would intervene, a darkness began to grow in my heart during each day of the next month in which I fixated on this thought: *If only I had arrived in time to save him*.

All of that changed on July 1. I was driving toward a family get-together at the home of Bill Schutt, whose son and my children had become the best of friends and who happened to be the zoologist who first identified the lamb bones in the *Titanic*'s soup-tureen concretion. The ride on the Long Island Expressway to his home was a straight line with only one turn, in Riverhead, and that day there was neither traffic nor any other reason for me to make a sudden wrong turn off our usual, well-traveled path—except for Paddy Brown, again.

I felt his peculiar presence (or imagined it again) just before and during my wrong turn off the expressway. As soon as I was off the highway, a man came running into the middle of the road, waving his arms and screaming for help. No more than a minute earlier, a car had struck an eight-year-old boy on a bicycle.

If only I had arrived in time to save him.

Scratch any cat; might you chase out a flea? Look into any coincidence too deeply; might you find a reason? Put any person in a moment of grave stress and in a moment of coincidence, and he might begin to wonder if the universe, Paddy Brown, or something else (call it what you will) is consciously teaching him a lesson.

The boy's name was Joseph. He was not wearing a bicycle helmet at the moment of impact. I could feel at once that the damage to his skull, his brain, and his upper spine was severe. I started compressions, and a woman who came running out of a car identified herself as a nurse. As she took the boy's wrist, she told me that she was beginning to detect a pulse. In this instance a pulse was horrifying news: the light of life was coming back into his veins but not into his eyes.

This time (a month, to the day), I had arrived in time; but now, by every indication, if this child lived, I would be saving him for a fate far worse than the final claustrophobic effects of lung cancer. Whether or not the universe was giving me a lesson, I felt in that moment as though Paddy were showing me what I already knew in the so-called logical left hemisphere of the brain but what I had failed during the past month to feel in my heart. "Here you are, Charlie," Paddy seemed to be saying, "just in time to save someone. Now, is this a good thing or a bad thing?"

In my mind, in what some might call an agnostic's prayer, I said, "Okay, kid. If this is not as bad as it looks and you think you can still use this body, then stay with me. But if it's as bad as it looks, it's okay if you go away."

I kept working, even after I felt him go. Perhaps the mind creates strange illusions under the incomparable stress of a child dying under your hands, but illusion or not, I felt a child's laughter (completely innocent and even soothing laughter) passing directly through my right shoulder. As little Joseph passed, it felt as though a gentle hand, almost as an afterthought, reached into my chest—to my heart—grabbed the darkness that had been growing within me for a month, and took it away with him. I never haunted myself again with *if only* about my father.

I never distinctly felt the presence of Paddy again, either. Inside, I had a vague feeling that he had seen what I needed to see, put me where I needed to be, taught me what I needed to be taught, and then either gone on to other errands or to peace.

Science is based on doubt—on trying to explain everything away and seeing what still stands afterward. I have maintained my agnosticism, but I often still wonder about what some of us have seen or felt at the *Titanic*, and especially at the stern.

31

Persevering

Masabumi Hosono—the man who was accused simultaneously of being the Japanese "coward" the women of boat 13 conspired to throw into the sea and Colonel Archibald Gracie's "stowaway" who seaman Ed Buley said entered the lifeboat dressed as a woman—arrived home in Japan with nothing except his own good word as a defense against what by then had become newspaper gossip. Almost immediately, Hosono was dismissed from his job. Up until 1912, his work had supported him quite well, as indicated by his "Schedule A" listing of gold coinage and possessions lost aboard the *Titanic*, valued at twenty-five hundred dollars in 1912 (equivalent to more than a hundred thousand dollars a century later).

After the accusations and the firing, Hosono made a request of his family and his friends that they refrain from speaking to him about the *Titanic* or what the newspapers and the local gossip council were saying about him. He understood that no matter what he said, people would see only what they wanted to see and believe what they wanted to believe. Hearing of it could only depress and distract him. Sorrow and distraction would prevent him from trying to cobble his career back together so that he could provide his wife and his children with a future worth having. Decades later, his daughter Fumiko wrote that her father's request was never violated, largely because his family and his friends knew that he was a private, strong-willed, hardworking man who would do everything within his power to rise above the gossip.

Fumiko's father was also a talented man. By 1915, even his detractors at the Ministry of Railways realized that they needed him, and they hired him away from his "freelance, nonregular jobs" and from his design and upkeep of a rare and beautiful garden that reminded visitors of island pinnacles and river valleys sculpted in miniature.

Soon he began collaborations with a number of artists, in particular a self-reliant outcast named Gyotei Mano. During the difficult gossip years, Hosono commissioned Mano to paint landscapes and golden dragons on detachable sliding screens, with the probable intent, his daughter believed, of carrying something beautiful with him to their new smaller home, if and when he had to sell the family house. Fumiko remembered the bamboo bushes and snow-capped Mount Fuji on eight different silk sheets set in solid rosewood frames. In particular, she remembered "a majestic dragon that had cloud-piercing gold eyes and claws—each, on either side of the large partitioning screen."

Eventually the Hosonos did have to move, to a house that Mr. Hosono designed and built near the Higashi-Nakano railway station in Nakano, Tokyo. With no guarantee that they would keep even this home, Hosono continued his collaboration with artists. He produced for each of his children two painted scrolls—among them Fumiko's long-remembered and cherished painting of pine trees and a flock of cranes set against the rising sun. Hosono was passing along not only his love of art and architecture but also gifts he hoped would become seeds to awaken any artistic talents in his children, or even in his children's children's children.

History tried to intervene again, naturally.

On September 1, 1923, the Great Kanto Earthquake, ranging in magnitude from 7.9 to 8.3, leveled most of Tokyo and its surrounding areas, including Nakano. The port city of Yokohama, forty-six miles away from Tokyo, was also leveled. According to survivors' accounts, the clay earth moved like a storm at sea for a minimum of four minutes. Thirty-seven miles from the epicenter, the tremors displaced Kamakura's Great Buddha statue almost two feet. The statue was carved from a single block of stone and weighed ninety-three tons. More than a hundred thousand people were killed.

Japan's newspapers at the time were no more reliable than America's Hearst newspapers of the same period, with rumors and accusations promptly "scooped" as news. Quake-clouded well water led to rumors that Korean immigrants were poisoning wells, and the rumors were printed as news. This led to vigilante roadblocks throughout Tokyo and Yokahama, where (until the army intervened), passersby were being stopped and tested for accents and other indicators of ethnic identity. Many who failed to pronounce words properly were killed; the lucky ones were turned back whence they had come. Chinese, Okinawans, and even Japanese citizens who spoke Hiroshima's distinctive lilting dialect were often identified as foreigners.

Hosono, a speaker of foreign languages who had naturally developed an accent, faced significant danger if he attempted to travel. He stayed safely at his small, mostly intact home through fifty-seven aftershocks and the typhoon that quickly followed. The house must have been designed quite well. Like a lifeboat, it rode the waves of liquefaction. Every member of his family survived. Even his silk artwork endured unharmed.

During the next two years, Hosono's talents were needed full-time for the repair of the railway system. After two years of repairs, he began teaching engineering and continued to do so until he was stricken suddenly ill in 1939 at the age of sixty-eight.

According to Fumiko, despite her father's illness and "just days before his death, he had the grades for all of his students ready. Unable to go to the college, a school official came to him and [Father] handed him the list of marks. The act moved the official quite deeply."

Six years later, on May 29, 1945, the region was leveled by one of World War II's largest B-29 firebomb raids. Once again, the Hosono family and the delicate silk paintings survived.

In the aftermath of World War II, Hosono's example of persevering, remaining fiercely independent no matter what anyone else thought, lived on within his family. Artistic abilities and a love of technology also seemed to live on. Hosono's grandson Haruomi Hosono became a very successful musician in the 1980s technoband YMO. An orchestrator of the group's electronic keyboard, Kae Matsumoto, also came from a family of survivor types, bringing together lineages from the *Titanic* and Hiroshima. Unlike most techno or new wave bands of the 1980s (famous for the "one-hit wonder" syndrome), YMO's popularity grew slowly and steadily, remaining very successful a hundred years after Masabumi Hosono had left the dock at Southampton.

32

Destination Unknown

If we Americans could find a way to coexist with the Russians—after decades of a declared willingness to incinerate each other and take the rest of the mammals, and the birds, and most of the trees with us— then anyone could find a way, and perhaps the survival value of human intelligence might be proved after all. "The first thing that must be asked about future man," said Charles Darwin in *The Descent of Man*, "is whether he will be alive, and will know how to keep alive, and not whether it is a good thing that he should be alive."

When I returned to the *Keldysh* in 2003, along with several NASA astrobiologists and most of the Expedition *Titanic XIII* team, there was much disagreement between Russian and American political leaders over the Iraq War. It did not matter. Aboard the *Keldysh*, the first words exchanged were a renewal of the vow that we were, and always would be, family.

Our mission on Expedition X-Treme Life was to explore and film the hydrothermal vent zones from the Azores all the way down to the equator. Roy Cullimore, Lori Johnston, and I had already observed the activities of more than twenty bacterial and three fungal species living within the *Titanic*'s rusticle community, among them the iron-loving bacteria. Most important, sulfur-metabolizing microbes called Archaea were present. The *Titanic*'s steel was sulfur-rich, and the microbial communities thriving around mid-ocean volcanic vents were sustained largely by an ecosystem based on hydrogen sulfide.

So it had been logical for us to suspect, all these years, that the *Titanic*'s rusticle consortium originated at vents hundreds of miles upwind of the *Titanic*. No one had yet proved that rusticles were living around iron-rich mineral deposits at the vents, but that was because no one ever set out to specifically look for them.

Our exploration of the *Titanic* had revealed that iron was not the only metal on which the rusticles thrived. Copper and zinc would serve just as well. The organism was very opportunistic and very adaptable, and the hydrothermal vents were becoming known as sources for all of the major metals (to such an extent that some of the most amazing and fragile biological communities on Earth were beginning, much to our alarm, to attract the attention of mining interests).

JULY 28, 2003
RUSSIAN RESEARCH VESSEL *KELDYSH*
EXPEDITION X-TREME LIFE

The NASA people just did not seem to understand the Russian tendency to sidestep high-tech bells and whistles and make everything in the *Mir*s able to be repaired on site, rather than having to flip switches and activate a redundant piece of equipment if its twin in the first compartment burned out. The Russian idea of redundancy was to have two *Mir*s, each with a mutual rescue capability. If all of the redundant equipment failed in the *Alvin* or the *Nautile* and surfacing became impossible, one had to hope that there was another submersible in the same ocean, no more than two days away.

It would take the NASA "high-techies" a bit of getting used to, but astronaut Michael Foale (a veteran of the orbital *Mir*), and the rest of us who continued to work with the Russians, had either been pre-adapted to or had carefully absorbed Russian-think, which amounted to thinking outside the box, every hour of every day.

One morning there had been some difficulty in trying to figure out how to hook a high-tech deep-ocean thermometer within camera-swivel view of the bot Jake so that the camera lens could read the very small markings. Someone had proposed designing a new lens or a new swivel arm with a magnifier. One of the *Keldysh* newcomers expressed a certain amount of panic over the possibility of not being able to tell if Jake (or worse, the *Mir*) was moving too close to a hydrothermal vent's stream of superheated water.

Keldysh veteran Mike Cameron pushed the electronic thermometer aside and dropped a box of Crayola crayons on the table. "Here is how we're going to do it," he said. "We mount a crayon near Jake's nose. If the wax begins to melt, back Jake off, then the cold water should solidify it instantly. If it melts again, back off again." That's Russian-think.

Captain Paul Mallery, of Ten-Ten House, had heard me talking often about the Russian approach to technology. With Russian-think on his mind, he sent me an e-mail for the crew. "[Here's] another example," he wrote, "of how sometimes we gain more if we are able to give up our stubborn thought limitations and think outside the box." The example was a question once used in a job interview. He was to imagine himself driving past a bus stop one night, through a gale of horizontal rain (and with the cell service out). There were three people at the bus stop: an old woman in ill health and on the verge of collapse and possible death, an old friend who had once saved his life, and the perfect partner—life's one true love. His car could carry only one passenger. Taking any one of them and leaving the other two behind presented both personal and moral dilemmas.

The solution was to give the car keys to the old friend and direct him toward the nearest hospital with the old woman, then stay behind with the woman of his dreams and wait for the bus. This sort of thinking applied even to the constantly emerging questions about cephalopods. One of the first things we had seen when we landed near the *Titanic*'s prow in 2002 was an octopus that had wings shaped like the ears of Dumbo the elephant, and for that reason it had affectionately been named by the biologists Dumbo. There was a beautiful winged cuttlefish hovering near the wooden eaves of the reception area and the red, spindly-armed octopus that had kept watch at my viewport, seemingly as curious about us as we were about it. They were among the most commanding of the predators. I had begun calling the world below "planet of the cephalopods." At the first vent zone we reached, about two-thirds of a mile down and still within the deep scattering layer, a five-foot-long Humboldt squid was seen in the distance, moving behind a sheet of shimmering hot water. It evidently did not like the lights of the *Mir-2*, because it swam up to the sub directly and very aggressively started slapping the lights. "Shades of [Captain] Nemo's *Nautilus* [in Jules Verne's novels]," I wrote to Arthur Clarke, who only a day earlier had written, in an e-mail, "Look out for the squid."

Later that night, Jim Cameron and I and some of the astrobiologists were standing on deck, talking about the remarkable intelligence exhibited by cephalopods, including the Humboldt squid and some of its insanely camouflage-prone octopus and cuttlefish cousins. "They have manipulative limbs every bit as good as our own," I said. "And they've certainly provided us with enough examples of memory, complex problem solving, even the occasional use of crude tools—enough to suggest that if their brains kept developing, one of them should have built a civilization."

The late paleontologist Stephen Jay Gould had once said that the greatest evolutionary step taken by humans was the one taken on two feet: it freed up the hands for carrying objects and making tools and thus force-fed the development of our brains. I did not agree. Octopi have "free hands," yet over the course of more than two hundred million years, they had not advanced.

All of us wondered why. I saw the difference between human beings and octopi in modes of reproduction. The most complex brains were large and energetically expensive, probably requiring a long gestation period in a placental mother who ate a lot of high-nutrient foods. A cephalopod's embryonic brain development was limited to whatever nutrients were supplied in the yolk of its eggs.

"Why else," I asked, "after being around longer than the dinosaurs, had they come this far in brain development, all those millions of years ago, and no farther?"

"What makes you so sure that they had come this far two hundred million years ago?" Cameron asked. "We primates evolved intelligence during a series of ice ages that had to rank as one of the most continually biologically stressful periods the planet had seen since the Permian and Cretaceous extinctions. What makes you so sure that four million years ago the cephalopods weren't all howler monkeys compared to what they have become today? What makes you so sure that under the same environmental stresses and pruning that more or less acted like rocket fuel for the development of *Australopithecus* or *Homo erectus*, cephalopods haven't been undergoing parallel change right along with us?"

I had never asked these questions. None of us had. And whether the possibility was right or wrong, who cared? It was a new way of looking at what we had been seeing all along and asking what we had never asked before. That was what counted. I thought about it, laughed, and said, "Wow."

There was nothing else to say. It was completely outside the box, and it was a perfectly good night for science.

AUGUST 1, 2003

Although the Archaea in the rusticle consortium were the same microbes that Bob Ballard's team had discovered at the hydrothermal vent zones in 1977, and although it seemed obvious that we would find rusticles at the vents, our first days of searching offshore of the Azores were fruitless, insofar as rusticles were concerned. Throughout the first week of the expedition, my inner theme song seemed to be the U2 classic, "I Still Haven't Found What I'm Looking For."

Then Jim and Mike Cameron found a whole rusticle reef thriving on an iron-rich overhang of rock. They insisted on keeping the *Mir* down an extra hour to sample a "rusticle stalactite" intact.

"No doubt of it," I wrote to Cullimore and Johnston. "The morphology is identical to the *Titanic*'s rusticle consortium: growth bands, fibrullar bundles, channels, reservoirs, span threads, iron-oxide 'shell.' So a mystery has been solved with reasonable certainty. The [microbial] cysts [that colonize the *Titanic* and other ships] are coming from the vents. This is amazing."

AUGUST 3, 2003

Sometimes the past really does have a way of sneaking up from behind and biting you in the butt. For nearly a year and a half, I had not experienced a recurrence of what was known in New York as "World Trade Center cough" and "ground zero lung." I had thought that the first incidents of asthma in my life, followed by two cases of bacterial pneumonia, were merely a temporary glitch that would never bother me again, so I packed an extra book and some equipment into the limited space available to me instead of the rescue inhaler and other medicines.

Dr. Glenn Singleman, our ship's surgeon, was prepared when my symptoms, after nearly eighteen months of quiescence, suddenly developed into a resilient and widespread wheeze across my lung fields. He had brought along an entire duffel bag filled with extra medications because "some stupid scientist can always be counted on to favor a reference book or a box of sampling equipment over lifesaving medicine." Then, more seriously, he asked, "You live in New York?"

I nodded.

"Did you go near the dust from 9/11?"

I explained, and he told me I must have been crazy to go in there. I tried to laugh it off, pointing out that this definition of *crazy* was coming from one of the men who had actually created the extreme sport of BASE jumping (parachuting from a high structure).

"You don't understand," Singleman said. "If you confine yourself to bed and follow every one of my instructions, I think I can get you well enough for your August 8 *Mir* dive. But I really shouldn't be clearing you, medically. I can clear you, just barely. But you'd better grab every good specimen and every good memory you can take with you from the 'Lost City' vents."

He told me to prepare my mind for a new reality: August 8, 2003, would be the last dive of my career. I would never see the *Titanic* again.

The Woods Hole, Massachusetts, scientist with whom I shared my cabin took up a Russian challenge that could never be won: he tried to match, shot for shot with four Russians, drinking a shipboard brew manufactured by the Marine Biology Department—a powerful new species of vodka with a unique and actually pleasant flavor. It's called Sheila. The scientist found out the next morning that "Sheila is a severe mistress."

The obvious stress of realizing that an important part of my career was over led my friend Lev to make repeated offers to me of Sheila; as in 2001, I said I could not make the "requisite" number of toasts and be able to do my job. He respected an expression of dedication to one's work and promised that we would share some of his food and only make a single toast to our friendship. The Russian stood by his promise, and whatever was in that single shot of Sheila actually did bring a sense of calm—even during my reception of the idea that the terrorists appeared to have now physically gotten a piece of me.

Sheila had perhaps the most colorful history of any high-alcohol concoction. During the 1995 filming expedition for the movie *Titanic*, in a world still lingering in the shadow of the Cold War, many parts of the *Keldysh* were off limits to Americans. There were a number of engineers aboard who had many hours to kill while the *Mir*s (and Jake's predecessor, Snoop Dog) were down at the *Titanic*. That's when one of the Marines discovered that Sheila was essentially 100 percent alcohol. He realized that when Sheila was combined with pure oxygen, it could actually be turned into an effective rocket fuel.

The rocket, built in secrecy by Americans on a Russian ship that was just coming out of its KGB years, was an impressive design. Oxygen tanks that could hold up to two thousand pounds per square inch were mated with a pressure tank for Sheila (which would be held under pressure by a bubble of inert compressed nitrogen). The design needed no pumps. Under pressure, only valves were required, as well as an igniter in the combustion chamber. After the fins were welded on, a control system was added, using a gyroscope from one of Jim Cameron's steady cams. The only remaining engineering challenge was timing the valves to open simultaneously, within the same tenth of a second. John-David Cameron and Big Lew Abernathy were scrounging below decks one night for spare parts, from which the timed trip mechanism could be built—and that's when Anatoly Sagalevich caught them and found the rocket.

During the 2001 expedition, John-David learned that the rocket had been dismantled but carefully stowed, having become a much laughed about and much cherished souvenir of the "crazy American and Canadian friends who filmed *Titanic*."

AUGUST 8, 2003

"The cup was half full," I told myself. The Lost City vent system had been discovered only three years before. Inorganic chemical reactions were venting dissolved carbonates, methane, ethane, butane, and sulfides. The hot carbonates crystallized into brilliant white towers of extremely porous rock standing more than two hundred feet tall—more than half the height of the Washington Monument and the Great Pyramid of Giza.

It was another planet down there. The dry weight of a Lost City rock sample was as much as 10 percent living material, ranging from bacteria to shrimplike ostracods. The best part of all was that during the day, at a depth of "only" one kilometer (almost two-thirds of a mile), the deep scattering layer scrapes the tops of the Lost City pinnacles the way low-lying clouds scrape the needles of the Chrysler Building and the Empire State Building.

This time, when we descended to the bed of the Atlantic, we were not merely counting organisms as we passed through the deep scattering layer at two feet per second. This time we were stopped within it: bioluminescent fish; the occasional large grouper; a tubular white worm no longer than a fingernail flapping wildly and swimming (bizarrely) sideways; and sheets of bacterial floc drifting past the viewport, many of them inhabited by absolutely stationary fish no more than a fraction of an inch long and so transparent as to be revealed only by their eyes at the ends of long spinal columns.

"Floaters" with dangling "baits," or traps, drifted by in fleetlike formation. Their fishing lines were rarely longer than a finger, and the hunters at the tops of the lures were invariably smaller than beans.

If the ocean surfaces were the mere skin of Earth, the empires beneath were rich with the unexpected. What at first appeared to be a fish approaching us turned out to be a large, bright red cousin of the common nautilus. But the coiled shell rippled as though it were made of a thick fleshy mantle instead of shell, and the mantle was strangely ornamented, like the shell of a paper nautilus. Yet the thing moved with all the grace and speed of a mackerel. It was difficult to believe; but when I double-checked with Sagalevich and cinematographer/explorer Vince Pace, they agreed: it looked like a cephalopod. We would never know what it really was without a capture—which on a gut level did not feel like the right thing to do. It was the only one we had seen and probably the only one anyone had ever seen, so what felt right this time was to take pictures, not samples.

As dusk fell upon the world above, the deep scattering layer left us and began migrating toward the surface. It also left behind a new realization: stragglers. Not all of the organisms migrated up, and the stragglers were just as strange as the migrants.

We would never know for sure what all of these stragglers were. The mysterious red cephalopod was among them, but at 9:18 p.m., when either it returned or one of its cousins showed up, filming the wildlife was not a priority. Eight minutes earlier, we had been caught in an avalanche from one of the pinnacles and we began losing hydraulics. Equipment was dislodged from the aft shelf, and I held it against my back until Pace was able to lift the metal boxes into their proper position and strap them down. It seemed to me that whatever hit us on the starboard side had pitched us forward only ten to fifteen degrees, but Pace insisted that it had been more than thirty degrees, because our equipment was bolted and strapped to accommodate high angles whenever we surfaced into rough seas.

We were losing hydraulic control and protective oil (and the remaining oil was heating up fast). Through the center port, Sagalevich saw another complication: a water sampler had crashed down among the *Mir-1*'s cables.

Sagalevich called out an alert to the *Mir-2* crew, announcing that we might need its help. Then he turned to me and said the words one never wants to hear from a Russian pilot: "We have problem. How are you?" Admitting the problem meant it was serious, and the question—coupled with a deep look into my eyes (then into Pace's)—really meant "How are you going to behave?"

I answered, "Biology. I'm going to do what I came here for," and I returned to my camera and my notebooks. It occurred to me that this was to be my last dive—my "retirement" dive—but I was not overly concerned that before the night was through, I would be feeling a strange kinship with Captain Edward J. Smith, for whom the *Titanic*'s maiden trip was to have been his "retirement" voyage.

I had full confidence in Sagalevich and his machines. He was, after all, the *Mir*s' chief designer. It seemed to me, as he cleared debris from external cables with the robot arm and repaired our hydraulics with an intensity of concentration rarely seen in a human being, that he was more concerned about losing face by not completing the work before the *Mir-2*'s lights came around the next pinnacle than about any possibility that this was a one-way trip.

Sagalevich beat the *Mir-2*. At 10:10 p.m., we were parked on the edge of a sheer cliff that dropped into what Lost City's discoverers had named the Atlantis Fracture Zone. Like hundreds of other such fractures, it ran perpendicular to the continental spreading center. The volcanic center extended literally from pole to pole, diving deep under Antarctica, where it had sprouted Mount Erebus.

My attention was drawn to a new mystery. At the cliff's edge and along the base of the nearest Lost City tower, I had seen white sea urchins, each with spines about ten centimeters (four inches) long. The spines seemed not to have afforded the urchins much protection. Scattered in every direction were little strewn fields of urchin needles, looking as though someone had dropped a whole planeload of white drinking straws. A crevice under my viewport, about one yard wide and slightly more than ankle deep, appeared to be an entire bedding plane of urchin spines and shell fragments—an echinoderm graveyard. Many of the spines, I noticed, had been broken, as though chewed and spat out.

Something had an appetite for sea urchins—something reasonably large and strong. Vertebrate or invertebrate? We could only guess, but none of us would have been shocked if it turned out to be something no one had yet seen.

If one had to be given a last dive, the Lost City site was the perfect place for it. In water clear enough to give the impression that we were flying helicopters through the air, the skyscraperlike pinnacles were a landscape so large and so beautiful that if I were given just one choice, either to fly into Earth orbit or to go back again into the deep, I would go back once more into the ever-black. If I were forced to choose between the *Titanic* and the Lost City, I'm not sure which one I would pick, but the Lost City might win.

That's how magical the day's exploration had been. We saw blizzards of marble-sized "stars," or dandelion seeds, each of which had snowy white arms branching from its center. The undersea dandelions were drifting microbial colonies of some sort—probably bacterial—but the avalanche and the broken sampler had precluded collection.

It was William Beebe's magical world squared down there; it was my wildest childhood dream, lived for real. But sooner or later you have to surface into the human world. Sooner or later you have to wake up.

August 9 came on like a thunderbolt, bringing with it news that my lungs were trying again to develop bacterial pneumonia. Dr. Singleman ordered a minimum two days of absolute bed rest in addition to increased prednisone dosing. During the discussions that followed, he pointed out that on an expedition hundreds of miles away from helicopter rescue, if a flare-up of this sort ever became uncontrollable, the entire expedition could be required to turn back. I had seen not only my last submersible dive but my last voyage as well.

As the 2005 expedition moved deep into its planning phase—with yet another new, smaller, and more agile generation of bots coming on line—the shock-cocoon events witnessed at the World Trade Center weighed more heavily than ever before on our thoughts about the *Titanic*. Shock cocoons, large and small, had shown up in every direction. They probably accompanied all catastrophic, explosive events, but they remained a persistent enigma.

One of the mission goals was to seek out new shock-cocooned chambers deep within the *Titanic*. Unfortunately, my attempts to understand the World Trade Center shock cocoons had added the unpredictability of the ground zero lung phenomenon to the equation and ultimately kept me ashore, but daily contact would be maintained with Roy Cullimore, Lori Johnston, and Jim Cameron.

This was the year we finally learned that the mysterious, mahogany-dwelling white worm of the first-class reception and dining area was neither entirely white nor a worm. In 2001, Georgyj Vinogradov had suspected that he saw "head features" reminiscent of sea cucumbers; yet pieces of elongated "worm" weaving in and out of mahogany burrows were so stretched out that it was difficult to tell where one worm began and another ended—so difficult, in fact, that it was possible to joke about a good reason for not sampling one of the worms with a clasper: "They're all one worm," Jim had said, "threaded through all the wood; and this worm is all that's holding the *Titanic* together. Cut that thread at any point, and the whole thing will unravel, causing the final collapse of *Titanic*."

The misnamed, misunderstood (and fortunately, not mistreated) white worm was finally identified when a minibot entered a first-class pantry room in the bow and revealed preserved wood still covering every wall. The fronts of the cabinets had either fallen off during the impact with the bottom or been eaten away by marine life. Inside, bone china plates and saucers were still neatly stacked behind vanished cabinet doors. On one side of a saucer stack, its entire body visible for the first time, lay a "white worm," with its head resting in the hole it had apparently eaten through a side panel.

Clearly, this was the same animal whose brethren had taken up residence in the reception area's black mahogany. Against the pantry's lighter wood, and with its body lying on a shelf (in relaxed compression rather than being stretched out), the lavender hue that artist and historian Ken Marschall had always assigned to the reception area's strange invaders was much more prominent. Its distinctive, luminous "side ports" and other elements of its morphology were unmistakable. Vinogradov was right: we had been observing echinoderm morphology all along. The misnamed and still poorly understood "white worms" were actually a type of sea cucumber never observed outside the *Titanic*. They were cousins of the starfish, flowerlike crinoids, and the black sea cucumbers that inhabited the plains outside for a radius of at least six miles.

The lavender sea cucumbers with the glowing rows of "ports" were not creatures of the plains. They were, like most of the animals seen inside the *Titanic*, different from those seen outside. At the Lost City vents, and along all of the major hydrothermal vent zones, our machines had glided over cracks often less than a yard across and dropping down deeper than our lights could reveal. Only now were minibots coming into existence that were small enough to navigate into those cracks—which girdled the entire planet, opening wherever the hydrothermal seams opened. These narrow nooks and crannies of Earth provided many tens of thousands of unexplored cubic miles, vast tracts of hidden surface area, and unknown nutrient sources. The *Titanic*'s interior was probably giving us a fleeting glimpse of what we would find when our bots finally descended into those nooks and crannies.

For almost a hundred years, discussions about the destructive forces at work the night the *Titanic* sank had focused on the power of the ship's

collision with the iceberg, but the iceberg was minuscule by comparison to the forces at work during the meteoritic impacts on the seabed.

In the bow section—which plunged to the bottom at a slower speed
than the stern and therefore impacted more "gently"—a thick iron pillar,
just outside the Turkish baths on F deck, was crushed out of line like a
large letter *C*. The expectation was that the bath chamber itself would be
crushed and shattered, just like the stairwell and corridor leading down
to it. Then, to everyone's astonishment, the minirobot, Gilligan, glided
beneath a perfectly intact wall and ceiling of vestibule wood. Turning
right, Gilligan entered a shock-cocooned room with intact tile walls and
unbroken couches and chairs that appeared to have floated to the ceiling
when the room flooded, then drifted gently to random positions on the
floor as high-pressure water squeezed into every air-filled microcavity in
the wood's cell structure. Every one of Maude Slocomb's polished ceramic
tiles was still lining the walls, their colors still vibrant. Gilded wood trim
and gilded lamps decorated the ceiling. The glass was unbroken, despite
the fact that everything outside the room had been completely destroyed.

"Can you imagine the concussive force of the ship hitting the bottom, and yet this room has survived?" Jim Cameron reflected, looking
at the gallery of Gilligan-eye views on his screens. "It's as if time has
just stopped. It's hard to imagine where we are—how deep we are, how
remote we are from the human world. And yet we find this beautiful
place, like a little church on the bottom of the ocean."

There were no currents bringing oxygenated water into Maude
Slocomb's Turkish baths; no "white worms" creating passages through
the wood; no white crabs, anemones, or gorgons. This appeared to be
a realm inhabited only by rusticle extrusions, which were emerging
through seams in the walls and growing toward the floor in clusters,
sometimes several yards long and rarely wider than a pencil, and quite
unlike the rusticle growths in the stairwell outside, which were generally thicker than the trunk of a small tree.

As with the Apollo program in the 1960s and as with the robot Elwood
in 2001, battery technology continued to be a black art with the mini-
robot fleet of 2005. On July 9, 2005, Jim Cameron wrote in an e-mail,
"Charlie, the four new bots are in trouble (three of them, anyway). Lost
three of them inside the wreck due to electronic failures, though hope
to recover two."

These were to be history's second and third undersea rescues of one
bot by another. The fantastic was becoming routine. "Managed to get

into the Turkish baths," Cameron continued, "for about one hour before vehicle failed. Exceptionally good state of preservation—like going into the tomb of Tutankhamun. Eerie and magnificent, and the colors were spectacular. Next leg, we are going out with the [mini] 'X-bots' plus [tried and tested] Jake and Elwood. Not taking any chances on live [Discovery Channel] show."

I replied, "Had fascinating scientific conference [about] rusticles with Roy, Lori. . . . It's not every day you find something that comes so close to defining a new kingdom of life. . . . The Consortia: [as you know], they are intensely symbiotic—so much so that we appear to be looking at a clear analogue of how tissue layers originated, back in the good old, old, old days. We are even seeing an immune system—which very effectively keeps 'outsiders' away from the rusticle consortium.

"And," I continued, "while we may disagree with Lynn Margulis's theory about bacteria (and not viruses) being the true culprits behind some viral epidemics—on this much, she has to be right: We are the multicellular result of bacterial symbiosis; we are all children of mud and bacteria. When we climbed out of the oceans, we took the chemical composition of seawater in our veins. We also carried along some of the pig-iron sludge, with the little Pacifics that carry oxygen to our hearts and our brains: Something like the biology of the rusticle lives on, in every atom of iron at the core of every molecule of hemoglobin."

On July 10, Cameron wrote, "I forgot to mention the most amazing find in the Turkish baths—the rooms are [as you and Ken Marschall hoped] completely sheltered from any currents; and they have [these] very thin rusticles (as thin as 4–6mm [about a fifth of an inch] in diameter), hanging straight down from the ceiling almost to the floor. We've seen these before (in the number 1 cargo hold), though maybe not so long and straight. But here's the kicker: A couple of them are growing *up* from the floor, and [they] end in a flowerlike cluster of tendrils, looking almost exactly like Triassic crinoids. Strange but true. No joke. I flew [the bot] all around one of them, couldn't believe it. Rusticles *cannot* grow *up*. But these do. Figure that one out. I was thinking about Roy and Lori while I was imaging them. They will go nuts for this one."

"Jim, I'm already going nuts for this one myself," I replied. "But believe it or not, it's not entirely surprising. We have some [rusticles] preserved from the 1996 [expedition] that actually did grow upward (but not much more than a couple of centimeters up). And when it suited them, they seemed to grow in every other direction. They [the "upstarts"] were sheltered in the curl of a completely twisted piece of steel.

"Similar structures were also imaged by the robot Robin [in 1993], growing inside the *Titanic*, on a pile of mail bags; but they were living under conditions similar to what you encountered with Jake [in 2001], in the forward crew quarters: Lots of bacterial floc [in places, more than ankle-deep]. The mailbag "reeds"—growing straight up from a layer of biofilm that enveloped the bags themselves—did not have a great deal of iron in their structure; and they were more in line with [another Archaea-including organism discovered in certain caves], called 'snotsicles.' This new discovery, in the Turkish baths, confirms what we (of team Rusticle) have been mostly guessing till now but could not be sure of, beyond speculation. [If proven], this is a pretty major discovery. Welcome to the pre-pre-Precambrian (the pre-Edicarian) [Period]. Welcome to 3 billion BC, inside the *Titanic*."

Cameron replied on Sunday, July 10, 2005, "Charlie, this was not a snotsicle—definitely rust-orange in color, thinner than a pencil, about one meter [yard] tall, perfectly straight, dividing into three or four tendrils at the top which splayed up and outward, curling slightly about 3–5 cm [almost 2 inches]. It was a rust-flower. I'll see if I can send you some video frames."

Like any good mystery, the video raised more questions than it answered. We could see brass lamps that still appeared to be polished—with their bulbs, of course, long ago imploded by water pressure. The idea of rusticle flowers growing up from the floor suggested something even more ancestral to plants and animals than we had dreamed. Cameron had asked for an explanation of how rusticle fronds could grow upward.

I supposed that the phenomenon could have started out like the soft reeds atop the mailbags, rising initially by growing buoyantly. Afterward, perhaps, the part of the consortium that "loved" iron increased in proportion, slowly adding iron oxide structural supports, like the "shell" that enclosed the standard rusticle sample.

However, a second and far less dramatic possibility had to be considered. I was working from a variation of an old Arthur Conan Doyle theme—actually, the opposite of Doyle. I started out not by eliminating the most improbable or impossible explanations but by believing the following instead: "We must first eliminate the more mundane and more likely possibilities. Then, whatever does not fall away (rusticles flowering up through the floor?), no matter how strange or impossible it may appear to be, must be the truth."

The most mundane explanation lay in the lamps hanging from the ceiling—some of them on wires that had pulled loose almost to the floor.

I wondered if the "rust flowers" in the Turkish baths could be rusticle-colonized wires on ceiling lamps that after hanging down for several decades, unfurled and unwound and finally broke under rusticle activity, falling to the floor with their rusticle-stiffened wires standing up. The strands at the break point might have unfurled farther as they added new layers of rusticle growth. Cullimore, Johnston, and a new explorer named Anthony El-Khouri saw evidence of a more natural branching pattern in the rust flowers, and the video revealed no sign of a lamp beneath the thin drifts of rusticle dust that had descended through the ceiling—and from which the mysterious growths appeared to have sprouted. El-Khouri's study of the video revealed three relevant trends:

1. When the robot camera panned toward the ceiling, a bronze lamp was filmed hanging down about a yard with its wiring exposed. The insulation appeared to be intact, and the wiring was entirely free of rusticles—this despite being surrounded by a little forest of unusually thin, long rusticles stretching down from the wooden beams around the lamp.

2. Another hanging wire, near a gilded wooden dome at one end of the room, was also rusticle-free, except for the very tip, where exposed metal (presumably copper) had sprouted a single rusticle orb. This indicated that the *Titanic*'s wire insulation was resilient (as in the cases of rusticle-free wires filmed throughout the Marconi shack and in Captain Smith's quarters), which meant that in order for the rust flowers on the floor to actually be colonized wire, the insulation would have been required to decay in a manner inconsistent with wires located elsewhere in the ship and even in the same room.

3. The upwardly sprouting rust flower that Cameron had circled with his bot, illuminating it for maximum resolution, was far from alone. El-Khouri pointed to "what appears to be a rust flower growing up from the base of a wooden [lounge] chair. Very strange. In fact, anywhere a rust flower [was photographed] touching the ground, there was something wooden very much in its vicinity. It's crazy, because you can just imagine the (albeit limited) dust on the floor acting like a soil full of 'seeds' of bacteria sprouting up literally like a garden of flowers. I think they're trying to increase their surface area in that anoxic room—like intestinal villi in a chamber of limited nutrients, absent of currents."

El-Khouri's observations pointed Occam's razor more toward a kinship with the growth patterns seen in the room of mailbags and bacterial "reeds" than with colonization of a preexisting wire skeleton. Cullimore provided another major piece of the puzzle: in at least one instance, a consortium he had seeded in a bed of rusticle dust and then fed with iron and organic nutrients grew upward from the bottom of an aquarium tank.

There was one means of settling the question once and for all time, in a matter of seconds, with nothing more than a magnifying glass.

"Is it possible," I had asked Jim Cameron, "to bring out a small sample [from the baths] on the next go? Even a *small* sample, without wounding the little beasties too badly? We really can't confirm unless we have one—only a centimeter-long sample should do the job. We can know immediately, just by looking at it, what we are dealing with."

He was sorry to report that this was not possible. "Charlie, so far the only sample taken in the Turkish baths is the one the *Titanic* took from our fleet. Bot 3 now resides there, in luxury."

In fifty million years, if paleontological minds should inherit the Earth after us, they would find the *Titanic* reduced to a thin band of fossilized materials in the same layers of sedimentary rock where windshield fragments, plastic dashboard dressing, and ceramic engine parts shall remain (along with bathroom tiles and toilets) as the most abundant indicator fossils of *Homo sapiens.* The paleontologists of remote futurity might also find (to their initial confusion) a twenty-first-century robot named Gilligan sandwiched between tiles from the Turkish baths.

Could Maude Slocomb or anyone else who entered the baths during that voyage have imagined that more than ninety years later, a tiny machine beyond anything Jules Verne had invented as fiction would enter this room and find it intact and perfectly familiar, nine-tenths of a league under the sea? Could anyone believe that on the decks above, and in this room, would emerge a bacterial wonderland, pregnant with mystery?

In 1996, Roy Cullimore had advised us all to remember that humans pulled iron ore out of the earth and fashioned it into the rivets, hull plates, and engine casings of the *Titanic.* Now the rusticle garden was dissolving the *Titanic,* cycling most of it back into the earth again as iron ore, sending some of it into the water column where it might even cycle into the fishes as hemoglobin. "What an amazing web," he said.

The Zen theologian Thich Nhat Hanh had written, "If you are a poet, you will see that there is a cloud in this piece of paper. Without a cloud, there will be no rain. Without the rain, the trees cannot grow; and without trees, we cannot make paper."

The *Titanic*, and its final unfailing return to the earth, had a similar lesson to teach—one of its many lessons: interdependence. There were nearly eternal cycles of water and nutrients and metals between sunlight and the sunless abyss. Even the dyes in the dresses Edith Russell had been importing from the Paris fashion show would eventually find their way into biological systems, if they hadn't already. In the deep, nothing really existed except the endless cycling of atoms. In the deep, there was the process of fossilization and eventually even the cycling of fossils by subduction into magma pools—tens of millions of years from now, in the case of the *Titanic*. But for now, there was only interdependence, And futurity. And the question of whether, as Darwin had put it, future humans would know how to keep alive.

In Masabumi Hosono's generation, large stone tablets were erected in Japan, adding to previous generations' stelae, marking the heights to which the 1923 and 1933 tsunamis had reached. Hundreds of similar tablets dating back as far as six centuries dotted the hills around coastal towns and cities, marking how far inland historic tsunamis had penetrated. Some of the markers described sea life washed far inland, leading occasionally to the naming of a town "Octopus Grounds." Other markers left specific warnings: "High dwellings are the peace and harmony of our descendants. Remember the calamity of the great tsunamis. Do not build any homes below this point."

As the generations passed and sea walls were designed to variously divert and even break the backs of tsunamis, the astonishing inertial power of advancing masses of water witnessed by past generations was forgotten, and many believed that modern engineering had advanced beyond the concerns of the warning stones. After complacency took root, the six Fukushima fission reactors were built below the level of tsunamis seen in Hosono's time. Worst-case-scenario earthquakes were planned for. Six reactors and their spent fuel-rod pools were protected by careful compartmentalization into six entirely separate containment buildings. Backup diesel generators, and batteries to back up the backups, seemed capable of guaranteeing that the reactors and the pools could stand up to every imaginable disaster scenario. Yet history teaches us that once we think we have thought of everything, nature will think of something else.

•

"*Titanic!*" the *Carpathia*'s Captain Rostron wrote in his 1931 memoir. "Of all the remarkable incidents connected with the short life of that

ship of destiny, not the least was her name. If you look in your diction-
ary, you'll find: 'Titans—A race of people vainly striving to overcome
the forces of nature.'" As he looked back in 1931 and drew that single
lesson from his encounter with history, it did not escape Rostron's
notice that he might have glimpsed the world to come.

Three decades after Rostron penned those words, Madeline Mellinger wrote to Walter Lord from the depths of Cold War politics,
humanity's first ascents into space, and the first signs that civilization
might one day outstrip the ability to provide itself with food, power,
and clean drinking water. "I hope you can find some light in this crazy,
dark world," she said. "Sometimes I wonder, as all thinking people
must: Where will it all end?"

Compartmentalization. Time and again, compartmentalization builds
complacency, kills humility, then fails to hold—from the *Titanic* and the
Britannic through the Twin Towers to Fukushima. In the year of
Fukushima and before the eve of the *Titanic*'s centennial, civilization
itself seemed on the verge of compartmentalizing into increasingly iso-
lationist factions whose leaders sought to further isolate themselves
behind the illusory watertight bulkhead of the "nuclear deterrent."

We are more fragile than we believe, but we are more powerful
than we understand, and that is civilization's onus. For an electronic
civilization pregnant with promise and peril and standing on the preci-
pice of either excelling or falling, nothing really does exist except a still
unrealized interdependence.

And the living, and the yet to be born.

Notes

The Lord/Pellegrino file consists of approximately 725 pages of letters, memoirs, and other correspondence from *Titanic* survivors and their families with Walter Lord and myself, along with discussion notes about the survivor accounts as illuminated by discoveries during the various *Titanic* expeditions. In addition, the file contains approximately two thousand pages of expedition log notes and discussions with key people in this book, including Robert Ballard and the Cameron brothers, the Tullochs, Barbara Shuttle, Roy Cullimore, Tom Dettweiler, and Lori Johnston. In 2001, the file was copied to the British Maritime Museum, the *Titanic* Historical Society, and James Cameron's historical research team. It is also being reproduced on Charlespellegrino.com (available for free download with a request that people make a donation to the Michael J. Fox Foundation or the Firefighters Burn Center). Below, the file is abbreviated as simply the L/P file, with page numbers and dates cited.

I. CONVERGENCE

On the origin and age of the ice field that drifted into the *Titanic*'s path: D. A. Meese et al., "The Greenland Ice Sheet Project 2 Depth-Age Scale: Methods and Results," *Journal of Geophysical Research* 102, no. C12 (1997): 26,411–26,423; M. De Angelis et al., "Primary Aerosol (Sea Salt and Soil Dust) Deposited in Greenland Ice during the Last Climatic Cycle: Comparison with East Antarctic Records," *Journal of Geophysical Research* 102, no. C12 (1997): 26,681–26,698.

The Hudson Strait or Labrador Current carries ice from as far north as Baffin Bay. Greenland and Baffin Bay ice, near the very bottom of the ice sheet, is strewn with gravel and can exceed a hundred thousand years in age. The extreme calm of the water in the *Titanic*'s path was emphasized by Charles H. Lightoller, transcript of audiograph interview, Nov. 1, 1936, p. 1.

John William Thompson's experience of the impact is contained in Wyn Craig Wade, *Titanic: End of a Dream* (New York: Penguin, 1979), 243–244. Charles Hendrickson reported his experience to the *British Inquiry into the Loss of the* Titanic, chaired by Lord Charles B. Mercey, May 9, 1912, pp. 116–117. Violet Jessop's description is recorded in her memoir, Titanic *Survivor* (London: Sheridan House,

1997), 125–126. Laura Francatelli, in the neighboring room, wrote about similar shivering walls on page 1 of her letter from the Ritz-Carlton Hotel, New York, to a family member named Mary Ann on Apr. 28, 1912, L/P file, pp. 433–437.

Albert Moss is recorded in Per Kristian Sebak, *Titanic: 31 Norwegian Destinies* (Oslo: Genesis Forlag, 1998), 28, 51, 59, 65, 75.

Conditions in the foremost boiler room at the moment of impact were reported in the *British Inquiry*, May 9, 1912, p. 116. The fire in the number 10 stokehold, the estimated temperature (1,300 degrees Fahrenheit), and the condition of the critical bulkhead were recorded by Fred Barrett, Charles Hendrickson, and Edward Wilding in the *British Inquiry*, May 7, 1912, pp. 57–59, 71, 122–123, and June 17, 1912, p. 528. What Barrett saw and did, the occurrence of impact just as he responded to the alarm, and the damage seen just two feet above the floor plates were recorded by Barrett in the *British Inquiry*, May 7, 1912, pp. 34, 57–58; *American Inquiry*, chaired by Senator Alden Smith, May 25, 1912, p. 1141; discussion with Walter Lord, Sept. 10, 1991, pp. 10–12, L/P file, pp. 96–98. Barrett reported the post-impact response of John ("Jack") Shepherd and George Beauchamp in boiler room number 5 to the *British Inquiry*, May 7, 1912, p. 59.

Heating problems, which caused Norman Chambers, Charles Stengel, James McGough, Jack Thayer, and others to leave their portholes open (a factor that quickened the rate of the *Titanic*'s sinking), were discussed with Walter Lord in "Artifact," series of discussion notes, p. 8, June 1993, L/P file, p. 38. Cases discussed included personal communication by Lord with Bertha Chambers (regarding the open porthole in stateroom E-7); also Stengel in the *American Inquiry*, Apr. 30, 1912, p. 981.

Chambers and McGough actually recalled ice falling through open portholes (noted in Lord's mapping of passengers and staterooms; L/P file map used from 1996 expedition onward), with the ice fall indoors mentioned in Walter Lord, *A Night to Remember* (New York: Holt, 1955), 5. Thayer reported his open porthole in the memoir he produced for his family, *Sinking of the SS* Titanic (Indian Orchard, MA: Titanic Historical Society, 1940). Refer also (with regard to the Thayer account) to Walter Lord, James Cameron, and Charles Pellegrino annotations in "The Archaeology of the *Titanic*: Reconstructing Falling Stars," in Jack Thayer, *In Their Own Words: Titanic*, http://www.charlespellegrino.com, p. 22.

On stateroom overheating: E. S. Kamuda, "F. Dent Ray: A *Titanic* First-Class Saloon Steward," *Titanic Commutator* 18, no. 5 (Jan. 1995). In a letter to E. Kamuda, Oct. 16, 1965, F. D. Ray wrote, "In Belfast, when the *Titanic* was being [made] ready for her first voyage—they found that the first-class staterooms near the engine room [were] too hot. So they had to insulate the walls near the engine room with extra walls behind which they packed granulated cork."

Ray was specifically addressing the mystery of why granulated cork was found drifting on the sea surface the day after the *Titanic* foundered and why three bodies recovered from the sea had their mouths filled with cork. More significant, Ray's account memorializes a quick and evidently unsuccessful fix, meant to correct a tendency toward stateroom overheating that was already known—a problem that would have existed even without the additional heating of E deck's floor plates by a coal bunker fire. Tragically, a significant number of portholes were left open as a means of air conditioning—at the worst possible moment and location (just above and often in front of the boilers, in the descending bow).

A secondary surge of impact effects and evidence of damage below the floor plates of boiler room number 4 were reported by George Cavel, *British Inquiry*, May 9, 1912, pp. 106–107.

George Kemish's record of conditions farther back, in boiler room number 2, appears in a letter to Lord, June 19, 1955, p. 2, L/P file, pp. 545–546. Impact conditions behind the boiler rooms at the steam engines were reported by Patrick Dillon to the *British Inquiry*, May 9, 1912, p. 98, and by F. Scott, May 10, 1912, pp. 130–131. Regarding additional openings to the sea, assistant purser Frank Prentice reported leaving his porthole open in his E-deck cabin in front of the engine room bulkhead and Charles Joughin's cabin: F. Prentice, undated interview transcript with Walter Lord, p. 2, L/P File, p. 649; Ken Marschall, personal communication, June 2010, L/P file, p. 129B.

Along Frank Prentice's deck, one of those closest to the waterline, the portholes were designed to close automatically unless physically held open, propped open, or swung upward and hooked open at approximately ninety degrees with a latch. However, if allowed to close while unlatched in the closed position, water pressure from the outside could push through these ports indoors. Wrote Marschall, L/P file, p. 129B, "If one opened it momentarily to look outside and didn't [latch] it closed again, it would swing back into an apparently closed attitude and would appear 'closed' today from the outside. So [short of an experiment to push on a random sample of E- and F-deck portholes with a robot arm to see if it pushes inward and is unlatched], we'll never know how many of the E- and F-deck portholes are un[latch]ed."

Madeline Mellinger recorded her experiences in several letters to Lord, beginning Jan. 13, 1962, L/P file, pp. 580, 592, 594, 596–597, 603–604. Madeline's thoughts about C. C. Jones at her table were mentioned in a letter dated Feb. 24, 1969, p. 9, L/P file, p. 596. Madeline's hope that Jones planned to become her stepfather: personal communication with Walter Lord, L/P file, p. 596. On the location of the Mellinger cabin on the same deck as the open Thayer and Chambers portholes: Mellinger letter, Feb. 24, 1969, part 2, p. 4, L/P file, p. 600.

Masabumi Hosono's case was featured in M. Findlay, "A Matter of Honor," *Voyage* 27, Winter 1998, p. 122, in which Hosono also records the extreme poverty he witnessed in Russia. George Tulloch (and Lord) addressed the Hosono and Laroche cases and examples of Harold Lowe's overt racism in a personal communication, 1996, during a pre–Expedition *Titanic VIII* conference. Colonel Archibald Gracie, in Jack Winocour, ed., *The Story of the* Titanic *as Told by Its Survivors* (New York: Dover, 1960), 194, 195, cited George Crowe's testimony to the American inquiry (*American Inquiry*, p. 615) as well as Charlotte Collier on Lowe's initial refusal to rescue an Asian man from the water until a woman and a child of boat 14 protested his behavior.

The little-known presence of an interracial couple aboard the *Titanic* (Joseph and Juliette Laroche) was reported by Oliver Mendez, "Mademoiselle Louise Laroche: A *Titanic* Survivor," Titanic *Commutator* 19, no. 2 (Aug. 1995): 40–47; Georges Michael, Titanic *Commutator* 24, no. 149 (Nov. 2000): 48; and Judith Geller, Titanic: *Women and Children First* (New York: W. W. Norton, 1998), 95.

Spencer Silverthorne's impression of the iceberg rising higher above the boat deck as it moved back was corroborated by George Rowe on the after-bridge. Silverthorne's account is transcribed from an interview with Lord, July 14, 1955, p. 1,

L/P file, p. 202. Rowe's observations appear in the *American Inquiry*, Apr. 25, 1912, p. 519, and in a letter to Lord, 1955, p. 1, L/P file, p. 317.

An estimated impact force equivalent to lifting the mass of fourteen Washington Monuments in a second was provided by J. Knapp to the *American Inquiry*, May 18, 1912, p. 1116. The total aggregate of punctures measuring twelve square feet was based on Edward Wilding's study of flooding rates in the *Titanic's* pierced compartments during the first ten minutes (before open portholes reached the sea and became contributing factors), as reported to the *British Inquiry*, June 7, 1912, p. 520.

The effect of the *Titanic* regarding the iceberg's side of the story: personal communication and brainstorming sessions with Robert Ballard (1985–1986), Tom Dettweiler (WHOI, 1986), James Powell (1986–1997), George Tulloch and William Garske (1996), Roy Cullimore (1996), and James Cameron (1996–present). Parks Stephenson (2005 and attachments to 2001 expedition log), along with Don Lynch and Ken Marschall (1996–2010) have emphasized possible "grounding" effects.

Damage consistent with the hole (in a probably dented plate) observed by Barrett in the empty coal bunker was examined at the center of a "dished-in" steel plate of the *Regent Sea* after it struck a small iceberg, called a "growler," in May 1993. Parks Stephenson, personal communication, Dec. 23, 2010, has expressed skepticism about ice itself being able to penetrate the *Titanic's* inch-thick steel plates by point-source impact. Stephenson also raises a valid argument that the observations of Silverthorne and Rowe at the aft end of the *Titanic* suggest that William Murdoch was able to order and execute final corrective maneuvers.

Advising that I must not miss this larger point, Stephenson wrote, "The ice impacted at the narrow [part of the] bow and if we understand the geometry of the collision correctly, the collision vector should have resulted in more damage where the ship [broadened] to its maximum width at the beam. However, it didn't—which means that, in A. B. Scarrott's words [description of impact, *British Inquiry*, May 3, 1912, p. 23], 'her stern was slewing off the iceberg.' This means, then, that Murdoch didn't just turn to port, but that he also reversed the rudder in order to save the beam and the stern (where the engineering spaces were) from being forced by the momentum of the ship hard into the berg."

2. FAR FROM OKAY

Location of stern section and high-mass debris at latitude 41 degrees 43 minutes north and longitude 49 degrees 56 minutes west: archaeological maps, 1996 and 2001 expeditions.

Warnings to the *Titanic* of ice at latitude 41 degrees 50 minutes north were produced at the *American Inquiry*, pp. 1114–1115. Witnesses to the report from the *Baltic*: J. Booth and S. Coughlan, eds., *Signals of Disaster* (compilation of Marconigrams received regarding the *Titanic*) (London: White Star, 1993), 14.

Parks Stephenson pointed to passages in the *American Inquiry*, Apr. 19, 1912, p. 68, and to the *British Inquiry*, May 20, 1912, p. 304, "About lunchtime on Apr. 14th—9 hours before the disaster—Captain Smith briefed his officers on the existence of ice ahead, in the *Titanic's* path, based on information stitched together from a number of ice warnings received earlier that morning. As soon as the *Titanic* crossed the 49th parallel [it] would effectively be in the vicinity of ice. Lightoller had 6th Officer Moody calculate when that would be. [The answer is 11 p.m.] The region of ice described by those acknowledged telegrams included the spot where the *Titanic* would later hit the iceberg."

Stephenson, personal communication, Dec. 23, 2010, concluded, therefore, that the *Mesaba* telegram and ultimately the *Californian*'s last-minute warning represented redundant information in this drama. "The real question," he added, "should be: Why did Smith not order extra precautions to be put into place (including extra lookouts closer to the water on the very head of the ship) as soon as the *Titanic* crossed the 49th parallel?"

Neshan Krekorian's sighting of icebergs through an open porthole, close to the waterline, was reported in George Behe, Titanic: *Safety, Speed, and Sacrifice* (Polo, IL: Transportation Trails, 1997), 62–63. Although Ken Marschall's comparative study of porthole construction on other ships of the period, including the *Titanic*'s two sister ships, emphasizes that on the lowest decks (E and F) the *Titanic*'s ports were probably designed to swing shut unless latched open, water might nonetheless have pushed through into the ship were they not latched closed: personal communication, 2010.

Marschall's opinion is that on a cold night, portholes that were closed would most likely have been latched closed—yet many portholes of a different design on the upper decks (C and D) were evidently left open. There was no reason for the ratio of open ports to be dissimilar along the lower decks, where weaker, thinner iron hooks (for the open position) were likelier to break when the bow crashed into the bottom of the sea, if they were not severed during subsequent decades by rusticle digestion (allowing the ports to drop shut). All E-deck ports currently appear to be closed; but given the approximately 17 percent of open ports on the next deck up, they may only *appear* to have been closed; L/P file, pp. 129B.

What Joseph Boxhall saw, at the critical moment, six decks above Krekorian: J. G. Boxhall, *American Inquiry*, Apr. 20, 1912, pp. 209, 228–229, and Apr. 29, 1912, pp. 907, 930; *British Inquiry*, May 22, 1912, p. 355. Quartermaster Robert Hitchens laid out for the *American Inquiry*, Apr. 24, 1912, pp. 449–450, a chronology in which William Murdoch ordered the wheel turned even before Boxhall heard the three warning bells from high atop the crow's nest and moved quickly toward the bridge.

An order to turn the wheel hard to starboard actually turned the rudder and the ship in a direction opposite the wheel, pointing the prow to port. Boxhall also gave testimony about the positions of instruments; however, Parks Stephenson pointed out (in a Dec. 23, 2010, letter to the author) that Boxhall had come from the brightly lit smoking room in the officers' quarters, and he had been passing deck lights on his path to the bridge; so he could not yet have had clear night vision by the time he entered the darkened bridge. Stephenson warned that this is something to keep in mind when evaluating what lever positions and instrument readings Boxhall reported seeing once he stepped onto the bridge, including Boxhall's observation (in contradiction of that of survivors in both the boiler rooms and the engine rooms) that according to instrument readings, the engines were slammed into full astern. According to Stephenson, the bridge should have been able to maintain at least some avoidance maneuverability during the critical seconds; the stopped propeller blades and the paralyzed rudder are probably, therefore, self-perpetuating textbook dogma.

The point was moot; there were too few seconds in which to respond. Hitchens testified that the ship was crushing the ice as he turned the wheel: *American Inquiry*, Apr. 24, 1912, p. 450.

Frederick Fleet told an American examiner that the impact occurred while he gave the warning to the bridge: *American Inquiry*, Apr. 23, 1912, pp. 320–321. He reiterated this for Charles Lightoller: Fleet, *American Inquiry*, Apr. 24, 1912, p. 362; Lightoller, *British Inquiry*, May 21, 1912, p. 343; Sir Ernest Shackleton, *Brtish Inquiry*, June 18, 1912, p. 723. Alfred Olliver was able to further narrow the exceedingly small time frame in which the bridge was forced to respond: *American Inquiry*, Apr. 25, 1912, pp. 526–528, 531–533; discussion with Walter Lord, Apr. 10, 1999, p. 3, L/P file, p. 48.

Joseph Scarrott's timing of events revealed passage by a second iceberg, after the *Titanic* briefly steamed forward again at half speed: J. Scarrott, *British Inquiry*, May 3, 1912, p. 23. On the steaming ahead again, after impact, eyewitness examples include L. Beesley, in Jack Winocour, ed., *The Story of the* Titanic *as Told by Its Survivors* (New York: Dover, 1960), p. 28.

August Wennerstrom and his friends were initially more amused than frightened, as recorded by Wyn Craig Wade, Titanic: *End of a Dream* (New York: Penguin, 1979), 248–249. This account was based on *Titanic* Historical Society papers—private letters of Wennerstrom collected by Wade.

Daniel Buckley took the impact much more seriously than the other men in the bow section, who played games with fallen ice during the first few minutes while bunks began to flood: *American Inquiry*, May 3, 1912, pp. 1019–1020; Natalie Wick, in Walter Lord, *A Night to Remember* (New York: Holt, 1955), p. 16.

In the next compartment in front of Buckley, Samuel Hemming began to discover the extent of the flooding: *British Inquiry*, May 24, 1912, p. 421.

3. A SLIGHT TREPIDATION

Madeline Mellinger was awakened by a steward banging loudly at the door, sprang immediately into action, and rescued her deaf mother. She reported this in a letter to Walter Lord, Feb. 24, 1969, p. 4, L/P file, pp. 598, 600.

As the Mellingers threaded their way up from second class, Madeline did not believe they were leaving their room for the last time, so she barely took notice that her mother was improperly dressed for freezing weather: letter to Lord, Oct. 31, 1955, L/P file, pp. 602, 603, 603C.

John Hardy recalled a strange question at the *American Inquiry*; he also recalled being roused by purser Reginald Barker from first class and seeing that the damage was serious, after which he closed additional watertight doors along F deck: *American Inquiry*, Apr. 25, 1912, pp. 587–588, 593.

At the top of the spiral stairs, a water fountain was installed by Thomas Andrews for the shifts working the coal-fired boilers. Not on the original plans, it was discovered during the 2001 robotic exploration of the *Titanic*'s interior. Violet Jessop spoke with extreme gratitude about the improvements "Tommy" had made for the stewards and coal gangs who rarely received any thought from management: Violet Jessop with John Maxtone Graham, *Violet Jessop*: Titanic *Survivor* (New York: Sheridan House, 1997), 102–103. Flooding submerged the fountain shortly after midnight: assessment by Expedition *Titanic* XIII, 2001.

Sir Ernest Shackleton expressed strong opinions about the sacrifice of safety for speed: *British Inquiry*, June 18, 1912, pp. 720–721. Emily Ryerson had expressed concerns to Bruce Ismay and felt rebuffed by him: letter to D. Brown on decision to testify, Apr. 18, 1913, p. 2, L/P file, pp. 327–328.

Juliette Laroche could deal with the prejudice of her time, but the *Titanic* itself disturbed her, as memorialized in a letter from Queenstown, preserved by her children and reported by Oliver Mendez, "Mademoiselle Louise Laroche: A Titanic Survivor," Titanic *Commutator* 19, no. 2 (Aug. 1995): 44–45. Juliette and the children departed in boat 10: Judith Geller, Titanic: *Women and Children First* (New York: W. W. Norton, 1998), 95–96.

Charles Lightoller was working on the false (and deadly) assumption that the new lifeboats were frail and could be launched only half full: John Hardy, *American Inquiry*, Apr. 25, 1912, p. 592; Lightoller, *American Inquiry*, Apr. 19, 1912, p. 77, and Apr. 24, 1912, p. 434. Lightoller was working under the further assumption that the lifeboats were not for adult males and people from third class: Lightoller, *American Inquiry*, Apr. 19, 1912, pp. 57, 71, 74–75, 1107; Lightoller, *British Inquiry*, May 21, 1912, p. 314.

Harold Lowe followed the Lightoller assumptions and added a barrier against nonwhites: Lowe, *American Inquiry*, Apr. 24, 1912, pp. 417–419. An "apology" of sorts by Lowe was logged in the *American Inquiry*, Apr. 30, 1912, p. 1100; he conceded that not all the dark-complexioned people against whom he drew his gun were Italians, so he was wrong to describe them all as Italians.

Ellen Betty Phillips, the unborn child whose future would be torn apart by the *Titanic*, is another of the *Titanic*'s least-known stories. Dennis Cocrane reported the saga of the Marshall necklace in "Love of the Sea," New York, International Gem and Jewelry Show, Inc., 1998. Further details on Ellen Betty Phillips: letters from John R. Hodges and E. B. Phillips, Apr. 27, 2001; "Life after the *Titanic*," *The West*, 2001; and Millvina Dean (whose mother was on the same lifeboat with Kate Phillips), personal communications, 1994, 1996, 2001.

As an example of how Henry Morley's story about leaving because of lung infections became believable to his family, and how common infections turned deadly all too easily in 1912, infection death rates in a single *Titanic* family were instructive: Violet Jessop with J. Maxtone Graham, *Violet Jessop:* Titanic *Survivor* 13, 19, 22–24, 26–27, 31–32, 34. The Pasteur Institute developed a treatment for diphtheria just in time to save Jessop's two younger brothers.

By five past midnight, Lawrence Beesley encountered the unforgettable sights and sounds of the library and the dining saloon, as described in his memoir, in Jack Winocour, ed., *The Story of the* Titanic *as Told by Its Survivors* (New York: Dover, 1960), p. 22.

Tracing the final resting places of the *Titanic*'s on-board mail was addressed with Walter Lord, personal communication, Sept. 13, 1993, L/P file, pp. 37, 60–63.

Masabumi Hosono's overly hasty departure from his room and its consequences were recorded in a letter to his wife written on *Titanic* stationery aboard the *Carpathia*: M. Findlay, "A Matter of Honor," *Voyage* 27, Winter 1998, p. 122.

Strange statements heard among the boat-deck runners were recorded in Helen Candee's unpublished memoir, *Sealed Orders*, May 1912, p. 2, L/P file, p. 172.

Violet Jessop had survived the collision between the *Olympic* and the *Hawke* seven months earlier, and though frightened by news that the *Titanic* might sink, she turned her attention to the safety and comfort of her passengers: Violet Jessop with J. Maxtone Graham, *Violet Jessop: Titanic Survivor* (New York: Sheridan House, 1997), 102–103, 106, 121, 126–127. This was affirmed by Annie Robinson at the *British Inquiry*, May 20, 1912, pp. 298–299, and in a letter by Jessop to a friend, July 27, 1958, L/P file, p. 539. The *Olympic-Hawke* incident can be referenced (with photos of the aftermath) in Robert Ballard, Titanic: *The Last Great Images* (Toronto: Madison Press, 2008), 50.

The curious encounter between Colonel Archibald Gracie and Frederick Wright was memorialized by Gracie in Jack Winocour, ed., *The Story of the Titanic as Told by Its Survivors* (New York: Dover, 1960), 119, and by Walter Lord, *A Night to Remember* (New York: Holt, 1955), 39.

A story about Jenny and her kittens safely departing the *Titanic* in Belfast and saving a scullion named Jim "Mulholland" when he followed them has turned out to be untrue. The actual story is contained in Violet Jessop with J. Maxtone Graham, *Violet Jessop:* Titanic *Survivor* (New York: Sheridan House, 1997), 118. The legend of Jenny and Jim went from an Internet blog to the *Belfast News* in 1997 (based on a story by ninety-two-year-old Paddy Scott, who claimed that his friend Jim Mulholland had been none other than Violet Jessop's friend Jim and that he had been saved by a cat's intuition). An article by Anne Hailes, published in the *Belfast News*, went to the Associated Press and the world—where it was eventually memorialized in such places as Marty Crisp's and Robert Papp's exquisitely illustrated book, *Titanicat* (Chelsea, MI: Sleeping Bear Press, 2008).

Jessop, a firsthand eyewitness, had a habit of changing the names of many people to protect them, including her own siblings; with great effort, John Maxtone Graham and Walter Lord were able to sort out the identities of her siblings, William Murdoch, Henry Sleeper Harper, and others, so Scott's naming of Jim Mulholland was itself a compass pointing toward the truth. Jessop stated very clearly that her friend Jim made the voyage along with the cats and that the real story did not end for them as happily as the legends of cyberspace would have it.

Charles Joughin organized his staff into a rescue effort, fully aware of the victimizing mathematics that had taken rule of the night: *British Inquiry*, May 10, 1912, pp. 140, 144–145; letter to Walter Lord, Nov. 2, 1955, p. 2, L/P file, p. 427. Joughin refused orders to take command of a lifeboat, decided that he would conduct rescues till the last possible minute, then follow Dr. Will O'Loughlin's advice to meet death indoors, deep within the ship, after drinking quickly and heavily: Walter Lord, transcript of conversations with Joughin, Sept. 13, 1993, p. 2, L/P file, p. 426.

Nearly a century later, deep-ocean archaeologists named an area of debris from Joughin's region (found near the stern section) "Hell's Kitchen," as noted in the documentary *Titanica*, made by the first Russian-American expedition, Stephen Low, IMAX, 1991.

4. NIGHT OF THE LIGHTNING DOLPHINS

Samuel Hemming's hatch is still wide open: Charles Pellegrino, video log, Expedition *Titanic XIII*, Sept. 22, 2001. The common rat-tailed fish, often seen lurking around the *Titanic*, is a perfect example of organisms we could see that remained around our bright searchlights because they don't see us. Parks Stephenson, in a letter to author, Dec. 24, 2010, wrote of his 2005 encounter: "I watched a rat-tail fish run smack into a projecting beam and then, startled, swim off in another direction. He didn't react to our presence the entire time. Not only are [these] fish blind, but they don't often see the submersibles as danger."

Our approach to the *Titanic* site during the Chinese Week of the Dead in 2001, the story of the service held (and its unanticipated result), and the arrival of Ralph White's lightning dolphins were recorded in Charles Pellegrino, written log, Expedition *Titanic XIII*, Aug. 2001, pp. 3, 9.

Practice sessions with robots occurred while we followed a mission profile originally outlined as part of the Space Cooperation Initiative: Charles Pellegrino, video log, Expedition *Titanic XIII*, Aug. 2001; Pellegrino, written log, Expedition *Titanic XIII*, Aug. 18, 2001, p. 2; Spark Matsunaga, *The Mars Project: Journeys beyond the Cold War* (New York: Hill and Wang, 1986); Jim Powell, Harrison Schmitt, and Charles Pellegrino, International Cooperation in Space Symposium, Boston, 1987; Jim Powell, Charles Pellegrino, and Jesse Stoff, "Final Crisis: The Ascent of Man," in *Darwin's Universe: Origins and Crises in the History of Life*, ed. Steve Bolt, 2nd ed. (Blue Ridge Summit, PA: TAB, 1987), 199–219.

The bronze plaque that Jim Cameron showed Lori Johnston and Lew Abernathy was photographed by Charles Pellegrino, written log, Expedition *Titanic XIII*, Aug. 2001, p. 148.

5. TRINITY

Masabumi Hosono's difficulties in reaching the lifeboats, as well as the segregation of the third class, the firemen, and the coal trimmers on the well decks, were recorded in Hosono's letter to his wife, Apr. 1912, reproduced in M. Findlay, "A Matter of Honor," *Voyage* 27, Winter 1998, p. 122, and during Olaus Abelseth's testimony to the *American Inquiry*, May 3, 1912, p. 1037.

Violet Jessop believed she saw the lights of another ship on the horizon: letter to a friend, July 27, 1958, pp. 2–3, L/P file, pp. 533–535] Jessop's recollections of her odd preparations to leave, under the watchful eye of her friend Stan, are preserved in Violet Jessop with J. Maxtone Graham, *Violet Jessop:* Titanic *Survivor* (New York: Sheridan House, 1997), 127–128.

In the interview notes of Walter Lord, July 1955, L/P file, p. 268, Maude Slocomb described her own sense of trepidation and gave a unique view of the Turkish baths and the horrible condition in which she found them at the beginning of the voyage. Ironically, the baths became one of the *Titanic*'s best-preserved interior regions. The water-resistant door next to the entrance of the cooling room was still closed, just as Joseph Wheat's account of having personally closed the door suggested it would be found. The tiles in the cooling room were intact except near a distortion of the starboard inboard wall, where bottom impact appeared to have sprung some of the tiles. Observations by Ken Marschall and Parks Stephenson, personal communication, 2005 expedition; P. Stephenson, "Titanic Wreck Observations, 2005," http://www.marconigraph.com, 2006, p. 5.

Celiney Yasbeck's escape, the fate of her husband, and her departure by force in boat 6 were detailed in a letter to Walter Lord, June 15, 1955, L/P file, pp. 223–230. Further insights into the Yasbeck story were provided in Judith Geller, Titanic: *Women and Children First* (New York: W. W. Norton, 1998), 179–181 (with details gleaned from White Star third-class passenger department interview,

Apr. 26, 1912). Lebanese men and women (as an exception) were quartered together in the bow, according to R. Bracken and J. White, "Lebanese Passengers," *Voyage* 27, Winter 1998, pp. 132–133. In a letter to Walter Lord, June 15, 1955, L/P file, pp. 224–227, Celiney Yasbeck Decker mentioned looking down into the "engine room" with her husband, but in a personal communication with Lord, she described a room full of machinery not very far from her cabin—which would be the boiler rooms; the engine rooms were hundreds of feet behind the front boiler rooms.

Boat 6 was the first lifeboat to leave on the port side, at 12:55 a.m., with a carrying capacity of sixty-five but only twenty-eight people aboard; on the other side of the ship, boat 7 reached the water with only twenty-eight people and a dog, according to the *American Inquiry*, digest of the testimony, pp. 1159–1163.

Boat 7 touched down at 12:45 a.m. Fred Barrett noted for the *British Inquiry*, May 7, 1912, pp. 2058–2059, that at about this time he was present for a probable cause of the *Titanic's* sudden list to the port side. Aboard boat 6, Molly Brown saw a great gush bursting suddenly through an open porthole. The gush was described by Brown to Colonel Gracie in Jack Winocour, ed., *The Story of the* Titanic *as Told by Its Survivors* (New York: Dover, 1960), 178. About the time of the shift and gush, Maude Slocomb's friend Joseph Wheat made a particularly dramatic escape: *British Inquiry*, May 16, 1912, pp. 241–242. Wheat had helped a Turkish bath assistant to close two F-deck bulkhead doors. About 12:45, he passed this way again, wanting to be sure that his friends had evacuated the front compartments. Water stopped him—it was running suddenly down the walls of F deck from E deck above. Wheat concluded for the British examiners that water had been shifting on E deck and falling down upon F deck from the starboard side. During the next ten minutes, boat 6 reached the sea surface, and water (evidently shifting from the starboard side) was seen bursting through an open porthole.

George Kemish, in a letter to Walter Lord, June 19, 1955, p. 9, L/P file, pp. 543, 560, wrote about the kindly stowaways hiding in the front cargo hold.

Edith Russell's experiences aboard the *Titanic*, and the final locations of objects in stateroom A-11, are described in her memoir for Walter Lord, Apr. 11, 1934, and in a letter from Lord, Feb. 11, 1987, communications file, Mar. 1978–Mar. 1988. Lord and Bill MacQuitty became close friends of hers and provided further details about her: Russell, personal communication to Lord, Apr. 28, 1956; J. Witter (smoke-room steward), letter to Lord, July 1957, L/P file, pp. 198–200 (on helping the woman with the toy pig into boat 11); Russell, BBC interview transcript, Apr. 14, 1970, L/P file, pp. 125–128 (with annotations and observations by Lord).

Russell had described for Lord the locking of her window and her bureau and the filling of her cup. Lord provided dictated annotations for Russell's actions in her room (in particular, with Russell's BBC interview), after he was shown video of a cup still intact in a cup holder near room A-11's dressing mirror, Oct. 2001, L/P file, p. 126.

In the spring of 1912, the *Titanic* was likely to become a forgotten ship. The launch of the *Titanic's* older twin, the *Olympic*, had indeed received almost all of the newsreel coverage. Had the *Titanic* not foundered during its maiden voyage, it would have remained the less famous of the two ships. (Indeed, most film footage used in documentaries about the *Titanic* is actually footage of the *Olympic*, not the *Titanic*, a fact that is quickly revealed by the lack of glassed-in windows on the *Olympic*'s promenade deck.)

The addition of more luxurious rooms with private promenade decks (the Cardeza and the Ismay suites), more first-class quarters near the smoking room (the Andrews suite), and a greater amount of decorative trim gave the *Titanic* an extra 1,004 tons of displacement over its twin and did legitimately allow it to be called the world's largest and most luxurious ship: Don Lynch and John Bruno, personal communication, pre–Expedition *Titanic XIII*, July 3, 2001.

The reaching of a critical limit in boiler room numbers 5 and 6 was highlighted during the testimony of Edward Wilding to the *British Inquiry*, June 7, 1912, pp. 528–529, 736. Fred Barrett described his attempt to close off the flooding in coal bunker number 10: *British Inquiry*, May 8, 1912, p. 71. The attempt was doomed to failure: Barrett, *American Inquiry*, May 25, 1912, p. 1141. He also provided key details about the eventual collapse of the dam between the two front boiler rooms: *British Inquiry*, May 7, 1912, pp. 60–61.

Barrett mentioned stopping the water in the number 10 coal bunker very early in the sinking: *British Inquiry*, May 7, 1912, p. 59. The water was entering through a small round hole about the size of a deck hose, and stalling the flow was as easy as closing the steel door on the empty coal bunker. The flood Barrett saw about 12:45 a.m. was much more significant than a mere release of water retained in the coal bunker. If the thinner steel of the coal bunker had been the only rupture at this time, once the accumulated water was released, there should have been nothing further to feed the flood or even to endanger John ("Jack") Shepherd and Herbert Harvey than the hose-size wound just behind the fire-damaged bulkhead.

The embrittled bulkhead itself most likely gave way along its base, specifically *because* of the sudden shift of water out of the coal bunker and away from the boiler room number 5 side of the dam. During the minutes leading up to the burst, engineer Shepherd fell into one of the keel's forty-four watertight compartments: Edward Wilding, *British Inquiry*, June 7, 1912, p. 521. Further details regarding Shepherd's injury and death were provided in a George Kemish letter to Walter Lord, June 19, 1955, p. 4, L/P file, pp. 543–560.

In 2005, one of James Cameron's robots finally provided insight into the evacuation of the two front boiler rooms, as discussed by Parks Stephenson, "Titanic Wreck Observations, 2005," http://www.marconigraph.com, 2006, p. 4. An open hatch at the top of boiler room number 5 would not, at this point, have contributed significantly to an increase in the rate of sinking. Water advancing from the front regions exerted a far greater impact than any overflow through the casing hatch that capped boiler room number 5.

On the effect of many tons of coal being removed from the the burning number 10 bunker: Fred Barrett, *British Inquiry*, May 8, 1912, p. 71. Lawrence Beesley appeared to have noticed this effect, resulting from the effort to completely empty a starboard bunker in boiler room number 5. He wrote of puzzlement over how, as the voyage progressed, the *Titanic* developed a significant list toward the port side.

"The purser remarked," Beesley reported, "that probably coal had been used mostly from the starboard side. . . . In view of the fact that the *Titanic* was cut open on the starboard side and before she sank listed so much to port that there was quite a chasm between her and the swinging [port side] lifeboats . . . the previous listing to port may be of interest": Beesley, in Jack Winocour, ed., *The Story of the Titanic as Told by Its Survivors* (New York: Dover, 1960), 20.

6. OF NATURE, NOT ABOVE IT

Bill Paxton, Big Lew Abernathy, and the early lessons of our exploration are recorded in Charles Pellegrino, written log and video log, Expedition *Titanic XIII*, Aug. 20–24, 2001. Paxton's response to Abernathy's question was a personal communication. Before his own first dive, Abernathy left a note for us on his desk. It read simply, "No regrets."

Artist-historian Ken Marschall managed to put a deeper sense of trepidation into Paxton, with his new "fingernail perspective" on the *Titanic*: Charles Pellegrino, written log, Expedition *Titanic XIII*, Aug. 21, 2001, pp. 16, 18. "I had always referred to the depth of water . . . Ten World Trade Center twin tower lengths": Charles Pellegrino, *Her Name*, Titanic (New York: Avon-Morrow, 1988), 92.

The acceleration of rusticle growth and the ominous population surges near the *Titanic* have been reported, beginning with the 1986–1996 comparisons: Charles Pellegrino and Roy Cullimore, "Rebirth of RMS *Titanic*: A Study of the Bioarchaeology of a Physically Disrupted Sunken Vessel," *Voyage*, Winter 1997, pp. 39–46; Henrietta Mann, "A Close-Up Look at *Titanic*'s Rusticles," *Voyage*, Winter 1997, pp. 47–48; Roy Cullimore, Charles Pellegrino, and Lori Johnston, "RMS *Titanic* and the Emergence of New Concepts on the Consortial Nature of Microbial Events," *Review of Environmental Contamination and Toxicology* 173 (2002): 117–141.

The same accelerated growth phenomenon has been recorded in the data and publications of the *Keldysh*'s Russian biologists: Charles Pellegrino, written log, Expedition *Titanic XIII*, Aug. 2001, p. 38. Regarding the unusually high biomass region into which the *Titanic* fell: Georgyj Vinogradov, in Pellegrino, written log, Expedition *Titanic XIII*, Aug. 2001, p. 38. Regarding the transformation of biological desert into jungle since the 1980s: Vinogradov, in Pellegrino, video log and written log, Expedition *Titanic XIII*, Aug. 2001, p. 26. The organisms (including the mysterious nests of rocks bound together in "silk"), sampled out to a three-kilometer radius (almost two miles) from the *Titanic*, are documented in the video log.

The evidence (including the doubling of rusticle growth rate during the prior seven cycles) indicates an increased nutrient throughput to the deep ocean: Lori Johnston and Charles Pellegrino, written log, Expedition *Titanic XIII*, pp. 38B–45. Georgyj Vinogradov agreed that the *Titanic*'s rusticles (and other organisms including Gorgonarians) seemed to have begun growing at an explosive rate, p. 26. This was memorialized by a study of Vinogradov's (point-bow) "gorgon" through the years: Pellegrino, written log, Expedition *Titanic XIII*, pp. 36–38; Georgyj M. Vinogradov, "Growth Rate of the Colony of a Deep-Water Gorgonarian *Chrysogoria agassisi*: *In situ* Observations," *Ophelia* 53 (Nov. 2000), pp. 101–103, expedition log, pp. 36–38A.

The discovery of bedposts and great quantities of intact wood inside the *Titanic*'s bow section is recorded in Charles Pellegrino, video log, Expedition *Titanic XIII*, Aug. 2001. "Rat-tailed fish patrolled the boilers . . . like the sentries to hell": Bill Paxton, in Pellegrino, written log, Expedition *Titanic XIII*, Aug. 2001, p. 22.

7. THE CASCADE POINT

Twelve forty-five a.m. marked a critical turning point in the *Titanic*'s sinking, characterized by a loss of what had, up to that moment, been a tenuous equilibrium. This was addressed, reluctantly, by Edward Wilding at the *British Inquiry*, June 7, 1912, p. 509. Equilibrium phases during the sinking were also discussed by electrical engineer and historian Paul J. Quinn, *Dusk to Dawn* (Hollis, NH: Fantail Press, 1999), 126. Quinn pointed out a credible alternative to Fred Barrett's perception that the 12:45 a.m. surge of water originated with a bulkhead failure. Quinn noted that the exhaust pipes and air intakes from boiler room numbers 5 and 6 converged upward toward the first smokestack, in the manner of a wishbone, just above E deck. This area of convergence (the exhaust chamber) could, according to Quinn, have "allowed the rising water in boiler room six to simply overflow into number five just like the analogy of an ice tray" (with water spilling from one compartment into another).

Although such duct overflows most likely occurred later in the sinking and to the rear (under the second smokestack, from boiler room number 4 into boiler room number 3), Barrett and Kemish escaped up through a hatch *atop* the boiler room number 5 casing—which would not have been possible if, prior to the loss of buoyancy in boiler room number 5, water was already pooled atop the hatch, almost halfway up E deck (at the point of exhaust-chamber convergence).

Moreover, under the duct-flooding scenario, the flooding in boiler room number 5 would have started slowly, then built steadily in force—with the flood coming down through the air and exhaust ducts and out through the mouths of the boilers, not from the direction of a bulkhead *between* the boilers, as reported by Barrett to the *American Inquiry*, May 25, 1912, p. 1141. Barrett was very clear about a sudden knocking noise, followed by a great wave that appeared to be shooting at him through the front bulkhead from a space between the boilers and not from the boilers themselves. All of this occurred with such rapidity that there was no time for Barrett and Kemish to attempt a rescue of John Shepherd and Herbert Harvey. During the next few minutes, boat 6 began lowering, and Molly Brown's observations are consistent with a rapid and significant loss of buoyancy in the bow section, with the ship taking on more water and beginning its shift from leaning to starboard to a portside list.

Edward Wilding's testimony at the *British Inquiry*, June 7, 1912, pp. 528–529, and June 19, 1912, pp. 736–737, divided the examiner and the commissioner on the use of mathematical figures alone in determining the breaking strength of the *Titanic*'s steel bulkheads and addressed (for the first and one of the few times) the bending strength of rivets and steel plates along the *interior* bulkheads (rather than the usual focus on the outer hull). Barrett reported that the slant of the deck was worsening considerably before water broke through to boiler room number 5: *British Inquiry*, May 7, 1912, pp. 2046–2049.

Daniel Buckley testified at the *American Inquiry*, May 3, 1912, pp. 1020–1022, about the confinement of third-class passengers. At the stern, Masabumi Hosono survived, like Buckley, by refusing to be confined, as recorded in his letter to his wife, Apr. 1912, reproduced in M. Findlay, "A Matter of Honor," *Voyage* 27, Winter 1998, p. 122. Anna Turja and several of her friends made a similar breakaway, detailed by Paul J. Quinn, *Dusk to Dawn*, Fantail Press (Hollis, NH: 1999), 123.

Harold Lowe had been forgotten and was initially left asleep in the officers' quarters, as he told the *British Inquiry*, May 22, 1912, pp. 366–367; British Consulate affidavit, New York, May 1912, L/P file, pp. 413–420. When he awoke and stood up, Lowe understood immediately that the slant of the deck was wrong: *American Inquiry*, Apr. 23, 1912, p. 387. Lowe's impression of a twelve- to fifteen-degree tilt was not accurate. Later in the sinking, when Lightoller swam toward the crow's nest from the submerging bridge, the *Titanic* measured only ten to eleven degrees down trim: Charles Pellegrino and Walter Lord, measurements made with models in water, 1987–1988.

About the time Lowe awoke and the first distress rocket detonated at 12:45 a.m., Lily Futrelle felt the deck tilt suddenly, as described in her interview with the *Boston Sunday Post*, Apr. 21, 1912, L/P file, p. 129.

Henry Harper reported in "The True Story of the Disaster," *Harper's Weekly*, Apr. 27, 1912, having watched the iceberg through his open porthole. When the robot Jake maneuvered into the Harper stateroom, D-33, the porthole was still open: Charles Pellegrino, video log, Expedition *Titanic XIII*, Aug. 2001; Don Lynch and Ken Marschall, *Ghosts of the Abyss* (Toronto: Madison Press, 2003), 102, 103.

Three starboard D-deck portholes near the Harper stateroom were also open, as confirmed by Ken Marschall, in a letter and maps discussing his census of open portholes in the bow section, June 30, 2010, L/P file, pp. 129B–130.

Thomas Patrick Dillon witnessed the opening of the watertight doors to boiler room number 4: *British Inquiry*, May 9, 1912, pp. 98–102. Edward Wilding defended this action: Wilding, *British Inquiry*, June 7, 1912, p. 529; Lightoller, *British Inquiry*, May 21, 1912, pp. 334–335.

Parks Stephenson, personal communication, Dec. 23, 2010, clarified the pumping power aft of boiler room 4: "The boiler [room number] 3 pump room was cross-connected via a ten-inch hose to help combat the rising flood waters in boiler room [number] 4 [up to and after the collapse of the sealed boiler room number 5]. Unlike boiler room [number] 5, where [a] single pump room was keeping ahead of the visible flooding before the failure of the bulkhead, the water in boiler room number 4 was rising despite two pump rooms working against it."

Charles Lightoller gave testimony suggesting that he helped to sink the ship faster, believing that a gangway door could be opened on a lower deck to off-load more passengers into lifeboats being sent down only half full: *British Inquiry*, May 21, 1912, pp. 314, 323.

Henry Harper's lifeboat (boat 3) reached the water about 1 a.m.: *American Inquiry*, Apr. 24, 1912, pp. 1159–1163; *British Inquiry*, pp. 399, 404. George Rowe said he fired the first rocket somewhere between 12:45 and 12:50 a.m. and had been instructed to fire rockets "every five or six minutes": letter to Walter Lord, 1955 (with annotations by Lord), L/P file, p. 319.

The number of people in boat 3: *American Inquiry*, results summary, pp. 1159–1163, lists forty passengers and ten crewmen; Colonel Archibald Gracie, in Jack Winocour, ed., *The Story of the* Titanic *as Told by Its Survivors* (New York: Dover, 1960), 234, lists forty people aboard. Henry Harper, "The True Story of the Disaster," *Harper's Weekly*, Apr. 27, 1912, described the tilt toward the port side and agreed with Gracie's total of forty people aboard.

The crew abided by Lightoller's plan to open a lower gangway door, as Norman Chambers testified to the *American Inquiry*, May 3, 1912, p. 1043. The opening of the portside D-deck door about this time probably occurred at least several minutes ahead of the boiler room number 5 collapse, the sudden shift to port, and the burst of water through a porthole near boat 6, as reported by Molly Brown to Colonel Gracie in Jack Winocour, ed., *The Story of the* Titanic *as Told by Its Survivors* (New York: Dover, 1960), 178.

Brown believed the gush came from a D-deck porthole; however, she was notoriously unsure of the *Titanic's* geography, even regarding the location of her own stateroom: James Cameron, *Ghosts of the Abyss*, IMAX, 2003. A census of D-deck openings renders Brown's identification of a D-deck port as the source of the gush unlikely. A known, open D-deck porthole just in front of the open gangway door would have been located near the bow of boat 6 as it was being lowered (possibly gushing directly into the boat).

Moreover, if this was the porthole described by Brown, she would most likely have seen (if it was already open) similar gushing activity at the open D-deck door—and certainly along other open D-deck portholes on either side of boat 6. Thus, she probably saw a gush from one of the lower, E-deck portholes, which were of a different construction and—having to be latched open in order to allow an outward gush if the *Titanic* began shifting to port—would have been more likely to produce only the single noticeable gush she reported, rather than a row of gushing ports, as would have been seen along D deck: Ken Marschall, census, June 30, 2010, L/P file, pp. 129B–130.

The E-deck portholes near boat 6's path of descent were occupied by forty-two stewards in a shared, multitiered bunk space, which was the sort of cramped room that often encouraged the latching open of a single porthole (as in the Krekorian account).

The sequence of events therefore favors a gush witnessed through an E-deck porthole, followed by portside flooding of the third-class recreation room through a front D-deck porthole (not much more than a couple of feet above the waterline at this time), followed by flooding through the open D-deck gangway door, during the minutes after boat 6 began rowing away from the *Titanic*.

8. EVERYTHING WAS AGAINST US

Charles Lightoller tried to defend his inadvisable action of opening a gangway door in the bow of a ship that was sinking by the bow: *British Inquiry*, May 21, 1912, pp. 314–315. Lightoller, who testified that he did not actually believe the ship was sinking, eventually found proof in a stairwell that the unthinkable really was occurring after all: Telediphone recording, Nov. 1, 1936 (transcription stamp dated March 23, 1956), pp. 2–3, L/P file, pp. 576–577; Walter Lord, *A Night to Remember* (New York: Holt, 1955), 61; Walter Lord, personal communications with Lightoller, 1927–1930, L/P file, p. 576.

Masabumi Hosono's boat (boat 10) launched at 1:10 a.m.: *American Inquiry*, p. 604. The portside list created a gap of three feet: Wyn Craig Wade, Titanic: *End of a Dream* (New York: Penguin, 1979), 292. At the *American Inquiry*, Apr. 19, 1912, p. 75, Lightoller asserted a belief that third class had no right to be on the boat deck and that boats were not for stewardesses either, an injunction that included Violet Jessop and Maude Slocomb.

Under Lightoller's and Lowe's rules, adolescent boys were forced out of the lifeboats: Wyn Craig Wade, Titanic: *End of a Dream* (New York: Penguin, 1979),

292. John Jacob Astor saved one of the boys, according to Madeline Astor: W. H. Dobbyn, letter to Robert Ferguson (the Astor Trust), May 15, 1912, L/P file, pp. 283–284. Even in the midst of such chaos, Lightoller insisted that lifeboats were being launched "as a precaution": Charles Lightoller, telediphone recording, Nov. 1, 1936, L/P file, p. 579; *British Inquiry*, May 20, 1912, pp. 222, 305, and May 21, 1912, p. 322.

The oars of the lifeboats revealed a bioluminescent effect that would have made icebergs visible had the water not been so unusually calm: Henry Sleeper Harper, "The True Story of the Disaster," *Harper's Weekly*, Apr. 27, 1912. Lightoller admitted to an ambition among the officers to see how fast the *Titanic* could really go: *American Inquiry*, Apr. 19, 1912, pp. 64, 67.

9. STALKING THE NIGHTMARE

The comparison of historian Don Lynch's notes with Walter Lord's mapping of passengers and staterooms, and the extensive Lord and Lynch contacts with survivors, reached its peak during Expedition *Titanic XIII*, as noted in Charles Pellegrino, written log, Aug. 2001, pp. 18, 19, 21. A possible mutation of memory was pointed out by Lynch with regard to Renee Harris in her interview with Lord, May 31, 1964, p. 1, L/P file, pp. 484, 485–502.

A corollary to the revelation of the sort of prejudice Renee Harris evidently faced from the Cardezas involved the behavior of Harold Lowe, reported by Charlotte Collier to Colonel Archibald Gracie in Jack Winocour, ed., *The Story of the* Titanic *as Told by Its Survivors* (New York: Dover, 1960), 195. "Ship of dreams" was a term invented after the sinking—"encapsulating," Parks Stephenson observed in a personal communication, Dec. 23, 2010, "in three short words: the 'myth of *Titanic*.'"

The events surrounding the two-and-a-half-mile swim and the pair of glasses headed down toward the *Medusa* and the *Mir*s are recorded in Charles Pellegrino's written log, Expedition *Titanic XIII*, Aug. 2001, p. 26, as well as the video log. Pages 39–40 of the written log indicate that some of the microbes in the rusticle consortium came from hundreds of miles away in the east, at the volcanic vent zones. Conversations with John-David Cameron, and being haunted by the opening paragraphs of *Rendezvous with Rama*, are personal experiences.

The sample bases from the area of boat 8 breaking into odd shapes and the observations on rusticle biology: Pellegrino, written log, Expedition *Titanic XIII*, Aug. 2001, pp. 39–70, 44–45 (illustrations and notes), 74. That the growth cycle reaches the approximate halfway mark during the summer and that August 2001 samples represent an interrupted cycle is a finding consistent with growth rings forming through an annual deep-ocean nutrient cycle.

A Russian scientist's strange response to cross-shaped rusticle substrates and a "rope-draped cross" from the boat 8 location: Pellegrino, written log, Expedition *Titanic XIII*, Aug. 2001, p. 58; letters from Rip MacKenzie, reproduced in Charles Pellegrino, *Ghosts of Vesuvius* (New York: HarperCollins, 2004), 380; Ken Marschall and Lew Abernathy, personal communications, Aug. 2001. Bill Paxton's creature at the boilers: Pellegrino, written log, Expedition *Titanic XIII*, Sept. 2001, p. 70D; unknowns of the deep: ibid., pp. 51, 73.

The continual revelation that much more wood had survived than previously believed, the discovery of strange "worms," and the fates of the grand stairway and

Edith Russell's stateroom: Pellegrino, written log, Expedition *Titanic XIII*, Sept. 2001, p. 79; James Cameron, *Ghosts of the Abyss*, IMAX, 2003 (DVD and supplemental materials).

10. POINTS OF DEPARTURE

Charles Lightoller continued to insist that everything had been against him: Telediphone recording, Nov. 1, 1936, p. 4, L/P file, p. 579. Fred Fleet indicated that if nothing else, confusion was certainly against them: *American Inquiry*, Apr. 23, 1912, p. 319. Fleet's replacement in the *Titanic*'s crow's nest was left there, completely forgotten, until the foremast on which the crow's nest was mounted approached the verge of beginning its submergence: George Hogg, *American Inquiry*, Apr. 25, 1912, pp. 577–578.

Violet Jessop identified the "Mason" in her memoir as Murdoch in a personal communication to Walter Lord, L/P file, p. 535. She noted that he assisted with lowering the portside boats. She also identified musician Jock Hume and the playing of Irving Berlin music along with, at some point, "Nearer My God to Thee." A further note on the music played was provided by Marjorie Newell Robb, personal communication, 1991, L/P file, p. 132.

Jessop saw Thomas Andrews throwing deck chairs and door rafts overboard with the assistance of a man identified by J. Maxtone Graham as Charles Joughin: Violet Jessop with J. Maxtone Graham, *Violet Jessop:* Titanic *Survivor* (New York: Sheridan House, 1997), 129, 131, 132. The L/P file includes Jessop's first draft of history, with annotations by Lord and Graham. These annotations of Jessop's recollections include a tabulation of Murdoch's presence at up to 75 percent of the rescues.

For Joughin's refusing Murdoch's order to save himself and Thomas Andrews's actions: Lord and Graham commenting on Jessop's observations, L/P file, pp. 703, 707, 708–710. The 66 to 75 percent figure is consistent with the prior Quinn chronology, revealing Murdoch as a key rescuer, in Paul J. Quinn, *Dusk to Dawn* (Hollis, NH: Fantail Press, 1999), 125, 178. The identifications of Murdoch aft and on the port side rely on people who personally knew him, including Jessop and Joughin, and not on people likely to have confused him with another officer. The Quinn analysis led us, during Expedition *Titanic XIII*, to add a line spoken by James Cameron in his film, *Ghosts of the Abyss*, honoring the all too frequently maligned Murdoch.

Annie Robinson's experience of a previous shipwreck appears in the *British Inquiry*, May 20, 1912, p. 299. Wyn Craig Wade, Titanic: *End of a Dream* (New York: Penguin, 1979), 280, described the accounts of new ropes and new paint jamming the davits, and Henry Sleeper Harper described the "biolumes" flashing to life in "The True Story of the Disaster," *Harper's Weekly*, Apr. 27, 1912.

George Harris's rescue efforts with Joughin, and his own ultimate rescue by Murdoch: letter from Harris to Bill MacQuitty, Dec. 16, 1956, with 1992 annotations, derived from MacQuitty's interview with Harris, L/P file, pp. 560–561; Charles Joughin, *British Inquiry*, May 10, 1912, p. 140.

Dr. Will O'Loughlin's unusual prescription for how to face death indoors after rescue work was completed: Charles Joughin, letter to Walter Lord, 1955, L/P file, p. 426; George Harris, letter to Bill MacQuitty, Dec. 16, 1956, L/P file, p. 561; letter from Mary Sloan to her sister, written aboard the SS *Lapland*, Apr. 27, 1912, p. 2, L/P file, pp. 310–311. The surgeon's "drink heavily" advice seemed universal, as noted by Walter Lord, Sept. 13, 1993, p. 4, L/P file, p. 33.

Maude Slocomb's rescue by Joseph Wheat, and her observations at one of the last boats: Wheat, *British Inquiry*, May 16, 1912, pp. 240–243; Slocomb, interview by Walter Lord, July 1955, L/P file, p. 268.

On the curious fate of George Rheims and Joe Loring: correspondence between Loring's daughter and Walter Lord, Apr. 1987, L/P file, pp. 421–423; letter from Rheims to his wife, Apr. 19, 1912, p. 1, L/P file, p. 232; Joseph Scarrott, *British Inquiry*, May 3, 1912, p. 23. The timing described in the Rheims account is indicative of two to three minutes between the impact and the first sighting of the iceberg on the starboard side, and it is consistent with Scarrott's account of what appeared to be a second iceberg sighted as the *Titanic* stopped. It is also consistent with several icebergs encountered by lifeboats casting off from the *Titanic*.

The sad case of young Alfred Rush was discussed in detail, as the full story became available from the Goldsmith family, by Walter Lord, Sept. 13, 1993, annotated transcript, pp. 10, 13, L/P file, pp. 40, 42A. In a letter from Frank Goldsmith to Walter Lord, Nov. 28, 1955, L/P file, p. 453, Goldsmith suggested that the boat he and his mother left the *Titanic* in was on the port side (boat D), not the starboard side (boat C).

The evidence points to a departure in boat C, however. Boat D departed about 2:05 a.m. while the port side of the bridge was submerging nearby (Goldsmith never reported seeing this). Boat C departed on the starboard side before boat D, yet still beyond the point at which the extreme list to port had taken control of the lowerings. On the port side, people had to step across a gap to boats that were leaning away from the ship: Charles Joughin, *British Inquiry*, May 10, 1912, p. 140. On the starboard side, the boats scraped against the *Titanic*'s hull while lowering.

In another letter from Goldsmith to Lord, Oct. 15, 1970, L/P file, p. 461, Goldsmith again described the intense list of the *Titanic* near the end, with the lifeboat leaning into the ship so hard that it caught at least three times on the rivets and plates—"nearly tipping us out into the water." However, he described the tilt in the wrong direction (to starboard), and though recalling correctly that his lifeboat must have left on the side of the ship opposite the tilt, he appeared to have reversed sides in his memory (from the starboard side to the port side and boat D). Further verification that Murdoch would have allowed sixteen-year-old Rush and even Frank Goldsmith's father into the starboard forward boat is recorded by Susanne Stormer, *The Biography of William McMaster Murdoch* (Kosel, Germany: Hans Christian Andersen, 1995), 114–115.

Don Lynch's poignant discussion of Thomas Andrews, Bruce Ismay, and the decision to remove extra lifeboats from the *Titanic*'s design was recorded by James Cameron, *Ghosts of the Abyss*, DVD, Walden Media/Disney, 2003.

The departure of Henry Harper's boat, the characterization of some men jumping into descending lifeboats as brave (depending on race or national origin), and the drawing of guns by officers against passengers: Henry Sleeper Harper, "The True Story of the Disaster," *Harper's Weekly*, Apr. 27, 1912; Masabumi Hosono, letter to his wife, Apr. 1912, in M. Findlay, "A Matter of Honor," *Voyage* 27, Winter 1998, pp. 122, 124.

The desperate measures adopted by William Murdoch and Charles Joughin at the aft portside lifeboats: Colonel Archibald Gracie, in Jack Winocour, ed., *The Story of the* Titanic *as Told by Its Survivors* (New York: Dover, 1960), 187; Charles Joughin, *British Inquiry*, May 10, 1912, p. 140.

Regarding the reference to the "penny dreadful" Morgan Robertson novels: Morgan Robertson was a weak stylist and, as was culturally acceptable at the time, openly anti-Semitic. Although several of his predictions came to naught, sometimes he had the uncanny knack of being more accurate than Nostradamus. In his novel *Beyond the Spectrum*, which he wrote in 1914, Japanese Americans were imprisoned in camps on U.S. soil, and Japan was defeated in a global air and naval war by America's use of a weapon that destroyed with a blinding light. The war began when Japanese planes bombed American bases in Manila and Hawaii on a December morning.

In 1898, Robertson had written *Futility*; it was about a ship called the *Titan* that sank one April night after striking an iceberg on the starboard side. "Fourteen years later," wrote Walter Lord in his preface to *A Night to Remember* (New York: Holt, 1955), "a British shipping company named the White Star Line built a ship remarkably like the one in Robertson's novel. The new liner was 66,000 tons displacement; Robertson's was 70,000. The real ship was 882.5 feet long; the fictional one was 800 feet. Both vessels were triple screw and could make 24–25 knots. Both could carry about 3,000 people, and both had enough lifeboats for only a fraction of this number. But, then, this didn't seem to matter because both were labeled 'unsinkable.'"

Charles Joughin's possible witnessing, at 1:20 a.m. of the first breaking of the ship, is recorded in his testimony to the *British Inquiry*, May 10, 1912, pp. 144–145. His actions and observations are further recorded in a personal communication with Lord, annotated with Lord's assessment of Joughin's subsequent last run through third class, snatching up children and refusing orders to save himself in a lifeboat: L/P file, pp. 31, 426.

Further indications of the ship's flooding conditions at this time were provided in a Frank Prentice interview by Walter Lord, p. 2, L/P file, p. 649, and the first real attempt to assess the role of open portholes was discussed by Ken Marschall, L/P file, p. 129B. Frank Prentice was one of the people aboard who mentioned having his porthole open at the moment of impact. It is unknown whether he latched it closed. He probably did, for the flood through the porthole would have been equal to about 10 percent of the initial iceberg damage, and water should thus have been pouring in, at 1:20 a.m., with the force of several fire hoses opened to full power.

Prentice's room was located just in front of Joughin's room, and surely Joughin would have noticed this as the source of the leak if water were gushing out of Prentice's door and down the slant of the deck, *away* from his room. Instead, Joughin reported to the *British Inquiry*, May 10, 1912, pp. 145, 147, that it was essentially a trickle coming *down* to his room, with no associated sound of a gush nearby. At 1:27 a.m., the *Titanic*'s two Marconi operators sent out a message hauntingly consistent with Joughin's observations, as noted by John Durant, a Marconi operator aboard the *Mount Temple*, to the *British Inquiry*, May 15, 1912, pp. 212–213.

There was much discussion in this portion of the *British Inquiry* about the Marconi operators' and the engineers' understanding of specifically which engine room was taking water at this time, with a focus on the reciprocating engine room (the entire front part of the reciprocating engine room did indeed break away). In the files of Bill MacQuitty, assembled for the City Heritage Collection, *Titanic* Marconi operator Harold Bride clarified that at approximately 1:30 a.m., he was sending out a warning about flooding in the aft engine rooms. He told the following to D. Hyslop et al., Titanic *Voices* (Southampton, UK: Southampton City Council, 1994), 150: "The list forward was increasing. [Jack] Phillips told me the wireless was growing weaker. The captain [who certainly knew an engine room from a boiler room, noting also that the dynamos were aft of the boilers] came and told us that our engine rooms were taking water and that the dynamos might not last much longer."

Masabumi Hosono's preparations for the end, and the events in boat 10, are recorded in his letter to his wife, Apr. 1912, in M. Findlay, "A Matter of Honor," *Voyage* 27, Winter 1998, p. 122; Charles Joughin, *British Inquiry*, May 10, 1912, p. 141; and William Burke, *American Inquiry*, Apr. 26, 1912, p. 822.

M. Findlay, "Solving the Mystery of Mr. Hosono's Lifeboat," *Voyage* 27, Winter 1998, pp. 124, 130, provides the last name of the man who entered boat 10 with Hosono: Krekorian. Colonel Archibald Gracie, in Jack Winocour, ed., *The Story of the* Titanic *as Told by Its Survivors* (New York: Dover, 1960), listed the last boats and the people in them: boat 10, p. 186; boat 14, p. 190; boat 4, pp. 202–203; boat D, p. 211; boat C, p. 258; and boat 13, p. 253.

Gracie automatically listed surviving men of non-Anglo-Saxon races and certain nationalities as "stowaways." In boat 4, Gracie listed a Frenchman as a "stowaway," but aside from the male crew assigned to the boat, all of the passengers were women and children except for three men who were described by Martha Stephenson as "dropped off the ship and . . . swimming towards us [as boat 4 pulled away]": Jack Winocour, ed., *The Story of the* Titanic *as Told by Its Survivors* (New York: Dover, 1960), 209. These appear to be the only three candidates for Gracie's branding of a French "stowaway."

In her letter to Colonel Gracie, Stephenson had written unfavorably about one of the jumper-swimmers: "One man was drunk and had a bottle of brandy in his pocket which the quartermaster promptly threw overboard and the drunken man was promptly thrown into the bottom of the boat and a blanket thrown over him." Gracie's comments about "the coolness, courage, and sense of duty . . . of my Anglo-Saxon race," appear on page 132 of Winocour.

Lawrence Beesley's account is also published in Winocour (pp. 37, 142, 253). On the same boat with Beesley was Millvina Dean's mother, who gives an account of the women in boat 13 who threatened violence against a nonwhite survivor: Roger Ailes interview with Millvina Dean and Charles Pellegrino, Fox News, Sept. 1994, L/P file, p. 662.

The long years of shame and ridicule that Hosono faced as a nonwhite male survivor because of Gracie and the press: "Letter Rectifies Decades of Shame of Japanese *Titanic* Survivor," *Arizona Daily Star*, Dec. 21, 1997, p. 20. Juliette Laroche and her two children were in the same boat with Hosono: O. Mendez, Titanic *Commutator* 24, no. 149 (Nov. 2000): 46–48; and Judith Geller, Titanic: *Women and Children First* (New York: W. W. Norton, 1998), 96.

In a lifeboat forward of Juliette Laroche and Hosono, Emily Ryerson witnessed an open D-deck porthole "and the water rushing in": affidavit, *American Inquiry*, p. 1107.

The bias against certain races and nationalities aboard the *Titanic* was so acceptable in Edwardian society as to be openly preached from the pulpit and published in such prominent papers as the *Brooklyn Daily Eagle*. In the published sermons, religious leaders took particular exception to the making of "mulatto" children by men like Joseph Laroche: "Dr. C. Parkhurst's Strong Words—Men and Religion: A Horrible Marine Massacre," *Brooklyn Daily Eagle*, Apr. 22, 1912, p. 3. One preacher, invoking the biblical prophet Ezekiel, blamed wealth: "Their silver and their gold shall not be able to deliver them," suggesting that God struck down the *Titanic* because its passengers were wealthy, notwithstanding the fact that the highest mortality was suffered by the poor. Celiney Yasbeck's observations from boat 6, and the census of women and children lost in third class, upholds this statistic: Judith Geller, Titanic: *Women and Children First* (New York: W. W. Norton, 1998), 181; Yasbeck, letter to Walter Lord, June 15, 1955, p. 3, L/P file, pp. 226–227.

Marjorie Newell watched lights going off throughout the ship: M. Newell Robb, personal communication, 1991; J. Fuoco, "Memories of a Terrible Night," Mystic Museum, 1991, L/P file, pp. 131–132. Referring to a possible attempt by the engineers to conserve power for the Marconi apparatus and the boat-deck lights, Bill MacQuitty cited a letter from Alfred White to the family of William Parr, June 21, 1912, L/P file, pp. 182–186. During the filming of *A Night to Remember*, MacQuitty learned additional details from family member Frank Johnston, including corroboration of White's story of having been instructed, near the end, to bring up more service power.

Possible archaeological corroboration of what Newell and White saw: Parks Stephenson recorded evidence of surge-and-burn effects during his 2005 dive. In a letter to author, Dec. 24, 2010, he wrote: "Just outside the Marconi Room, we found an electrical distribution panel that had suffered a brief fire, melting some (but not all) fuse holders and scorching a portion of the panel. The dousing of the lights could be due to something similar—a localized electrical casualty could cause some lights to fail while others stayed on."

11. THE GEOMETRY OF SHADOWS

Robot footage and the fate of the *Titanic*'s grand stairway: Charles Pellegrino, written log, Expedition *Titanic XIII*, Sept. 2001, pp. 86–87. Robert Ballard, *Titanic: The Last Great Images* (Toronto: Madison Press, 2007), pp. 56–57, described the discovery of metal framing consistent with a central portion of the grand stairway dome, lying in the debris field. Crystal dome fragments (clearly from the large, front grand stairway) were imaged in trace amounts at the bottom of the mostly empty grand stairwell by robots in James Cameron, *Last Secrets of the Titanic*, Discovery Channel, 2005.

There was a rear grand stairway with a similar crystal dome, so the possibility is fifty-fifty that the crystal dome frame discovered by Ballard could be from either stairway. The rear stairway was only two decks deep, so the greater probability is that any floating stairway wreckage described by Marjorie Newell, 1991 interview notes, L/P file, p. 131, and others, as encountered by the *Titanic*'s lifeboats, originated from the larger, front grand staircase.

The velocity of the down-blast effect and its destructive power comes from an analysis of James Cameron's 1995 expedition results (robot Snoop Dog); Charles Pellegrino, written log, Expedition *Ocean Voyager*, *Titanic VIII*, June 19, 1997, L/P file, supplemental log notes; investigation into bioarchaeology of *Titanic*, 1996–1997: Pellegrino and Tom Dettweiler, written log, Expedition *Titanic VIII*, Aug. 2001, pp. 11–18; Pellegrino, written log, Expedition *Titanic XIII*, Aug. 2001, pp. 88–90.

The passenger room numbers given in this book are based on Walter Lord's revision of the Cave list, with additional survival accounts of room listings added by Don Lynch's contacts with survivors, which jointly became the basis for the room map used during Expedition *Titanic XIII* in 2001: Charles Pellegrino, *Ghosts of the* Titanic (New York: HarperCollins, 2000).

The condition of the staterooms and the corridors and the discussion of bones at the *Titanic* site: Pellegrino, written log, Expedition *Titanic XIII*, Aug. 2001, pp. 90, 92, 150. Shreds of clothing in the soup-tureen concretion and instances of biological preservation at the *Titanic*: Pellegrino, written log, Expedition *Titanic VIII*, 1996, pp. 16, 18; Pellegrino, video log, Expedition *Titanic VIII*, 1996.

Identification of lamb bones by Bill Schutt, 1997. Rusticle samples, confirmed calcium-absorbing and -secreting invertebrates at the *Titanic*'s depth, and close-up of rusticle inhabitants at the starboard bow: Lori Johnston and Charles Pellegrino, video log, Expedition *Titanic XIII*, Sept. 22, 2001.

The two notes written on shrunken Styrofoam coffee cups are from Expedition *Titanic XIII*'s dive 7, Sept. 10, 2001. The stages in descent to the *Titanic* are from Charles Pellegrino, dive 7 field notes, Expedition *Titanic XIII*, Sept. 10, 2001, pp. 103, 108–110.

Observations and experiences at the *Titanic*'s stern: Pellegrino, written log, Expedition *Titanic XIII*, Sept. 10, 2001, pp. 116–120, and post–dive 7 discussion notes. It was determined that the stern hit at approximately sixty miles per hour at approximately a thirty- to forty-five-degree angle, with the rudder embedding first. The front end of the stern still had between 80 and 120 feet to travel before striking the bottom at almost 90 feet per second.

The down-blast effect did not strike the front part of the stern and stop its rotation until the entire stern section became level with the bottom—an interval that allowed roughly one second for the front part to continue rotating, between thirty and forty feet, out of line with the embedded aft end. The electrical anomalies for both the *Mir*s and the robot Medusa at 4:12 p.m., reported by Lori Johnston at mission control: Charles Pellegrino, dive 7 field notes, Expedition *Titanic XIII*, Sept. 10, 2001, pp. 104, 113.

Thoughts as the davit bitt and the boat 8 railing were being prepared for their return to the *Titanic*: Charles Pellegrino, post–dive 7 letters to Mary Leung, Expedition *Titanic XIII*, Sept. 11, 2001, 3 a.m.; also written log, pp. 115B–122, 186. Prior referenced experimental materials include the following books by Charles Pellegrino: *Flying to Valhalla* (New York: Avon-Morrow, 1993), 97; (as coauthor with J. A. Stoff) *Chronic Fatigue Syndrome*, 2nd ed. (New York: HarperCollins, 1992), 295; *Return to Sodom and Gomorrah* (New York: HarperCollins, 1994), 209; (with G. Zebrowski, coauthor) *The Killing Star* (New York: Avon-Morrow, 1995); *Dust* (New York: Avon-Morrow, 1998), 309, 414; *Her Name*, Titanic (New York: Avon-Morrow, 1998), 93.

12. HOW MUCH DOES DARKNESS WEIGH?

Rip MacKenzie's question and the answers he received: Charles Pellegrino, written log, Expedition *Titanic XIII*, July 29, 2001, pp. 123–126; Charles Pellegrino, *Ghosts of Vesuvius* (New York: HarperCollins, 2004), 380–381.

Roy Cullimore's answer: Pellegrino, written log, Expedition *Titanic XIII*, p. 125. Mervyn Fernando's answer: Fernando, *Whither Humankind?* (Pilliyandah, Sri Lanka: Subodhi Institute, 2009), 10, 11, 17, 19, 22. My own answer: Pellegrino, written log, Expedition *Titanic XIII*, Sept. 11, 2001, p. 118. Fernando on Teilhard and the saving of civilization: personal communication. Lori Johnston's question about hearing "the quiet voices" at the stern: Charles Pellegrino, photo log and notes, Expedition *Titanic XIII*, Sept. 10–11, 2001.

13. THE 46TH PSALM

The story of Shaneene Abi-Saab Wahabe was published by R. Bracken and J. White, "A Journey from Lebanon," *Voyage* 27, Winter 1998, pp. 132–134. David Vartanian's story, as told by his daughter, was published by P. T. Dattilo, "A Daughter Remembers, *Titanic* David," Titanic *Commutator* 23, no. 145 (1999): 28, 29. Eugene Daly's story of survival after being corralled below the decks in the stern was recorded in the notes of Dr. F. Blackmarr aboard the *Carpathia*, and these were published in the Titanic *Commutato* 22, no. 3 (Jan. 1999): 27.

Anna Sjoblom's story about barriers against the third class: letter to Walter Lord, July 18, 1955, L/P file, pp. 192–195. A passenger named Olaus Abelseth corroborated Sjoblom's observations at the *American Inquiry*, May 3, 1912, p. 1037. Sjoblom provided additional details, including the observation of many hundreds of feet of rope strewn along the boat deck: letter to the *Tacoma Daily News*, Apr. 30, 1912, quoted by Paul J. Quinn, *Dusk to Dawn* (Hollis, NH: Fantail Press, 1999), 183. James Cameron, personal communication, 2005, confirmed that nearly three hundred feet of rope were unfurled onto the decks by each lifeboat launching from precisely reconstructed davits during the filming of *Titanic*.

What Violet Jessop saw in the end kept her both horrified and strangely transfixed: V. Jessop in transcript, annotated by W. Lord and J. M. Graham, L/P file, p. 710. Lily Futrelle's view was reported by her in a letter to the *Boston Sunday Post*, Apr. 21, 1912. Charlotte Collier and her suddenly fatherless daughter, Marjorie, witnessed almost equally opposite behaviors by Harold Lowe and William Murdoch. They also witnessed mournfully beautiful bioluminescent effects, created by *Titanic*-generated currents, as archived by Charlotte Collier in D. Hyslop et al., Titanic *Voices* (Southampton, UK: Southampton City Council, 1994), 134–137. The troubles with boat 2 in the *Titanic*'s currents were reported by J. G. Boxhall at the *American Inquiry*, Apr. 22, 1912, pp. 242–243.

The *Titanic* at 2:05 a.m.: Walter Lord, letter to Captain T. Barnett, Oct. 8, 1990, L/P file, p. 78. Regarding the last of eight rockets, at 1:20 a.m.: Arthur Bright, *American Inquiry*, Apr. 26, 1912, p. 832.

Joe Loring and George Rheims at 2:05 a.m.: Rheims, letter to his wife, Apr. 19, 1912, and Walter Lord, personal communication with the Loring and Rheims descendants, L/P file, pp. 57–58, 232–234, 421–424. On similar, final choices facing Jack Thayer: Thayer, *Sinking of the SS* Titanic (Indian Orchard, MA: *Titanic* Historical Society, 1940), 14, 19–20.

Referencing the fading deck lights and the decreasing chances of swimming to a lifeboat in the dark: Hugh Woolner, letter to a friend, Apr. 26, 1912, p. 4, L/P file, p. 149; J. Thayer, personal communication to Walter Lord, L/P file, p. 58.

On the *Titanic*'s briefly changing list—port to starboard and back again to port—about 1:20 a.m.: Charles Lightoller, *British Inquiry*, May 21, 1912, p. 316.

Hugh Woolner's last sighting of William Murdoch: Woolner, letter to a friend, Apr. 1912, p. 4, L/P file, p. 149.

Colonel Archibald Gracie recalled working with Murdoch almost till the end: Jack Winocour, ed., *The Story of the* Titanic *as Told by Its Survivors* (New York: Dover, 1960), 137–138, 211, 213. Gracie also mentioned a man named Frederick Hoyt swimming to boat D, along with Woolner and Bjornstrom Steffansen. Boat D was one of the few boats lowered with the *Titanic*'s foredeck close enough to the water to allow at least five people to believe that jumping and swimming could be safely attempted.

Joseph Duquemin dove into the water with a friend, but only Duquemin made it to boat D; his mention of diving from the front port side in "waist-deep" water was consistent with conditions about the time of Woolner's departure: *Guernsey Evening Press*, May 2, 1912, L/P file, p. 150. On the date of the article, Duquemin was still recovering in a hospital, evidently from the effects of hypothermia compounding circulation problems arising from early-stage diabetes. Family records (http://www.ancestry.com) indicate that one of his legs was soon amputated.

Lightoller's firing of an early warning shot was reported by Gracie, *American Inquiry*, Apr. 27, 1912, pp. 991–992. Gracie also reported the throwing down of boat A in Jack Winocour, ed., *The Story of the* Titanic *as Told by Its Survivors* (New York: Dover, 1960), 137. Gracie passed John Collins after abandoning efforts to launch boat A in favor of racing the water uphill, toward the stern: Collins, *American Inquiry*, Apr. 25, 1912, p. 628.

Murdoch continued to struggle with his team to launch boat A: Richard Norris Williams II, letter to Walter Lord, Apr. 27, 1962, p. 2, L/P file, p. 179; Williams, letter to *Main Line Life* (a shipping magazine), Dec. 18, 1957, reprinted in Paul J. Quinn, *Dusk to Dawn* (Hollis, NH: Fantail Press, 1999), 233–234.

The pandemonium on the same part of the boat deck, within this same time frame: Jack Thayer, *Sinking of the SS* Titanic (Indian Orchard, MA: *Titanic* Historical Society, 1940), 21–22; Thayer, personal communication with Walter Lord, reported by Lord, April 10, 1991, L/P file, p. 59.

Eugene Daly witnessed warning shots escalating to shootings at boat A: letter to his sister, Maggie, Apr. 1912, reprinted in Walter Lord, *The Night Lives On* (New York: William Morrow, 1986), 128–129. Carl Olof Jansen also witnessed part of a shooting event: Jansen, letter quoted in Wyn Craig Wade, Titanic: *End of a Dream* (New York: Penguin, 1979), 91. George Rheims appeared to have a particularly close-up view of the shootings: Rheims, letter to his wife, Apr. 19, 1912; Walter Lord, notes, L/P file, pp. 57–58, 234–235.

Jack Thayer had an impression, as the final plunge began, that the ship was breaking up: Thayer, *Sinking of the SS* Titanic (Indian Orchard, MA: *Titanic* Historical Society, 1940), 22, 24, 32; Thayer, letter to Judge Charles Long, Apr. 23, 1912, reprinted in Jack Winocour, ed., *The Story of the* Titanic *as Told by Its Survivors* (New York: Dover, 1960), 221.

Watching from boat D, Arthur Bright noticed that the lights were burning only very dimly near Thayer's part of the ship: Bright, *American Inquiry*, Apr. 27, 1912, p. 839.

Thayer's friend, Richard Norris Williams, witnessed large, shadowy parts of the ship falling to the deck: Williams, personal communication to Walter Lord, 1962, L/P file, p. 179.

14. THE TRUTH ABOUT WILLIAM MURDOCH

On the significance of boat A survivors who witnessed shootings: Walter Lord and Charles Pellegrino summary and discussion, Apr. 1991, L/P file, pp. 57–59. The evidence was historically sound, but it revealed only part of Murdoch and his last stand. Relevant expedition log notes and recollections are compiled in Charles Pellegrino, *Ghosts of Vesuvius* (New York: HarperCollins, 2004), 394–396. The rest of the story was uncovered by Paul J. Quinn, *Dusk to Dawn* (Hollis, NH: Fantail Press, 1999). Jim Cameron and Don Lynch were impressed with the Quinn analysis: Cameron, *Ghosts of the Abyss*, IMAX/Walden Media, 2003.

In 1995, Susanne Stormer published her biography of William Murdoch: *The Biography of William McMaster Murdoch* (Kosel, Germany: Hans Christian Andersen, 1995), 61–62, 121. The Stormer book was written with input from William Murdoch's relatives, Scott, Siv, and Harry Murdoch, who supplied letters and other family documents. Later, inside the *Mir-2* and aboard the *Titanic*, a letter was written to William Murdoch in a copy of the Stormer book: Charles Pellegrino, written log, Expedition *Titanic XIII*, Sept. 10, 2001.

Jessop, who was among the many saved by Murdoch, was perplexed by the final breakup of the *Titanic*: Violet Jessop with J. Maxtone Graham, *Violet Jessop:* Titanic *Survivor* (New York: Sheridan House, 1997), 133.

George Harris and Maude Slocomb watched from boat 11 with Edith Russell: Harris, letter to Bill MacQuitty, Dec. 16, 1956; Harris, interview by Bill Mac-Quitty, detailed by MacQuitty in 1992, L/P file, pp. 560–561; Slocomb, interview by Walter Lord, July 1965, L/P file, p. 268; Russell, in Walter Lord, reproduced in "In Their Own Words: *Titanic* Passengers," Apr. 1934, pp. 4–5, http://www .charlespellegrino.com; Walter Lord, letter covering the Russell account, Feb. 11, 1987; Russell, BBC interview, Apr. 14, 1970, L/P file, p. 127.

The rift between Millvina Dean and Ellen (Betty) Phillips began in a lifeboat while one was only an infant and the other was yet to be born: E. Phillips, personal communication with John Hodges, "In Their Own Words: *Titanic* Passengers," Apr. 2001, http://www.charlespellegrino.com.

15. TO DREAM ON THE SHIP OF SORROWS

At 3:30 a.m. aboard the *Keldysh*, the cleaning of the two *Titanic* "crosses" was memorialized in Charles Pellegrino, photo log and notes, Expedition *Titanic XIII*, Sept. 10–11, 2001; personal experiences with family members (cousins Donna and Sharon). Captain Paddy Brown's at-home and on-the-job habits: personal communication with friends Olinda Cedeno and Mary Leung, members of the Brown family, and Ladder 3. His fights with the "red devil" and the rescue of Jessica Rubenstein: anonymous, in eulogy read by Mike Daly, St. Patrick's Cathedral, New York, Nov. 9, 2001.

The "How Much Does Darkness Weigh?" conference and Roy Cullimore's comments about "a sense of justice": Charles Pellegrino, written log, Expedition *Titanic XIII*, p. 126; personal communication with Roy Cullimore, Aug. 2001. The actions of Atta and Abdulaziz in Maine, while we prepared for dive 7 and history's first rescue of one robot by another: Reporters and editors of *Der Spiegel, Inside 9–11* (New York: St. Martin's Press, 2002), 2, 26. Events aboard the *Keldysh*: Pellegrino, written log, Expedition *Titanic XIII*, Sept. 11, 2001, pp. 103–145.

An hour and a half behind *Titanic* time, in New York, Paddy Brown signed in: artifacts at 3 House of the fire department (the chalkboard and journal, on which the crew signed in for the last time). The story of the close-knit members of two families, located on Flights 11 and 175 and inside the Twin Towers: H. McClure (friend of the two families), personal communication, 2002; Reporters and editors of *Der Spiegel, Inside 9–11* (New York: St. Martin's Press, 2002), 36–38, 41, 68–70.

About the time Flight 175 became airborne, we placed the two "crosses" in the *Titanic* sample return tray and launched the *Mir-1*: Pellegrino, photo log and notes, Expedition *Titanic XIII*, Sept. 11, 2001. Event impact collapse timing, and seismic results: *The 9/11 Commission Report* (New York: W. W. Norton, 2004); Lamont Geophysical Observatory, Palisades, New York.

16. FALLING STARS

Information about Ruth McCourt and Ron Clifford, personal communication with Holly McClure. Mary Leung, looking east across the river, wishing it was not real and pleading for Jim Cameron to yell, "Cut!": Leung, personal communication. The *Keldysh*, the International Space Station, and the Antarctic overwinter team were among the most isolated outposts of humanity on September 11, 2001, at 10:40 a.m. *Titanic* time. No clear video reached us, and news of family members and friends safe or missing trickled in slowly, over the course of two days: Charles Pellegrino, personal experiences; Pellegrino, written log, Expedition *Titanic XIII*, Sept. 11–13, 2001, pp. 123–130; Pellegrino, *Keldysh-Mir* communications log, Sept. 11–13, 2001, pp. 132–133. Continuing biomedical research in the deep-ocean pharmacy referenced in Pellegrino, e-mail to Ed Bishop from the *Keldysh*, Sept. 13, 2001, p. 146.

17. MOVEMENTS OF FIRE AND ICE

William Murdoch and the tragic practice of "cracking on": Susanne Stormer, *The Biography of William McMaster Murdoch* (Kosel, Germany: Hans Christian Andersen, 1995), 60–61, 160; George Rowe, letter to Walter Lord, 1955, L/P file, pp. 317–318. Murdoch to Samuel Hemming: Hemming, *British Inquiry*, May 24, 1912, p. 421.

Aboard the *Keldysh*, the Americans reflected on the number of warnings that had been missed: Eleanor Hill, *New Jersey Record*, Sept. 19, 2002; R. Schlesinger and W. Washington, *Boston Globe*, May 17, 2002. Regarding Jim Cameron's insistence that "it is not 11:40 p.m.": Charles Pellegrino, written log, Expedition *Titanic XIII*, logged Sept. 21, 2001, pp. 259–260.

18. FRAILTY

Note: The chapter title is a nod to the film of the same name starring Bill Paxton. The Yeltsin event (1995) is recounted in the film *Countdown to Zero*, National Geographic Channel, 2011. The last warning to the *Titanic*, from the *Californian*, was affirmed by C. F. Evans, *British Inquiry*, May 15, 1912, p. 202.

Charles Lightoller discussed in 1936 how he and Samuel Hemming had worked to free boat B as the final plunge began; Hemming, who had insisted all along that there was plenty of time, decided that time might actually have been running out after all: Jack Winocour, ed., *The Story of the* Titanic *as Told by Its Survivors* (New York: Dover, 1960), p. 297; Hemming, *American Inquiry*, Apr. 23, 1912, p. 666; Hemming, *British Inquiry*, May 24, 1912, p. 422.

Lightoller's critical observations in determining the angle between the bridge and the crow's nest—and his remarkable escape: *American Inquiry*, Apr. 24, 1912, pp. 72, 90, 94; *British Inquiry*, May 21, 1912, p. 318; Winocour, *The Story of the* Titanic, pp. 297, 299.

On the fall of the first smokestack: James Cameron, "Thayer: The Dance of the Smokestacks," in Jack Thayer, *In Their Own Words:* Titanic, http://www .charlespellegrino.com. Thayer also spoke of a smokestack falling near boat B in his *Sinking of the SS* Titanic (Indian Orchard, MA: Titanic Historical Society, 1940), 24.

Thayer has often been attached to sensational newspaper reports and to a series of drawings, attributed to him, describing the ship breaking apart in such a manner that the bow's tip resurfaced near him and among the falling smokestacks. In *Sinking of the SS* Titanic, 24, 25, Thayer described parts of the ship, including the second funnel and some of the upper-deck "superstructure," splitting apart and buckling upward as the region around the officers, quarters and the crystal dome submerged. He did not believe the ship itself actually broke in two—and especially not at a point near the first two smokestacks and the grand stairway in such a manner as to draw the tip of the bow being pulled all the way back to his location. The drawings attributed to Thayer, made famous after the Ballard expeditions really did prove that the *Titanic* broke in two, were sketched in 1912 by reporter L. D. Skidmon of Brooklyn, based on second-hand information.

Eugene Daly surfaced from the final plunge into horrors that were described by him to Dr. Frank Blackmarr on the rescue ship *Carpathia* and published by J. T. Harper, "Dr. Frank Blackmarr's Remarkable Scrapbook," Titanic *Commutator* 22, no. 3 (Jan. 1999): 27.

Almost two decades later, Lightoller told what he had heard people calling to one another during those last minutes: Lightoller, personal communication to Walter Lord, L/P file, p. 575. Anthony El-Khouri, in an e-mail to Charles Pellegrino, Jan. 11, 2011, speculated about what Lightoller must have felt when he heard those calls and why he felt it.

Thayer reported that despite the horror, he was entranced: Thayer, *Sinking of the SS* Titanic (Indian Orchard, MA: *Titanic* Historical Society, 1940), 25. August Wennerstrom's account was recorded in Wyn Craig Wade, Titanic: *End of a Dream* (New York: Penguin, 1979), 314.

George Rheims wrote of having barely escaped tangled ropes in a letter to his wife, Apr. 19, 1912, L/P file, pp. 232–234; annotation by James Cameron on ropes left on decks by exact reproduction of the *Titanic's* lifeboats, Aug. 2001, p. 233.

Alfred White's last actions in the engine room, and his escape via the fourth smokestack, were detailed in a letter to Rev. M. Langley (brother-in-law of William Parr), June 21, 1912. The letter was forwarded to Bill MacQuitty and Walter Lord by family member Frank Johnston, Nov. 20, 1956. Notes about additional family recollections were provided by MacQuitty in 1990, L/P file, pp. 182–186.

Thomas Patrick Dillon reported that the clocks in the engine room had not yet been reset and were off by about fifteen minutes (and perhaps more, up to half an hour): *British Inquiry*, May 9, 1912, p. 99. Consequently, when White specifies 1 a.m., he, like Dillon, means at least 1:15. When White states that the ship began lurching down at "twenty of two," he is almost certainly talking about the plunge that began with the boiler room number 4 collapse, between 2:00 and 2:10 a.m. (and closer to the latter). One of the enduring engine-room enigmas of the night was the steam source for electrical power late into the sinking: Parks Stephenson, "*Titanic* Wreck Observations, 2005," http://www.mconigraph.com, 2006, p. 5.

Charles Joughin, after his rescue work was finished, followed the doctor's orders for facing the last minutes ("drink heavily") and stepped into history as a medical enigma: He first contacted Lord by letter, Nov. 2, 1955, L/P file, pp. 425–427, 429. Lord reported on his conversations with Joughin on Sept. 13, 1993, L/P file, pp. 31–32, 38.

Joughin told the examiners that during the forty to forty-five minutes leading up to the breakup, he saw a leak and heard cracking in a region between the third and fourth smokestacks: *British Inquiry*, May 10, 1912, pp. 145, 148. Joughin clarified that he first heard a loud cracking sound a few minutes after he had been to his room and discovered a leak about 1:30 a.m. Joughin also clarified that the breakup of the ship and the rush of people toward the stern occurred after 2 a.m. Thomas Patrick Dillon described his escape from the severed stern for the *British Inquiry*, May 9, 1912, pp. 98–101.

The story of Howard Irwin and Henry Sutehall's journey: Matt Tulloch, personal communication, June 14, 1995, L/P file, pp. 670–678; Barbara Shuttle, personal communications, 2004–2010; and Dave Shuttle and Barbara Shuttle, "Pearl and Howard: Recovered Artifacts Recall a Story of Tragic Love," *Voyage* 31, Winter 2000, pp. 151–154.

George Kemish's escape: letter to Walter Lord, June 19, 1955, L/P file, pp. 554, 560. Kemish reached boat 9, commanded by James McGough, as noted by Colonel Archibald Gracie in Jack Winocour, ed., *The Story of the* Titanic *as Told by Its Survivors* (New York: Dover, 1960), 248. An important contribution of the Kemish letter is that it sheds light on the kidnapping of Howard Irwin. Martha Stephenson's recollections were recorded in a letter to Gracie in 1912, reproduced in Winocour, p. 209.

In boat 14, the crew lied about the source of the screams, as recalled by Madeline Mellinger: *Toronto Star*, Apr. 15, 1974, L/P file, p. 578.

Observations from boat 16 were recorded by Violet Jessop and Lily Futrelle, Lord annotations of Jessop memoir, 1999, L/P file, pp. 709, 711.

Arthur Bright testified that he witnessed lights in portholes after the stern broke away: *American Inquiry*, Apr. 27, 1912, pp. 833, 837, 840–841. Thomas Ranger and George Cavell reported the same phenomenon to the *British Inquiry*, May 9, 1912, pp. 104–105, 107. In boat 10, Edward Buley also noted the impossible persistence of portside lights: *American Inquiry*, Apr. 25, 1912, pp. 610, 612. Buley, who would disappear into history as a casualty of World War I, became the chief antagonist of Masabumi Hosono: Buley, *American Inquiry*, Apr. 25, 1912, p. 613; Hosono, "Letter Rectifies Decades of Shame," *Arizona Star*, Dec. 21, 1997 (courtesy of Carl J. White); M. Findlay, "A Matter of Honor," *Voyage* 27, Winter 1998, p. 124.

Frank Evans saw the breakup of the *Titanic* from Hosono's boat and described it in detail: *American Inquiry*, Apr. 26, 1912, p. 753.

19. A CREVICE IN TIME

Events aboard the *Keldysh* immediately after 9/11: Charles Pellegrino, e-mail to Arthur C. Clarke, Sept. 13, 2001; Pellegrino, written log, Expedition *Titanic XIII*,

Sept. 11–13, 2001, pp. 146, 178; communications shack log and video log for these dates (pp. 103–105); James Cameron, *Ghosts of the Abyss* (DVD).

On the origin of a study in column collapse, down-blast, volcano physics, and a decision to enter ground zero at the expedition's end: Charles Pellegrino, in Haraldur Sigurddson, *American Vesuvius*, Towers Productions, History Channel, 2006. Nomenclature scale for explosive events developed by Charles Scheffield and others: Charles Pellegrino, *Ghosts of Vesuvius* (New York: HarperCollins, 2004), 62–63.

The figure of twelve thousand pounds per square inch, within the regions of the central World Trade Center column collapses, was determined by metallurgical studies of damage to the barrels of service guns worn by police officers killed in the towers. Forces ranged both above and below this number, depending on such variables as radius from the core of the column collapse, shielding effects, and even shock cocooning. This was a force approximately equivalent to twice the force pressing in on the hulls of the *Mir*s at the *Titanic*'s depth.

Aboard the *Keldysh*, John-David Cameron warned against entering the toxic plumes of the World Trade Center: Cameron, personal communication and shared experiences with Lew Abernathy, Expedition *Titanic XIII*, Sept. 2001. "Remember Dr. O'Loughlin" and a lesson in not following the ship's surgeon's advice: Pellegrino, letters to Arthur C. Clarke, in written log, Expedition *Titanic XIII*, Sept. 13, 16, 2001, pp. 175, 180.

Aboard the *Keldysh*, a drawing was faxed from P.S. 26 in Queens: Pellegrino, written log, Expedition *Titanic XIII*, Sept. 20, 2001, p. 220.

Discovery of the number 1 cargo hatch cover, further study of the stern section, and implications for World Trade Center down-blast studies: Charles Pellegrino and James Cameron, field notes and written log, Expedition *Titanic XIII*, Sept. 21, 2001, pp. 226–228; Roy Cullimore, Charles Pellegrino, and Lori Johnston, "RMS *Titanic* and the Emergence of New Concepts on the Consortial Nature of Microbial Events," *Environmental Contamination and Toxicology* 173 (2002): 132–134; Ken Marschall and Charles Pellegrino, written log, Expedition *Titanic XIII*, debris field map and stern section.

While at sea, preparing for a comparative study of volcano physics at the World Trade Center, we received from the navy fresh comparative material from the wreck of the *Ehime Maru*: written log, Expedition *Titanic XIII*, Sept. 2001, dive 7 frontmatter. The next day, Jim Cameron opened the production meeting with a surprise—sending me back again to the *Titanic*: Pellegrino, written log, Expedition *Titanic XIII*, Sept. 22, 2001, pp. 265–266.

20. DARK CIRCLE

In the deep, even the most insignificant fungus seemed eager to teach: Charles Pellegrino, letter to friends S. Sittenreich and F. Kakugawa, Mar. 2, 2011.

Revelations of Alfred White's retrograde amnesia and the real horrors of boat A: Alfred White, letters to family of William Parr, contact of family with Bill MacQuitty, June 1, 1912, Nov. 20, 1956, L/P file, pp. 124, 182–186; George Rheims, letter to his wife, Apr. 19, 1912, annotated by Walter Lord and James Cameron, L/P file, pp. 57–58, 232–236; Richard Norris Williams, letter to Walter Lord, Apr. 27, 1962, L/P file, p. 179.

More details about the improbable escape and the medical enigma of Charles Joughin: Joughin, *British Inquiry*, May 10, 1912, pp. 142, 145, 148; Joughin, personal communication to Walter Lord, discussed by Lord, Sept. 13, 1993, L/P file, p. 38B. On hypothermia and the hazards of warming from the extremities: Barbara M. Medlin and Rich Robles (*Keldysh* staff), personal communication, 2001. On the actual measurement of the surface area and volume ratios in such processes: Charles Pellegrino, "The Role of Dessication Pressures and Surface Area/Volume Relationships . . . Implications for Adaptation to Land," *Crustaceana* 47, no. 3 (1984): 251–268, http://victoria.Icon.ac.nz/vwebv/searchBasic.

Following these same mathematical principles, Joughin's unorthodox way of warming himself (and *surviving* it) compounds the mystery: Captain J. J. Anderson, letter to Walter Lord, Jan. 1956, L/P file, p. 429. August Wennerstrom's harrowing odyssey aboard boat A was recorded in undated unpublished papers, sourced courtesy of Wennerstrom's family in Wyn Craig Wade, Titanic: *End of a Dream* (New York: Penguin, 1979), 248–249, 299, 313–314, 320. Fellow survivor David Vartanian's boat A experience was reported by Philip T. Dattilo, "A Daughter Remembers *Titanic* David," Titanic *Commutator* 23, no. 145 (1999): 28, 29.

George Rheims described the dead and the dying in boat A, leading up to the rescue of Vartanian: letter to his wife, Apr. 19, 1912, p. 4, L/P file, p. 238. The only woman to survive sinking with the *Titanic* was discovered by Walter Lord to be a boat A survivor, Rosa Abbott: Walter Lord, personal communication, 1986; Judith Geller, Titanic: *Women and Children First* (New York: W. W. Norton, 1998), 142.

Albert Moss's arrival at the overturned boat B was recorded in Per Kristian Sebak, Titanic: *31 Norwegian Destinies* (Oslo: Genesis Forlag, 1998), 88–89. This boat was Charles Lightoller's command: Lightoller, in Jack Winocour, ed., *The Story of the* Titanic *as Told by Its Survivors* (New York: Dover, 1960), 301.

Celiney Yasbeck estimated that her boat was within five minutes' rowing distance of the circle of dying people, but the officer in charge would not move nearer: Yasbeck, letter to Walter Lord, June 15, 1955, pp. 3, 4, L/P file, pp. 226–229; Helen Candee to Colonel Archibald Gracie, in Winocour, 301.

Boat 11 was another that did not move nearer: Edith Russell, unpublished memoir with letter to Walter Lord, Apr. 11, 1934, annotated by Lord, Feb. 11, 1987, communications file, Mar. 1978–Mar. 1988, pp. 6, 7. In boat 5, Herbert Pitman allowed himself to be overruled by his passengers: Pitman, *American Inquiry*, Apr. 19, 1912, pp. 283, 284; survivor C. H. Behr, letter written for his family's scrapbook, undated, L/P file, p. 211.

Don Lynch's chilling explanation for the behavior of the women in Pitman's boat: Charles Pellegrino, written log, Expedition *Titanic XIII*, Aug. 2001, as the result of a personal communication with Lynch. Violet Jessop's observations in boat 16 and the behavior of Mary Hewlett: Violet Jessop with J. Maxtone Graham, *Violet Jessop:* Titanic *Survivor* (New York: Sheridan House, 1997), 138; M. Hewlett, letter to her sister, May 30, 1912, L/P file, p. 444. Not all of the women shared Hewlett's attitude, such as in the case of an odd coincidence recorded in Captain Arthur Rostron's 1939 account, *The Loss of the* Titanic (Indian Orchard, MA: Titanic Historical Society, 1975), 16–17.

Frank Prentice on the idle lifeboats: Prentice interview with Walter Lord, undated, L/P file, pp. 659, 660; Augustus H. Weikman, *American Inquiry*, Apr. 24, 1912, p. 1099. Edward John Buley (Hosono's accuser) had witnessed people trying to construct rafts, as he told the *American Inquiry*, Apr. 25, 1912, pp. 606, 609–611. Weikman survived on one of the rafts.

By 3:20 a.m., Harold Lowe pulled the Buley-Hosono boat together with several others and prepared to row back with boat 14 in search of survivors: Buley, *American Inquiry*, Apr. 25, 1912, p. 606. While transferring passengers, Lowe overlooked Charlotte Collier and her daughter, who were still in his rescue boat: Collier, in D. Hyslop et al., Titanic *Voices* (Southampton, UK: Southampton City Council, 1994), 133, 137.

Collier wrote that her feet were in several inches of water; this was consistent with another passenger's account to Gracie that boat 14 struck the water hard enough to be damaged and had developed a slow leak: Jack Winocour, ed., *The Story of the* Titanic *as Told by Its Survivors* (New York: Dover, 1960), 197.

Lowe discovered to his horror that he had waited too long before returning to the site of the sinking: Lowe, *American Inquiry*, Apr. 23, 1912, p. 410. His boat began grating up against hundreds of frozen bodies: Joseph Scarrott, *British Inquiry*, May 3, 1912, pp. 25–26. The electric torch Lowe brought with him was described in Winocour, 197. Collier's experience in the circle of death is preserved in D. Hyslop et al., Titanic *Voices* (Southampton, UK: Southampton City Council, 1994), 137–138.

The initial refusal of Lowe to rescue a nonwhite survivor who was clinging to floating wreckage was revealed over the course of several weeks in 1912: George Crowe, *American Inquiry*, Apr. 25, 1912, p. 616; Collier, *American Semi-Monthly*, May 1912.

The Collier passage was sanitized for reproduction in D. Hyslop et al., Titanic *Voices* (Southampton, UK: Southampton City Council, 1994), 76, but it was mostly restored there on page 76; it was also reproduced in its original form by Gracie in Jack Winocour, ed., *The Story of the* Titanic *as Told by Its Survivors* (New York: Dover, 1960), 195. It was also reproduced in its entirety in "Biography of Harold Godfrey Lowe," *Encyclopedia Titanica*, 1. The only lesson that Lowe seems to have learned from this experience was to cease cursing Asians and denigrate Italians instead: *American Inquiry*, Apr. 19, 1912, p. 408; Buley (who went back with Lowe in boat 14), *American Inquiry*, Apr. 25, 1912, p. 613.

21. EXPLORERS, GRAVES, AND LOVERS

The velocity of the *Titanic's* bow section, upon impact with the bottom: B. Matsen, *The* Titanic's *Last Secrets* (New York: Twelve, 2008), 35, 41. Analysis of impact-generated "jetting trenches" and craters: Charles Pellegrino, video log, Expedition *Titanic XIII*, Sept. 22, 2001. Additional data: Sinking of the *Ocean Voyager* and its terminal velocity in the Gulf of Oman: Tom Dettweiler, James Cameron, and John-David Cameron, personal communication, 2002.

Analysis of rusticle concreted (preserved) cross-sections of the *Titanic's* "Hell's Kitchen" and starboard stern ejected-materials blanket: Charles Pellegrino and Roy Cullimore, written log and video log, Expedition *Titanic VIII*, 1996, and post-expedition notes, Apr. 13, 1997; Pellegrino and Cullimore, in William Garske, "How Did the *Titanic* Really Sink?" *Voyage* 25, 1997, p. 43.

Eyewitness accounts of people trapped in the *Titanic's* stern: Gus Cohen, as recollected from personal communication, as noted by Walter Lord, Sept. 13, 1993, p. 4, L/P file, p. 33. Alfred White had also reported seeing people deep inside the ship, gathered in prayer: communication from family members to Walter Lord and Bill MacQuitty, 1955–1956, L/P file, p. 184; pre-expedition

Titanic VIII conference, 1996, L/P file, pp. 687–688. On the growth of rusticles at and around the stern: glacier-like flows from rusticle sources are especially prominent in black-and-white Argo photos of a broken-away crane near aft port side of the stern debris, 1986.

On bioconcretions, the 1996 soup-tureen discovery, and the breakthrough study of the *Titanic*'s rusticle reef with Roy Cullimore: Charles Pellegrino, written and video logs, Expedition *Titanic VIII*, 1996; written log, pp. 1, 4B, 5, 12, 13, 16, 90; William Garske, "How Did the *Titanic* Really Sink?" *Voyage* 25, 1997, pp. 39–46. The gold-covered band remnant was found surrounding a mammalian bone consistent with the base of a human finger. More specifically, the copper-gold band appeared to have grown outward from the base of the third bone from the tip of a finger, called the proximal phalanx. The base of this bone was mostly missing at the break point in the concretion. The expansion of disintegrating copper from the bone into anoxic mud had continued backward and hardened over the base of the next bone—the bone actually found in the tureen concretion—which was the forepart of the palm itself, called a metacarpal.

On the equipment sent to probe the *Titanic* during Expedition *Titanic VIII*: Charles Pellegrino, video log, Expedition *Titanic VIII*, Aug. 1996. Discussion of bilateral bow damage under sediment: Charles Pellegrino, Roy Cullimore, William Garske, and Bill Lange. Debris field map: Paul Henry Nargeolet, George Tulloch, Roy Cullimore, Ken Marschall, and Charles Pellegrino, by aid of Argo footage enhanced by B. Lange, WHOI, 1997. The Georgia sheriff comment is credited to Bill Engfer, personal communication, 1997.

The high-resolution sonar results were first described by William Garske, "How Did the *Titanic* Really Sink?" *Voyage* 25, 1997, pp. 29–31. Paul Henry Nargeolet and Paul Matthias's results from the port side, indicating that most of the bow section damage seen had resulted from the deep-ocean crash, was discussed in B. Martzen, *Titanic's Last Secrets* (New York: Twelve, 2008), 36. On the biological pathways of iron and water through rusticles: Roy Cullimore and Lori Johnston, "*Titanic*: The Biological Odyssey," *Voyage* 32, 2000, p. 174.

The fate of the Rice family aboard the *Titanic*: Eugene Rice, personal communication, 2002, and by Don Lynch, letters to author, 2002. Rice participated in framing the dirty bomb protocol for the New York fire department: R. Meo, *My Turn on the Front Lines* (Victoria, BC: Trafford, 2009), 436–437.

Bertha Mulvihil was an eyewitness to the loss of the Rice and Goodwin families and published her account in *Providence Daily Journal*, Apr. 20, 1912, L/P file, p. 709. Rosa Abbott witnessed and experienced what happened to the Sages and other third-class families on the stern: Abbott was a case study by Walter Lord, 1987, personal communication; Abbott, letter to Emily Goldsmith, Mar. 1, 1914, L/P file, p. 457; Judith Geller, Titanic: *Women and Children First* (New York: W. W. Norton, 1988), 141–145.

On the discovery of Howard Irwin's steamer trunk: Barbara Shuttle, letter to author and notes, Sept. 10, 2004, L/P file, p. 103; Barbara Shuttle and Dave Shuttle, *The Musician's Trunk* (unpublished).

The *Titanic* became one of the very first shipwrecks to yield readable paper after nearly a century. The presence of additional intact paper in the *Titanic*'s mail room was indicated by the robot Robin: George Tulloch, video log, Expedition *Titanic V*, 1993. This discovery supported the conclusions of a Walter Lord and

Charles Pellegrino study pinpointing locations and possible fates of letters written during the voyage, identifying places where robot probes should seek out survivable paper, April 10, 1991, L/P file, pp. 60–63.

"It's amazing how close we [might] have been to losing the story forever": Barbara Shuttle, letter to author, Nov. 20, 2009, p. 1. On the reducing environment inside Howard Irwin's trunk: Charles Pellegrino and Matt Tulloch, IP-3 Laboratory photos and video, France, 1995, L/P file, pp. 670–678. Pearl Shuttle's career as a musician from Hamilton, Ontario, and her doomed love were described in David Shuttle and Barbara Shuttle, "Pearl and Howard," *Voyage* 31, Winter 2000, pp. 151–154, and by Barbara Shuttle, personal communication, 2000–2011.

22. TERMINAL VELOCITY

Dive 10, the discoveries made, the number 1 cargo hatch accident, and the Big Lew Abernathy law: Charles Pellegrino, written log and video log, Expedition *Titanic XIII*, Sept. 22, 2001, pp. 267a, 271, 274–275, 276, 278–280, 369.

23. LAYING THE MUSIC TO REST

The distress call from the *Titanic* reporting "engine room" flooding: Captain Arthur Rostron, *British Inquiry*, June 21, 1912, p. 741. The last signal from the *Titanic*, reported by the *Virginian*, was always a puzzle. Walter Lord and I wondered for a long time what two V's meant, until a possible solution was inspired by the film *A Clockwork Orange*: three dots and a dash, transmitted twice, was the opening of Beethoven's Fifth Symphony, representing death knocking at the door—twice. The last curious signal was first cited in Walter Lord, *A Night to Remember* (New York: Holt, 1955), 92. The monitoring of the *Titanic*'s dying electric spark was detailed by J. H. Moore of the *Mount Temple*, *American Inquiry*, Apr. 27, 1912, pp. 776–777, and in "Digest of Marconigram Messages," *American Inquiry*, p. 1138.

Celiney Yasbeck's boat was among those that came upon the horrifying and mysterious wreck of the floating stairway: Marjorie Newell, personal communication, recorded 1991, L/P file, p. 131. The rescue of the overturned boat B, under Lightoller's command, is detailed in several major firsthand accounts: survivor F. Clench, *American Inquiry*, Apr. 25, 1912, p. 639; Walter Lord, boat 4 discussion notes with author, Sept. 10, 1991, L/P file, p. 90; Jack Thayer letter to Colonel Archibald Gracie, in Jack Winocour, ed., *The Story of the* Titanic *as Told by Its Survivors* (New York: Dover, 1960), 222; Charles Lightoller, in Winocour, 301–302.

Madeline Mellinger and her mother, in boat 12, were present for the rescue of boat B. Madeline, in a letter to Lord, Oct. 1955, described the rescue and the saving of Lightoller himself. Walter Lord, personal communication, Sept. 10, 1991, described how Madeline came into possession of Lightoller's whistle. He also described the rift that later developed over the whistle. L/P file, pp. 89–90, 578–579, 602, 603–613.

Lightoller's whistle was willed by Lord to the British National Maritime Museum, May 2002. Lord can reasonably be argued to have earned the privilege of being the only person besides Lightoller himself to have blown the whistle since the night the *Titanic* went down. They should remain the last two people to do so.

The crowding aboard the rescue ship *Carpathia*, and the immediate resegregation of the classes as they boarded from the lifeboats: Edith Russell, personal communication to Bill MacQuitty, 1995, L/P file, p. 155. Oliver Mendez reported the Laroche family's oral history in "Mademoiselle Louise Laroche: A *Titanic* Survivor," Titanic *Commutator* 19, no. 2 (Aug. 1995): 44, 45.

Additional information was obtained by R. Bracken and M. Findlay, "*Titanic*'s Very Youngest Survivors," *Voyage* 27, Winter 1998, 155, and by Oliver Mendez, Titanic *Commutator*, Oct. 1995, 45.

Mendez referred to a recollection by Juliette Laroche that either a countess or someone with the title "Lady" was aboard her lifeboat, possibly suggesting that she was not—in accordance with Judith Geller, Titanic: *Women and Children First* (New York: W. W. Norton, 1998), 96—in boat 10 but was in boat 8, which contained someone named Countess Rothe. Geller's listing is almost certainly the proper one. The Laroche boat was clearly one of the last ones lowered on the port side; it was so crowded that Juliette was unable to lift her feet from a shallow pool of freezing water in the bottom (about midkeel) or to move to another part of the boat (Mendez, p. 45).

Boat 10 was completely filled, with more than sixty people, and it departed under chaotic conditions that included a rough splash-down: Frank Evans, *American Inquiry*, Apr. 25, 1912, p. 677. Boat 8 cast off with only twenty-eight aboard, during a time of so little chaos that many passengers were still denying the danger. There were no children and no second-class passengers reported in boat 8: Colonel Archibald Gracie, in Jack Winocour, ed., *The Story of the* Titanic *as Told by Its Survivors* (New York: Dover, 1960), 184; William Burke, *American Inquiry*, Apr. 28, 1912, p. 822.

In boat 8, a passenger named M. S. White complained about every minor detail, including members of the crew smoking, but she never mentioned water in the bottom of the boat or overcrowding: affidavit, *American Inquiry*, p. 1008. Further observations on the almost immediate resegregation of second- and third-class survivors from first-class survivors: Marjorie Newell Robb, personal communication, 1991, L/P file, p. 131.

On Simonne Laroche's recollections of the tall woman with the musical toy pig (Edith Russell) and a strategy that diverted attention from the Laroche children's African ancestry: Judith Geller, Titanic: *Women and Children First* (New York: W. W. Norton, 1998), 95, 97, 98, 100; Russell, personal communication with Bill MacQuitty and Walter Lord, around 1956, L/P file, p. 128.

On the music heard that night, and the prolonged belief in Colonel Gracie's insistence that "Nearer My God to Thee" was never played: H. C. Candee, unpublished memoir titled *Sealed Orders*, May 1912, L/P file, p. 173; Walter Lord, *The Night Lives On* (New York: William Morrow, 1986), 138; Roland Hind, personal communication with Lord and MacQuitty, Aug. 1, 1956, L/P, pp. 511–512.

Lawrence Beesley told MacQuitty that for many, memories of "that night" were unhealthy: Bill MacQuitty, personal communication, pre-expedition conference, *Titanic VIII*, 1996, L/P file, pp. 690, 692. Beesley might have been right, in cases that included Jack Thayer: Jack Thayer III obituary, *Philadelphia Inquirer*, Sept. 23, 1945. Marjorie Collier's friend, twelve-year-old Bertha Watts, had managed to keep the *Titanic* out of her thoughts even when the Ballard team discovered the wreck in 1985, as told by Judith Geller, Titanic: *Women and Children First* (New York: W. W. Norton, 1998), 101, 102.

24. A FURY SCORNED

The experiences of Masabumi Hosono (maligned by Edward John Buley as a man who survived the "women and children first" rule by dressing as a woman) and Kate Phillips (pregnant out of wedlock) were recorded as early as 1912. On Hosono: Ed Buley, *American Inquiry*, Apr. 25, 1912, p. 613; M. Findlay, "A Matter of Honor," *Voyage* 27, Winter 1998, p. 122. On Kate's daughter: R. Hodges, "Life after the *Titanic*," letter and enclosure to author, Apr. 27, 2001.

George Rheims's story was finally clarified for his family in correspondence between Patterson-Knight and Walter Lord, Apr. 1987, L/P file, pp. 421–424.

During the filming of *A Night to Remember*, Bill MacQuitty was under such constant attack by the Ismay family that he reported actually getting "that 'bad dog' feeling." It meant a great deal to him, therefore, when actual survivors reviewed early edited versions of the film and told him that he was getting the story right: Bill MacQuitty, personal communication with Walter Lord and author, pre-expedition conference, *Titanic VIII*, 1996, L/P file, pp. 691–692.

25. SLEEPING IN LIGHT

The violence of the stern section's arrival on the bottom turned out to be greater than we imagined: Charles Pellegrino, written log, Expedition *Titanic XIII*, Sept. 25, 2001, pp. 282–283. The last *Mir* was on its way up from stern exploration: Pellegrino, written log, Expedition *Titanic XIII*, Sept. 26, 2001, pp. 278, 280, 283, 285. The ominous beauty of the white rainbow and history repeating itself: Charles Pellegrino and James Cameron, supplemental post-expedition notes, Expedition *Titanic VIII*, 1996, quoted also in Pellegrino, *Ghosts of the* Titanic (New York: HarperCollins, 2000), 141.

26. COMING HOME TO SHOCK COCOONS

The drawings made by the children were included in the written log, Expedition *Titanic XIII*, Sept. 2001, last pages (Oct. 1, 2001).

At the World Trade Center, the same down-blast and surge effects seen at the *Titanic* were immediately apparent, including, at Vesey Street, an exact shape I had seen at the stern, as documented in the World Trade Center video log, mapping perimeter of surge-cloud zones, Nov. 3, 2001.

Comparative study sources included the following: sectioned and sampled steel beam presently on display at the Liberty Street Tribute Center, ground zero, New York; *The 9/11 Commission Report* on metallurgical results and surge-cloud velocities; J. P. Delgado et al., *The Archaeology of the Atomic Bomb* (Santa Fe, NM: Southwest Cultural Resources Center, 1991), 27, 89, 95–97; Charles Pellegrino, field notes; World Trade Center dust samples, microscopic examination (optical) scanning, electron microscope (and microprobe) analysis, New York's Suffolk County crime lab, 2005; NASA/Jet Propulsion laboratory white papers, 2002–2005.

See also Haraldur Sigurddson et al., "The Eruption of Vesuvius in AD 79," *National Geographic Research* 1 (1985): 332–387. That the Herculaneum phenomena are instructive for understanding the World Trade Center and *Titanic* surge-cloud (gravity current) physics was discussed extensively with G. Mastrolerenzo, personal communication, 2005, who had published surge-cloud findings in "Herculaneum Victims of Vesuvius in A.D. 79," *Nature*, Apr. 12, 2001.

The capricious nature and fluid mechanics of surge clouds: Haraldur Sigurddson, *American Vesuvius*, Towers Productions, History Channel, 2006; T. H. Druitt,

"Pyroclastic Density Currents," in *The Physics of Explosive Volcanic Eruptions*, ed. J. S. Gilbert and R. S. Sparks (London: Geological Society, 1998), 145–182; and Robert Ballard and Ken Marschall, *Exploring the* Titanic (London: Scholastic, 1993), 54.

27. THE LONG NIGHT OF ELLEN BETTY PHILLIPS

When I wrote *Her Name*, Titanic (New York: Avon-Morrow, 1988), I was not really writing about a ship at all, but about a beautiful child, abused, who came to a terrible fate. This, and Amber's story, were discussed in a letter to Roy Cullimore, Sept. 18, 2007. Ellen Phillips gave an account of her early years for the *Daily Mail* and the *White Star Journal*, Sept. 2002, reproduced in its entirety in *Encyclopedia Titanica* (using the name Ellen used when she was married, "Mary Walker"), Nov. 9, 2005, with additional material published by Judith Geller, Titanic: *Women and Children First* (New York: W. W. Norton, 1998), 133.

In later years, Ellen Phillips obsessed on her birthdate, believing she must actually have been conceived on the *Titanic* itself: Ellen Phillips and G. Hodges to the author, 2000, 2001. Her life with loving grandparents and later with a cruel mother: *West*, 1998, 11–12.

Ellen Phillips attributed her mother's behavior to the shock of the *Titanic*, but the Russians aboard the *Keldysh* interpreted a cruel mother's actions to her having possessed a mean streak from the start. Lev and Anatoly Sagalevich, during the *Keldysh* hydrothermal vent expedition in 2003, explained to me that a reason Russians like to drink with a person before deciding if there is a professional future is that "drunkenness and mental illness reveal the real person." The two keys given to Ellen by her mother from the *Titanic* turned out to be simple steel ring keys, with no White Star Line insignias or room numbers engraved. They appear to have been trunk keys.

In later years, Ellen was forced by near poverty to sell the blue sapphire and diamond necklace her father had brought aboard the *Titanic*: J. R. Hodges, personal communication and letters to author, Sept. 5, 2000, Apr. 27, 2001. Although a rift had by then developed between Ellen and Millvina Dean, Dean eventually came to Ellen's defense: Dean, personal communication with author, 1994–2005.

28. THE THIEVING MAGPIES

Thomas Andrews, who had designed the *Titanic* from the keel up, was overruled on the "excess" of lifeboats he had built into the plan: James Cameron, *Ghosts of the Abyss*, IMAX (DVD, Walden Media), 2003. Lessons learned and forgotten resurfaced with the money-saving rewriting of building codes in 1968 that had been enacted after the Triangle Shirtwaist Factory fire: D. Peterson (Verizon), personal communication, 2001, 2011; Paul Mallery, personal communication. Repeating old mistakes of the *Titanic* with the World Trade Center escape systems: J. Dwyer and K. Flynn, *102 Minutes* (New York: Holt, 2005), 107–110.

29. MONSTERS DOWN THERE

The fates of Albert Moss (heading toward his third shipwreck) and David Vartanian were reported by Per Kristian Sebak, Titanic: *31 Norwegian Destinies* (Oslo: Genesis Forlag, 1998), and by Philip Dattilio, "A Daughter Remembers *Titanic* David," Titanic *Commutator* 23, no. 145 (1999): 30.

The heating problems that had compelled Jack Thayer and many others to leave their portholes open were repeated for the *Britannic*, more or less neutralizing new safety features: *Britannic* issue, Titanic *Commutator* 20, no. 1 (July 1996): 32. Analysis of improvements from the *Titanic* to the *Britannic*: J. H. McCarthy and T. Foecke, *New Forensic Discoveries: What Really Sank the* Titanic (New York: Citadel Press, 2008), 20. The new lifeboat arrangements became one of the *Britannic's* few saving graces: Ken Marschall and Robert G. Ballard, *Lost Liners* (New York: Madison Press, 1997), 124.

Violet Jessop's famous "Oh no, not again" moment aboard the *Britannic* was told to J. M. Graham and personal communication with Walter Lord, date unknown. The sealing of the *Britannic's* fate, brought about by open portholes, was confirmed by Ken Marschall and Robert G. Ballard, *Lost Liners* (New York: Madison Press, 1997), 118–122, 127–131. This was discussed by B. Matsen, *The* Titanic's *Last Secrets* (New York: Twelve, 2008), 252–254. Captain Charles Bartlett and the *Britannic's* lookouts concluded that their ship had struck a mine, rather than been struck by a torpedo. The torpedoes of this period left clear tracks of white bubbles, and neither Bartlett nor his lookouts had seen a torpedo track. See also J. H. McCarthy and T. Foeke, *New Forensic Evidence: What Really Sank the* Titanic (New York: Citadel Press, 2008), 20.

Ken Marschall's *NR-1* dive to the *Britannic* is detailed in Marschall, "Descent to Another World," Titanic *Commutator* 20, no.1 (July 1996): 50–74. Differences in the condition of the *Britannic's* bow and the *Titanic's* (with the latter exposed to a powerful column collapse and down-blast effect, and the former not) were highlighted by intact mushroom vents near the *Britannic's* front cargo cranes, compared to Parks Stephenson's 2005 photographs of an identical vent from the same place on the *Titanic*, pressed into the shape of a deck bollard as one might press a piece of aluminum foil into the shape of a quarter by rubbing it down over the contours of George Washington with a pencil eraser.

Jessop's recall of the first ten minutes of the *Britannic's* run toward the Isle of Kea, the disastrous lowering of the lifeboats, her last view of the *Britannic*, and the toppling of the smokestacks: her diary, with annotations about physical aspects of the sinking by Bill MacQuitty, Walter Lord, and Charles Pellegrino, 1996, L/P file, pp. 716–732; see also Violet Jessop with J. Maxtone Graham, *Violet Jessop: Titanic Survivor* (New York: Sheridan House, 1997), 175–177.

The escape of the chief engineer and his team from the *Britannic*, along the same path Alfred White took aboard the *Titanic*: Ken Marschall and Robert G. Ballard, *Lost Liners* (New York: Madison Press, 1997), 132–133.

While Jessop awaited rescue, and while the engines of the *Titanic's* twin finally died, the chief engineer and several of his crew followed the same path to escape, seeming almost impossible, that Alfred White had followed aboard the *Titanic*, and which would perplex historian Walter Lord several decades later. They climbed up an escape path in the casing of the fourth funnel and dove from its outer ladder as the stern rolled slowly onto one side and dropped the funnel into the sea with surprising gentleness. The engineers proved that it was indeed possible to survive along "the White path," just as White said it had been. The fates of Charles Lightoller and Albert Moss: Lightoller, in Walter Lord, *The Night Lives On* (New York: William Morrow, 1986), 192–193; Moss, in Per Kristian Sebak, Titanic: *31 Norwegian Destinies* (Oslo: Genesis Forlag, 1998), 158–159. Jessop's following decades were scarcely less colorful, as recorded in letters to Walter Lord, 1958–1969, L/P file, pp. 533–542; Violet Jessop with J. Maxtone

Graham, *Violet Jessop: Titanic Survivor* (New York: Sheridan House, 1997), 188, 190, 192, 198. Jessop's memoir is well worth reading even for its chapters that are not about the *Titanic*, for they compare well with Jane Austen. Of particular note-worthiness is chapter 32, "The Jinrikisha Man," one of the saddest stories ever written about true devotion and endless love. The *almost* (so near and yet so far) first meeting of triple *Olympic*-class shipwreck survivor Violet Jessop and Walter Lord aboard the *Olympic* in July 1926 is memorialized in an inscribed photo of Lord beginning to study his favorite subject at age nine, L/P file, p. 1.

J. Chatterton, Carl Spencer, and the Shadow Divers unit at the *Britannic*: B. Matsen, *The* Titanic's *Last Secrets* (New York: Twelve, 2008), 245, 252–255. Chatterton's and a colleague's encounter with illness as an apparent result of rusticle infection at the *Britannic*: Roy Cullimore, Lori Johnston, and Mark Newman, personal communication, 2005–2012; Matsen, 259.

In 2008, Carl Spencer, the polymath explorer, was working with the microbiologists: Roy Cullimore, letter to author, Nov. 2010; Roy Cullimore and Lori Johnston, personal communication. Tests had already shown a tremendous acceleration of rusticle reefing on the *Britannic*: Cullimore and Johnston, "Microbial Evaluation of the Potential at-Site Corrosion of the Steels Used in the Construction of HMSS *Britannic*," *Forensic Microbial Service*, Droycon Bioconcepts Inc., Saskatchewan, Canada, Jan 12, 2011.

After setting the new GUCCI rack and two new bacterial etching experiments on the *Britannic*, Spencer's rebreather system malfunctioned: Cullimore, letter to author, Nov. 11, 2010; Johnston, letters to author, Jan. 2011 and Feb. 14, 2011. The *National Geographic* support ship was equipped with a portable hyperbaric chamber, but Spencer never revived: Carl Spencer death inquest outcome, Feb. 14, 2011.

30. GHOSTS OF THE ABYSS

Notes on how the aftermath of a trauma (as in the case described by Ellen Betty Phillips) can eat away at one's heart as badly as the event itself: Charles Pellegrino, video log, WTC surge cloud effect survey.

Ten-Ten House "apparitions" and "ghosts of the imagination": John Morabito, personal communications, 2002–2005. Events, second and third time, "saved" by Paddy Brown: Charles Pellegrino, John Pellegrino, family history.

31. PERSEVERING

On Masabumi Hosono and his family during the century after the *Titanic*: Fumiko Hosono, in M. Findlay, "The Fateful Voyage of Masabumi Hosono," *Voyage* 27, Winter 1998, pp. 128–129; Kae Matsumoto and Hideo Nakamura, letters to author, Feb. and Mar. 2011.

Unlike most techno or new wave bands of the 1980s, YMO's popularity grew slowly and steadily: http://www.youtube.com/watch?v=sJgtyMbfYAY&feature= relted. Their 2011 hit (in homage to Masabumi Hosono's perseverance) was titled "You've Got to Help Yourself."

32. DESTINATION UNKNOWN

Return to the *Keldysh* in 2003 and Captain Paul Mallery's lesson to the *Keldysh* about thinking outside the box: Paul Mallery, e-mail log, Expedition *X-Treme Life*, July 23, 2003, p. 16, July 28, 2003, pp. 22–23.

"Russian-think," applied by James Cameron to the evolution of the cephalopods: Charles Pellegrino, correspondence with Arthur C. Clarke, e-mail log, Expedition *X-Treme Life*, July 31, 2003, p. 40. James Cameron, *Keldysh* crew, and NASA astrobiology team, personal communications, Expedition *X-Treme Life*, July 31, 2003.

The search for hydrothermal vent origins of the *Titanic*'s rusticle reef: Charles Pellegrino, written log, Expedition *X-Treme Life*, July 31, 2003, pp. 39, 47–49.

A recurrence of "World Trade Center cough" at sea and the news from our ship's surgeon, Dr. Glenn Singleman, that I would never see the *Titanic* again: Pellegrino, written log, Expedition *X-Treme Life*, Aug. 3, 2003, pp. 20, 43. Mary Leung, e-mail to author, Expedition *X-Treme Life*, Aug 6, 2003, p. 62.

The colorful history of "rocket fuel" in a drink called Sheila: Pellegrino, written log, Expedition *Titanic XIII*, Sept. 23, 2001, p. 272.

"The cup is half full," I told myself, as I prepared for the last dive of my career: Pellegrino, written log, Expedition *X-Treme Life*, Aug. 7–8, 2003, pp. 46, 67, 68. Abiotic organic material forms the base of the Lost City food chain: G. Prokurowski et al., "Abiotic Lost City Organics," *Science*, Feb. 1, 2008; S. Perkins et al., "Sea Floor Chemistry: Life's Building Blocks Made Inorganically [Lost City Vents]," *Science News*, Feb. 2, 2008.

Discovery of Lost City: *Science News*, July 14, 2000. Investigation of hydrothermal vents, abiotic matter in carbonaceous meteorites (pioneered by H. C. Urey, B. Nagy, and C. E. Folsome), with implications for subsurface seas of certain moons of Jupiter and Saturn (especially Titan and Enceladus): Charles Pellegrino and Jesse Stoff, notes and correspondence, J. Stoff, R. Ballard, 1978; *Darwin's Universe: Origins and Crises in the History of Life*, 2nd ed. (New York: Van Nostrand Reinhold, 1983).

The Lost City dive was documented in Pellegrino, dive log and video log, Expedition *X-Treme Life*, Aug. 8. 2003, pp. 79–130.

Ground zero lung, preparations (as land crew) for the 2005 *Titanic* expedition: Charles Pellegrino, Paul Mallery, et al., written log, Expedition *X-Treme Life*, Aug. 6–14, 2003, pp. 57, 58, 60, 61, 62B, 75, 77, 92, 102, 103, 104, 107, 108.

Revelations about the *Titanic*'s misnamed, misunderstood (and fortunately not mistreated) white worm: James Cameron, *Last Mysteries of the* Titanic, Discovery Channel, 2005. Other 2005 expedition notes relevant to shock cocoons, breakup of the *Titanic*, and sea floor impact: James Cameron, letters to C. Pellegrino and R. Long, in "Archaeology of the *Titanic*," *Explorers*, Part 3, http://www.charlespellegrino.com, pp. 5, 7, 11, 12, 17–18, 37.

The discovery of more shock-cocooned chambers inside the *Titanic* and a new rusticle morphology: James Cameron and Charles Pellegrino, in "Archaeology of the *Titanic*," *Explorers*, Part 2, http://www.charlespellegrino.com, pp. 1–4; Lynn Margulis interview, *Discover*, Apr. 2011, pp. 66–71.

The same "electron racetrack" found in hemoglobin is found throughout nature, the chief difference being the metal at the center of the "racetrack": magnesium for plants, copper for insects, and iron for birds and mammals. On the *Titanic*, we have seen that the rusticle makes use of whatever metals are available: iron, copper, and zinc. The mystery of "rusticle flowers" in Maude Slocomb's Turkish baths was discussed by James Cameron, Charles Pellegrino, Roy Cullimore, Lori Johnston, and Anthony El-Khouri in correspondence beginning in Apr. 2011.

El-Khouri's study of the rusticle flower video revealed three relevant trends: El-Khouri, letter to author, Apr. 25, 2011; Cullimore, letter to author, Apr. 26, 2011. Cullimore's observations pointed Occam's razor toward a "rust flower" kinship with the anoxic microbial reeds growing on (and protecting) the *Titanic*'s mail bags, and his photos show rusticles growing *up*, in the laboratory. The nutrient base was ferro-rich narrow-spectrum fatty acids. Cullimore relied on iron-reducing bacteria (from rusticles) to start the oxidative-reductive cycle and switched to ferrous as required.

Cullimore's observations about bacterially produced iron deposits having been made into *Titanic*'s steel, being returned now to the earth as iron ore again, by microbiology: Pellegrino and Cullimore, video log, Expedition *Titanic VIII*, 1996.

Humans repeat history again. In Masabumi Hosono's generation, large stone tablets were erected warning of the heights reached by tsunamis: J. Alabaster, "Tsunami-Hit Towns Forgot Warnings from Ancestors," Associated Press, Apr. 6, 2011; A. Revkin, "Limits of Disaster Memory, Even Etched in Stone," *New York Times*, Apr. 8, 2011.

Guglielmo Marconi, whose apparatus was largely responsible for saving those who escaped the *Titanic* in lifeboats, noted how often the lessons of the past tended to be ignored, and he was much distressed by the sinking of the *Titanic* and by subsequent avoidable repetitions: Gioia Marconi Braga (his daughter), letter to author (with family memoir and letters), Aug. 10, 1995; Degna Marconi, *My Father Marconi* (New York: McGraw-Hill, 1962), 198.

Marconi was originally invited by the White Star Line as a special guest for the maiden voyage, but his work required him to be in New York three days ahead of the *Titanic*, so he booked earlier passage on the *Lusitania* instead. Although he was never involved in a shipwreck himself, his daughter Gioia noted that ships her father changed his mind about sailing on sank when he would have been on them, and ships on which he actually sailed sank later.

Captain Arthur Rostron's and Madeline Mellinger's closing thoughts about the *Titanic*: Rostron, *The Loss of the* Titanic (Indian Orchard, MA: Titanic Historical Society, 1931), 27; Mellinger letter to Walter Lord, 1961, L/P file, p. 595.

Index